Ibn Khaldūn and the Arab Origi
of Civilisation and Power

Annalisa Verza

Ibn Khaldūn and the Arab Origins of the Sociology of Civilisation and Power

Springer

Annalisa Verza
University of Bologna
Bologna, Italy

ISBN 978-3-030-70341-7 ISBN 978-3-030-70339-4 (eBook)
https://doi.org/10.1007/978-3-030-70339-4

This Springer imprint is published by the registered company Springer Nature Switzerland AG.
The registered company address is: Gewerbestrasse 11, 6330 Cham, Switzerland

Foreword

Historiography on Ibn Khaldūn has been an uninterrupted success for a long time now, and even in Italy it is no longer a subject reserved for a select circle of insiders but is beginning to interest a wider public. This monograph by Annalisa Verza is therefore welcome and significant.

Although Verza does not have an institutional Arabist background, being instead professor of sociology and philosophy of law at the University of Bologna, this has not been an obstacle to her research which, on the contrary, comes through as extremely precise, and acutely cognizant of the problems posed by the interpretation of Ibn Khaldūn's complex technical language.

I think that, as Verza argues, the analytical tools provided by the great sociologist, philosopher and historian Ibn Khaldūn have lost none of their freshness and sharpness, and still remain fully capable of helping us understand contemporary Western civilisation. This same point has also been aptly captured in the title of a book by the Moroccan philosopher Mohammed Aziz Lahbabi, *Ibn Khaldoun notre contemporain.*

In contrast, it is interesting to remember how, in the Arab world and in Europe alike, Ibn Khaldūn has been consigned to oblivion for centuries. He died in 1406, and only in the nineteenth century did his fortune swing back in his favour, first with Quatremere's edition of the *Muqaddimah*, and then with the increasing interest that scholars have taken in his work, not only in the West but subsequently also, and especially, in the Islamic Arab world.

Today, Ibn Khaldūn has become a true icon of Arab scholarship, and although not everyone appreciates the modernity of his method, he continues to remain a reference point in the search for Arab identity and in its effort to reflect on its historical past.

Our contemporary society has been characterised as "a liquid society," but I would push this metaphor a little further by calling ours a "liquefied society." This is to say that the Arab-Islamic world is suffering as a result of the globalisation that is extending its reach across all the cultures over which the Western world dominates, and also as a result of the crisis that is affecting knowledge, the economy and religion across Europe and in the so-called Western world, where even consolidated models, such as those of representative democracy, appear to be in need of revision. To this end, Ibn Khaldūn's work can be very useful in understanding what methods can be used to rediscover the cohesion that is getting lost in such a liquid, or liquefied, society.

In fact, the central concept in Ibn Khaldūn's sociological and historical thought, namely, the concept of *'aṣabiyya* (group spirit), was intended precisely to identify what processes and what dynamics could lead from the crisis of a society to its reconstitution. There is no social distancing in Ibn Khaldūn's reconstruction, but a close weaving of relations. And while it is true that his perspective is cyclical, it cannot be considered simply repetitive. In fact, he believed that with the passing of time, something of the previous social and civil conquests would remain in the legacy handed down to later generations.

Annalisa Verza reads this process, projects it forward and, above all, brings it into comparison with a political system whose real meaning the Western world has, in my opinion too, lost sight of: political and legal liberalism.

There is no doubt that Ibn Khaldūn was not a liberal, at least not in any of the ways in which this term can be interpreted in light of the categories of European-Western political thought. According to the Maghrebi thinker, the engine of history and the driving force behind historical evolution lies in conflict. Conflict takes place among the forces of the various group spirits that clash with each other, but also between those who wield power and those who are subjected to it and suffer its consequences, between nomadism and sedentariness, between Bedouin and city culture, between religion and state. All these dialectical elements make possible a transformation which, as noted, preserves and protects the best achievements of the past even in the course of cyclical evolution. As has been suggested within a certain strand of contemporary historiography, Ibn Khaldūn took the view that history's engine is to be found in violence. Even so, violence is to be understood not only as a display and deployment of brute force, bringing about the destruction of what seemed to be consolidated, but also as a positive force, in which conflict becomes the instrument through which society finds a way to evolve. The study of Ibn Khaldūn's thought makes it possible to directly link sociology and history to law, and this is certainly a particularly stimulating characteristic of Annalisa Verza's work.

Much work still needs to be done on the semantisation of power, on the need to find a language that could adequately define concepts as fundamental and controversial for Islamic political thought as those of *mulk* (kingdom, kingship) and *khilafa* (caliphate), or even that of *retrospective utopia*, referring to the prevailing tendency to see the past as a model on which to build the future. These are speculative nodes, very much present in Ibn Khaldūn, which can help us identify the limits of Islamic political language, and to do so by outlining a broad cultural framework in which the sciences, the arts, the economic system and the legal system come to intertwine fruitfully. Even if such a process of revision still remains largely augural today, it could enable us to lay new foundations on which to revise and rebuild the whole contemporary political-legal system—a system that, I repeat, seems to me to be in serious crisis, in the West and elsewhere.

Another pivotal concept in Ibn Khaldūn's reflection is that of justice, and certainly justice is a pillar that must innervate not only the philosophy of law but also the day-to-day management of power and the relationship between power and law. All these elements are appropriately outlined in Annalisa Verza's book, providing a general picture that, while certainly suggesting openings for further investigation in detail, proves convincing.

A last point I would like to underline concerns Ibn Khaldūn's role in relation to colonialism and the coexistence, so difficult today, of different cultural models and religions, together with the abiding resurgence of racist and xenophobic tendencies and drives.

This is a subject that runs through Annalisa Verza's entire book, and I believe that this is the perspective the author offers for the future, pointing out the need to revisit several obsolete paradigms and to question ancient and consolidated categories so as to make them more suitable for the contemporary reality.

However, how could Ibn Khaldūn be able to suggest these interpretive tools? And how could he manage to be so topical? The answer, in my opinion, lies in his realism. He nurtured a thoroughly realistic philosophical vision, which left nothing to the imagination. In this sense, in addition to highlighting the role of conflict, as we earlier did, it is especially enlightening to link Ibn Khaldūn to Machiavelli, as has been done by Moroccan scholars such as Abdallah Laroui and Muhammad Jabiri. Machiavelli remains, in my opinion, the gold standard for all those who want to understand how politics ought to be conducted and how states ought to be governed. The question is not so much whether democracy is superior to authoritarianism or republicanism to princedom. At issue, rather, is the problem of understanding politics, and consequently the interrelationships between political science and law, appreciating that politics are not governed by moralistic elements, but by the need to deal with concrete situations that require decisions at once rapid and practical.

I believe that Annalisa Verza's book provides remarkable insights for reconstructing a renewed vision of the relationship between institutions, societies and individuals, and it is really interesting that a Western-educated scholar should have the sensitivity to find a solid guide, and an exceptionally creative and useful counterpoint, in a "medieval" Arab Muslim thinker like our Ibn Khaldūn.

Milan, 13 July 2020

University of Napoli l'Orientale, Naples, Italy
Massimo Campanini

University of Trento, Trento, Italy

The original version of this book was revised. Typographical errors involving incorrect names with special characters have been updated throughout the book. The correction to this book is available at: https://doi.org/10.1007/978-3-030-70339-4_6.

Preface

This book is the far-removed outcome of an encounter that took place in Tunis, on an August day some years ago, with a green door. In that summer I was studying Arabic at the *Bourguiba Institut des Langues Vivantes*, and the school guide, who had organised a tour of the city centre for that day, pointed with pride at the door of the native home of Ibn Khaldūn, "the world's first sociologist," the same figure who, immortalised in a bronze statue, towered over Place de l'Indépendance. And so that green door, somewhat like the mossy opening in the rock that, on his sixth voyage, by chance led the mariner Sinbad to discover Serendip, opened up a new perspective for me that, through a long and challenging voyage, has led me here.

This book is thus dedicated to an analysis of the philosophico-sociologico-political thought of Maghrebin thinker Ibn Khaldūn,[1] an author who, as early as the fourteenth century and despite working in a context which was far-removed from the historico-cultural conditions of the Western Enlightenment, elaborated a work of such breadth, richness and depth as to prompt one of his greatest admirers—the great historian Arnold Toynbee—to state, with words of boundless extolment, that:

> He has conceived and formulated a philosophy of history which is undoubtedly the greatest work of its kind that has ever yet been created by any mind in any time and place (Toynbee [1934] 1962: 322. Cf. Issawi 1950: Preface).

In fact, his "theory of civilisation" (*'ilm al-'umrān*)—the "new science" that Ibn Khaldūn formulated in 1377—, deserves to be recognised as a great classic, a pioneering work worthy of a place of honour in the landscape of the modern social sciences, even within the Western syllabus of the sociological conceptions that are relevant to politics and law.

Many scholars, when discovering this extraordinary and complex author, have not concealed their astonishment at finding that a medieval Maghrebin author had not only already clearly outlined, but also effectively interconnected, in an extremely

---

[1] According to the transliteration system adopted here, the correct rendering of his name would be *Ibn Ḫaldūn*. However, I have decided to adopt the more widely used spelling of Ibn Khaldūn.

rich and complex analysis, analytical concepts that in the West, from the nineteenth century onwards, have been detonators of authentic revolutions of thought.

In many cases, from the very earliest times since its rediscovery, this has spawned a widespread temptation to read his thought in analogy to that of specific Western authors. And so, not only has Ibn Khaldūn been seen as a keen anticipator of a rational and sociological analysis of society, but it has also been hypothesised that his work may have directly inspired that of authors like Niccolò Machiavelli, Giambattista Vico, Auguste Comte, Karl Marx and Émile Durkheim.

And after all, the illuminating concepts and the deepest, most seminal insights that human culture has grasped, should be conceived of, perhaps, less as the product and creation of the independent and endogenous mental paths charted by single scholars, developed in the *hortus conclusus* of their thoughts, and more as ideas that are floating "in the air," ready to be seized "on the fly" by minds that have proved capable of elevating themselves to the right place at the right time. And, perhaps, it is also for this reason that the history of the development of ideas rarely follows a linear path, but rather often proceeds by fits and starts, advancing and retreating, with possible leaps forward and instances of "passing on the baton," in ways conditioned by the countless variations of the causal factors produced by the multiform combinatory logic of reality.

In any event, after the first wave of writings, aimed at enthusiastically stressing his modernity (at times, in an anachronistic and uncontextualised way), the singularity of Ibn Khaldūn's thought and, above all, the close proximity between many of his ideas and those of many Western social theorists have sparked different kinds of reactions among critics.

On the one hand, some of these critics, like Muhsin Mahdi (1957), Abdesselam Cheddadi (2006) and Stephen Frederic Dale (2015a), have attempted to bind Ibn Khaldūn and the Western social theorists through a single unifying thread, arguing that the analogies that bring them together would descend from both having Aristotle's thought as a common source. More precisely, the Maghrebin thinker was supposed to have been influenced by Aristotle's writings on physics (as, in his time, Aristotle's political writings were not available in Arabic), which had allegedly inspired the underlying structure of his "cyclical" thought. At the same time, in Europe, Aristotelian thought had given rise to a long wave of reflexion, starting out with the ferment generated at the University of Paris by the Arabic translations of his writings commented by Averroes, which proved to be fundamental for Thomas Aquinas's thought. Then, further and later, this very Aristotelian thread, going through the Scottish Enlightenment, would end up influencing the development of the social sciences.[2]

[2]In actual fact, that Ibn Khaldūn's writings were the outcome of a transposition and application of an Aristotelian scheme is no more than a fascinating supposition—one that, moreover, is often accompanied by a philological-reductive tendency to downplay the innovative import of his thought.

On the other hand, a completely different reaction to Ibn Khaldūn's thought has led other scholars—most notably Taha Hussein (1918, 75), but also, more recently, Claude Horrut (2006, 173–83)—to deny Ibn Khaldūn any possible qualification as a sociologist, in the name of a reductive definition of sociology as constitutively tied to secularisation. Thus, only because in the nineteenth century, in Europe, sociology had been conceived in a European secularist milieu, this aspect has been rigidly considered as a *conditio sine qua non* of the definition.

But to deny (Pomian 2006, 232) that Ibn Khaldūn's work can also be described as "sociological" on the ground that its author lived in the thirteenth century, and (what is more!) in the very Islamic Maghreb, is a *non sequitur,* a methodological fallacy that places the definition ahead of the reality it sets out to define. On the contrary, precisely the advisability of tweaking our initial definition of sociology in this sense, broadening the horizon of its conditions of possibility and development, is, indeed, one of the benefits that could be derived from an unbiased evaluation of Ibn Khaldūn's work. In fact, this author's work has in the first place shown that sociology does not necessarily require its scholars to be secularised or lay, as long as they are equipped with a distinct *forma mentis,* capable of reconciling religiously grounded thought with rationally grounded thought—what Arab culture defines as the "*'aql-naql mindset*" (Dhaouadi 2005; Dale 2015a, 288–99).

Precisely this way of structuring thought is what, half a millennium before the "official" birth of sociology, effectively enabled Ibn Khaldūn to work out a whole series of concepts that we consider to be distinctly tied to "our" rational scientific thought: concepts relating, for example, to social solidarity, the scientific methodology for investigating social factors, the economic phenomenon now known as the Laffer curve (Laffer 2004), the unleashing of desires tied to the availability of luxury goods, or the relationship between society and power and between power and its symbols.

But the fact that, in the theses of Ibn Khaldūn, concepts could be found which are in many respects similar to those much later and independently developed in Western culture and sociology of politics and of society—and which we accordingly consider as peculiar of "our own" Western, secular culture—also carries with it a second important implication. The very fact that Ibn Khaldūn, proceeding from a cultural and biographical basis that was profoundly religious and tied to Islam, could grasp and bring into focus some sociological and philosophico-political insights that the West also elaborated as its own, reveals the profound foundational and apical contacts that exist between the roots of these two macro-cultures. These cannot be ignored, despite the essentialist claims that see Islam and the West as necessarily and radically alien[3] (Verza 2013).

On the other hand, however, it would also be risky to reduce his relevance to that of being only a "precursor" of Western sociological thought. In fact, unless such a

[3]Not only do some of the most vociferous fringes of Islam categorically insist on this aspect (see, for example, the sort of "nativism" that forms the basis of the project to "Islamicise knowledge" (Syed Farid Alatas 2014, ch. 3)), but also many Western voices.

reading of his work is taken with due caution, the peculiarity of his theory—with its own originality, resting on the autogenous balance of its different components—would risk being wasted into the most superficial anachronism, as the strength and plausibility of his theory lies not only in the single insights that make it up, but also, and especially, in the way these are interconnected and made to rest on one another.

If, in his insistence on the environmental relativity of human character traits, theoretical elements can be found which are typical of Montesquieu's thought, for example, this is not a reason for reducing Ibn Khaldūn to a "Montesquieu of the Arabs." Likewise, if his analysis of the material basis of historical development conjures up a Marxist vision of history, the different cultural and social contexts and perspectives that frame the two sets of theses are significant enough to decisively rule out the plausibility of labelling Ibn Khaldūn as a materialist thinker (in the Marxist sense), ahead of his own time.[4] And any such reductions are to be excluded, not for any lack of comparable insights underpinning his thesis, but because these very elements are fitted together by him in a theory, a "symphony," which is original and distinctive to him, and which cannot be stretched and reduced to that of other authors without losing much of its own peculiarity.

Thus, precisely in order not to second a reception of this author flattened into a vision of him as an anticipator of other thinkers, it has been decided here to avoid setting up this work on a comparative plane, favouring a critical commentary instead, along with a presentation of his theory, and leaving it to the reader (apart from a few scattered references) to relish the pleasure of personally discovering the many points of possible analogy, symmetry and anticipation that come to light while reading this author.

Ibn Khaldūn was an Arab thinker of the fourteenth century. Not only was he a believer, but also a Malikite judge and (I am deliberately saying "and" and not "but") he was possessed of an ironclad logical apparatus. At the same time, he was also—although this might seem to clash with his rationality—authentically and originally "inspired" in the proper sense of the term,[5] as he was careful to stress. In the 5 months of frenetic writing during which his massive work was completed in the solitude of a retreat in the desert, far from any access to libraries, his spirit was overtaken—as he himself would write—by the irresistible inspiration of a torrential flood of words and ideas (Ibn Khaldūn [1980] 1995, 142; 2002: 151).[6]

---

[4]This idea has been put forward by Lacoste, for example.

[5]The value of the inspiration that made him write his masterpiece is something that Ibn Khaldūn very much insisted on, and with good reason: the added value given by this inspirational element will become clearer when (cf. *infra*, ch. IV, sect. 4.1) his thesis on the different types of intelligence is expounded. In fact, in his fascinating reconstruction of the "three worlds," the Maghrebin author described the intellectual world as populated with "ideas," existing by themselves, and attainable only by those who might be capable of elevating themselves to their height.

[6]Also in his treatise on Sufism (2017: 22–27) Ibn Khaldūn insisted on the importance of inspiration, distinguishing acquired science (*al-'ilm al-kasbī*), inspired science (*ilhām*) and revelation (*waḥy*).

By the way, at a time very close to Ibn Khaldūn's, even Dante[7] ([1316] 1988: canto XXIV, 52–54) (also an author, in exile, of a masterpiece distinguished by an immense architecture) underlined the generative importance of inspiration for his work (his "poetic manifesto" is well-known: "*i' mi son un che, quando Amor mi spira, noto, e a quel modo ch'e' ditta dentro vo significando*")—which somehow strengthens the view that the greatest ideas could be truly already there, floating and wafting "in the air,"[8] waiting to be grasped by inspired minds.

On the other hand, perhaps it is precisely owing to the astounding modernity and originality of his thought that, to this day and however much he may be the object of a thriving and internally variegated galaxy of learned "Khaldunian studies,"[9] Ibn Khaldūn still remains a thinker barely included in the classic curricula in sociological and philosophical thought, both general and specifically concerned with the law. Yet, precisely on account of his status as a "great absentee," all too often expunged, as if by *lapsus*, from the official narrative through which the flow of the theoretical history of thought on society and its forms of government unfolds, Ibn Khaldūn must today be reprised and regarded as an author who is still to be addressed in dialogue, investigated and turned to for answers.[10] Unless his ideas and theories are fully integrated into the general framework of theoretical thought on government and society, an important and unresolved gap in the history of thought would remain unfilled, and important theoretical potentialities would remain latent.

Given the unprecedented import and depth of his theory and his originality, along with his anticipative capacity, it becomes therefore urgent to fully recognise this Maghrebin thinker for the place he undoubtedly deserves in the philosophy and sociology of civilisations (or in the landscape of their "precursors," assuming that we wish to retain the idea that sociology was first conceived in the West in the nineteenth century—an idea that, at this point, cannot be taken for granted at all). Such recognition would thus dismiss the widespread albeit tacit tendency to think that Arab culture is, and must continue to be, constitutively "alien" to the trajectory charted by "official" culture, and that its study should be the exclusive province of specialists in the "niche" of "Oriental" studies.[11] On the contrary, the importance of

---

[7]The contacts between Dante's thought and the Islamic world, following the reconstruction offered by Miguel Asín Palacio ([1919] 2014), devoted to Islamic eschatology in the *Divine Comedy*, are probably very profound.

[8]Even the history of science and technology abounds with cases of techniques and discoveries that have been "seized" and intuited, by different researchers, in different places and at different times.

[9]A 1981 bibliography devoted to him already listed more than 700 works (al-Azmeh 1981: 229–324): this number must have at least doubled by now.

[10]Alatas (2020, 77): "While Ibn Khaldūn was taken seriously by European sociologists in the late 19th century and early 20th century, he was excluded from the sociological canon as it became established after the Second World War." See also Dale (2015b: 54).

[11]For example, see also Kalpakian (2008), according to whom Ibn Khaldūn's work also belongs to the domain of international relations theory.

Ibn Khaldūn's thought demonstrates[12] that we should rather think of a single line of reflection, at once Western and Oriental, ideally unifiable into a comprehensive thread.

But in addition to originating from a desire to redeem Ibn Khaldūn's thought from a neglect that does not do justice to its value, this study also springs from the conviction that the knowledge of Ibn Khaldūn's work would also be important for us, here and now: in fact, his thought could provide us with particularly useful insights, for two reasons, at least.

In the first place, his theoretical work represents an important and direct expression of Islamic culture—a culture that, for us and especially today, has acquired a particular importance, especially in the light of the recent increase in migration flows to Europe. In this perspective, his work could, in fact, endow us with precious teachings about this culture: about its distinctive internal dynamics, its roots and foundational values, and its specificities.

Especially from the 1980s, the demographic and cultural changes brought about by immigration and by multicultural policies have led to an ever greater opening to the Islamic world in the public forum, especially in Europe. Yet, while this phenomenon, in the social sciences, has for the most part been addressed as a subject matter for the sociology of migrations or for Islamic studies (for the most part, anthropologically or politically focused, and mainly centred on the threat and genesis of religious fundamentalism), the underlying "sociology"—the one that supplies the theoretical frameworks and the basic interpretive lens though which the world is studied—has remained essentially and distinctly Western. If, then, Islam is today much more relevant to sociological studies, it is so mainly as an object to be studied—that is, in a way that is still too impermeable to welcoming the intellectual *perspectives* developed by its culture. But for a full understanding of Islam, it is not sufficient to make it into an object of study: it would be advisable to also be open to assessing the interpretation of the world offered by a perspective that was born within that culture. For this reason, too, a deeper knowledge of the thought developed by an author like Ibn Khaldūn proves to be particularly precious.

But, in the second place and even more importantly, his theory also concerns us because of the diagnosis of our society that it enables us to do. In fact, I am convinced that his thesis can help us understand what is happening to our civilisation today, at what point it now finds itself in the course of its developmental arc, and what its evolution is bound to be.

In fact, the potentially universal (or universalisable) scope and significance of the ancient, yet extraordinarily current paradigm he built—once consciously decontextualised, separated, and abstracted from the fourteenth-century Maghrebin reality in which it was developed (and so long as all undue anachronism is avoided: Chaouch 2008)—opens the way to its possibly fruitful and revealing applicability even to the current historico-political context (cf. Aubert 2016, 54), which today, in a

[12] Attesting to that fact are the many studies that are currently being devoted to it, especially in countries where translations of his work are more accessible, as in France.

difficult dialogue, is engaging the West with that very Islamic world which almost seven centuries ago gave birth to Ibn Khaldūn.

The last part of this work will therefore aim to understand, through a philosophico-sociological prism, how the study of Khaldūn's work may be useful to us today by shedding new, original light on the likely trajectory—not only axiological but also political and historical—which the current multicultural configuration of our society is now taking, helping us to understand and frame much of what is happening in our world today, and, perhaps, in time also to identify—thanks to its lesson (*'ibar*) sourced from the history of the past—possible suggestions for its better management and care.

In this text, as a rule, I will be referring to the excellent translation of the *Muqaddima* done by Franz Rosenthal, first published in an unabridged edition in three volumes (Ibn Khaldūn 1958) and then issued in an abridged edition (Ibn Khaldūn [1967] 2005). But in order to make it easier to find passages, in the *Muqaddima*, also for readers using the French edition published by de Slane (Ibn Khaldūn 1862–1868), Monteil (Ibn Khaldūn 1967–1968) or Cheddadi (Ibn Khaldūn 2002), reference will be made to the partitions (chapters and sections) into which the text was divided by Ibn Khaldūn himself. When quoting verbatim from the *Muqaddima*, the source will be provided not only by specifying the textual partition but also by pinpointing the quotation to the specific page numbers of the two editions of Franz Rosenthal's translation.

Bologna, Italy Annalisa Verza

References

(A) Ibn Khaldūn's Works

Ibn Khaldūn. 1862–1868. *Les Prolégomènes d'Ibn Khaldoun* (ed. William Mac Guckin de Slane). Paris: Librairie orientaliste Paul Geuthner.

———. 1958. *The Muqaddimah: An Introduction to History* (ed. Franz Rosenthal). 3 Voll. New Jersey: Princeton University Press.

———. 1967–1968. *Discours sur l'histoire universelle*, (ed. Vincent Monteil). 3 Voll. Beyrouth: Commission libanaise pour la traduction des chefs-d'oeuvre et Sinbad.

———. [1980] 1995. *Le voyage d'Occident et d'Orient* (ed. Abdesselam Cheddadi). Paris: Sindbad.

———. 2002. *Le Livre des Exemples. I. Autobiographie, Muqaddima* (ed. Abdesselam Cheddadi). Paris: Gallimard.

———. [1967] 2005. *The Muqaddimah: An Introduction to History* (ed. Franz Rosenthal), abridged edition. Princeton: Princeton University Press.

———. 2017. *Ibn Khaldūn on Sufism. Remedy for the Questioner in Search of Answers* (trans. Yumna Ozer). Cambridge: The Islamic Texts Society.

(B) Other Works

Alatas, Syed Farid. 2014. Applying Ibn Khaldūn. *The Recovery of a Lost Tradition in Sociology*. London: Routledge.

Alatas, Syed Farid. 2020. The Contemporary Significance of Ibn Khaldūn for Decolonial Sociology: Methodological and Theoretical Dimensions. *Tajseer. Qatar University Press* 1 (2): 75–98.

Alighieri, Dante. [1316] 1988. *La Divina Commedia: Purgatorio*. Milano: Garzanti.

al-Azmeh, Aziz. 1981. *Ibn Khaldūn in Modern Scholarship: A Study in Orientalism*. London: Third World Research Centre.

Asín Palacio, Miguel. [1919] 2014. *Dante e l'Islam*. Milano: Luni editrice.

Aubert, Bruno. 2016. Au delà d'Ibn Khaldūn. La tragédie arabe n'est pas fatale. *Esprit* 5: 53–59.

Chaouch, Khalid. 2008. Ibn Khaldūn, in Spite of Himself. *The Journal of North African Studies* 13 (3): 279–291.

Cheddadi, Abdesselam. 2006. *Ibn Khaldūn. L'homme et le théoricien de la civilisation*. Paris: Gallimard.

Dale, Stephen Frederic. 2015a. *The Orange Trees of Marrakesh. Ibn Khaldūn and the Science of Man*. Cambridge, MA: Harvard University Press.

Dale, Stephen Frederic. 2015b. Return to Ibn Khaldūn–Again. *Review of Middle East Studies* 49 (1): 48–55.

Dhaouadi, Mahmoud. 2005. The ʿIbar: Lessons of Ibn Khaldūn's ʻUmrān Mind. *Contemporary Sociology,* 34/6: *Essays on Ibn Khaldūn*: 585–589.

Horrut, Claude. 2006. *Ibn Khaldūn, un Islam des "Lumières"*. Paris: Les Éditions Complexes.

Hussein, Taha. 1918. *Étude analitique et critique de la philosophie sociale d'Ibn Khaldoun*. Paris: Pedone.

Issawi, Charles. 1950. Preface. In *An Arab Philosophy of History*, ed. Charles Issawi. London: Murray.

Kalpakian, Jack. 2008. Ibn Khaldūn's Influence on Current International Relations Theory. *The Journal of North African Studies* 13 (3): 357–370.

Laffer, Arthur. 2004. The Laffer Curve: Past, Present, and Future. *Executive Summary Backgrounder No. 1765*: 1–18. s3.amazonaws.com/thf_media/2004/pdf/bg1765.pdf. Accessed 17 Sept 2020.

Mahdi, Muhsin. 1957. *Ibn Khaldūn's Philosophy of History*. Chicago: University of Chicago Press.

Pomian, Krzysztof. 2006. *Ibn Khaldūn au prisme de l'Occident*. Paris: Gallimard.

Toynbee, Arnold. [1934] 1962. *A Study of History. Vol. III: The Growths of Civilizations*. New York: Oxford University Press.

Verza, Annalisa. 2013. Western and Islamic Values: A "False" Contraposition. *ARSP* 99 (2): 173–185.

Acknowledgements

As one might imagine, this work, having been born out of a sincere passion and admiration for an author I came across thanks to the serendipity of chance (or of destiny), has also revealed itself to be singularly long and difficult on account of the intersectionality between the sociological, philosophical, historical, linguistic and cultural perspectives with which it has been necessary to deal. At the same time, however, this complexity has also been an opportunity of great enrichment for me. In fact, I am convinced that it is especially when we engage with what is different from ourselves that the results become fruitful—as in the realm of nature, also in the realm of thought, where different ideas can afford a real exchange.

Last but not least, I come now to the most pleasant task: thanking all those colleagues who, over the course of the several years required by the development of this book, have supported this project, from different perspectives and in connection with different aspects of the research it involved.

First of all, heartfelt thanks to Alberto Artosi, Franz Belvisi, Massimo Campanini, René Foqué, Gustavo Gozzi, Alberto Jori, Claudio Luzzati, Enrico Pattaro, Valerio Pocar and Sandra Tugnoli, for reading all or parts of this book, or for discussing it with me over the course of its writing: the comments and observations they shared with me greatly contributed to its improvement.

Special thanks go to Roberta Denaro, who kindly checked large part of the work I did when transliterating Arabic terms and who has provided me with valuable tips in that regard. Of course, all responsibility for any remaining inaccuracy rests solely with me.

I am also deeply grateful to Carla Faralli and Vincenzo Ferrari, for their appreciation of this project.

In structuring this book, I have also benefited from the suggestions and input I received from various colleagues during three conferences that gave me the opportunity to present parts of this work in progress. The first was the conference held by the Italian Society for the Philosophy of Law (SIFD) in September 2016, where I had stimulating discussions with Pio Marconi, Antonio Punzi, Simona Sagnotti and Franco Todescan.

Another important conference for this project was *Sicily, al-Andalus and the Maghreb: Writing in Times of Turmoil*, organised by Nicola Carpentieri at the Universitat Autònoma de Barcelona in May 2017: this was especially valuable in framing my work within the cultural context of Islam in the Middle Ages, and made it possible for me to get feedback from scholars in this field, such as Giovanna Calasso, Nicola Carpentieri, Francesca Maria Corrao, Roberta Denaro, Nora S. Eggen, Jonas Elbousty and William Granara, all of whom I greatly thank.

Finally, I drew much benefit from *The Shape of Return*, a stimulating conference on the cyclical conceptions of history, held in September 2017 at ICI Berlin and organised by Francesco Giusti and Daniel Reeve: my grateful thanks go to them, as well as to all the other participants, for the many and useful comments they offered.

I should further thank the publisher Franco Angeli, for giving me permission to publish this work in English, Clelia Boscolo, for her help in revising the present English translation, and all my friends and colleagues at CIRSFID-Alma Human AI. The privilege of working in a research centre which provides an opportunity to exchange ideas with colleagues on an informal, daily basis, is an important added value that, even if it may not translate into specific and detailed ad hoc comments, always and in any event works in the background to strengthen research, greatly contributing to its development.

But my final, as well as my greatest and most heartfelt thanks, go to Edoardo and to our children, Emanuele and Elisa: like background painting, their "colouring" fills this entire book.

Contents

About the Author

Annalisa Verza is associate professor of Sociology and Philosophy of Law at the University of Bologna. Her main research areas concern liberalism and multiculturalism, the relationship between Islamic culture and fundamental rights, legal feminism and the impact of digital technology on our society's democratic processes.

Chapter 1
The Rediscovery of Ibn Khaldūn's Work

Abstract This chapter deals with the connections between the genesis of *Muqaddima*—Ibn Khaldūn's masterpiece—and the most significant moments in its author's eventful life.

It then traces the history of the rediscovery of his work, first through Ottoman culture, and then through Orientalism of Europe, until its first translations, published precisely when European sociology was taking its first steps.

Space is also devoted to contextualising the *Muqaddima*, considered here against the backdrop of its author's Islamic culture and the tradition of philosophical rationalism, that he gathers and reinterprets. Particular attention is devoted to the examination of the hypothesis, put forward by some exegetes, of a possible influence on the basic structure of the *Muqaddima* of Aristotle's Physics.

Finally, attention is paid to the ambivalence of the attitude taken, in successive waves, by Ibn Khaldūn's critics, both in Europe and in the Arab world, as well as to the thesis of the direct influence of the *Muqaddima* on the works of the fathers of European sociology.

1.1 Ibn Khaldūn and His Time: A "Nomad" in Space and in Thought

Born in Tunis on 27 May 1332, Ibn Khaldūn ('Abd-ar-Raḥmān Abū Zayd ibn Muḥammad ibn Muḥammad Ibn Ḫaldūn al-Ḥaḍramī) was not only one of the most important historians from the Arab world of all times, but also one of its greatest thinkers. At once a man of thought and action—politician, diplomat, historian, man of letters, poet, scholar, law teacher and Maliki judge—next to Avicenna (Ibn Sīnā) and Averroes (Ibn Rušd) he can be regarded as one of the Muslim theorists whose thought has most deeply penetrated and influenced the general culture of the West.

A. Verza, *Ibn Khaldūn and the Arab Origins of the Sociology of Civilisation and Power*, https://doi.org/10.1007/978-3-030-70339-4_1

In fact, the depth of his thought, nourished by the richness and variety of his direct experiences, not only made him an attentive and enlightened expert of the past and present of his own world, but also enabled him to transcend the specificity of his contingent time and space, comprehending it within the framework of a more general scheme endowed with constant elements, encompassing, in a process of continuous transformation, both the history of the past and its projection into the future.

Not unlike the great traveller Ibn Baṭṭūṭa, with whom he was acquainted, Ibn Khaldūn himself was exposed to the broader cultural experience of those whose circumstances, by personal or family fortune, destine them to a life constantly on the move, and, thus, develop an eager curiosity to make sense of the world about them. In this respect, there was a twofold aspect to his travels—at once geographic and intellectual.

His family, that of the Banū Khaldūn, had also been accustomed to moving from place to place for generations, and was, thus, alert to the instability that seemed to mark its fate.[1] Originally from Yemen, as is attested by the last part of its name (i.e., its *nisba*, indicating that one of Ibn Khaldūn's ancestors, named al-Ḥaḍramī, came from Ḥaḍramawt, a coastal region of Yemen), in the eighth century, the early age of Muslim conquest, with its troops on the Prophet's side, his family made its way to the land of al-Andalus,[2] which, in 712, was wrested from the Visigoth rule. There it settled and, until the thirteenth century, it held some of the highest government posts, first in Carmona and then in Seville.

Reference to this family is also made by Andalusian historian Ibn Ḥayyān, who, in his extensive *al-Muqtabis,* traces the long Sevillian history of the Banū Khaldūn family, which maintained a position of power (al-Yaaqubi 2006, 320) not only throughout the Umayyad period—and so until 1031—, but also in the subsequent politically fragmented period of the *Reyes de Tayfas* (kings of the principalities in the territories held by the Umayyad Andalusian dynasty),[3] the independent sovereigns who ruled for about half a century.

But even after this five-century span, the comfortable position the family had secured did not quell its distinctive propensity to cast a wider, restless searching gaze on the world. So, in 1228, it took the farsighted decision to leave its possessions behind and migrate once again, heading for Tunis (at the time, the capital of Ifrīqiya, held by the Hafsid dynasty, which came into power after the Abbasid dynasty) just before the Christian *Reconquista* of Andalusia and, in particular, the reconquest of Seville in 1248.

Having reached Ifrīqiya, the prosperous Banū Khaldūn acquired various territories south of Tunis, as well as many houses in the Tunis district where the

[1]On the history of his family, see al-Yaaqubi (2006).

[2]For this reason, as had been promised, blessings would remain on its family and descendants until the day of resurrection.

[3]The *Reyes de Tayfas* "opened the gates" to the later arrival of governors of non-Arab descent coming from the Maghreb, enlisted to provide military support in fighting the threat posed by Spain's Christian Muslims.

Andalusians resided.[4] In one of these, to this day still marked with a plaque, in 1332, Ibn Khaldūn was born. The young man, following in his father's footsteps, was destined to be brought up as an *adīb*—a "man of culture"—in Islamic law and in all sciences. He thus studied classic Arabic, the Koran, law, and literature with the best scholars of the time. Particularly important, in light of the strong influence he exerted on his pupil (Nassar 1964, 103–14; Pizzi 1985, 29), was philosopher Abū 'Abd Allāh Muḥammad Ibn Ibrāhīm al-Ābilī,[5] descending from a family originally from Avila, in Spain (whence he was named). Mathematician and philosopher, al-Ābilī had moved closer to the great thinkers Avicenna (Ibn Sīnā) and Averroes (Ibn Rušd)—despite the strong anti-rationalist bias that dominated the region at the time of the Hafsids in Tunis and the Marinids in Fez (Nassar 1964, 29). His rational approach, which can be appreciated even in the path he planned to follow when teaching the intellectual sciences to the young Ibn Khaldūn, proved to be crucial for his training. Starting out with mathematics (Ibn Khaldūn [1980] 1995), logic (Aristotelian logic, known through the Arabic translations of the *Organon*), and the study of other curricular subjects, he methodically guided his pupil to the study of philosophy. Thus, he progressively disclosed to his quick intellect the very "encyclopaedic" breadth of views that would later be reflected in Chapter VI of the *Muqaddima*, a chapter devoted to offering, after a comprehensive overview of the level reached by the arts (in Chapter V), a full picture of the sciences developed in his time, examined in relation to the dynamic characteristics of the society which produced them.[6]

At the age of 20 Ibn Khaldūn was hired by Abū Isḥāq to serve as *khaṭīb al-alāma* in the Hafsid court in Tunis, where, in this capacity, he was entrusted with writing the ritual formula of the praise to God as an epigraph, between the *Basmala* and the main body of text, in fine calligraphy, in correspondence and official documents. At this court, he began to become acquainted with the reality of government, an institution that—as he would later stress himself—is designed to prevent all injustices "except its own."[7]

In Tunis, however, between 1348 and 1349, in the short span of a couple of years, the traumas of the black plague, and the famine that followed it, radically changed the reality of his world. This ravaging turn of events proved to be decisive in

---

[4]To this day, this remains the name of the Tunis road that runs from the Zaitūna Mosque to the Husainid mausoleum.

[5]Al-Ābilī was deeply knowledgeable about the works of Averroes, Avicenna, al-Fārābī, and al-Rāzī, and commented on all of them. Cf. Lacoste ([1966] 1998, 55).

[6]In Ibn Khaldūn's scheme—anticipating, in a sense, the much later project which, through a different perspective, prompted Auguste Comte's *Treatise on Sociology*—the sciences are framed as a sort of "luxury" that can be developed only at the more mature stages of civilisation.

[7]*Muqaddima* II, 7. Ibn Khaldūn (1958, Vol. I: 262). Ibn Khaldūn ([1967] 2005, 97): "Mutual aggression of people in towns and cities is averted by the authorities and the governments, which hold back the masses under their control from attacks upon each other. They are, thus, prevented by the influence of force and governmental authority from mutual injustice, save such injustice as comes from the ruler himself."

prompting him to move elsewhere once again. As he himself commented in the introduction to his *Muqaddima*, "the entire inhabited world changed." (*Muqaddima*: The Introduction. Ibn Khaldūn 1958, Vol. I: 64. Ibn Khaldūn [1967] 2005, 30).

> [A destructive plague] devastated nations and caused populations to vanish. It swallowed up many of the good things of civilizations and wiped them out. It overtook dynasties at the time of their senility, when they had reached the limit of their duration. It lessened their power and curtailed their influence. It weakened their authority. Their situation approached the point of annihilation and dissolution. Civilizations decreased with the decrease of mankind. Cities and buildings were laid waste, roads and way signs were obliterated, settlements and mansions became empty, dynasties and tribes grew weak. (Ibid.).

The plague, soon followed by a terrible famine, killed his kin, many of his friends, and nearly all of his teachers. The words Ibn Khaldūn uses to describe the great pestilence are strong—a rare occurrence in his lean and "mathematical" prose—and filled with quivering emotion, although, as is the rule in his thought, never too far from a ratiocinating endeavour: "It was as if the voice of existence in the world had called out for oblivion and restriction, and the world had responded to its call."[8]

Shortly thereafter, without any feeling of regret, the young Ibn Khaldūn left his first position, which he perceived to be much below his abilities, with the ambition to find a more active role in the politics of his time. This marked the beginning of his life as a traveller, but also as an attentive and keen observer of a world that, between destructions and rebirths, was going through an utterly critical phase in its history, before his very eyes. As we can read in the *Muqaddima*, the destructive reach of the black plague had already set in motion his urgency to find explanations for the unfolding of historical events, and this urgency was soon to lead to something innovative.[9] In fact, in the face of such sweeping changes in conditions, Ibn Khaldūn writes, "there is need [...] that someone should systematically set down the situation of the world." (*Muqaddima*: The Introduction. Ibn Khaldūn 1958, Vol. I: 65. Ibn Khaldūn [1967] 2005, 30).

His decision to leave would soon cause him to take part in the administrative, political, and legal life of the different reigns that stretched across North Africa and Granada, but also, inevitably, in that world's power intrigues and alliance games. In the pell-mell of such affairs, not only did he play a direct role—owing to which he would intermittently be elevated to the greatest honours or (depending on the alternating play of political forces, as they vied for power) forced into prison—but he also, and especially, acted as an attentive and analytical decoder of the dynamics and deeply underlying causes of the changes taking place in such contexts.

---

[8] *Muqaddima*: The Introduction. Ibn Khaldūn (1958, Vol. I: 64). Ibn Khaldūn ([1967] 2005, 30). Even then, with words of great evocative power, Ibn Khaldūn tried to offer a somehow rationalising explanation for the phenomenon: In this passage, his explanation takes on a singularly Malthusian cast.

[9] A parallel can be drawn here with Boccaccio: in his *Decameron* the same pestilence was the backdrop against which his Florentine story-tellers retreated to the countryside, where they would fill their time and thoughts with novellas.

His activity is historically situated in the period which followed the fall of the Almohad caliphate (al-Muwaḥḥidūn), which had managed to unify Tunisia, Morocco, and Spain into a single powerful reign where the intellectual sciences had prospered: in the twelfth century, the Almohad courts had provided the environment in which thinkers like Averroes (Ibn Rušd) and Abubekar (Ibn Ṭufayl) could develop their theories. Once this dynasty fell, North Africa was split up (and would continue in this way until the mid-sixteenth century) among various Arabised Berber dynasties (Turroni 2002, 29), such as the Hafsids, based in Tunis and ruling over Ifrīqiya (present-day Tunisia, beyond the region east of Algeria); the Zayyanids (Abd al-Wadids), based in Tlemcen; and the Marinids, in the Maghreb, based in Fez.

Luckily, a specific record of Ibn Khaldūn's quicksilver ups and downs in this constantly changing world comes to us by his own hand: in fact, he was also the first Arab author to write an autobiography.[10] His *Ta'rīf bi-Ibn Ḫaldūn wa-riḥlatuhu ġarban wa-šarqan* (*Biography of Ibn Khaldūn and of his travels across the West and the East*),[11] updated by Ibn Khaldūn until the year before his death, in 1406, is an exceptional document that matches the chronicler's work with a conscious and intelligent[12] "intersectional" glance comparing the Maghreb and the Mashriq (as the title itself specifies).

Aimed at documenting the importance of the historical and geographic contexts to explain political events, his *Ta'rīf* represents a very important basis to understand the world in which Ibn Khaldūn operated, both physically and intellectually. In part modelled after the *riḥla*, a classic travel-writing genre made famous by Ibn Baṭṭūṭa, Ibn Khaldūn's *Ta'rīf* departed from its model taking on characteristics of its own, that make it even more valuable: instead of turning to curious and marvellous elements, it focuses on particular details and seemingly irrelevant "fine-grained" elements of everyday life that, however much they may generally have been considered unworthy of a savant's attention, turn up to be actually profoundly revealing of his world. Likewise, not only are dates and events reported in his *Ta'rīf*, but also systematically arranged (with scientific attention, as always) along the conceptual axis of the transition from rural to urban society (Pomian 2006, 185), thus ideally intertwining the themes and reflections developed in his main work.

---

[10]But he was not the first *Muslim* autobiographer: cf. Fischel (1952, 14–17).

[11]As Fischel (1952) has clarified, the *Ta'rīf* was initially conceived as an integral part of the *Kitāb al-'Ibar*, and only towards the end of his life did Ibn Khaldūn decide to treat it as an independent work. The *Ta'rīf* was published in 1370 in Cairo in an Arabic version edited by Muḥammad Tawit at-Tanji. In the nineteenth century a French translation was published, prefacing De Slane's translation of the *Muqaddima* (Ibn Khaldūn 1862–1868). In 1980 Abdesselam Cheddadi provided a new French translation as a self-standing work (Ibn Khaldūn [1980]1995), but leaving out its poetic part, which was then included in a newer translation in Ibn Khaldūn 2002. On his "intellectual biography," see also Irwin (2018).

[12]Baali (1988, 3–4) writes that Ibn Khaldūn seems to have been the only Muslim author to have written frankly, in his *Ta'rīf*, about his secular activities, and that this unprecedented feature of this work, realistic and absolutely not idealised, is likely to have subsequently made him the object of much criticism.

So, thanks to this document, we know that Ibn Khaldūn, as an active player in the government politics of the majority of the North African and Andalusian dynasties of his time, necessarily witnessed, directly and at first hand, their continuous, fragile, and critical series of alternating successions. In particular, he was a direct participant in the political events that developed in the Marinid court of Abū ʿInān in Fez (where he first arrived in 1352 after al-Ābilī, his only teacher and friend to have survived the plague), where he served as judge in the *Maẓālim* court;[13] in Mohamed V's Nasrid court in Granada (in 1363), where he served as a court diplomat; in the Castilian court of the Christian king Peter the Cruel (in 1364), who offered to return his family's ancient possessions to him if he accepted a move to Seville; in the court of emir Abū 'Abd Allāh Muḥammad in Béjaïa, in Algeria (in 1365), where he served as chamberlain and Malikite judge (*qāḍı*); and then in the court of emir Abū l-ʿAbbās of Constantine, in Algeria and in the court of Abū Ḥammū Mūsā II of Tlemcen, also in Algeria, where he succeeded in establishing important relations with the local Berber tribes [The Banū Khaldūn family may itself have had a Berber kinship (Lawrence 2005, vii)], following a mission ordered by the sovereign, and where he was offered a position as prime minister.

In fact, not only was the world he knew and in which he moved wide, but also particularly varied, unstable, and complex.

One of Ibn Khaldūn's first European commentators, Gaston Bouthoul[14] (1930, 49–50), clearly described the political and social fragmentation which characterised North Africa at the time, and the profound challenge of the effort to manage all those different political alliances. In fact, the cities, especially along the coast, did enjoy a sufficient level of civilisation, but the countryside was vulnerable to the violent incursions of the nomadic tribes,[15]—warlike, untameable, and ever-ready to stake claims to power—which represented for all governments a worrisome element of unpredictability. The mountain Berbers (Khroumirians, Kabylians, Chleuhs, and so on), for their part, lived in almost complete independence, considering that rarely did the troops of the ruling powers dare to venture into their areas. Finally, the desert lands were inhabited by peoples who were even more disquieting, fierce, and prone to religious fanaticism in the form of the cult of those who would later be known as *Marabouts*.[16] As Ibn Khaldūn would later stress, the inhabitants of the cities, albeit culturally more advanced, revealed by contrast a more pliant character and had completely lost their warlike inclination. On the contrary, they were accustomed to entrusting their own defence to the city militia[17] and to the city walls (as, unlike the

[13]The *Maẓālim* court had been instituted to protect ordinary citizens from abuses of power.

[14]Along with Louise Weiss, Gaston Bouthoul was the founder of polemology. He also wrote (Bouthoul 1934) the preface to the second edition of De Slane's translation.

[15]There were also seminomadic, equally insubordinate tribes.

[16]Men shrouded in a halo of sacredness, regarded as "saints" and equipped with magical-religious powers, venerated even in their tombs.

[17]In some cases, under specific agreements, protection was also entrusted to the nomads who surrounded the cities.

nomads, they did not have the option of fleeing in retreat if they lost in battle), and so they found themselves having to yield to whatever group might take power. In fact, for the same reasons, they proved to be extraordinarily passive even when confronted with Tamerlane's conquests (Lavisse and Rambaud 1898).

The very instability intrinsic to this situation[18] might have worked as a key element in stimulating Ibn Khaldūn's need to steer his analysis not so much (as in the Platonic-Aristotelian philosophical tradition) toward a reflection on the characteristics of the best possible form of state, as toward an examination of the actual processes through which political power is gained and the dynamics through which it is subsequently lost.

It was precisely after gaining so much experience, in the Maghreb as well as in Europe (a context which, to his eyes, had shown the same power dynamics which he had observed in the Maghreb, and which had also been struck, to an even greater degree than the Maghreb, by the same wave of the black plague), that the urgency of his scientific "mandate," and his need to set down the details of his historical analysis, pushed him toward a truce.

In 1375, the sultan of Tlemcen sent him on a mission to the tribe of the Awlād ʿArīf, in western Algeria, close to present-day Oran. Once he got there, however, Ibn Khaldūn asked to stay, as a guest and friend of the tribe. This stay, spent with his family in the Berber fortress of Qalʿat Ibn Salāma under the protection of the Awlād ʿArīf, lasted almost 4 years, from 1375 to 1378.

During this period, in a few very intense months of feverish inspiration[19] from July to November 1377 (as stated in his autobiography, but also in the closing lines of the *Muqaddima* itself),[20] far from libraries, texts, and schools, Ibn Khaldūn wrote the first draft of the *Muqaddima*—the first volume of his massive *Kitāb al-ʿIbar* (*Book of Lessons*).[21] This seven-volume historical work was meant to revolutionise the structure and function, and consequently also the style, of history writing itself.

In his *Taʿrīf* Ibn Khaldūn (2002, 151) describes the torrential flow of the rapture that, in the short span of those few months, prompted his hand to pen the

---

[18]Bouthoul (1930, 50–51) suggests that this instability can in part explain both the progressive decadence of North Africa, and the fact that the only moments of stability in its history were determined by the support of foreign powers (as in the case of Byzantine domination, or that of the Aghlabid princes backed by the emirs of the Orient).

[19]In several places in the *Muqaddima*, as well as in his autobiography, Ibn Khaldūn insisted that he did write his work in a spell of exceptional inspiration.

[20]*Muqaddima*, Concluding Remark. Ibn Khaldūn (1958, Vol. III: 481). Ibn Khaldūn ([1967] 2005, 459): "I completed the composition and draft of this first part, before revision and correction, in a period of five months ending in the middle of the year 779 [November 1377]." From his autobiography (Ibn Khaldūn 2002) we know that he went back to expanding the *Muqaddima* from 1378 to 1382, and that he continued to refine it until his death in Cairo in 1406.

[21]The title, in its extended form, might be translated as follows: "*Book of Lessons, Record of Beginnings and Events in the History of the Arabs, Persians and Berbers, and Their Powerful Contemporaries*."

Muqaddima, when speaking of "words and ideas pouring into my head like cream in a churn, until the finished product was ready."[22]

Once he completed his *Muqaddima*, however, Ibn Khaldūn fell seriously ill (Ibn Khaldūn 2002, 152), to the extent that he was afraid to die. For health reasons, then, but also because of the need to consult other writings for his inquiry, after this moment of retreat he decided to return to urban life, and hence, inevitably, back to the rough and tumble of political life: in fact, as he writes in the *Muqaddima*: "It should be known that it is difficult and impossible to escape (from official life) after having once been in it."[23]

Thus, at the end of 1378, he first returned to Tunis, at the court of the Hafsid sultan Abū l-'Abbās, to whom he offered a copy of his work. Abū l-'Abbās granted him the honour of being appointed as a teacher at the University of al-Zaytūna—which he did with great success. However, he soon came to realise that he was privy to too many political secrets to be able to safely stay in the city for long, and so, in order to escape the envy and plotting of local government circles (in Ibn Khaldūn's own words, "*the scorpions of intrigue*") (Ibn Khaldūn [1967] 2005, 20. *Muqaddima*, The Introduction. Ibn Khaldūn 1958, Vol. I, 31), he took leave, with the excuse of carrying out his pilgrimage to Mecca, when in fact he was heading for Egypt. He arrived there in the Autumn of 1382.

Ibn Khaldūn settled first in Alexandria and then, permanently, in Cairo (enthusiastically described as the "metropolis of the world, garden of the universe": Ibn Khaldūn 2002, 162), where, precisely in that fateful year 1382, power had passed from the Turkish Mamluks of the Bahri dynasty to the Circassian Mamluks under al-Ẓāhir Sayf al-Dīn Barqūq. In Cairo Ibn Khaldūn, apart from his pilgrimage to Mecca (which he actually accomplished later on) and various diplomatic missions entrusted upon him, spent the rest of his life. Here he was well received by the sultan, but at the same time, almost because of an implacable nemesis, he attracted deep resentments among the courtiers. In 1384 Ibn Khaldūn received the honour of being appointed *gran qāḍī*, but in July of the same year he had to endure the terrible tragedy of the loss of his family in a shipwreck off the coast of Alexandria. His wife and five sons, along with some attendants who were very close to them, having set sail from Tunis, were going to join him in Cairo. In fact, there are still doubts whether their death in the shipwreck was merely bad luck, or whether it was somehow connected with the hatred from which Ibn Khaldūn had just fled (Horrut 2006, 96). According to Goumeziane (2006, 27), Ibn Khaldūn was left with only two

[22]Franz Rosenthal (1958, liii). The torrent metaphor—the idea of words flooding in—is retained in the French translation: "J'en achevai l'introduction [*al-Muqaddima*] selon cette manière originale qui me fut inspirée dans cette retraite: des torrents de mots et d'idées se déversèrent sur mon esprit et y furent agités jusqu'à ce que j'en eusse extrait la crème et élaboré les produits" (Ibn Khaldūn 2002, 151).

[23]Ibn Khaldūn ([1967] 2005, 236); *Muqaddima* III, 39; Ibn Khaldūn (1958, Vol. II, 99–100). In fact, as Ibn Khaldūn explained, "rulers [...] want to avoid the chance that someone (outside) might come to know (their secrets) and their circumstances (through such persons), and they are averse to letting them become the servants of others."

children, who had not left with their mother, and who would reach him a few months later.

In Egypt, Ibn Khaldūn once again found himself thrust into the fray of political life and of its highs and lows. Once more, he found himself being cyclically honoured and envied: honoured as a Malikite *gran qāḍī*, as a highly regarded and followed teacher of law at the al-Qamḥiyya *madrasa*, and also as a diplomat, serving the local sovereign; then envied, as is reported in detail in his autobiography, as he ended up attracting animosity by his rigorous and incorruptible spirit, closely adhering to Islamic law and unwilling to give in to favouritism or to make the pretrial agreements customarily entered into by the local powerful men.

In fact, Ibn Khaldūn, on account of his intransigence, drew the ire of a high number of highly placed individuals who, being accustomed to rigged trials, could not countenance the prospect of losing a case. As he wrote in his *Ta'rīf*,[24] it was standard practice for emirs to resort to "loyal" judges who would confine themselves to seconding and giving written form to the judgements prepared in advance by the emirs' secretaries. As a result of the complaints raised in reaction to his "inconceivable" and uncompromising stringency, Ibn Khaldūn would regularly be relieved of his duties, and he was even brought to trial (fortunately, with a favourable outcome). His cherished independence of judgment and his freedom from conformism was also reflected in his outward choices, such as his continuing to wear a "different" garb even in Egypt, signalling his Maghrebin-Andalusian origin (Franz Rosenthal 1984; Fischel 1952, 70–71 n. 54), rather than blending into the new context by wearing the lighter Egyptian attire.

Ibn Khaldūn also directed one of the leading Sufi convents in North Africa—that of Baybars—and Sufism, which he discusses with great proficiency even in his *Muqaddima,*[25] became the subject of a separate work (Ibn Khaldūn 2017) which he wrote with the title "*Šifā' al-sā'il li-tahḏīb al-masā'il*" (*The Satisfaction of Those Who Inquire into the Solution of Problems*).

In the last three decades of his life, he never stopped revising and perfecting his *Kitāb al-'Ibar*, writing several manuscript versions, slightly different from one another, which were entrusted to different libraries across the Maghreb and Egypt. Even his eastbound pilgrimage to Mecca, which he made in 1387, thereafter visiting Jerusalem, Hebron, and Bethlehem, became a source for his historical investigation,

[24] As he himself wrote in his autobiography: "Je respectais strictement l'égalité des parties, défendant le droit du plus faible, repoussant toute intercession, j'examinais soigneusement les explications des plaideurs, vérifiais l'honorabilité des témoins. Car parmi ceux-ci, il y en avait d'honnêtes et de malhonnêtes, le bon grain se mêlant à l'ivraie. Et comme ils se prévalaient de leurs liens avec les puissants [ahl ash sahwka], les juges fermaient les yeux sur leurs vices et se gardaient de les censurer [...]. Le mal empirait sans cesse; les prévarications, les falsifications répandaient partout les scandales" (Ibn Khaldūn [1980] 1995). Cf. Ibn Khaldūn (2002, 154).

[25] As Fromherz emphasises (2010), Ibn Khaldūn learned much about Sufism from his older friend and colleague from Granada Ibn al-Khaṭīb, who wrote a treatise on the subject (*The Garden of the Definition of Supreme Love*). See Fromherz, Allen James (2010: 95, n. 68). See also Al-Azmeh, Aziz (2003: 6, n. 8) .

enabling him to fill some gaps in his historical knowledge relating to the non-Arab rulers of these lands and to the Turkish dynasties.

In 1394 Ibn Khaldūn sent a copy of his *Kitāb al-'Ibar* to Merinid sultan Abū Fāris 'Abd al-ʿAzīz in Fez. This two-volume manuscript, still held in Fez in the library of the Qarawiyīne mosque, is distinguished by a peculiarity: At the end, Ibn Khaldūn placed some poems and songs, written in the local dialect. In 1396 (the same year in which he visited Jerusalem) Ibn Khaldūn sent another copy of his work to Marrakesh as a gift for the city's library.

In the meantime, the first volume of the *Kitāb*, the *Muqaddima*, was gaining currency as a book taught in separate lessons to large numbers of students.

Finally, in 1400, towards the end of his life and aged almost 70, Ibn Khaldūn, still serving as a diplomatic representative, met face to face with the greatest and most feared conqueror and destructor of his time (who, in addition, vividly and powerfully exemplified Ibn Khaldūn's own theories about the destructive and conquering power of nomadic groups): Tamerlane. Tamerlane, of Tartar descent, for two decades, through a series of military conquests accompanied by destruction and cruel massacres, and following in the footsteps of his Mongol predecessor Genghis Khan, had been pursuing a plan of universal sovereignty.

In that year Ibn Khaldūn was assigned the task of accompanying the successor to Barqūq, Nāṣir al-Dīn Faraj, to the city of Damascus (which was then under Egyptian protection), as Tamerlane, leading his Tartar troops together with the Mongol tribes whose lineage went back to Genghis Khan, was making his way back to conquer Aleppo, and Damascus was at risk of falling under his attack. Yet, as soon as Ibn Khaldūn and Nāṣir al-Dīn Faraj entered Syria, rumours of a series of attempted revolts in Egypt reached the ear of the sovereign who, thus, found himself forced to hastily return to Egypt, along with most of his retinue, entrusting Ibn Khaldūn, left with a few other courtiers, with the extremely sensitive and perilous diplomatic mission of interacting with the great and cruel conqueror.

The intense meeting with Tamerlane took place on 10 January 1401, in a tent outside the walls of Damascus (Speake [2003] 2014, 582), and is recounted in minute detail in Ibn Khaldūn's autobiography. As he arrived, with a wealth of gifts to tilt the negotiations in favour of Damascus, Tamerlane had him immediately placed under arrest along with his entourage, with the intention, as was expected, of putting all of them to death.

But then, the historical and political theories he had developed about *'aṣabiyya* and the dynasties' cycle of conquest and demise, properly hinted at by Ibn Khaldūn, intrigued Tamerlane, who became captivated by the discussion. Certainly interested in these theories' practical applications in view of his project of conquest, Tamerlane—who would later be described by Ibn Khaldūn ([1980] 1995, 246) as "very intelligent and perspicuous, and tireless in discussing what he knew and even what he didn't know"—wanted to learn more from the scholar he was conversing with.[26] After all, Tamerlane himself could not, in turn, fail to fascinate Ibn Khaldūn. In fact Tamerlane, with the story of his conquests, seemed to embody the central thesis set out in Ibn Khaldūn's theory (Ibn Khaldūn [1980] 1995, 234), according to which a leader's rise to power (and also, proportionately, the extent of the realm he will conquer) is linked to the intensity of the solidal cohesion (what Ibn Khaldūn calls *'aṣabiyya*) of the group from which he emerges as a "champion." Thus Tamerlane, keen to gain a better understanding of this uniquely original theorist of power, withdrew his earlier order to have him killed, and for 35 days took him along as a guest and interlocutor in a quick-paced, tightly strung dialogue. In those days, among other things, he also asked Ibn Khaldūn to write a historical and geographical treatise on North Africa for him.

Despite this, Damascus was destined to go up in flames, and that is precisely what happened. Still, it was perhaps because of the influence of Ibn Khaldūn that Tamerlane continued his advance by steering towards Anatolia, without heading first for Egypt, which consequently was spared from the destruction.

Tamerlane was so impressed by these theories and information that, in the end, he proposed that Ibn Khaldūn stay permanently with him; nevertheless, Ibn Khaldūn succeeded in diplomatically declining the offer without consequence.

In the winter of 1401, Ibn Khaldūn took leave from Tamerlane and, in mid-March, he could go back to his teaching in Cairo. Here, the *Muqaddima* had already become the subject of a specifically dedicated theoretical course for throngs of students.[27] In addition to his teaching, he also went back to serving as a judge.

In Cairo 5 years later, on 17 March 1406, after his sixth appointment as *qāḍī*, the life of a man who, in words and deeds, had taken up in an exceptional way the challenges of an exceptional time, came to an end. His body still rests there, in the Sufi cemetery in Cairo, just outside the Bāb al-Naṣr gate. His writings also lay to rest—mostly consigned to oblivion in the libraries of North Africa, where he had ensured their preservation—until they were rediscovered half a millennium later.

---

[26] Ibn Khaldūn's autobiographical account of his meeting with Tamerlane has been translated into English in W. J. Fischel (1952), who enriched the text with interesting comments. A partial Italian translation can be found in Pizzi (1985).

[27] Even the pace of the *Muqaddima*, based on a pattern of propositions and demonstrations, shows that it might have been conceived from the outset by Ibn Khaldūn as a textbook to be taught.

1.2 The Rediscovery of the *Muqaddima* Five Centuries Later

Ibn Khaldūn's *Muqaddima* is the theoretical introduction[28]—and hence, from a socio-philosophical standpoint, the most interesting volume—of a complex, seven-volume work, the *Kitāb al-'Ibar* (*Book of Lessons, Record of Beginnings and Events in the History of the Arabs, Persians and Berbers, and Their Powerful Contemporaries*), aimed at analysing, with surprisingly modern and innovative criteria, the history of the rise and fall of civilisations, with particular—but not exclusive—reference to North Africa.

Across its 1600 pages,[29] this *Introduction* develops an original and detailed thesis aimed at explaining the dynamics that shape the historical spans of the political forces that take turns in the government of society. In it we find a paradigm of social history at once universal, in the eternal cyclic progression it depicts, and granularly fragmented in the manifold makeup of the environmental, cultural, technological, and religious variables by which every single cultural-spatiotemporal crossroads is defined.

In the preface to his work, Ibn Khaldūn expressed the hope that in the future it might be studied, improved, and perfected in light of the consolidation of the philosophico-historico-sociological discipline that he was aware he was pioneering: if "the capital of knowledge that an individual scholar has to offer is small" (*Muqaddima*, Foreword. Ibn Khaldūn 1958, Vol. I, 14. Ibn Khaldūn [1967] 2005, 9), it is to the entire community of scholars that Ibn Khaldūn wished to entrust the development of his great insight.

This heartfelt hope in a future development of his "new science" is also reiterated in the closing lines of the *Muqaddima*, where Ibn Khaldūn wrote:

> Perhaps some later (scholar), aided by the divine gifts of a sound mind and of solid scholarship, will penetrate into these problems in greater detail than we did here. A person who creates a new discipline does not have the task of enumerating all the problems connected with it. His successors, then, may gradually add more problems, until the discipline is completely (presented). (*Muqaddima*, Concluding Remark. Ibn Khaldūn 1958, Vol. III, 481. Ibn Khaldūn [1967] 2005, 459).

However, it would be a long time before his hope could be fulfilled. In fact, for almost two centuries, his theory would be doomed to exist only in a "latent state," without giving rise to any school of thought, finding almost no theoretical or concrete application (Cheddadi 2006, 169–88), and failing to find fertile ground on which to flourish and give fruit. In a word, the trade-off for his originality and his extreme modernity, which he evidently expressed too early, was that for a long time he should remain a sequestered "voice in the desert"—not understood, much less

[28]This is the meaning of the term *Muqaddima*.

[29]The French translation runs to 1632 pages. Rosenthal's three-volume English translation is 1547 pages long.

culturally integrated in his environment, and destined to be heeded and put to use only many centuries later.

It may be that some responsibility for sealing this fate for his work lay with its scarce or even non-existent inclination to praise the sovereign or idealise the ruling powers—and, in fact, the political realism expressed in the work was scarcely flattering to the Arab élite its readers belonged to. It is certainly plausible to think that, in an authoritarian context which, for political reasons, was interested in an apologetic history (*tā'rīḫ*), complacent and conventional, a reading of history like Ibn Khaldūn's, at once rational and tied to real facts, could prove unseemly and even disturbing. So, the many manuscripts he sent around would remain virtually ignored until their rediscovery several centuries later.

Until then, there would be only a few, well-known exceptions to this "shelving" of his oeuvre.

The themes and structure of Ibn Khaldūn's work have been used, for example, in the *Badā'i al-silk* (*The Wonders of State Conduct and the Nature of Kingship*), by Abū Muḥammad Ibn al-Azraq (fifteenth century), who was himself a Malikite *qāḍī*, and who, like Ibn Khaldūn, spent the last years of his life in Cairo. In fact, not only does his work on power echo Ibn Khaldūn's arguments, but, in many passages, it quotes directly from the *Muqaddima* (Abdesselem 1983).

The most important exception to his oblivion, however, undoubtedly lies in the wide use made of Ibn Khaldūn's theory in Turkish historico-political culture (Bombaci 1969). In fact, various scholars in Istanbul, interested in understanding the way the empire might evolve in light of the predictive power provided by Ibn Khaldūn's model, gathered dozens of manuscripts of the work (four of which written when Ibn Khaldūn was still alive), still kept today in the Topkapi Palace (Pizzi 1985, 60).

It was especially famous historian and geographer Kātib Çelebi (1609–1657) who engaged with Ibn Khaldūn's theory by explicit reference to his texts. As Fleischer (1983) notes, for example, he took up Ibn Khaldūn's analogy between the phases in human life and those in political life. He did so for the purpose of showing how the Ottoman Empire proved to be the exception to the rule—in virtue of its ability to flourish anew after Tamerlane's conquest, reaching its highest splendour in the seventeenth century, and to escape the grip of the Khaldunian "fate" of the dynasties' inevitable fall in ordinary times.[30] In the same way, Ibn Khaldūn's scheme was widely used by historians inspired by Çelebi,[31] such as Muṣtafa Na'īmā (1655–1716) and eighteenth-century historian Ahmed Resmī Efendi (1700–1783).

Again, in Turkey—the empire which seemed to represent the most successful embodiment of Ibn Khaldūn's rational state—Pirizāde Efendi (1674–1749), in 1730, worked on the first translation of Ibn Khaldūn's work (a partial translation, limited to

[30] This argument is presented in particular in the work *Kašf al-ẓunūn*.

[31] Ibn Khaldūn's work inspired Muṣtafa Na'īmā's *History* (*Tā'rīḫ*), which discusses the cyclical theory of history and the conflict between sedentary and nomadic social organisations, and, in general, influenced the thought of Ahmed Resmī Efendi.

the first five chapters), written in Turkish and published in Cairo (Franz Rosenthal 1958, cvii–cviii): this translation would subsequently be an important waymark on the path to the European discovery of Ibn Khaldūn.

Although, in the meantime, a Latin translation of Tamerlane's biography by Ibn ʿArabšāh (1389–1450) was published (in 1636 in Leiden, printed by Jacob Golius), and this translation mentioned Ibn Khaldūn by name, it was decidedly mainly through the mediation of Çelebi that Ibn Khaldūn's work truly came to be known in Europe. In actual fact, this did not happen, as one might think, through Spain, which in the Old Continent was the historical heir to Arabic culture. The relaunch came by way of France, where Barthelémy D'Herbelot (1625–1695), an Orientalist who was studying the work of Çelebi, inserted Ibn Khaldūn's name and a short and rather basic biography in his 1697 *Bibliothèque orientale, ou dictionnaire universel contenant tout ce qui regarde la connaissance des peuples de l'Orient*. This biography largely consisted of an abridged translation of the *Kašf al-ẓunūn*, a great bibliographic work written by Çelebi. However, the French Enlightenment of the time was not yet ready to appreciate culture coming from Islam. At best, a few decades hence, this culture would come to be regarded as the "exotic" backdrop to Montesquieu's *Persian Letters*.

Not until the subsequent century, with a weakening Ottoman Empire and the connected prospects of European conquests, would an interest in the East be rekindled. And in this period, too, it was thanks to the European contacts with Turkey that, once more, Ibn Khaldūn's ideas resurfaced in Europe, finally igniting interest in him in the West—and thence, retroactively, also in the Arab world itself.

In fact, as early as 1810, Antoine Isaac Silvestre de Sacy (1758–1838), a professor of Persian and Arabic, published his *Relation de l'Egipte par Abdellatif, médecin arabe de Bagdad*, which contained the first French translation of excerpts from the *Muqaddima*, together with an introduction to his work. Then in 1816, in his *Biographie universelle* ([1816] 1843), he published a biography of Ibn Khaldūn, and finally, in 1826, he translated other excerpts of Ibn Khaldūn's work in his *Chrestomathie arabe* (Silvestre de Sacy [1826–1827] 2012).

In the same period, precisely on the basis of that partial Turkish translation of Ibn Khaldūn's work which had been done almost a century earlier by Pirizāde Efendi, Austrian scholar of Islam and historian of the Ottoman Empire Joseph von Hammer-Purgstall (1774–1856) also devoted new attention to Ibn Khaldūn. In two studies (Hammer-Purgstall 1812, 1818) which, for the first time, dealt with Ibn Khaldūn directly and made extensive reference to translated parts of the *Muqaddima*, he presented his theories (Hammer-Purgstall 1812, 360), describing Ibn Khaldūn (with a curious chronological inversion) as "*the Montesquieu of the Arabs*."

And while, between 1867 and 1868, the Arab world had received its first complete edition (Ibn Khaldūn 1867–1868) of the *Kitāb al-ʻIbar*, based on the original manuscript that Ibn Khaldūn had sent to Fez, edited by Naṣr al-Hūrīnī and published in Būlāq/Cairo,[32] another complete edition had come out a few years earlier in Europe: Étienne Quatremère (1782–1857) had published the unabridged Arabic text of the *Muqaddima* (Ibn Khaldūn 1858), planning to work on its first French translation later on.

Unfortunately, before he could devote himself to this project, he died. A few years later, however, on the basis of Quatremère's edition and of the previous Turkish translations, this project was undertaken and brought to completion in three volumes (Ibn Khaldūn 1862–1868, 1865, 1868) by his disciple, Baron William Mac Guckin de Slane (1801–1878). A French-speaking Irish Orientalist, de Slane had previously published not only a translation of the *Ta'rīf* (Ibn Khaldūn 1844), but also, between 1847 and 1851 (at the request of the French minister of war), the Arabic edition (Ibn Khaldūn 1847–1851) of the "Maghrebin" historical part of the *Kitāb* (corresponding to Books VI and VII).

Later on, some scholars (Pizzi 1985, 93; Ḥamès, 1999, 171; Salama 2011, 77–101) pointed out the profound influence of the colonialist perspective of the period on this translation. For example, they showed how eager de Slane had been to highlight the criticisms that Ibn Khaldūn addressed at the "nomads." Furthermore, he had translated the corresponding term with "Arabs" (Pizzi 1985, 63), in such a way as to justify—apparently, with the backing of Ibn Khaldūn, himself an Arab—the possible arguments in favour of colonial government that were directed against the peoples of North Africa and the Middle East, regarded as politically immature and incapable of self-government.

For a long time, de Slane's translation of the *Muqaddima*, commented in detail by Reinhart Dozy as early as 1869 and by Alessio Bombaci in 1949, remained the only European translation available: it was republished as a photostatic reprint in Paris in 1934–1938 with an introduction by Gaston Bouthoul, and it would serve as the basis for Khaldunian studies for almost a century, until other important translations came out.

A first abridged translation into English by Charles Issawi came out in 1950 with the title *An Arab Philosophy of History*. The most important complete translations of the *Muqaddima*, however, would be carried out in the mid-twentieth century by Franz Rosenthal (Ibn Khaldūn 1958) into English and by Vincent Monteil (working with experts appointed by a UNESCO committee) (Ibn Khaldūn 1967–1968) into French, respectively. Both were based on a 1402 manuscript containing an initial note signed by Ibn Khaldūn, discovered by Rosenthal himself in Istanbul at the Ātif Efendi library. This is the last of Ibn Khaldūn's manuscripts to have survived and is regarded as the most accurate of them all, since it had been completed only a few years before his death.

In particular, the excellent English translation done by Franz Rosenthal, director of the Semitic languages department at Yale University—a translation expressly

[32]This seven volumes edition reproduced, in its first volume, the text of the *Muqaddima* which had been previously published, always in Būlāq/Cairo, in 1857: this was one of the first works published by an Arab publishing house.

conceived to adhere as close as possible to the linguistic form of the original, and to the particular terminology that Ibn Khaldūn accurately developed for his "new science"[33]—proved to be decisive in giving currency to Ibn Khaldūn's thought in the English-speaking world.

A further and later translation which, too, is worthy of note, is the one done in 2002 by Abdesselam Cheddadi (Ibn Khaldūn 2002), who, in addition to being a translator, ranks among the most respected contemporary experts on Ibn Khaldūn's thought.[34]

Starting from these translations, Khaldunian studies have been increasing. There have been some scholars, such as Bruce B. Lawrence,[35] who have claimed that the success of Ibn Khaldūn's rediscovery was essentially only due to European Orientalism and to its desire to discover the exotic expression of a culture "other" from Western culture in his work, rather than an important piece of a shared intellectual tradition binding together ancient Greeks, Muslims, and Europeans.

But to debunk this hypothesis it should suffice to point out (in addition to the previously mentioned influence and deep regard that Ibn Khaldūn's masterpiece already enjoyed since the fifteenth century in Ottoman political culture) that, after its rediscovery, a great number of studies flourished in which Ibn Khaldūn was considered as a modern thinker and a precursor of Western sociology. These acknowledgements, paid by numerous European scholars to the Maghrebin thinker, went well beyond an Orientalist perspective, recognising his clearly anticipative import instead, and from the outset. Moreover, in the Muslim world, by that time, he was recognised, directly, as the "founder" of Arab sociology.[36]

It is true that his work has sometimes been interpreted as a brilliant but idiosyncratic product of Arab culture, stressing its "otherness" relative to Western thought: we can see this in the first commentary of Ibn Khaldūn's work, written in 1834 by Swede Gråberg Graf von Hemsö (1776–1847), an Arabist and consul in Morocco and Tripoli, but also in the 1907 commentary by Reynold A. Nicholson (1868–1945). Both are certainly laudatory, but are aimed at underlying the uniqueness and specificities of Ibn Khaldūn's thought against the backdrop of a Muslim landscape described as bleak and dispiriting.

On the contrary, however, he has more often been acclaimed, in light of the wide-ranging scope of his insights (encompassing much more than the Maghrebin context of the time), as a precursor of sociology and as a "philosopher" of history and of society.

---

[33]In relation to the language he chiselled, Ibn Khaldūn wrote in his autobiography (Ibn Khaldūn 1951: 240 l. 10) that he had to "domesticate" the raw and refractory Arabic language, to make it useful for his work.

[34]It bears mentioning, too, that there is also an Italian translation of part of the *Muqaddima,* carried out by Giancarlo Pizzi (1985), and a translation of ch. 4 edited by Francesca Forte (2020).

[35]"To speak of Ibn Khaldūn and Islamic Ideology [...] is to acknowledge [...] the emergence of Ibn Khaldūn within Orientalism" (Lawrence 1983, 154). Cf. Lawrence (1984).

[36]This is so even if some sociological traits can also be found in Averroes's commentary of Plato's *Republic* (Cruz Hernández 2003, 72).

In fact, the *Muqaddima* had made its debut on the official scene of the European socio-political debate precisely at the time of the incubation, and subsequent birth, of the sociological sciences in Europe. At the time of the first translations by Silvestre de Sacy and von Hammer-Purgstall, the spread of Saint-Simon's thought in France was still in full swing. At the time of de Slane's unabridged translation, Saint-Simonianism was still guiding the *Société d'Études du Canal de Suez*, founded in 1846 by Prosper Enfantin, Saint-Simon's main disciple; likewise, Auguste Comte's *Course in Positive Philosophy* (1855) and Karl Marx's *Communist Manifesto* (1848) had only recently seen the light. Similarly, precisely in those years, the publication of Spencer's *Synthetic Philosophy* was being undertaken in England (its ten volumes would be published between 1862 and 1897), while Durkheim in France was still working on his *Division of Labour in Society* (1893).

The cultural landscape in which the *Muqaddima* made its entrance, then, was primed to take a keen and particular interest in a work that, though it had been written five centuries earlier, presented some aspects of surprising topicality and unexpected intersection with the theories on society that were being developed or discussed precisely at that time. So much so, that some scholars have also advanced various hypotheses on the possibility that the fathers of sociology might have been directly influenced, in their thinking, by their acquaintance with Ibn Khaldūn's theses. And in fact, the similarities, including structural ones, with the work of Auguste Comte, for example, are undeniably surprising, so much so that in 1879 a scholar like Alfred von Kremer (1828–1889) carried out an in-depth investigation into Ibn Khaldūn's "science of cultures": not only did it hail Ibn Khaldūn as the true founder of the science of civil societies (sociology), but also speculated that Auguste Comte might have had first-hand knowledge of his ideas.

In turn, Gråber de Hemsö, in his study, hypothesised that Niccolò Machiavelli might have come to know of Ibn Khaldūn's work through Ḥasan al-Wazzān (a Berber-Andalusian scholar who was baptised in Rome as Giovanni Leone de' Medici, also known as Leone l'Africano (1485–1537), and who taught in Bologna in the sixteenth century), and that this knowledge might have profoundly influenced Machiavelli's thought.

The conflict-theory sociologist Ludwig Gumplowicz, for his part, deeply impressed by Ibn Khaldūn's "social philosophy" and clearly influenced by it in relation to his own theory of the "cycles of conquest," published in Innsbruck a work containing an essay where Ibn Khaldūn was defined as an "Arab sociologist," and also as one who had superseded Vico ahead of Vico's time (Gumplowicz 1925, 90; 113).

Similar appreciations of Ibn Khaldūn as an *ante litteram* Arab sociologist have come from Franz Oppenheimer (1922–1935, vol. II, 173ff.; vol. IV, 251ff.); René Maunier (1915); Pitirim A. Sorokin (1962: 20), who defined the *Muqaddima* as "the earliest systematic treatise both in sociology and in rural-urban sociology"; and Harry Elmer Barnes and Howard Becker (1961, vol. 2, 706–8), who saw in him a conflict theorist and who particularly appreciated his ability to underline the causal explanations of social phenomena in an age when "providential" explanations of history still held primacy. Meanwhile, in Italy, in an 1896 essay published in *La*

Riforma Sociale, Guglielmo Ferrero defined Ibn Khaldūn "*an Arab sociologist of the 14th century,*" greater than Vico and Machiavelli, and the inventor of the sociological concept of civilisation.

Nor should we discount the words of admiration written by historian Arnold Toynbee ([1934] 1962, 322), who, after comparing Ibn Khaldūn to Thucydides and Machiavelli, was unconditional in his praise of Ibn Khaldūn's work.

Other important authors also expressed high praise for Ibn Khaldūn's work. A case in point is the great anthropologist Ernest Gellner (1995, 202), who described him as one of the great thinkers—perhaps *the* greatest—in the social sciences, supporting the idea that his work had influenced the thought of Masqueray, Durkheim, and Evans-Pritchard.

Starting in the 1930s, however, other investigations—by Benedetto Croce (1932), in particular—focused on the importance of reading Ibn Khaldūn within the context of his age and his world, picking out, for example, his deep religiosity, also proven by his emphasising and fully hypostatising, in seamless continuity with the Muslim tradition, the period of the first "well-guided" caliphs. This was the direction taken, for example, in the investigations by Hamilton A. R. Gibb (1933) and Francesco Gabrieli ([1930] 1984).[37]

Meanwhile Islam, in its modernising push, had been receptive to the Western writings where, through the distorting lens of colonial interests, Ibn Khaldūn had been depicted as the "Montesquieu of the East." Now, especially as the former colonies were gaining their independence, it started reclaiming Ibn Khaldūn's legacy as its own, celebrating it, at the same time, as the original source of all sociological knowledge, whose beginnings were, accordingly, proudly stated as having been conceived in North Africa, and, hence, as "homegrown," rather than as imported from Europe.

In particular, one of the founders of the *Nahḍa* (Arab modernism), Egyptian Rifāʿa Al-Ṭahṭāwī (1801–1873), not only reimagined Ibn Khaldūn's idea of *'aṣabiyya* by likening it to the patriotism of his own nationalist view (Hourani 1962, 78ff.; see also Lahbabi 1987[38]), but also, significantly and provokingly, turned the old and well-known judgment expressed by von Hammer-Purgstall on its head, defining Montesquieu "a Western Ibn Khaldūn." At the same time, he stressed the important role that in Ibn Khaldūn's thought is played by the peculiar balance between religious faith and rationality, which in Arabic is termed *ʿaql-naql.*

Beginning in the nineteenth century, then, even the Arab world took a renewed interest in Ibn Khaldūn's political ideas. In 1910 in Cairo, next to the "traditionalist" University of al-Azhar, a new "secular" university opened, which in 1914 awarded its first PhD to the blind scholar Taha Hussein. Hussein was then sent to Paris, to the Sorbonne, to work on a doctoral dissertation on Ibn Khaldūn's thought with the

---

[37]Francesco Gabrieli's father, Giuseppe Gabrieli (1923), also devoted much attention to Ibn Khaldūn.

[38]Lahbabi (1987, 138): "Son manichéisme dénote la réaction d'amertume d'un penseur 'patriote' et aigri."

supervision of Émile Durkheim[39] and Orientalist Paul Casanova. This study (Hussein 1918; Celarent 2013), which decisively relaunched Ibn Khaldūn's "reappropriation" by the Arab world (Pizzi 1985, 75), interpreted Ibn Khaldūn (also quoting Francesco Gabrieli's work) by situating him in a rationalist current that had been running through universal thought, yet, at the same time, establishing his deep roots in the Islamic culture of his time and suggesting that he was not so much a sociologist as a "philosopher of society."

Furthermore, an important role in giving life to this current of "rediscovery" of Ibn Khaldūn has been played by the international colloquia devoted to him that were held in Cairo and in Rabat in 1962, in Rabat and in Algiers in 1978, and in Tunis in 1980 and 1982.[40] In these colloquia the tendency was increasingly to emphasise not the aspects in which Ibn Khaldūn was directly "in dialogue" with Western culture, but rather the contextual aspects and the historical, geographic, religious, and linguistic specificity that marked him out as an Arab thinker. An example of this orientation can be found in Ahmed Abdesselem's work (1983) on the *Muqaddima*, where he has forcefully insisted on defining Ibn Khaldūn's thought as being clearly articulated within the cultural categories of his own time. According to Abdesselem, even in the construction of his innovative intellectual science Ibn Khaldūn was likely to have drawn his material entirely from the sedimented cultural legacy of his world, without betraying the cultural heritage that it was part of.

Meanwhile, the understanding of Ibn Khaldūn as a "forerunner" of Western sociology and an inspiring force behind it continued to be debated, especially in Europe.

Assessing whether the knowledge of Ibn Khaldūn's thought actually influenced the thinking of various Western precursors, fathers, and developers of sociology in a determining way, is something that would require not only an in-depth comparative analysis of the various points of contact and assonance between Ibn Khaldūn's ideas and those of these other authors, but also specific historico-biographical data.

At any rate, the element that apparently most astonished the Western thinkers who looked at Ibn Khaldūn's writings (and also, in many cases, the North African thinkers) was precisely the clear comparability of his theses—in terms of methods, themes, and basic intuitions—with the more advanced Western sociological thought of the nineteenth and twentieth centuries.

In fact, half a millennium in advance, this monumental Maghrebin and Muslim author developed and integrated in his work many of the most important sociological concepts which would be theorised much later in the West (even while proceeding from an "Oriental" basis, and regardless of the secular historico-cultural presuppositions that informed our Enlightenment): from Montesquieu's idea of the fundamental influence that the geographic, climatic, economic, and cultural environments

[39]As Barbara Celarent (2013) reports, Durkheim died shortly before Hussein could discuss his thesis in January 1918.

[40]Further colloquia devoted to him were subsequently held in France as well: Horrut (2006, 222–23).

exert on the character of populations, to the idea of the generative importance of social solidarity and of the different quality that the latter assumes in different demographic contexts (clearly, a Durkheimian theme); from Vico's idea of the existence in history of a cyclical scheme of renewal and decay (*corsi e ricorsi*), to Marx's idea that the historical transition from one form of social and economic organisation to the next dialectically derives from the contradictions (especially those tied to material factors) intrinsic to each single phase; and much else besides.

With this—which represents one of the most stimulating aspects of his thought—Ibn Khaldūn provides the historical demonstration of how it has been (and still is) possible to arrange these same concepts by linking them up within a unifying theory, not only original, but also perfectly compatible with the deep and unshakeable Muslim faith of an incorruptible and sincere Shariatic judge of the Malikite school, despite the peremptoriness with which our culture regards secularism as the *conditio sine qua non* for the birth of the social sciences.

1.3 The Cultural Context of the Time

1.3.1 Ibn Khaldūn Against the Background of the Islamic Tradition

There is certainly no doubt that Ibn Khaldūn's "new science," despite its great originality and the absolute novelty of its objectives and methodology, must have been fostered by the categories of thought, sensibility, and concerns of the society of its own time. Reflecting the debates present in that society and its intellectual atmosphere, it certainly helped, as the scholar Abdesselam Cheddadi (2006, 461) has commented, to make "his society visible to itself."

Through a particularly effective simile, Cheddadi (2006, 462) has compared the *Muqaddima* to the great mosques of the early centuries of Islam such as the Umayyads in Damascus or the Mosque-Cathedral of Córdoba, the Mezquita. These mosques are, indeed, both uniquely original, but equally eclectic by virtue of their ability to include, in an "Arab" way, building techniques, materials, and motifs borrowed from other traditions (Syrian, Byzantine, Visigoth, and probably also Roman), while finally achieving an impression of great harmony in their individuality.

In the same way, the originality of Ibn Khaldūn's thought certainly relied on the foundation of his own culture, developed in previous centuries and continually revisited—to the extent of incorporating elements from other traditions—by a pan-Arabic world which, as Ibn Khaldūn himself observed with thinly veiled bitterness,[41] was at that time beginning to decline. In fact, while fourteenth-century

[41]See the text of one of the first versions of the *Muqaddima* written in Qal'at Ibn Salāma between 1375 and 1377—Manuscript A, VII preamble (Ibn Khaldūn 2002, 1207)—subsequently removed

Islam was increasingly losing its dynamism, at the same time Christianity, having left the long Middle Ages behind, was leaping forward into modernity. There were already some 40 universities in Europe, and by that time—after their first flourishing (Pomian 2006, 23) prompted by the ground-breaking teachings of Saint Thomas Aquinas (1225–1274), Saint Bonaventure (1221–1274), Roger Bacon (1214–1294), Duns Scotus (1268–1308), and great jurists such as Accursius (1182–1260)—they were progressively developing. As Cheddadi comments, Islam was therefore experiencing a distressing sense of being "eclipsed"—a sense that, by reaction, translated into distinct hostility toward philosophy, coupled with a defensive retreat into religion.[42]

Thus, the study of "traditional" sciences—that is, those based on a religious-legal foundation—was the first essential element in the education of the young Ibn Khaldūn. As Franz Rosenthal (1958, lxxxvi) among others has observed, much of the foundational material used for his work is directly drawn from Islamic legal tradition (in particular, the Malikite tradition) or, in any case, inspired by it. However, if Ibn Khaldūn certainly started out from such material, it is also true that—"a brilliant and errant thinker" as he has been described (Brunschvig 1947, 391; Talbi 2002, 854)—, he used it creatively as no one before him had done, and this originality enabled him to contribute to building a science based on an entirely new investigative perspective. As Rosenthal (1958, lxxxvi) comments: "Yet [...] the *Muqaddimah* was profoundly original and constituted a new departure in scholarly research."

In fact, it was the ingenuity of his insight that enabled him to couple the disciplines that had formed his spirit with the very many political experiences he had known, and through which he had become aware of the "inner meaning" of history. In this way, he managed to channel these disciplines and his experience into a broad scientific project which opened up a range of different research avenues, not only historical but also philosophical, sociological, economic, and beyond, thus melding into one coherent picture the two great streams of scientific research that the culture of his time endeavoured to keep separate: the traditional sciences, on the one hand, and the intellectual sciences, on the other.

In fact, while the traditional sciences certainly merged together in the genesis of his work, equally important to it was the contribution that came from his study of grammar, rhetoric, mathematics, and above all—thanks to his teacher al-Ābilī[43]—philosophical method and perspective, which greatly informed Ibn Khaldūn's work,

---

from later versions of the work completed in Cairo between 1385 and 1396 (perhaps, owing to the hope aroused in him by the lively and active vitality that could be sensed and experienced in that city): "A notre époque, nous constatons une sorte de déplacement de la civilisation du sud vers le nord." For a comment on the order in which the different versions of the work were written, see Ibn Khaldūn 2002, 1292–1301.

[42]See Cheddadi 2006, 225, speaking "d'une crispation autur de la religion."

[43]Ibn Khaldūn, in his autobiography, described al-Ābilī as a "great master of the sciences based on reason" (Ibn Khaldūn [1980] 1995, 48).

despite the great scepticism towards philosophy expressed by the socio-cultural environment in which he was working.

It is precisely this happy convergence of many perspectives, gathered during his education and life experiences, coupled with his open, analytical spirit and his own uncommon freedom of thought, that perhaps explains how he came to conceive such an innovative project as the scientific study of human history, society, and civilisation. Such a project, distinct, in its originality, from both Aristotelian philosophy and the thought of great Muslim philosophers such as Avicenna, Averroes, and al-Rāzī, had to wait for a figure such as Saint-Simon to be envisaged in the nineteenth century in the Western world.

The Arab world had come to know philosophy almost fortuitously in the ninth century. The first translations of the Greek authors were born initially out of an interest in the Greeks' knowledge of the natural sciences (physics, astronomy, mathematics, etc.). After that, for completeness' sake, various theoretical works of the Greeks were translated as well. Until that time (and even later, until about the tenth century) the ethical and political world views of both Islam and Christianity were articulated mainly in religious terms, bypassing rational research—if not, often, even discouraging it.

In fact, as Ibn Khaldūn stressed in the *Muqaddima* (VI, 42), the most important philosophical contributions in Arab culture were developed in the preceding centuries by non-Arab Muslim scholars, or by thinkers of Arabic lineage but not language, educated by non-Arab teachers. Ibn Khaldūn explains this phenomenon on the basis of the fact that the Arabs were initially devoid of a sedentary culture, and that subsequently, even after they had taken power, they continued to disdain intellectual work, considering it as a "craft" and, hence, an occupation whose standing lay below the dignity of their lineage. It was not only the case that the fundamental translation of Greek works, done in the early centuries of Islam (especially in the ninth century, spurred on by the Abbasid caliph of Baghdad al-Ma'mūn,[44] who in 832 founded the Bayt al-ḥikma, or *House of Wisdom*), had mostly been made possible by the work of mainly Christian, Jewish, and "pagan" Arabic-speaking translators.

Even the scholars belonging to the Muslim cultural sphere whose work had been opened up to Ibn Khaldūn by his teacher (Nassar 1964) were themselves, for the most part, non-Arab. For example, twelfth-century thinker Faḫr al-Dīn al-Rāzī (1149–1209), who, in his *Tafsīr al-Kabīr*, or *Large Commentary* on the Quran, had maintained the rationalistic thesis according to which facts drawn from tradition alone (from the *ḥadīṯ*)[45] can only be considered as a basis of presumption and can never give any certainty,[46] was Persian. Another important rationalist thinker,

[44]As Ibn Khaldūn reminds us, Al-Ma'mūn was the same caliph who attempted, but failed, to take down the pyramids of Egypt (*Muqaddima* IV, 4).

[45]The *ḥadīṯ* (plural *aḥadīṯ*) is the tradition, generally handed down through a series of transmitters bearing the word of the original witnesses, that concerns the examples and sayings offered by the prophet Muhammad.

[46]In the context of Khaldunian historiography, this concept would then be reflected in his recommendation that historical tradition be used cautiously and selectively. Furthermore, in vol. IV of his

antonomastically referred to as the "Second Teacher," was Turkish logician and philosopher al-Fārābī (872–951). Al-Fārābī had commented on the *Organon* by Aristotle (the philosopher—*al-ḥakīm*—par excellence), assessing the use of logic as the main tool of scientific analysis. Thus, he had reformulated philosophy in such a way as to bring it into accord with the emphasis that Islamic culture places on the community, in view of the happiness of Muslims understood as a political group, rather than on the individual. Central to that aim was his work on the "ideal city," *al-Madīna al-fāḍila*. In the thinking of al-Fārābī, philosophy found its place within religion:[47] hence, the true prophet-lawgiver should also be a philosopher-king.[48] Among other things, Ibn Khaldūn borrowed from al-Fārābī the cosmogony underpinning his vision of the unbroken chain, described in the first part of his work, that links up minerals, plants, animals, and, finally, man.

Also of great importance was the Persian Neoplatonic encyclopaedic philosopher and physician Avicenna (Ibn Sīnā, 980–1037). Avicenna wrote, among other works, the *Book of Healing*, where he refined al-Fārābī's work and held that the intellects which influence the events of the world, all of them created by God, are arranged within a descending ontological and normative hierarchy that also assigns a place to man, who is distinguished from these intellects by virtue of his material component. God gave his law to Muhammad for the benefit of man in a "dense formula," and it was man's task to understand it by using his intellect.[49]

Soon after, however, an increasingly rigid attitude towards philosophy found especially powerful expression in the occasionalist theology propounded by the Persian philosopher and Ashʿarite theologian al-Ġazālī (1058–1111). In his treatise *The Incoherence of the Philosophers*, al-Ġazālī directly criticised al-Fārābī and Avicenna, and in so doing also indirectly dismissed Aristotelian metaphysics, however much he himself used Aristotle's own logic in so doing.

Maṭālib, al-Rāzī advances the idea of the existence of an infinite universe (a multiverse) inhabited by many worlds similar to our own, all of them created by God.

[47]In the *Supreme Prayer of al-Fārābī* (*Du'ā' 'aẓīm*), for example, rationality as a tool of knowledge, philosophical thought and logical rigour are coupled with a recognition of the imponderable superiority of God, the first cause and prime-mover of all things. Published in a critical edition by Muhsin Mahdi (al-Fārābī 1986, 89–92) on the basis of a manuscript found in the Süleymaniye Library in Istanbul, it reads as follows in the English translation by Ibrahim Kalin (2017a): "Show me the truth as truth and inspire me to follow it. Show me the falsehood as falsehood and forbid me from believing and following it. Refine my soul with the clay of the hyle (the first matter). You are the Primary Cause!" and in its closing it reads: "O God! Show my soul the true forms of the invisible in its dreams and transform it from seeing nightmares to seeing goodness and veritable glad tidings in its dreams. Clean it from the dirt that has afflicted its senses and delusive imagination. Remove from it the muddiness of the natural world."

[48]Al-Fārābī held that man is capable of understanding "intelligible forms" channelled through God by way of the sensations, the imagination, and the intellect. Cf. Strauss and Cropsey ([1963] 1972, 184).

[49]Other important representatives of the intellectual sciences—who also, strictly speaking, were non-Arab—were Avempace, born in Zaragoza, and Ibn Ṭufayl, born in Guadix.

According to the Persian thinker reason, and the principle of causality in which it grounds its own reconstructions of the real, should not be recognised as a valid and reliable tool of knowledge:[50] rather, it is God, the cause of all events, who is also, at the same time, a direct cause of our knowledge of them.[51] For this reason, al-Ġazālī believed that even the observation of an appreciable relation of consequentiality between one element and another could never, in any event, entail the existence of a certain and necessary causal relation between the two elements. In other words, the causal nexus could not be considered a reliable source of knowledge.

An echo of this vision can be descried in Ibn Khaldūn. In fact, in relation to his embracing of philosophical thought—particularly as far as Aristotelian philosophy is concerned—his attitude does show the ambivalence typical of his time. If on the one hand, in the *Muqaddima*, Ibn Khaldūn based his study on logic and inductive reasoning—and this is precisely one of the great "revolutions" of knowledge he brought to the study of history—, on the other he also explicitly held that logic could prove to be a source of ideas contrary to religion. Consequently, he argued that it should never be taught to students before instilling in them a firm knowledge of the religious sciences (*Muqaddima* VI, 30).

Furthermore, while his commitment to the universalism of reason and the rigour of logic can clearly be appreciated in the adoption of the method on which he founded his "new science," on the other hand, in a partial move toward the theses advanced by al-Ġazālī, there also emerges in his work his concern to establish clear limits and borderlines between what it is possible for our human faculties to know, and what lies, instead, beyond their ken, such knowledge being reserved for divine revelation. In fact, Ibn Khaldūn himself stated that we are not endowed with an ability to know how causes "ultimately" truly affect the things which are caused, and that for this reason Muslims have rightly been commanded to renounce any speculation on such matters (*Muqaddima* VI, 30).

However, it is important to clarify from the start that in Ibn Khaldūn this limitation and this mistrust do not take over the whole of scientific and philosophical research, but are rather understood by him as being in force *only within the province of metaphysics* (for only this discipline is what, in a proper sense, he terms *falsafa*, isolating it, with pejorative overtones, from the rest of *ḥikma,* the general philosophical discipline). The world of natural phenomena is not involved in this.

Ibn Khaldūn, therefore, conceived reason as a legitimate tool, although only within the scope of its natural limits, which are set by the investigation and interpretation of the elements of the physical world and are based on empiricism and observation. For Ibn Khaldūn, the important implication of the non-necessariness of a radical epistemological break between the religious option

[50]This position, after all, also found support in the judgments expressed by the Christian Church of the twelfth century on the relation between religion and reason: only a century later would the two elements find, in scholasticism, a reconciliation that would allot a greater role to reason, all the while respecting religion.

[51]Compare the view much later taken by David Hume (Norton and Taylor 2011).

and the rationalistic one (Hamès 1999, 175) comes from this "division" of spheres. As Stephen Dale (2015a, 103) has commented: "God, in this latter Greco-Islamic context is the prime-mover and not al-Ġazālī's God of small things."

In fact, in relation to the social and earthly phenomena that form the object of his inquiry, the idea that everything possesses a nature or essence which determines a development that can be rationally grasped is not only reflected, as we will see, in the entire model of his cyclical history of human civilisations. It also profoundly influences his own expository methodology, structured according to a rigorous architecture aimed at reproducing the order of anteriority that, on a synoptic level, is found in the objective world. This order is expressed not only in Ibn Khaldūn's ordering and exposition of the domains of knowledge,[52] but also in the discussion of every single element in his explanations. These typically proceed from the framing of the problem to its solution in successive stages until its complete demonstration (Talbi 1973, 37): *faqad tabayyana anna* (the Latin QED, or *quod erat demonstrandum*). In fact, Ibn Khaldūn employs the demonstrative method (*burhān*, or rational demonstration) in each minute analysis of facts,[53] staggered according to a rhythm of premises and demonstrations similar to that of mathematics.

If, then, Ibn Khaldūn's thinking on the question of the metaphysical foundation of creation recalls that of al-Ġazālī, on everything else it reveals itself to be closer to the work of al-Ġazālī's "great adversary": the Berber philosopher, physician, and mathematician Averroes of Córdoba (Ibn Rušd, 1126–1198), the great proponent of Aristotle's thought who, especially in his *Incoherence of the Incoherence*, used rational thinking to confute al-Ġazālī's occasionalist theology.[54]

A jurist and theologian by training, Averroes had commented on the works of Aristotle for the caliph Abū Yūsuf Yaʿqūb al-Manṣūr, making the point that if philosophy had continued to be regarded merely as theology's maidservant, it would never have been able to find answers beyond what is literally described in religious terms. What Averroes was saying, in other words, is that, while it was a duty of all Muslims to follow Islam, those endowed with higher forms of philosophical ability were similarly duty-bound to develop their own thought by also pursuing this other form of knowledge.

[52]In fact, in his work Ibn Khaldūn attempts to systematically present all the relevant topics of inquiry of his time, covering (in chap. VI) even alchemy, chemistry, astrology, and numerology. Hodgson (1974, vol. 2, 479–80) describes his work as "a self-consistent body of demonstrable generalisations about historical change, generalisations which would, in turn, be based on premises taken from the demonstrated results of 'higher,' i.e., more abstract, sciences—in this case chiefly biology, psychology, and geography."

[53]Following Aristotle, even Ibn Khaldūn considers rational demonstration as a procedure of reasoning aimed at yielding certainties—this, in contrast to dialectics (*jadal*), or disputation, aimed at prevailing over a contender, as well as to rhetoric (*ḫiṭāba*), aimed at persuading others; poetry (*šiʿr*), aimed at providing inspiration; and sophism (*safsaṭa*), aimed at confusing one's adversary.

[54]On Averroes, see Campanini (2007), Butterworth (1972).

In the Muslim world, the perspective which understood demonstrative rational reasoning as fully reconcilable with religious faith was greatly revitalised thanks to his teaching, so much so that, as the scholar Stephen Frederic Dale (2015a, 263) has commented, Averroes can be said to have been the first important link between the philosophical cultures of North Africa, Andalusia, and Europe.

However, the *opposite* orientation ineluctably prevailed in his world, and Averroes eventually fell into disgrace towards the end of his life, and saw his books burned at the request of the *ʿulemā*, just before being forced to go into exile. He died in Marrakesh.[55]

Copies of his works, however, with his commentaries on Aristotle, were preserved by his students and went on to become some of the most authoritative textual sources on Aristotelian thought in Medieval Europe. They were read and discussed by Thomas Aquinas at the Sorbonne in Paris[56]—a university that played a key role in the spread of Greek philosophy—and, through Aquinas, they played an important role in the rebirth of universities in the Latin West, until they also came to influence—through a long chain of intellectual legacies, as cited by Dale (2015a, ch. VI)[57]—Italian Renaissance thought and, later still, the work of many European Enlightenment and post-Enlightenment thinkers.[58]

In North Africa, on the other hand, Averroes's theses and, in particular, his articulation of the concepts of nature and causality, perhaps bore their main fruit precisely in the thought of Ibn Khaldūn, where, in the *Muqaddima*, they contributed to the formation of the new science of civilisation built on a rational basis.

Meanwhile, the contact with Aristotle's rationalistic philosophy had also set in motion a new current of rational study applied to the law. This current had especially found expression in an innovative theological school: that of the Muʿtazilites. Prominent here was al-Kindī (801–873), an Iraqi jurist and philosopher who

---

[55]The story is also the subject of a film titled *al-Massir* (1997), directed by the Egyptian director Youssef Chahine.

[56]His work would later be placed on the *Index of Forbidden Books* (see Horrut 2006, 142).

[57]Indeed, Dale brings out a whole series of interesting analogies between Ibn Khaldūn and Montesquieu as to the structure and method of their work, ascribing to both a common Aristotelian-Averroist root, generally characterised, as Dale says, by a deep interweaving of *logos* and *peira* and by a vision of society as a "natural fact" (Durkheim 1994, 45). This common root can also be found in the Scottish Enlightenment, and in particular in the work of David Hume (in view of the analogies between Hume's view of human nature and the arguments expressed by Ibn Khaldūn); in Adam Smith (owing to his vision of the interconnection of economic and social factors in leading to the division of labour, a thesis that had been anticipated by Ibn Khaldūn); and, later, in Durkheim's sociology (especially considering how his distinction of the two kinds of solidarity can be traced back to Ibn Khaldūn's insight on the transformation of the force of social cohesion in the two models of social organization). Despite the differing politico-historico-social backgrounds of all these authors, they all "inhabited the same philosophical world" (Dale 2015a, 275), a world which, at root, was Aristotelian. On the influence of classical Greek philosophy on Montesquieu, see Shackleton (1961, 264–303).

[58]Durkheim (1999) himself expressly linked the ideas developed in sociology to the great classic philosophical ideas—foremost among them, those of Aristotle.

commented on Greek, Persian, and Indian thinkers: it was al-Kindī's view that "we should not [...] be ashamed to recognize truth and assimilate it, from whatever quarter it may reach us, even though it may come from earlier generations and foreign people" (Fakhry 1970, 23).

As early as the ninth century, the Muʿtazilites argued for the importance of using reason and logic in the interpretation of religious/legal concepts. This view, which later found a place to flourish in the Christian West,[59] came to a halt in the tenth century in the world in which it was born, when the stranglehold upon the interpretation of history known as the "closing of the gates of *ijtihād*"[60] (Verza 2008, 217–18) was reached. The rationalistic approach, then, met with serious opposition from several quarters: as the growing interest in philosophy threatened the hegemony of traditional theologians, both in Islam and in Christianity, an extensive and divisive debate on the relation between rationality and revealed religion sprang up (DeBoer 1965, 211–12).

In Christianity, these two divergent paths, eventually, came to be reconciled in the work of Thomas Aquinas, who argued that no necessary conflict existed between revelation and reason (both understood as valid pathways to God). In Islam, however, the traditional thesis, staunchly voluntarist and occasionalist, prevailed, championed especially by the towering figure of Al-Ġazālī, who placed philosophy below revealed religion (ibid.; Miller 1975, 46). The pejorative overtones (Horrut 2006, 142)[61] of the term *falsafa*, juxtaposed with the more neutral-sounding *ḥikma,* clearly testified as to this defensive entrenchment. We can also find this term in the *Muqaddima*, where Ibn Khaldūn is invariably careful to distance himself from it.

After that, in the early thirteenth-century Arabic-speaking world, that broader intellectual ferment produced by the impact of rationalistic philosophy lost its motive power,[62] both in the East (with the rise to power of the Seljuk Turks) and

[59]As previously said, it did so with scholasticism, which, in the universities, sparked the interest ignited by the commentaries written by Muslim philosophers who, like Averroes (Schacht 1974)—challenging the control exerted by theological authority over the limits of intellectual endeavours—had carried forward the work of the Muʿtazilites.

[60]Such is that phase of history beyond which *the ijtihād*, i.e., independent interpretation and reasoning in law—initially allowed to all members of the community of the faithful, later only to the class of doctors of the law—ceased to apply, to be replaced only by the "conforming imitation" of the interpretations produced up to that moment. It is interesting that Ibn Khaldūn called this phenomenon, instead, "closing of the doors of *khilāf*," where the latter is the opinion held on religious matters. See Ahmad (2003, 46).

[61]On the relation between *ḥikma* and *falsafa*, see also Cheddadi (2006, 204ff).

[62]Moḥammed al-Jabri ([1976–1991] 1996, 135) observed that afterwards, while the Orient by and large embraced the path charted by al-Ġazālī and Avicenna, getting mired in the problem of the relation between religion and faith, Ibn Khaldūn inherited the legacy of Averroes and of that brand of rationalism that can treat philosophy separately from religion (the same legacy subsequently inherited by the West): "After Averroes, we Arabs effectively lived in the margins of history (in inertia and decline) because we clung to the Avicennian moment from the time that al-Ġazālī conferred on him a right of citizenship in Islam. The Europeans, by contrast, lived their own history, because they knew how to appropriate Averroes and to live in the Averroist moment up to our own time." (my translation).

in the Arab West with the loss of Andalusia, which led to the break-up of the intellectual élite (including Ibn Khaldūn's family) (Horrut 2006, 142).

Ibn Khaldūn, while still coming to terms with the gradual disappearance in the Maghreb of the cultivation of the intellectual sciences, learned that the philosophical sciences were flourishing in Christian lands to the north:

> We hear that the intellectual sciences are still amply represented among the inhabitants of the East, in particular in the non-Arab 'Iraq and, farther east, in Transoxiana. [...] We further hear now that the philosophical sciences are greatly cultivated in the land of Rome and along the adjacent northern shore of the country of the European Christians.

This observation, however, came with an understandable tinge of hurt pride, prompting him to close the passage by wryly commenting, "God knows better what exists there." (*Muqaddima* VI, 18. Ibn Khaldūn 1958, vol. III, 117–18; Ibn Khaldūn [1967] 2005, 375).

1.3.2 A Possible Inspiration from Aristotelian Physics

For Ibn Khaldūn there is no innate knowledge:[63] yet, on an epistemological level, and by way of sound intuition, man can perceive that he is part of three different worlds (*Muqaddima* VI, 4).

The first is the world of sensory perception; the second, deducible from our observation of our capacity to think and gain scientific knowledge of things, is the intellectual world, that of ideas.[64] Then there is a third, spiritual world, which can be accessed only in exceptional circumstances and expresses a supernatural knowledge inspired from above, voiced particularly by way of prophecy.[65]

This distinction, as Turroni (2002, 84) observes, contributes to enabling Ibn Khaldūn's neat separation of the world of science, in its own boundaries, and the world of revealed religion—and this without bringing them into contradiction and without diminishing the value of either. In fact, while to Ibn Khaldūn philosophy is harmful to religion insofar as it improperly makes inroads into the metaphysical—this is the *falsafa* with which he takes issue—, the remaining area of speculation and the intellectual science of wisdom, belonging in the second world, is fully legitimate, as long as it does not encroach on metaphysics. This is the area of the *ḥikma*

---

[63]That is the comment that makes up the title of the sixth paragraph of chapter VI.

[64]Rational knowledge goes through three steps: external perception, internal perception and thought, the last of which involves three types of operations (*'aql*): discerning ones, from which we get concepts; experimental ones, yielding judgments; and speculative ones, through which concepts and judgments are combined to generate new knowledge. In both rational thought and supernatural knowledge (based on intuition, or *wijdān*), as well as in prophecy (a gift of God), sensory experience is bypassed. See *infra*, ch. IV.

[65]As Lakhsassi (1979) stresses, there are also some sciences, albeit imperfect ones, which can be traced to the third type of soul: these are the "spiritual" sciences of Sufism, and they also include the magical, talismanic, and divinatory sciences, among others.

(*al-'ulūm al-'akliyya al-ḥikmiyya*), and it is precisely within it (*Muqaddima* Foreword), and no longer in the field of literary tradition, that he sets his work.

However, this framing of his own historical project—stated from the outset, in its Foreword, as a work of rational knowledge—entailed a re-drawing of its own meaning and underlying values: it would no longer have mainly stylistic goals, but would rather be aimed at a rational search for the truth,[66] and at understanding the constant laws which, as a matter of fact, regulate political aggregates.

At that time the political outlook of Christian scholars (mostly clerics, jurists, and university professors) was filtered, on a theoretical level, not only through the perspective of the *Corpus Iuris Iustinianeum* (which was essential for the philosophy and practice of law and politics, as well as for the development of a secular spirit: see Lagarde 1956–1970), but also through reference to the three models of government presented in Aristotle's *Politics*. These models were already classic: Aristotle's political work had been known to Christian Europeans since the thirteenth century, thanks to a translation into Latin by Guillaume de Moerbeke upon which Thomas Aquinas commented shortly after its publication. Categories and themes were drawn from them which centred on the problem of types of government, on the relation between the ruled and rulers, and on the definition of the best form of government, justice, rights, and citizenship. The models were a long way from dealing with the idea of society's cyclical growth and corruption: on the contrary, they were interested in promoting the idea of society's unity and endurance (Pomian 2006, 95).[67]

At that time, however, neither the *Corpus Iuris Iustinianeum* nor Aristotle's ethico-political works had been translated into Arabic—although, under the title *Politics*, a book thought to be attributable to Aristotle was at the time in circulation. In fact, this was a completely different, spurious work, known as *Sirr al-asrār* (*Secretum secretorum*): Ibn Khaldūn himself makes a doubting reference to it in the foreword to his *Muqaddima*, showing that he did not believe that attribution to be accurate. From this perspective, then, Ibn Khaldūn's frame of mind, on the level of political reflection, was less "boxed in": he was freer and less constrained than the Latin clerics and university academicians.[68]

Some translations of the works of Plato and Galen (Turroni 2002, 80) were in circulation in the Arab world at that time, but, apart from his works on logic, the

---

[66]Pomian (2006, 78) observes that this assertion made in the Foreword to Ibn Khaldūn's *Muqaddima* may well mark the first time that history and science have ever been mentioned together within the span of the same sentence.

[67]Thus for example, in that same period in Italy, the Paduan professor and jurist Baldus de Ubaldis (1327–1400), in line with his teacher, Bartolus de Saxoferrato (1314–1357), was justifying self-government by cities such as Genoa and Venice by virtue of its effectiveness as "interstitial," even within the *de jure* extension of the empire's jurisdiction. Bartolus had previously defined a city capable of self-government as an immortal corporation, continuing to exist even through the coming and going of the natural persons who make it up. His thought would later influence that of Ernst Kantorowicz (1989, 218).

[68]As Pomian (2006, 221) observes, at that time in the Christian world a freer spirit, closer to Ibn Khaldūn's, can be found in Boccaccio's *Decameron*, in Franco Sacchetti's *Trecentonovelle*, and in Geoffrey Chaucer's *Canterbury Tales*.

books of the "First Teacher" translated into Arabic and in circulation—and thus presumably known to, or knowable, by Ibn Khaldūn either directly or through commentators—were his scientific works: those on physics, for example, which had also been widely commented on not only by al-Fārābī, but also by Avicenna.[69]

It was precisely these writings on physics, if we are to follow the fascinating thesis advanced by scholars such as Pomian and Dale (and also Cheddadi 2006, ch. IV), that are said to have played an important role in Ibn Khaldūn's work, serving as a source of inspiration "exogenous" to the Arab world, in the general structuring of his thought. This influence could particularly have been exercised by the thesis set out in the *De generatione et corruptione*, an Aristotelian work devoted to understanding whether things come into being causally through being produced from prime matter, or whether everything is generated by way of alteration—a question previously addressed by Aristotle in his *Physics*.

In the *Physics*, having defined nature as the complex of all things that have in themselves "the principle of movement and rest," Aristotle argued that created things behave in conformity with their nature. As Dale notes, we could identify a main pillar of Ibn Khaldūn's theory[70] in the idea that it is possible to identify a proper nature of things—an essential condition for conceiving the possibility of predicting their future trajectory, physical or historical, in both an explicative and a predictive sense.

Thus, according to Dale, Ibn Khaldūn had the ingenious insight of taking the Aristotelian idea that each thing possesses a nature by which its development is determined, and applying this idea to the study of the forms of transformation of society, joining the categories of Aristotelian physics to the data furnished by his own political experience and by his historical knowledge of life in North Africa, so as to ultimately arrive at a completely unprecedented theory of society and of its metamorphoses.

Aristotle's *De generatione et corruptione*, which had been translated into Arabic in the second half of the ninth century, traced the causes of natural things' cycles of generation and corruption to the circular movement of Earth's celestial sphere.[71] For Aristotle, the decomposition and re-composition of complex bodies and the transmutation of the elements into each other—that is, generation and corruption—follow each other in continuous succession because the eternal movement of the heavens along the ecliptic, by turns attracts and repels the principle that generates growth by proximity, and corrupts by distancing. On that basis, Aristotle concluded that there

---

[69]In the section devoted to physics (*Muqaddima* VI, 23), Ibn Khaldūn makes reference, for the most part, to the popular *Book of Healing*, in which Avicenna (Ibn Sīnā) had, in his own turn, assigned a central role to the notion of causality. This work too, according to Dale, could have been used by Ibn Khaldūn as a source through which to access the Aristotelian concepts of causality, nature, and accident.

[70]As Dale (2015a, 24) notes, Ibn Khaldūn uses the term *ṭabi'a* (meaning, precisely, "nature") more than any other Muslim thinker of the time, and he also often uses the Aristotelian expression *al-taqaddum bi 'l-ṭab'*, meaning "prior by nature."

[71]This does not, in any event, imply that any reference was being made to astrology, which was extraneous to the Aristotelian conception and was rejected by Ibn Khaldūn.

is, in effect, an order proper to each thing and that the duration of each life is measured in a cycle, shorter or longer depending on circumstances (Aristotle 2013, 336b, 10–15).

Ibn Khaldūn thought that human societies also have a part to play in the order which God imparted on nature: so, there must be the possibility of applying the Aristotelian scheme to human societies, too.[72] In fact, in one of the first versions of the *Muqaddima* (what Cheddadi calls Manuscript A) Ibn Khaldūn writes:

> The conditions of these elemental worlds are subject to generation and corruption. When something belonging to these worlds reaches a point of extreme corruption, we should expect it to make the passage to generation. In the same way, if it reaches a point of extreme generation, it must make the passage to corruption. [...] If that is how it goes for material things, it must be the same for conditions and for states. When conditions of corruption become prevalent in the world, and functions unravel, and that which makes it up, meaning the order of human society, becomes dispersed, and corruption in this whole process reaches an extreme point, then we have to expect the transformation of this entire order, union, and harmony, and the beginning of a new order.[73]

In Ibn Khaldūn's cycle of generation and corruption, as applied to society, various clues make it possible to understand the point in the cycle at which the polity lay. As we will see, the most important of these clues is the durability of the moral virtues especially developed at the tribal stage: those of group solidarity, courage, and "fortitude/prowess"; the practice of living on what is necessary and no more; and the virtue of solidary closeness among society's members and between the leader and the governed. With the progressive weakening of these virtues, the phase of demise comes closer, in a corrupting process affecting not only the community as a whole, but also its members, as well as their characters and dispositions.

In order to understand the characteristics of these social cycles, however, it is essential to have a good understanding of the present and a capacity for observation, together with a good knowledge of history, enabling us to understand the cyclic

---

[72]Ibn Khaldūn writes that all created things—minerals, plants, and animals, including humans—are subject to this same law, and the same also goes for all human conditions. *Muqaddima* II, 14. Ibn Khaldūn (1958, vol. I, 278). Ibn Khaldūn ([1967] 2005, 105): "The same applies to the conditions that affect created things, and especially to the conditions that affect man." Pomian (2006, 96) notes that even the Paduan historian Albertino Mussato (1261–1329) used the categories of the *De generatione*, albeit not systematically, to compare human society to the human body, both being subject to corruption.

[73]Ibn Khaldūn (2002, 1244): "Les conditions de ces mondes élémentaires sont sujettes à la génération et à la corruption. Quand une chose appartenant à ces mondes parvient à la corruption extrême, on doit s'attendre à son passage à la génération. De même, si elle parvient à la génération extrême, elle passe à la corruption. [...] S'il en est ainsi dans les choses matérielles, il doit en être de même dans les conditions et les États. Quand les conditions de la corruption dominent le monde, que la fonction de direction se dérègle, que ce qui la constitue, c'est à dire l'ordre de la société humaine, se disperse, et que la corruption en tout cela atteint son point extrême, on doit alors s'attendre à la transformation de ce bon ordre, de cette union et de cette harmonie, et au retour au commencement de l'ordre."

recurrence of the past—provided that its data be reliable and well checked. That is why another aspect that is central to Ibn Khaldūn's work lays in the criterion of historical truth.

In fact, the cyclicality of time which, for Ibn Khaldūn, governs all things in our world, is not to be intended as a deterministic return to sameness but rather as implying a continuous "swing" between predefined phases, where transitions between the two occur. It is from this perspective that an understanding of the past—of history as a repository of useful examples—can be made to work as a source of instruction for the future. Hence the reasoning behind the title of his work, which refers, in its entirety, to the "instructive examples" of the past, thus underlying—in what today we might call a stimulus to "sociological imagination"—their potential usefulness as warnings and as training tools for the future.

Therefore, if Ibn Khaldūn qualifies at all as an "Aristotelian" author, this is not for reprising, or commenting upon, Aristotle (which he only occasionally does), but for taking advantage of Aristotle's categories, albeit with the aim of investigating a topic to which Aristotle himself never considered applying them.

Is this enough to define Ibn Khaldūn as an "Aristotelian"? Perhaps. In any case, apart from this question, the idea that he could have drawn the initial insight for his socio-dynamic theory from a totally different area of investigation—that of the laws of physics—suggests a parallel with the insight that subsequently, in Europe, provided the basis for the birth of sociology: the idea that the same robustness of the method for investigating the laws of the natural world could be carried over to a new province—the investigation of society.

However valid this may be, the hypothesis of Ibn Khaldūn's insight having an Aristotelian root is seductive, especially insofar as it makes it possible to rationalise and make comprehensible the analogy between Ibn Khaldūn's ideas and those of the social thinkers active from the nineteenth century onwards to whom he has been compared.

In fact, this exceptional similarity has been explained by the scholars advancing this thesis as implied by the commonality of the logical and philosophical approach used by both—that is, the approach of the "first teacher" *par excellence*. Aristotelian thought influenced both the Maghrebin thinker (indirectly, through his "rationalist" teacher al-Ābilī, but also directly, through the works of Aristotle translated into Arabic that were, then, available) and European culture. In the latter, in particular, Aristotelianism was disseminated through the research activity stimulated at the University of Paris (particularly from the second millennium on) by Averroes's commentaries on Aristotle, to which Thomas Aquinas, as we have seen, devoted his observations, ultimately exerting an influence lasting up to modern times.

Incidentally, this reduction of Ibn Khaldūn's cyclical theory (in which every state of affairs is understood as a mutation and development from a previous state) to an Aristotelian "seed" also seems to reaffirm, on a metatheoretical level, this very idea of causality, as it reframes Ibn Khaldūn's theory merely as a pre-programmed development of elements already present, *in nuce*, in Aristotelian thought.

However, this attempt to reduce the originality of this striking author to one of "our" schemes, treating it as a kind of "cultural *déjà vu*," is perplexing to the extent that it ends up "normalising" his originality, and diminishes his thesis to a development, however marginal it may be, of *Western* philosophy—that is, to an unfolding of ideas already present in classical thought.

Certainly, the seed of Aristotelian rationalism and its categories must inevitably have influenced *all* Western thinkers. Yet, it is singularly curious that great pains have been taken to stress that such a legacy exists in particular in the thought of Ibn Khaldūn (even despite the simple hypotheticality of the conceptual links said to underlie the possible passage from the sphere of physics to that of politics). It is almost as if this amounts to explain the "Khaldunian phenomenon" in a way which, more reassuringly, relocates its "phenomenonality" into the realm of the familiar.

Furthermore, there is no direct evidence that Ibn Khaldūn's cyclic scheme, as seductively suggested, is far from an original insight and merely an application (however ingenious) of something borrowed from Aristotle's *De generatione*. In point of fact, Ibn Khaldūn does at times also refer specifically to Aristotelian physics (*Muqaddima* VI, 23), but in doing so he does not make these links; more generally, he almost never mentions Aristotle as a source for his central ideas (even if, in general, scrupulousness in citing sources and rigour in referencing schemes and readings—especially, historical ones—is one of the key points of his methodology). In fact, the *Muqaddima* contains various and explicit statements to the contrary, where Ibn Khaldūn proudly distances himself from the *falāsifa*.

Most importantly, however, it is certain that Ibn Khaldūn repeatedly stresses the *absolute novelty* of his new science, thereby claiming originality for the insight and intellectual intuition which, coupled with attention to detail and rigorous observation, produced his masterpiece.

If we follow his narration of the genesis of the work to the end, one cannot fail to be impressed by his description of how he came to grasp these ideas. It is as if they had literally been "delivered" to him in a flood of inspiration during 5 months of work and creativity that we can imagine as having been overwhelming. This almost suggests that this "onrush" of ideas never before conceived came to him and made his intellect—already tempered in the intellectual gymnasium of his mentor and teacher al-Ābilī and, therefore, already distinguished by the "colouring" imparted by familiarity with philosophical discipline—a human discharger of conceptual energies, perhaps plummeting from the heights of the world of "ideas."

1.4 Overlaid Interpretive Currents

1.4.1 Successive and Dichotomic Interpretive Waves

As we have seen, Ibn Khaldūn was "rediscovered" in a period when the social sciences were going through a formative stage. An overview of the studies dedicated to him shows us how from the outset the first interpretations of his work were already polarised, as Alatas writes (2013: 104), around very different types of attitudes.

More to the point, it becomes apparent that at different times, and under the impulse of different ideological-cultural forces (Forte 2005), interpretations have been applied to his complex work in order to emphasise (or, in some cases, to devalue) some aspects instead of others—in a way that has revealed, in many cases, the political nature of these readings themselves above all (Boukraa 2008; Patriarca 2019).

For example, as Francesca Forte (2005: 185) points out, it is instructive to see how a different light is cast onto him even in the conferences devoted to him in the Arab world, especially from the 1960s onwards.

Thus, in the *Social Sciences Congress* on Ibn Khaldūn in 1962 in Cairo, perhaps in the wake of many European studies that in previous decades had been devoted to him as a "forerunner" of the new social sciences,[74] he was celebrated in precisely these terms: as a modern thinker, founder of sociology, author of the first sociological study in Arab civilisation and, because of the "law" of social phenomena he developed, as a precursor of theorists such as Montesquieu, Spencer, and Comte.

In this context, Ibn Khaldūn was presented as an author who could stand on an equal footing with contemporary European authors—as had been argued by authoritative scholars such as Ludwig Gumplowicz (1925, 90–114), Franz Oppenheimer (1922–1935, vol. II, 173ff.; vol. IV, 251ff.) (whom Becker and Barnes had even defined as a "resurrector of Ibn Khaldūn"), Guglielmo Ferrero (1896), and also Alfred von Kremer (1879) and René Maunier (1915), as well as Becker and Barnes ([1938] 1961, 706–8),[75] who had hailed Ibn Khaldūn as the first of the sociologists.

In later years, by contrast, there increasingly emerged a Khaldunian exegesis concerned to reconnect him to the specificity of his Islamic culture, as if to imply that it was impossible to conceive a single cultural path of Greco-Arab origin characterised by similarities and variations, and that Arab culture necessarily had to be set in contradiction to Western culture, essentially transformed into something "other" and obdurately cleaving to its own distinctive traits. As early as the colloquium held in 1978 in Algiers, the emphasis fell on the ability of Ibn Khaldūn to couple rationalist endeavour with religion in his work, through its particular epistemology—a line of interpretation that was developed in particular by thinkers like Moḥammed 'Abed al-Jabri ([1976–1991] 1996) and Nassif Nassar (1967).

However, the "defensive" need to situate his work in its own historical, cultural, and religious context most emphatically began to prevail at the 1979 Rabat colloquium and continued through to the end of the twentieth century. This is still a thriving interpretive trend [elements of it can be recognised even in the work of contemporary exegetes like Claude Horrut (2006) and Robert Irwin (2018)]—and

[74]As Bouthoul had commented, European scientific thought was, at that time, eager to read itself through the image reflected in others. Bouthoul 1930: 172: "La pensée scientifique française et européenne est avide de se lire (en miroir) chez d'autres."

[75]In the chapter "Struggle over 'The Struggle for Existence,'" Harry E. Barnes (1948, 25–26) further argued that, preceding Vico, Ibn Khaldūn had founded the philosophy of history by underscoring the oneness and continuity of the historical process, in contrast to the staticness informing the Christian historiography of his time.

such a line of interpretation has often reached the point of denying, or at least deliberately downplaying, the status of originality of his work. For example, the Arab (though British-trained) historian Aziz al-Azmeh (1981, 160; cf. Campanini 2005b, 21, n. 1) denies Ibn Khaldūn's modernity and confines his thought strictly within the cultural boundaries of his time. Even earlier, though, Taha Hussein (1918; cf. Celarent 2003)[76]—who was certainly influential because, among other reasons, he was among the first commentators to emerge in the Arab world after the "rediscovery" of Ibn Khaldūn—went in the same direction, minimising Ibn Khaldūn's techniques as mere applications of the traditional *uṣūl al-fiqh*, the formal criticism of sacred texts. Even Enan (2007, 99–100) had claimed that some of Ibn Khaldūn's themes had previously been treated by al-Fārābī and the Iḫwān al-ṣafā'[77] (in particular in their *Epistles*, as stated by Mahmud Isma'il ([1976] 1996), who went so far as to accuse Ibn Khaldūn of plagiarism).[78]

We can therefore see how, in the face of the temptation to devise ideologically "colonising" readings of Ibn Khaldūn's work (consider the influence that Europe's colonial history may have exerted on the European reception of his work, or consider the ferment sparked by the birth of disciplines like sociology precisely at the time when his work was being rediscovered), an equal and contrary trend emerged from the opposite side—beginning, in particular, with the Rabat colloquium. This trend produced an onrush of readings geared toward dissolving the originality of his theory (an originality deriving from its overall view, its objectives, and the mutual relations between its parts) into a meticulous analysis of its many components already present in the cultural context out of which it had emerged, in order to completely reabsorb it into the tradition on which it was founded.

As Cheddadi comments, this tendency can be understood if we consider how the praise of Ibn Khaldūn's singularity, coupled with the tendency to read him as an utterly exceptional thinker (and the latter tendency was not only Western, but also Islamic), paradoxically helped overshadow the rest of Arabic-Islamic tradition, thereby "embodying, in the heart of the agonizing East, the triumph of the West" (Cheddadi [1980] 1995, 26).

It is true that, from the outset, there had been commentators capable of offering objective and non-Eurocentric assessments: Robert Flint ([1893] 2010), for example, enthusiastically described Ibn Khaldūn as a unique theorist of history for his originality in the overall landscape of Muslim and European classical and medieval

---

[76]Horrut (2006, 112) writes that Taha Hussein, finding Ibn Khaldūn's project too unreligious, neglected to adequately appreciate its scientific merit, being instead concerned to judge Ibn Khaldūn as a man who was even willing to bend religion and morality to his own ambitious dreams (Hussein 1918, 23–24). Taha Hussein, furthermore, denied that Ibn Khaldūn could be described as a sociologist, insofar as his object of study was, in Hussein's assessment, too narrowly defined.

[77]Literally, the "brethren of purity": they formed in the tenth century an intellectual Muslim circle, particularly rooted in Iraq. This circle produced a sort of philosophico-religious encyclopaedia.

[78]In reality, as Alatas (2013, 21) critically points out, these themes were treated in a strictly philosophical way by these authors, whereas Ibn Khaldūn frames them within a scientific perspective.

thought; similarly, the historian of science George Sarton ([1927] 1962), in his *Introduction to the History of Science*, rated him as a "giant" among the pygmies of "our" common Greco-Arabic tradition.

We already find, however, a different tone in the commentaries of the earliest Khaldunian scholars. The previously cited Gråberg Graf von Hemsö (1835, 387–88) and Reynold A. Nicholson (1907, 438–39), for example, praised Ibn Khaldūn for being able, more than any other Muslim historian, to distance himself from the prejudices of Islam. Even the Spanish philosopher José Ortega y Gasset ([1934] 1976–1978), in a 1934 article where he used Ibn Khaldūn's paradigm to explain the apparent chaos of the continual hostilities that had unfolded for four centuries in Melilla (a North African city that Spain conquered in 1497), exalted Ibn Khaldūn as a surprising anomaly within his own cultural landscape.[79]

In short, as an exception that proves the rule, the appreciation of the "modernity" and atypicality of Ibn Khaldūn's work seemed to have the effect of obscuring all the traditional (and, therefore, not "modern") cultural apparatus from which it had emerged.

This "shadow effect," for example, was certainly evident in the words of great praise with which Arnold Toynbee exalted Ibn Khaldūn, on the one hand comparing him to Thucydides and Machiavelli, while on the other juxtaposing his work with the intellectual output of the time, judged, by contrast, as being empty and depleted. In fact, as Toynbee commented:

> The last member of our Pleiad of historians is 'Abd-ar-Raḥmān Abū Zayd ibn Muḥammad ibn Muḥammad Ibn Khaldūn al-Ḥaḍramī (1332–1406)—an Arabic genius who achieved in a single "acquiescence" of less than four years' length, out of a fifty-four years' span of adult working life, a life-work in the shape of a piece of literature which can bear comparison with the work of a Thucydides or the work of a Machiavelli for both breadth and profundity of vision as well as for sheer intellectual power. Ibn Khaldūn's star shines the more brightly by contrast with the foil of darkness against which it flashes out; for while Thucydides and Machiavelli and Clarendon are all brilliant representatives of brilliant times and places, Ibn Khaldūn is the sole point of light in his quarter of the firmament. He is indeed the one outstanding personality in the history of a civilization whose social life on the whole was "solitary, poor, nasty, brutish, and short." In his chosen field of intellectual activity he appears to have been inspired by no predecessors and to have found no kindred souls among his contemporaries and to have kindled no answering spark of inspiration in any successors; and yet, in the Prolegomena (*Muqaddimāt*) to his *Universal History* he has conceived and formulated a philosophy of history which is undoubtedly the greatest work of its kind that has ever yet been created by any mind in any time or place. (Toynbee [1934] 1962, 321–22)

After all, these were precisely the years in which the debate on the "Orientalist" thesis advanced by Edward Said (1978) sprang up. He accused the reading and reconstruction of the culture of the Muslim world advanced by dominant Western thinking, and the accompanying literature devoted to that subject, of being

[79]Ortega y Gasset's essay considers the *Muqaddima* a work of both sociology and philosophy (actually the *first* philosophy) of history. In particular, according to Ortega y Gasset, Ibn Khaldūn's theory is the only one that can explain phenomena such as the emergence of the Saudi state and of Wahhabite religious fanaticism.

essentially aimed, by way of contrast, at celebrating Western culture and furthering the imperialist and colonialist cultural subjugation of the "East."[80]

It is precisely to such an approach that the Arab world responded, to a certain extent, by countering with a kind of rigid and defensive "nativism" (see, for example, the project of "Islamization of knowledge" launched in Mecca in 1977 on the basis of the ideas propounded by Seyyed Nasr and carried forward by al-Faruqi (Alatas 2014, 58–62)), aimed at denying any overlap between methodologies and concepts developed in the Western and Muslim worlds. In such an essentially culturalist undertaking, Ibn Khaldūn's work could not but represent an "uncomfortable" hindrance because of the difficulty of easily placing it within an exclusive "box."

So much so that, as Megherbi (1971, 44–49) observes, it is perhaps a consequence of Ibn Khaldūn's atypicality and intellectual nonconformism that in the Arab world itself, even if the study of his work falls within the curricular purview of many North African countries (such as Tunisia, Algeria, and Morocco), he has often been taught and greeted polemically and censoriously.

This spirit led to the endorsement of theses such as those put forward by Taha Hussein (1918), Mahmud Isma'il ([1976] 1996), or the jurist Ernest Enan (2007), which arraigned the Tunisian author as ignorant, egocentric, and anti-Arab (particularly, on account of some of his observations on nomadic populations), and even went so far as to criticise him (because of the many places in which he lived) for alleged opportunism and *patriotic* disloyalty. Their bias, here, is clear: this last line of criticism is anachronistic in the extreme, as it relates to a time and space in history that are still far removed from the conceptualisation of the idea of "homeland" (Bouthoul 1930, 47–48, 79; Megherbi 1971, 28; Talbi 2002, 851), and in which "betrayal" was, accordingly, only conceivable in essentially inter-subjective terms, or as apostasy, but could certainly not be linked to the fact of serving one sovereign and then another.[81]

Therefore, as Alatas (2014, 43) observes,[82] if Eurocentric bias has in point of fact acted as an obstacle to including Ibn Khaldūn in the sociological curriculum taught in the West, on the other hand, not even the "anti-imperialist" reaction, eventually, facilitated his popularity in the Arab world.

So it is that, torn between the vanity of the "theorising" trend on the one hand, and the intellectual jealousy (or, on the contrary, rejection) of the "contextualising" trend on the other (Forte 2005, 186), Ibn Khaldun's work has often risked being alternately

[80]In reality, as Miller (1975) observed, it is precisely through the appreciation and work of "enlightened Orientalists" such as Franz Rosenthal that Ibn Khaldūn's work is now known.

[81]On the contrary, precisely this very detachment of his may have been an important factor enabling him to observe and, thus, scientifically develop his new science.

[82]Precisely in order to restore Ibn Khaldūn's deserved position in the sociological curriculum, in 2011 Alatas (2011) devoted the opening chapter of the *Wiley-Blackwell Companion to Major Social Theorists* (Ritzer and Stepnisky 2011) to him. Ibn Khaldūn has also been included in a few other anthologies (Chambliss 1954; Hughes-Warrington 2008; Heath and Kaldis 2017).

misunderstood and forced by some scholars into interpretations tending to overplay its secular nature, or, on the contrary, belittled in its originality and greatness.[83]

One example of this can be observed in the reading offered of his strictly empirical assertion that political unity does not necessarily require religion and prophecy. On the one hand, an author like Kamil Ayad (1930, 51–3, 143), interpreting this assertion in an anti-theological sense, went so far as to argue that in Ibn Khaldūn's thinking religion figures as no more than a socio-psychological process. Similarly, even Erwin Rosenthal, while recognising that Ibn Khaldūn was a believer, considered his observation that royal authority can exist without religious backing as evidence of Ibn Khaldūn's independent thought, "free of theological trammels" (Rosenthal 1932, 58, 12), and aimed at considering religion as only one factor among many in the study of the state.

On the other hand, the Orientalist Hamilton A. R. Gibb (1933) commented that in making this observation Ibn Khaldūn simply applied the methods of earlier Sunni jurists and philosophers such as the orthodox scholar Ibn Taymiyya, who had also argued, half a century before Ibn Khaldūn, for the possibility of human association and political power of being independent of the guidance of prophecy and religion.

If it is true that Ibn Khaldūn certainly needs to be understood and contextualised within his time and tradition,[84] this must not go so far as to obscure the originality and emphatically deny the innovative thrust of the complex syntax of his work (Capezzone 2020). That would amount to a great loss. In fact, many aspects of his theory, although rooted, in their genealogy, in the cultural fabric of their time and space (and that goes for any theory: every thinker is a child of his or her own time), can nevertheless be taken out of their context and applied to others (Walzer 1963). As Gierer (2001, 8) has stressed, "too much emphasis on particular details may obscure interesting general features rather than uncovering and elucidating them."

Certainly, a failure to contextualise can lead to naiveté and hasty conclusions, both of which are to be avoided. On the other hand, though, even the unduly sterilising perspective of radical relativism (according to which culture is to be understood exclusively in its own context, where it must be enclosed and boxed up) should be avoided, especially with regard to such a theory as Ibn Khaldun's—in itself, "an immense and complex work embodied in a text of extraordinary homogeneousness and coherence,"[85] abounding in intellectual surprises elusive to any form of synthesis. In actual fact, it is difficult, even today, to deny admiration to its astounding originality, even if we want to dampen the enthusiasm of his first discoverers and concede how much we owe to the needs of historical contextualisation.

[83]Turroni (2005, 126) comments that the current tendency is to understate his originality owing to the limited scope of his historical categories, which, in her assessment, are mostly good for describing change in tribal societies.

[84]In reality, any theoretical work is obviously *also* the outcome and reflection of the cultural substrata out of which it grows. But that is not to say that it is *only* that.

[85]In the French original: "travail immense et complexe dans un texte d'une extraordinaire homogéneité et cohérence" (Cheddadi 2006, 241).

1.4.2 *Ibn Khaldūn as a "Forerunner" of the Social Sciences*

There are many points of contact between Ibn Khaldūn's ideas and those of the early sociologists. Many scholars have carried out studies comparing his work to that of other thinkers (Alatas 2013, 140–41). Thus, for example, Ibn Khaldūn has been compared to Durkheim by 'Izzat (1952), Gellner (1981, 86–98), and Turner (1971); to Machiavelli by Stowasser (1983) and Laroui (1987); to Comte by Baali (1986); and to Marx and Engels by Baali and Price (1982) and Lacoste ([1966] 1998).[86] Ibn Khaldūn's historical method has also been compared to Marc Bloch and Lucien Febvre's French school of the *Annales*.[87] In short, the idea that Ibn Khaldūn may have had a direct influence on Western sociological thought is certainly a recurrent hypothesis, and it undoubtedly stands on solid ground at least as far as one of the authors with whom a comparison most immediately suggests itself, Émile Durkheim, is concerned. In fact, Durkheim was certainly familiar with his work, having supervised the doctoral thesis on Ibn Khaldūn that Taha Hussein submitted at the Sorbonne.

We can only speak, instead, of the *possibility* that Auguste Comte might have been acquainted with Ibn Khaldūn's works—a possibility that, at any rate, is not to be ruled out, considering that at the time Comte was writing, not only was the *Muqaddima* already available in various Arabic, Turkish, French and German editions, but he also had Egyptian students. Therefore, as Fuad Baali has suggested, Comte might have become aware of Ibn Khaldūn (and discussed his ideas) through these students (Baali (1988, 24) makes explicit reference to a pupil of Comte named Mazhar Beg).[88]

In addition to the previously cited Alfred von Kremer (1879), even on the non-European side of Khaldunian studies there have been authors—such as 'Abd al-'Azīz 'Izzat, with his 1947 thesis titled "Ibn Khaldoun et sa science sociale"—who have specifically conjectured that Auguste Comte knew of Ibn Khaldūn's work and was influenced by it. Alatas (2014, 47) suggests that Comte may also have indirectly learned of Ibn Khaldūn's theses in another way, through the works of

[86]By virtue of his historical method, he has also been compared to Thucydides, by Lenn Evan Goodman (1972).

[87]See Dale (2015a, 284–87). In fact, even Bloch, a pupil of Émile Durkheim, conceived history as the history of societies, that is, of groups organised by the core element of their social cohesion. Furthermore, Bloch too believed in the power of the social structure to mould its own characteristics, as reflected, for example in its laws, vocabulary, and human activity. And, finally, like Durkheim and Ibn Khaldūn, Block also linked the increase in social density to economic development and the division of labour.

[88]Fuad Baali (1986, 29–32) points out eight characteristics that Ibn Khaldūn shared with Comte: both believed they had forged a new science; both sought to mark the exit from a phase of metaphysical and non-rational explanations of the world; both wanted to discover the predictive laws of social life; both recognised the important contribution that history makes to an understanding of the past and the future; both used a historical and non-statistical method; both distinguished their sciences from what had come before; both held that human nature was everywhere the same; and both recognised the central importance of social change.

Montesquieu; the latter, in turn, may have come to know them not only directly through Arabic texts, but also, as Gates claims,[89] more indirectly, through Jean-Baptiste Chardin's then-popular *Voyages en Perse et autres lieux de l'Orient* (1686), which was certainly familiar to Montesquieu, and which took up some Khaldunian theses, particularly those to do with climate.

Even some of Friedrich Engels' writings, such as his *History of Early Christianity*,[90] take up themes and even reproduce expressions that, as Alatas (2014, 47–48) maintains, appear to have been borrowed from Ibn Khaldūn's *Muqaddima*. Neither is it unlikely that Engels was familiar with this work (Bosquet 1969, 124–25), as he may have had access to it through French translations by Silvestre de Sacy and de Slane, as well as through von Hammer-Purgstall's German translation.

Even Karl Marx, as Hopkins (1990, 12) claims, was certainly familiar with de Slane's translation[91] and expressed some ideas that had already been set out by Ibn Khaldūn, such as the thesis that human beings, embedded in their different modes of production, "inevitably enter into definite relations, which are independent of their will, namely, relations of production appropriate to a given stage in the development of their material forces of production" (Marx [1859] 1970, 20).

The importance of Ibn Khaldūn's contribution is also recognised in the economic sciences. Joseph Schumpeter (1954), for example, mentions Ibn Khaldūn as the single exception to the "Schumpeterian gap"—referring to the long, five-century period following the development of Thomistic thought when economic analysis remained dormant—, and Joseph Spengler (1964, 285–86; 289; 297–303) hailed Ibn Khaldūn as the greatest economist of the Islamic Middle Ages. Moreover, Arthur Laffer, credited for theorising what has come to be known as the Laffer Curve, expressly declares he took the concept directly from Ibn Khaldūn's writings.[92]

However, as Gaston Bouthoul noted, when Western culture, in the nineteenth century, became a seedbed for the social sciences, and the critical moment came to bring these sciences into comparison with the coherent and systematic framework developed by Ibn Khaldūn, it became a widespread response to approach this comparison not with an open, explorative mind, but by enveloping his theory within the West's own thinking, and subsuming it within its own categories (sometimes even, in certain respects, unscrupulously):

---

[89]Gates (1967, 422): "A theory of climate which had reached a dead end in Europe was suddenly revitalized by a contribution from the East, giving new impetus to western social philosophy."

[90]Engels ([1894] 1975, 276): "All these movements are clothed in religion but they have their source in economic causes."

[91]Hopkins (1990, 12) points out that Marx mentions de Slane's translation in some of his notes written in Algeria in the early 1880s.

[92]"The Laffer Curve, by the way, was not invented by me. For example, Ibn Khaldūn, a fourteenth-century Muslim philosopher, wrote in his work *The Muqaddimah*: 'It should be known that at the beginning of the dynasty, taxation yields a large revenue from small assessments. At the end of the dynasty, taxation yields a small revenue from large assessments'" (Laffer 2004). For a recent article on the Laffer curve, see Orsi et al. (2013). For a recent appreciation of Ibn Khaldūn's economic thought, see also Rizliyah and Chachi (2020).

> Steeped in an overabundance of secularising evolutionary ideas about the development of societies, the thinking Europe of the mid-19th century co-opted from other cultures and continents those thinkers who seemed to confirm its own visions, repainting them in the guise of a general law.[93]

From this perspective, Ibn Khaldūn's thought—in the first phase of its "rediscovery," ranging roughly from the nineteenth century to the 1930s (Turroni 2002, 41)—was held up as a model that could "validate" the new theories, especially sociological, that were taking hold in the intellectual world. Even Bouthoul's own assessment is clearly reflective of this parallelism. For the father of polemology, just as the grand sociological system developed by Comte and Spencer marked the conclusion of three centuries of philosophical speculation in Europe, so the last grand system that closed the "season" of Arab thought had been the clearly sociological one developed by Ibn Khaldūn (Bouthoul 1934, xxv). Clearly watermarked and dominant in this image was Comte's classic tripartite scheme, under which the positive scientific system[94] was presented as "bookending" the journey that had begun with the most "immature" theological and metaphysical phases.

This underlying logic, thus, led Bouthoul, in his analysis, to stress Ibn Khaldūn's exceptionality in being able to "free himself," as Hamès comments,[95] from the Islamic theological interpretation of history.[96] Starting from the background of the Comtian scheme of progress, Bouthoul surreptitiously constructed a somewhat incorrect circular equation according to which if Ibn Khaldūn, labelled as a positivist thinker, based his theorising on rational thought, this could have only happened on condition that he uprooted himself from the theological and metaphysical thought that had preceded him. This was supposed to prove that theology needed to be set aside so as to make room for the intellectual sciences. That transition, as Bouthoul implied, never took place, in general, in Islamic culture, incapable as it was of culturally working toward a rebirth in the way that, instead, happened on the other shore of the Mediterranean.[97]

---

[93]"Engagée dans une surenchère d'idées évolutionnistes sécularisantes quant'à la marche des sociétés, l'Europe pensante du milieu du 19 siècle annexe les penseurs d'autres cultures et d'autres continents qui lui paraissent venir conforter ses propres vues en leur conférant une apparence de loi générale" (Bouthoul 1930, 173).

[94]Bouthoul (ibid.) compares Ibn Khaldūn to Descartes.

[95]As Constant Hamès (1999, 173) explains, the same kind of interpretation can later be descried in Ernest Renan's account of Averroes (Renan and al-Afghani 1883), who is considered not in his entirety but only for his Aristotelianism, until the implicit conclusion is reached that if the secular scientific spirit, which in the West enabled the progress of philosophy and science, at one point in Islam died out, responsibility for that loss of vitality is essentially to be laid on the rigid influence of the Muslim religion.

[96]Bouthoul (1930) deliberately speaks of "theology" in this context, avoiding the term "religion," since the latter was reserved by Comte for his own positivist religion as expounded in his *Cathéchisme positiviste* (Comte [1852] 2009).

[97]With regard to this conclusion, Horrut (2006, 109) complains that: "La conclusion est fortement ethnocentrique et campe un historien musulman rétrograde." In reality, it is likely that Bouthoul merely reported and adopted an observation made by Ibn Khaldūn himself, who regretted

Thus, as Voyé and Billiet (1999, 15–16) observe, although Ibn Khaldūn embraced a non-contradictory view of the universe in which reason and religion could coexist without having to reduce one to the other (Hamès 1999, 174), the first encounter between Islam and sociology came, in some way, to be read in a de-Islamised way through the interpretative reach that portrayed him as an atheist, if not scientifically anti-religious, thinker.

Even in the Islamic world, a great thinker like Muhsin Mahdi,[98] facing up to the "double valence" of Ibn Khaldūn as a great representative of rational scientific thought on the one hand, yet, on the other, as a believer explicitly committed to the observance of religious dogmas with regard to revealed truths, has felt prompted to conclude that Ibn Khaldūn must have been nothing less than a "crypto-philosopher."[99] In other words, Mahdi depicted him as a philosopher through and through who, for reasons of social acceptability and prudence, had to "camouflage" and protect himself by inserting ad hoc, in the *Muqaddima* (especially in chapter VI), explicit and strong "injections" of orthodox religious thought.

In so doing Mahdi took up the interpretive lens of philosophy as "reticent writing" that, in the late 1930s, Leo Strauss (1941; [1939] 1998, 294–305; Campanini 2004, 65–67) proposed, particularly for the purpose of interpreting other authors, such as Maimonides and Spinoza. According to this, two different discursive planes should be distinguished in the thought of many philosophers who lived in precarious times from the point of view of freedom of thought: one "esoteric," for the "initiates," and one "exoteric," "camouflaged," for others.

A similar kind of reading, according to Claude Horrut,[100] underlies the approach taken by various commentators such as Georges Labica,[101] Jamel Eddine Benchheick (1965), and especially Yves Lacoste (1984) (an anti-colonialist scholar mostly interested in a reading of the *Muqaddima* that might explain the reasons for the under-development of the Maghreb), who have offered a "materialist" and political reading of Ibn Khaldūn's work. This reading is also aimed at unravelling the knot of the coexistence, in Ibn Khaldūn, of a strictly rational perspective and an explicit religiosity, minimising or denying the import of the latter.

(*Muqaddima* VI, 18) the fact that the stand-off of civilization in the Maghreb and Spain had also put an end, there, to the flourishing of scientific disciplines.

[98]Muhsin Mahdi (1957) holds that, owing to the characteristics of his study of society, Ibn Khaldūn should be situated within the Aristotelian philosophical tradition, and in particular in that of the *falsafa* associated with al-Fārābī and Averroes, in contraposition to the Neoplatonic tradition associated with Avicenna and al-Ġazālī.

[99]With regard to this hypothetical crypto-philosophy, Leïla Babès (2011, 94) claimed that the same evident discrepancy between the absolute legal-theological purity of Islam (the kingdom of *da'wa*, the mission and proclamation of truth) and its real history, characterised by violence, corruption, and internal revolutions (the kingdom of *dawla*, the multi-faceted worldly management of power), could not but require an interpretative split.

[100]Horrut (2006, 104–8) condemns this operation as an act of "imperial colonialism."

[101]Labica (1968, 202): "l'Islam du point de vue politique ne serait que l'expression idéologique d'une structure économique et sociale en voie de dépassement."

In fact, on the one hand, these Marxist readings have highlighted the author's ability to anticipate themes that would much later become characteristic of historical materialism, such as the dialectical concept of history, the close relation between modes of production and social structure, and the power that economic forces wield in shaping individual attitudes and social relations (Kalin 2016). On the other hand, though, they have solved the conundrum of the annoying coexistence in Ibn Khaldūn of two radically different perspectives—rationality and religious thought—by stripping out one of the two kernels of the discussion. Consistently with this, they read the frequent religious "interpolations" as no more than a facade aimed at making people accept a thesis which, in reality, is essentially based on Aristotelian and Averroist thought and on a pre-Marxist methodology, nourished only by materialism, dialectics, and history.

A clarification is, however, in order: if the interpretive distortion that has been imposed on Ibn Khaldūn, in an effort to recast him as an "atheist," or at least as a secular thinker, ought to be set aside as an anachronistic and imperialist conceit, this line of criticism should not, on the other hand, be extended to overwhelm the recognition of his role as a forerunner of sociology—or, better, as already a sociologist in his own right.

Claude Horrut, for example, encounters this difficulty in commenting on Fuad Baali's claim that Ibn Khaldūn, the first thinker to have laid the groundwork for a sociology at once theoretical and empirical, anticipated Comte, Durkheim, and Malinowski. According to Horrut, reading an author like Ibn Khaldūn as a forerunner of these other authors is necessarily tantamount to unduly and forcibly projecting onto an author of the fourteenth century the standards of contemporary sociology (Horrut 2006, 110).

In reality, one thing does not imply the other. Highlighting an anticipation of insights and content cannot constitute, here, either distortion or anachronism, unless we assume a working definition of sociology as necessarily an Enlightenment product: precisely the assumption that Ibn Khaldūn's work succeeds in disproving.

References

(A) Ibn Khaldūn's Works

Ibn Khaldūn. 1844. Autobiographie d'Ibn Khaldoun (ed. William Mac Guckin de Slane). *Journal Asiatique* III: 5–60; 187–210; 291–308; 325–353.

———. 1847–1851. *Histoire des Berbères et des dynasties musulmanes de l'Afrique septentrionale* (ed. William Mac Guckin de Slane). 2 Voll. Algers: Imprimerie du Gouvernement.

———. 1857. *Muqaddimat Ibn Khaldūn*. Il Cairo: Būlāq.

———. 1858. *Prolégomènes D'Ebn-Khaldoun* (ed. M. Quatremère). Paris: Benjamin Duprat.

———. 1862–1868. *Les Prolégomènes d'Ibn Khaldoun* (ed. William Mac Guckin de Slane). Paris: Librairie orientaliste Paul Geuthner.

———. 1867–1868. *Kitāb al-'Ibar* (ed. Naṣr al-Hūrīnī). Il Cairo: Būlāq.

———. 1950. *An Arab Philosophy of History* (ed. Charles Issawi). London: Murray.

———. 1951. *Ta'rīf bi-Ibn Ḫaldūn wa-riḥlatuhu ġarban wa-šarqan* (ed. Muḥammad Tawit al-Tanji). Cairo: Lajnat al-Ta'lif wa-al-Tarjamah wa-al-Nashr.

———. 1958. *The Muqaddimah: An Introduction to History* (ed. Franz Rosenthal). 3 Voll. New Jersey: Princeton University Press.
———. 1967–1968. *Discours sur l'histoire universelle*, (ed. Vincent Monteil). 3 Voll. Beyrouth: Commission libanaise pour la traduction des chefs-d'oeuvre et Sinbad.
———. [1959] 1990. *Šifā' al-sā'il li-tahḏīb al-masā'il* (ed. Abū Yaarub Marzouki). Tunis: al-Dar al-Àrabiyah lil-Kitāb.
———. [1980] 1995. *Le voyage d'Occident et d'Orient* (ed. Abdesselam Cheddadi). Paris: Sindbad.
———. 2002. *Le Livre des Exemples. I. Autobiographie, Muqaddima* (ed. Abdesselam Cheddadi). Paris: Gallimard.
———. [1967] 2005. *The Muqaddimah: An Introduction to History* (ed. Franz Rosenthal), abridged edition. Princeton: Princeton University Press.
———. 2017. *Ibn Khaldūn on Sufism. Remedy for the Questioner in Search of Answers* (trans. Yumna Ozer). Cambridge: The Islamic Texts Society.

(B) Other Works

Abdesselem, Ahmed. 1983. *Ibn Khaldūn et ses lecteurs*. Paris: Presses Universitaires de France.
Ahmad, Zaid. 2003. *The Epistemology of Ibn Khaldūn*. London: RoutledgeCurzon.
Alatas, Syed Farid. 2011. Ibn Khaldūn. In *Wiley-Blackwell Companion to Major Social Theorists*, eds. George Ritzer and Jeffrey Stepnisky, 12–29. Malden, MA: Wiley-Blackwell.
———. 2013. *Ibn Khaldūn*. Oxford: Oxford Centre for Islamic Studies.
———. 2014. *Applying Ibn Khaldūn. The Recovery of a Lost Tradition in Sociology*. London: Routledge.
al-Azmeh, Aziz. 1981. *Ibn Khaldūn in Modern Scholarship: A Study in Orientalism*. London: Third World Research Centre.
———. 1982. *Ibn Khaldūn: An Essay in Reinterpretation*. Budapest: Central European University Press.
al-Fārābī, Abū Nasr. [X-XI century] 1986. *Kitāb al-millah wa nuṣūṣ ukhrā* (ed. Muhsin Mahdi). Beirut: Dar-El-Mashreq.
al-Jabri, Mohammed 'Abed. [1976, 1991] 1996. *La ragione araba*. Milano: Feltrinelli.
al-Yaaqubi, Husayn. 2006. The Banū Khaldūn: From Seville to Tunisia. In *Ibn Khaldūn. The Mediterranean in the 14th Century. Rise and Fall of the Empires. Studies*, ed. Noemí García Millán, 316–331. Seville: Fundación José Manuel Lara.
Aristotle. [350 B.C.]2013. *La generazione e la corruzione*. Milano: Bompiani.
Ayad, Kamil. 1930. *Die Geschichts- und Gesellschaftslehre Ibn Ḫaldūns*. Stuttgart und Berlin: Cotta.
Baali, Fuad. 1986. *Ilm al-'Umrān and Sociology: A Comparative Study*. Kuwait: Annals of the Faculty of Arts, Kuwait University.
———. 1988. *Society, State, and Urbanism: Ibn Khaldūn's Sociological Thought*. Lanham: University Press of America.
Baali, Fuad, and Brian Price. 1982. Ibn Khaldūn and Karl Marx: On Socio-Historical Change. *Iqbal Review* 23 (1): 17–36.
Babès, Leïla. 2011. *L'utopie de l'islam. La religion contre l'État*. Armand Colin: Paris.
Barnes, Harry E. 1948. Ancient and Medieval Social Philosophy. In *An Introduction to the History of Social Philosophy*, ed. H.E. Barnes, 3–28. Chicago: Chicago University Press.
Becker, Howard, and Harry E. Barnes, [1938] 1961. *Social Thought from Lore to Science*. 3 Voll. New York: Dover.
Bencheick, Jamel E. 1965. Esquisse d'une sociologie de la religion chez Ibn Khaldūn. *La Pensée* 123: 3–23.
Bombaci, Alessio. 1949. Postille alla traduzione della Muqaddimah di Ibn Ḫaldūn. *AION* III: 439–472.

———. 1969. *Letteratura turca*. Firenze: Sansoni.

Bosquet, Georges-H. 1969. Marx et Engels se sont-ils intéressés aux questions islamiques? *Studia Islamica* 30: 119–130.

Boukraa, Ridha. 2008. The Khaldunian concept of 'Umran/Ijtimaa in Light of the Current Paradigm of Post-Modern Society. *The Journal of North African Studies* 13 (3): 317–326.

Bouthoul, Gaston. 1930. *Ibn-Khaldoun. Sa philosophie sociale*. Librairie Orientaliste Paul Geuthner: Paris.

———. 1934. Ibn Khaldoun. Préface à la nouvelle édition des Prolégomènes. In Ibn Khaldūn, *Les Prolégomènes d'Ibn Khaldoun* (ed. William Mac Guckin de Slane). Paris: Geuthner.

Brunschvig, Robert. 1947. *La Berbérie orientale sous les Hafsides*. Adrien Maisonneuve: Tome II. Paris.

Butterworth, Charles. 1972. Averroës, Politics and Opinion. *The American Political Science Review*: 894–901.

Campanini, Massimo. 2004. *Introduzione alla filosofia islamica*. Roma-Bari: Laterza.

———. 2005b. *Ibn Khaldūn: la Muqaddima, la storia, la civiltà, il potere*. In *Studies on Ibn Khaldūn*, ed. Massimo Campanini, 9–48. Milano: Polimetrica.

———. 2007. *Averroè. Bologna: il Mulino.*

Capezzone, Leonardo. 2020. The City and the Law. Aspects of Ibn Khaldūn's critique of the philosophers. *Philological Encounters* 5: 4–24.

Celarent, Barbara. 2013. Taha Hussein, La philosophie sociale d'Ibn Khaldoun. *American Journal of Sociology* 119: 894–902.

Chambliss, Rollin. 1954. *Social Thought: From Hammurabi to Comte*. New York: Dryden Press.

Chardin, Jean-Baptiste. 1686. *Travels into Perse and the East Indies*. Vol. I. London: folio.

Cheddadi, Abdesselam. 1980. Le système du pouvoir en Islam d'après Ibn Khaldoun. *Annales. Économies, Sociétés, Civilisations* 35: 534–550.

———. [1980] 1995. Lectures d'Ibn Khaldūn. In Ibn Khaldūn, *Le voyage d'Occident e d'Orient, Autobiographie* (ed. Abdesselam Cheddadi), 9–26. Paris: Sinbad.

———. 2006. *Ibn Khaldūn. L'homme et le théoricien de la civilisation*. Paris: Gallimard.

Comte, Auguste. 1855. *Positive Philosophy*. New York: Calvin Blanchard.

———. [1852] 2009. *Cathéchisme positiviste*. Paris: Sandre.

Croce, Benedetto. 1932. Recensione di M. K. Ayad, *Die Geschichts–und Gesellschaftslehre Ibn Ḫaldūns*, Stuttgart, Berlin, Cotta. *La critica* XXX: 213–214.

Cruz Hernández, Miguel. 2003. Siete interrogantes en la historia del pensamiento. *Revista Española de Filosofía Medieval* 10: 69–73.

Dale, Stephen Frederic. 2015a. *The Orange Trees of Marrakesh. Ibn Khaldūn and the Science of Man*. Cambridge, MA: Harvard University Press.

DeBoer, Tjitze J. [1901] 1965. *The History of Philosophy in Islam*. New York: Dover.

Dozy, Reinhart. 1869. Compte-rendue des "Prolégomènes d'Ibn Khaldoun", texte Arabe par E. Quatremère, traduit par de Slane. *Journal Asiatique* XIV (6): 133–218.

Durkheim, Émile. 1893. *De la division du travail social*. Paris: Presses Universitaires de France.

———. 1994. *Course in Sociology, Opening Lecture*. In *Émile Durkheim on Institutional Analysis*, ed. Mark Traugott. Chicago: University of Chicago Press.

———. [1895] 1999. *Les règles de la méthode sociologique*. Paris: Flammarion.

Enan, Mohammad Abdullah. [1941] 2007. *Ibn Khaldūn: His Life and Works*. Kuala Lumpur: The Other Press.

Engels, Frederick. [1894] 1975. *On the History of Early Christianity*. In Marx & Engels, *On Religion*. Moscow: Progress.

Fakhry, Majid. 1970. *A History of Islamic Philosophy*. New York: Columbia University Press.

Ferrero, Guglielmo. 1896. Un sociologo arabo del secolo XIV: Ibn Khaldoun. *La riforma sociale* 6: 221–235.

Fischel, Walter J. 1952. *Ibn Khaldūn and Tamerlane*. Berkeley: University of California Press.

Fleischer, Cornell. 1983. Royal Authority, Dynastic Cyclism and "Ibn Khaldūnism" in Sixteenth Century Ottoman Letters. *Journal of Asian and African Studies* 18: 198–220.

Flint, Robert. [1893] 2010. *History of the Philosophy of History*. Memphis, TN: General Books.

Forte, Francesca. 2005. Per una nuova storiografia khalduniana. In *Studies on Ibn Khaldūn*, ed. Massimo Campanini, 181–199. Milano: Polimetrica.
———. 2020. *Ibn Khaldūn: Antologia della Muqaddima*. Milano: Jaca Books.
Fromherz, Allen James. 2010. *Ibn Khaldūn: Life and Times*. Edinburgh: Edinburgh University Press.
Gabrieli, Giuseppe. 1923. Saggio di bibliografia e concordanza della storia di Ibn Ḫaldūn. *Rivista degli Studi Orientali, X*: 169–211.
Gabrieli, Francesco. [1930] 1984. Il concetto di 'aṣabiyya' nel pensiero storico di Ibn Khaldūn. In *L'Islam nella storia*, ed. Francesco Gabrieli, 211–252. Bari: Dedalo.
Gates, Warren E. 1967. The Spread of Ibn Khaldūn's Ideas on Climate and Culture. *Journal of the History of Ideas* 28: 415–422.
Gellner, Ernest. 1981. *Cohesion and Identity: the Maghreb from Ibn Khaldūn to Émile Durkheim*. In *Muslim Society*, ed. Ernest Gellner. Cambridge: Cambridge University Press.
———. 1995. *Anthropology and Politics. Revolution in the Sacred Grove*. Oxford: Blackwell.
Gibb, Hamilton A.R. 1933. The Islamic Background of Ibn Khaldūn's Political Theory. *Bulletin of the School of Oriental Studies* VII: 23–31.
Gierer, Alfred. 2001. Ibn Khaldūn on Solidarity ("Asabiyah")–Modern Science on Cooperativeness and Empathy: A Comparison. *Philosophia Naturalis* 38: 91–104.
Goodman, Lenn Evan. 1972. Ibn Khaldūn and Thucydides. *Journal of the American Oriental Society* 92 (2): 250–270.
Goumeziane, Smaïl. 2006. *Ibn Khaldoun, un génie maghrébien*. Paris: Non lieu.
Gumplowicz, Ludwig. 1925. *Soziologische Essays*. Innsbruck: Universitäts- Verlag Wagner.
Hamès, Constant. 1999. Islam et Sociologie: Une rencontre qui n'a pas eu lieu? In *Sociology and Religions. An Ambiguous Relationship*, eds. Liliane Voyé and Jaak Billiet, 171–182. Leuven: Leuven University Press.
Heath, Eugene, and Byron Kaldis. 2017. *Wealth, Commerce and Philosophy: Foundational Thinkers and Business Ethics*. Chicago: The University of Chicago Press.
Hodgson, Marshall G.S. 1974. *The Venture of Islam: Conscience and History in a World Civilization*. Chicago: University of Chicago Press.
Hopkins, Nicholas. 1990. Engels and Ibn Khaldūn. *Alif. Journal of Comparative Poetics* 10: 9–18.
Horrut, Claude. 2006. *Ibn Khaldūn, un Islam des "Lumières"*. Paris: Les Éditions Complexes.
Hourani, Albert. 1962. *Arabic Thought in the Liberal Age 1798-1939*. Cambridge: Cambridge University Press.
Hughes-Warrington, Marnie. 2008. *Fifty Key-Thinkers on History*. London: Routledge.
Hussein, Taha. 1918. *Étude analitique et critique de la philosophie sociale d'Ibn Khaldoun*. Paris: Pedone.
Irwin, Robert. 2018. *Ibn Khaldūn. An Intellectual Biography*. Princeton: Princeton University Press.
Isma'il, Mahmud. [1976] 1996. *Nihāyat usṭūrat naẓarīyāt Ibn Khaldūn: muqtabasah min Rasā'il Ikhwān al-ṣafā*. Al-Manṣūrah: 'Āmir lil-Ṭibā'ah wa-al-Nashr.
'Izzat, 'Abd al-'Aziz. 1947. *Ibn Khaldoun et sa science sociale*. Cairo: Université de Fouad.
———. 1952. *Étude comparée d'Ibn Khaldūn et Durkheim*. Cairo: al-Maktabat al-Anglo al-Misriyya.
Kalin, Ibrahim. 2016, December 10. Ibn Khaldūn has a Message for Us. *Daily Sabah Columns*. https://www.dailysabah.com/columns/ibrahim-kalin/2016/12/10/ibn-khaldun-has-a-message-for-us. Accessed 17 Sept 2020.
———. 2017a, January 6. Al-Fārābī Prayer. *Daily Sabah Columns*. https://www.dailysabah.com/columns/ibrahim-kalin/2017/01/07/al-farabis. Accessed 17 Sept 2020.
Kantorowicz, Ernst. 1989. *Les deux corps du roi. Essai sur la théologie politique au Moyen Âge*. Paris: Gallimard.
Labica, Georges. 1968. *Politique et religion chez Ibn Khaldūn*. Alger: SNED.
Lacoste, Yves. [1966] 1998. *Ibn Khaldoun, Naissance de l'Histoire, passé du Tiers Monde*. Paris: La Decouverte.

Laffer, Arthur. 2004. The Laffer Curve: Past, Present, and Future. *Executive Summary Backgrounder No. 1765*: 1–18. s3.amazonaws.com/thf_media/2004/pdf/bg1765.pdf. Accessed 17 Sept 2020.

Lagarde, Georges de. [1934] 1956–1970. *La naissance de l'esprit laïque au déclin du Moyen Âge*. Louvain: E. Nauvelaerts.

Lahbabi, Mohamed-Aziz. 1987. *Ibn Khaldūn: notre contemporain*. Paris: L'Harmattan.

Lakhsassi, Abderrahman. 1979. Ibn Khaldūn and the Classification of the Science. *The Maghreb Review* 4 (1): 21–25.

Lavisse, Ernest, and Alfred Rambaud. 1898. *Histoire générale*, Tome X. Paris: Armand Colin & Cie.

Lawrence, Bruce B. 1983. Ibn Khaldūn and Islamic Ideology. *Journal of Asian and African Studies, XVIII* 3–4: 154–165.

———. 1984. *Ibn Khaldūn and Islamic Ideology*. Leiden: Brill.

———. 2005. *Introduction to the 2005 Edition*. In Ibn Khaldūn, *The Muqaddimah: An Introduction to History* (ed. Franz Rosenthal), abridged edition, vii–xxv. Princeton: Princeton University Press.

Laroui, Abdallah. 1987. *Islam et modernité*. Paris: La Découverte.

Mahdi, Muhsin. 1957. *Ibn Khaldūn's Philosophy of History*. Chicago: University of Chicago Press.

Marx, Karl. 1848. *Manifesto of the Communist Party*. London: Burghard.

———. [1859] 1970. *A Contribution to the Critique of Political Economy*. Moscow: Progress Publishers.

Maunier, René. 1915. Les idées sociologiques d'un philosophe arabe au XIV siècle. *Revue internationale de sociologie* 23: 142–154.

Megherbi, Abdelghani. 1971. *La pensée sociologique d'Ibn Khaldoun*. SNED: Alger.

Miller, John H. 1975. *Ibn Khaldūn and Machiavelli: an Examination of Paradigms*. Manhattan, KS: Master's Thesis, Kansas State University.

Nassar, Nassif. 1964. *Le maître d'Ibn Khaldūn, Al-Ābilī*, 103–114. XX: *Studia Islamica*.

———. 1967. *La pensée realiste d'Ibn Khaldūn*. Paris: Presses Universitaires de France.

Nicholson, Reynold A. 1907. *A Literary History of the Arabs*. Cambridge: Cambridge University Press.

Norton, David F., and Jacqueline Taylor (eds.). [1993] 2011. *The Cambridge Companion to Hume*. Cambridge: Cambridge University Press.

Oppenheimer, Franz. 1922–1935. *System der Soziologie*. Jena: G. Fisher.

Orsi, Renzo, Davide Raggi, and Francesco Turrino. 2013, December 13. Ridurre le tasse si deve. *Lavoce.info*. http://www.lavoce.info/archives/15593/ridurre-le-tasse-pressione-fiscale-curva-di-laffer/. Accessed 17 Sept 2020.

Ortega y Gasset, José. [1934] 1976–1978. Abenjaldún nos revela el secreto: pensamientos sobre África Minor. *Revista del Instituto Egipcio de Estudios Islámicos en Madrid* 19: 95–114.

Patriarca, Giovanni. 2019. El eterno retorno de la Asabiyyah. Ibn Jaldún y la teoría política contemporánea. *Daimon. Revista International de filosofía* 76: 139–153.

Pizzi, Giancarlo. 1985. *Ibn Ḫaldūn e la Muqaddima: una filosofia della storia*. Milano: All'insegna del pesce d'oro.

Pomian, Krzysztof. 2006. *Ibn Khaldūn au prisme de l'Occident*. Paris: Gallimard.

Renan, Ernest, and Djamal ad-Din al-Afghani. 1883. *Le journal des débats*: 1–17. http://blogs.histoireglobale.com/wp-content/uploads/2011/10/Renan-al-Afghani.pdf. Accessed 17 Sept 2020.

Ritzer, George, and Jeffrey Stepnisky. 2011. *Wiley-Blackwell Companion to Major Social Theorists*. Malden, MA: Wiley-Blackwell.

Rizliyah, Siti, and Abdelkader Chachi. 2020. The relevance of Ibn Khaldūn's economic thought. *Turkish Journal of Islamic Economics* 7 (2): 76–96.

Rosenthal, Erwin. 1932. *Ibn Khaldūns Gedanken über den Staat. Ein Beitrag zur Geschichte der mittelalterlichen Staatlehre*. Oldenbourg: Munich.

Rosenthal, Franz. 1958. *Preface to Ibn Khaldūn*. In Ibn Khaldūn, *The Muqaddimah: An Introduction to History* (ed. Franz Rosenthal). Vol. I, xxix–cxv. Princeton: Princeton University Press.

———. 1984. Ibn Khaldūn in His Time. In *Ibn Khaldūn and Islamic Ideology*, ed. Bruce B. Lawrence, 16–24. Leiden: Brill.

Said, Edward. 1978. *Orientalism*. London: Penguin.

Salama, Mohammad. 2011. *Islam, Orientalism and Intellectual History. Modernity and the Politics of Exclusion since Ibn Khaldūn*. London York: I. B. Tauris.

Sarton, George. [1927] 1962. *Introduction to the History of Science*. Baltimore, MD: Williams and Wilkins Company.

Schacht, Joseph (ed.). 1974. *The Legacy of Islam*. Oxford: Clarendon Press.

Schumpeter, Joseph. 1954. *History of Economic Analysis*. New York: Oxford University Press.

Shackleton, Robert. 1961. *Montesquieu*. London: Oxford University Press.

Silvestre de Sacy, Antoine Isaac. 1810. Extraits de Prolégomènes d'Ebn Khaldoun. In *Relation de l'Egipte par Abdellatif, médecin arabe de Bagdad*, ed. Antoine Isaac Silvestre de Sacy, 509–524 (translation); 558–564 (Arabic text). Paris: Treuttel & Würtz.

Silvestre de Sacy, Antoine Isaac. [1816] 1843. Ibn Khaldoun. In *Biographie universelle ancienne et moderne*, ed. Antoine Isaac Silvestre de Sacy, Tome XX. Paris: A. Thoisniers Deplace.

———. [1826–1827] 2012. *Chrestomatie arabe, ou extraits de divers écrivains arabes*. Paris: Ulan Press.

Sorokin, Pitirim A. [1947] 1962. *Society, Culture, and Personality*. New York: Cooper Square.

Speake, Jennifer. [2003] 2014. *Literature of Travel and Exploration. An Encyclopedia*. London: Routledge.

Spengler, Joseph. 1964. Economic Thought of Islam: Ibn Khaldūn. *Comparative Studies in Society and History* 6: 268–306.

Stowasser, Barbara. 1983. *Religion and Political Development: Some Comparative Ideas on Ibn Khaldūn and Machiavelli*. Washington, DC: Center for Contemporary Arab Studies.

Strauss, Leo. 1941. Persecution and the Art of Writing. *Social Research* VIII (4): 488–504.

———. [1939] 1998. *L'insegnamento esoterico*. In Leo Strauss, *Gerusalemme e Atene*. Torino: Einaudi.

Strauss, Leo, and Joseph Cropsey. [1963] 1972. *History of Political Philosophy*. Chicago: Rand McNally and Co.

Talbi, Mohamed. 1973. *Ibn Ḫaldūn et l'histoire*. Tunis: Maison Tunisienne de l'Édition.

———. 2002. Ibn Khaldoun. *Encyclopédie de l'Islam*, t. III, 849–855. Leiden: Brill.

Toynbee, Arnold. [1934] 1962. *A Study of History. Vol. III: The Growths of Civilizations*. New York: Oxford University Press.

Turner, Bryan S. 1971. Sociological Founders and Precursors: the Theories of Religion of Émile Durkheim, Fustel de Coulanges and Ibn Khaldūn. *Religion* 1: 32–48.

Turroni, Giuliana. 2002. *Il mondo della storia secondo Ibn Khaldūn*. Roma: Jouvence.

———. 2005. Ibn Khaldūn: penseur classique de l'islam laïque. In *Studies on Ibn Khaldūn*, ed. Massimo Campanini, 123–144. Milano: Polimetrica.

Verza, Annalisa. 2008. Islam e diritti umani: tra rigidità strutturali e radici interne. In *Diritti umani. Trasformazioni e reazioni*, ed. Silvia Vida, 211–225. Bologna: Bononia University Press.

von Hammer-Purgstall, Joseph. 1812. *Über den Verfall des Islam nach den ersten drei Jahrhunderten der Hidschra*. Wien: Anton Schmid.

———. 1818. *Extraits d'Ibn Khaldūn*. In *Fundgruben des Orients*, ed. Joseph von Hammer-Purgstall, Vol. 6, 301–307, 362–364. Wien: Anton Schmid.

von Hemsö, Gråberg, and Chevalier Jakob Grefve. 1835. An Account of the Great Historical Work of the African Philosopher Ibn Khaldūn. *Transactions of the Royal Asiatic Society of Great Britain and Ireland* 3 (3): 387–404.

von Kremer, Alfred. 1879. Ibn Chaldun and seine Kulturgeschichte der Islamischen Reiche. *Sitzungberichte der Kaiserlichen Akademie der Wissenschaften, Philosoph.-histor. Klasse* 93: 581–634.

Voyé, Liliane, and Jaak Billiet. 1999. Introduction. In *Sociology and Religions. An Ambiguous Relationship*, eds. Liliane Voyé and Jaak Billiet, 9–16. Leuven: Leuven University Press.

Walzer, Richard. 1963. Aspects of Islamic Political Thought: Al-Fārābī and Ibn Xaldūn. *Oriens* 16: 40–60.

Chapter 2
Sense and Form of a "New History"

Abstract This chapter focuses on the novelty of Ibn Khaldūn's approach to history and, in particular, on the role played by the profound political and social instability of his time in stimulating the urgency of a general revision and restructuring of historical endeavours. Therefore, it addresses Ibn Khaldūn's criticism of the Islamic approach of his time to history, and also examines the innovative methodology he proposed, as well as all the cognitive and moral requirements he showed were necessary premises for a rational and objective understanding of historical development, capable of grasping its "inner meaning." In Ibn Khaldūn such a method, informed by a rigorous rationality, does not conflict with his profound and sincere Islamic faith, but virtuously combines with it thanks to a particular *forma mentis* called, in Arabic, *'aql-naql*, identifying the two different approaches as pertaining to the separate domains of the natural world, and metaphysics.

Finally, on a meta-scientific level, the chapter focuses on how, in Ibn Khaldūn's work, the different dimensions of historical, sociological-empirical, philosophical, and religious understanding intertwine and strengthen each other, thus producing a complex and revealing vision of the cycles of history. As the latter, thus, acquires a predictable character, the historical examples from the past (*'ibar*) are offered in Ibn Khaldūn's book as instructive paradigms, enabling man to understand his present and foresee its immediate future developments.

2.1 Chaos as a Spur of Theoretical Order

The complex reformulation of history in Ibn Khaldūn's work was prompted by a need for a scientific approach and objectivity which was, in itself, revolutionary at the time, and that certainly found in itself its own raison d'être. Yet, it must have been the necessity to respond to much deeper and personal generative needs, that prompted him to work out such a radical reformulation of the coordinates of history.

The new and revolutionary intuition at the basis of his enterprise was the idea that, behind the continuous flow of political changes, predetermined "laws," like those of

A. Verza, *Ibn Khaldūn and the Arab Origins of the Sociology of Civilisation and Power*, https://doi.org/10.1007/978-3-030-70339-4_2

nature, were at work, framing history within a cyclical and comprehensive dynamic scheme.

Ibn Khaldūn was a Muslim believer, immersed in a culture which was centred around the authority of tradition, and not on the logico-rationalistic reasoning proper to the Greek tradition. Religious tradition dictated the core values in law, in ethics, and in the historical and historiographical enterprise, and the presence of cognitive limits impassable for human intelligence was well emphasised. Starting from that context, thus, only an exceptionally pressing practical urgency could have prompted him to move beyond that vision and to explore new intellectual landscapes, in order independently to develop an original theory of history in which even the regressive movements, the involution and, eventually, the decline of an entire world might in some way be redeemed by their rational explicability.

Between 1348 and 1349 the terrible black plague ravaging nearby towns reached Tunis, decimating the population. Its destructive effect was horrific: as Ibn Khaldūn commented, it "devastated nations and caused populations to vanish. It swallowed up many of the good things of civilisation and wiped them out." (*Muqaddima*, The Introduction; Ibn Khaldūn 1958, vol. 1, 64; Ibn Khaldūn [1967] 2005, 30). Completing its destructive action, and in consequence of the inevitable neglect of agricultural work which came in its wake, a further calamity raged in the following year: a devastating famine which, in turn, claimed a great many lives as well.

Thomas Spragens argued in *Understanding Political Theory*, that "political theories are like pearls: they are not produced without an irritant," and in fact that "most political theories [...] are written as an attempt to deal with some very real and urgent problems" (Spragens 1976, 20). It can be hypothesised that precisely this element may have been the spark that would soon prompt the great historian and theorist of sociodynamics Ibn Khaldūn, at that time only 16 years old, to embark on his intellectual project.

Regarding the devastation caused by the disease, he wrote, in fact, that "it was as if the voice of existence in the world had called out for oblivion and restriction, and the world had responded to its call." (*Muqaddima*, The Introduction; Ibn Khaldūn 1958, vol. 1, 64; Ibn Khaldūn [1967] 2005, 30). This comment is striking not only for its singularly poignant and emphatic tone (at least, if compared with the usually measured and analytical style of his prose).[1] It also expresses the determined resolve to find an ultimate meaning even in tragedies such as the epidemic and the deadly famine that had plagued his world. In fact, like a revealing warning light,[2] this comment gives us a first glimpse into that peculiar intent to understand and sort into their proper place all the elements of history within a complex, but understandable, rational system, which would characterise his entire work. This attitude, through a combination of both direct observation and rational speculation, would lead him to

[1]As we learn from Ibn Khaldūn's autobiography, he was a poet as well.

[2]Some have seen Malthusian anticipations in this parenthetical passage: see Bouthoul (1930, 38), Boulakia (1971, 1117).

develop an original science aimed at grasping the hitherto untapped "inner meaning" of history.

However, the constant precariousness of the political life of the time, in addition to Ibn Khaldūn's own personal story, must also have prompted this need to find a concealed order within the confused historical changeability of his world. In fact, his own life was chequered by a continuous series of achievements and losses, crises and rebirths, court honours, and imprisonments, which took their turn amid the exceedingly deep political instability of his time, as different dynasties and alliances ceaselessly re-combined.

All this background supports the idea that his long and detailed "theoretical introduction" to history (the *Muqaddima*) could be also read as a rationalising response to the "irritant" represented by the great social and political instability of his world. This instability was not only due to the chaos that followed the terrible scourge of the black plague, but also to a broader set of socio-political factors, all elements precipitating an urgent need for reflection which Ibn Khaldūn clearly expresses at the beginning of his work:

> When there is a general change of conditions, it is as if the entire creation had changed and the whole world been altered, as if it were a new and repeated creation, a world brought into existence anew. Therefore, there is need at this time that someone should systematically set down the situation of the world among all regions and races, as well as the customs and sectarian beliefs that have changed for their adherents, doing for this age what al-Mas'ūdī[3] did for his. (*Muqaddima*, The Introduction; Ibn Khaldūn 1958, vol. 1, 65; Ibn Khaldūn [1967] 2005, 30).

On the one hand, here, Ibn Khaldūn's reference to Mas'ūdī's "encyclopaedic" work already programmatically anticipated the systematic breadth he would later impart to the *Muqaddima* (especially in its sixth chapter). On the other, his remark on the destructive (almost resuscitative) effect of the great scourge, and his own attempt to understand these events within the framework of the historico-cultural situation of his time, reveal the key role that such concrete historical shocks must have played in alerting him to the need for a new approach to the study of history.

The purpose of identifying an intrinsic rationality of history—something reassuring, at least insofar as it would make it possible intellectually to define and map out the course of events, and to make them intelligible within a framework that imparted to them some kind of predictability—was, in a sense, the only possibly

[3]Abū al-Ḥasan 'Alī Mas'ūdī, almost certainly a Muʿtazilite, was a scholar and a restless traveller who lived in the tenth century, the period during which the Arab civilisation reached its apogee. Among other works, he wrote a famous treatise ([10th cent.] 1861–1877), the *Murūj al-Ḏahab* (*The Meadows of Gold*), that would exert in his world, in the centuries to follow, a significant influence on geography and historiography (so much so that he has been described by orientalists as the "Herodotus of the Arabs"). In his approach to knowledge he was also open to non-Arab culture—this, in keeping with the Muʿtazilite tenet that logic can reconcile faith and reason. In relation to many aspect of his biography, and in his scientific ambitions, Ibn Khaldūn seems to follow in al-Mas'ūdī's footsteps. And, in fact, he recognises his predecessor's huge importance, even as he charts a new course, his "new" science being original, compared with his predecessor's encyclopaedism.

rational way to cope with the increasingly pressing urgency of his world. Precisely this must have been the motivational springboard that prompted Ibn Khaldūn to develop an extraordinarily modern model of history, intended to be not only new and original, but also (*Muqaddima*, Preliminary Remarks: Ibn Khaldūn 1958, vol. I, 77; Ibn Khaldūn [1967] 2005, 39) "extremely useful." In fact, in his view, not only was an objective quest for historical truth in itself a necessary enterprise, but he further entrusted to history the crucial task of helping us understand the truth beneath the ceaseless instability that dynamically characterises the social and political world.

Returning to Spragens's observation, therefore, it must have been the stimulus of such "irritants" that provided the conditions for his elaboration of the "new science," to which the mission of making sense of the chaos and of the "panicked," ubiquitous instability of his time could be entrusted, carrying forward this renewed vision of the historical enterprise. Yet, it was precisely on account of its brilliant modernity and innovativeness, that this science was subsequently doomed (everywhere, except in Turkey) to remain an isolated model for a long time.

2.2 Criticism of the Errors of the Past

According to Taha Hussein (1918, cf. Laroui 1999), the methods by which Ibn Khaldūn proceeded in his hermeneutic endeavour simply took us back to his practice as a Muslim judge, accustomed to reasoning on his sources by relying on hermeneutical instruments such as reasoning by analogy (known as *qiyās*), and the interpretive effort (*ra'y*). Therefore, his methods, far from being truly innovative, essentially reflected instruments already present in the culture of his time.

However, while it *is* true that these elements can effectively be found *in nuce* in his work, there is reason to object to such a belittling analysis. In fact, the ambitious objective of the *Muqaddima* expressed an unprecedented scholarly effort, radically distant not only from the historical tradition of the time, but also from the influential philosophical paradigms of the "Second Teacher," Al-Fārābī, who, in the popular work *al-Madīna al-fāḍila* (*The Perfectly Virtuous City*)—a utopian rather than scientific work—viewed society essentially from the Platonic perspective of the quest for the best and most ethical way of governing.

It should also be remembered that, as we have seen, the *Politics* of the "First Teacher" Aristotle had not yet been translated into Arabic at the time, although another book on "Politics" was erroneously attributed to him, despite many doubts (Ibn Khaldūn himself distinctly queried this attribution). This book was organised on the basis of the widespread medieval model (of Persian origin: see Lambton [1954] 1980; Campanini 2005b: 28–29) of the "*Specula principum*,"[4] and was considered

[4] Also known, in the Europe of Germanic influence, as "*Fürstenspiegel*."

by Ibn Khaldūn not only as spurious, but also as rhetorically circular, superficial, unenlightening, and lacking in organicity.[5]

Moving on from this entire context, Ibn Khaldūn refined a new approach in Muslim history, innovatively understood by him as a discipline no longer rooted in tradition but in rationality (*ḥikma*, not *falsafa*), and aimed at grasping, under the surface of events, the nature of society as it is, and not as it should be.

The entire construction takes its starting point from a criticism directed, first of all, against the tendency, typical of medieval Islam, to report history (*ḫabar*, the central concept in traditional Arab historiography, traditionally referred to the event and its narration at the same time) in a poetic and fantastic way. Events were customarily explained by using nonchalant references to supernatural, miraculous, or marvellous forces, and often uncritically handed down, from one source to the next (Coltman Brown 1981: 22), without any objective validation of their truth in the light of hard facts, expunging from the historical sphere rationality and methodological accuracy.

The *Muqaddima* opens (*Muqaddima*, Foreword; Ibn Khaldūn 1958, Vol. I: 6; Ibn Khaldūn [1967] 2005, 5) with the statement that "on the surface history is no more than *information* about political events, dynasties, and occurrences of the remote past, elegantly presented and spiced with proverbs." However—as Ibn Khaldūn pointed out—previous historians had mostly limited themselves to reporting data and information taken from tradition, without sifting them through the filter of rationality and understanding them through the prism of the knowledge of the nature of things. Operating, thus, without any speculative capacity, and without any effort at historical penetration, they often deviated from reality, getting lost "in the desert of baseless assumptions and errors" (*Muqaddima*, The Introduction; Ibn Khaldūn 1958, Vol. I: 16; Ibn Khaldūn [1967] 2005: 11).

In short, in his time still, in the name of a blind respect for tradition, the historical discipline neglected to separate from historical accounts spurious elements and untrue gossip, initially added by "persons who had no right to occupy themselves with history" (*Muqaddima*, Foreword; Ibn Khaldūn 1958, Vol. I: 6; Ibn Khaldūn [1967] 2005, 5), and then lazily repeated by successive generations of historians. In this way, Ibn Khaldūn complained, not only "Strays got into the flock, bits of shell were mixed with the nut, truth was adulterated with lies," but the very meaning of historical transmission was emptied from within.

---

[5]In the Pseudo-Politics, the circle (*Muqaddima*, Preliminary Remarks; Ibn Khaldūn 1958, Vol. I: 81–82; Ibn Khaldūn [1967] 2005, 41) goes as follows: "[...] the world is a garden the fence of which is the dynasty. The dynasty is an authority through which life is given to proper behaviour. Proper behaviour is a policy directed by the ruler. The ruler is an institution supported by the soldiers. The soldiers are helpers who are maintained by money. Money is substance brought together by the subjects. The subjects are servants who are protected by justice. Justice is something familiar, and through it, the world persists. The world is a garden [...]." The *specula principum* are political works addressed to the formation of the "good ruler," structured sometimes, as in this case, on the basis of circular statements: Lambton ([1954] 1980).

Simply emulating like "parrots" (*Muqaddima*, Foreword; Ibn Khaldūn 1958, Vol. I: 9; Ibn Khaldūn [1967] 2005, 7) the explanations given by the historians of the past, happy to endorse any unfounded and unworkable analogies (*Muqaddima*, The Introduction; Ibn Khaldūn 1958, Vol. I: 58; Ibn Khaldūn [1967] 2005, 26), and not at all interested in considering intervening changes in customs and circumstances, and the way these changes influenced events, those lazy interpreters had reduced the historical *ḫabar* to a mere form depleted of any substance, transmitting, thus, a type of knowledge equivalent to pure ignorance.

But even if blind faith in tradition is a "hereditary" trait of human beings, said Ibn Khaldūn (*Muqaddima*, Foreword; Ibn Khaldūn 1958, Vol. I: 7; Ibn Khaldūn [1967] 2005, 5), nevertheless:

> the pasture of stupidity is unwholesome for mankind. No one can stand up against the authority of truth, and the evil of falsehood is to be fought with enlightening speculation.

Certainly, respect and obedience to tradition were religious imperatives for Ibn Khaldūn, a sincere believer; this respect, however, had to be owed not to an empty formula, but to the Truth (*ḥaqq*[6]), and the only means to discern what was true, at least in the historical and social sphere, was provided by rational demonstration.[7] As Ibn Khaldūn (*Muqaddima*, Foreword; Ibn Khaldūn 1958, Vol. I: 15–16; Ibn Khaldūn [1967] 2005, 11) wrote, in fact,

> [If the historian] trusts historical information in its plain transmitted form and has no clear knowledge of the principles resulting from custom, the fundamental facts of politics, the nature of civilisation, or the condition governing human social organisation, and if, furthermore, he does not evaluate remote or ancient material through comparison with near or contemporary material, he often cannot avoid [...] deviating from the path of truth.

Therefore, if Ibn Khaldūn aimed at understanding the "inner meaning" of history, to achieve this purpose tradition, rather than being subverted, had to be well interpreted—and this required the use of strict criteria in the sifting of sources in the first place.

First of all, the *ḫabar* needed to be verified: much attention had to be paid to the correspondence between history and facts. In this regard, Ibn Khaldūn offers examples taken from past stories, handed down by several persons as reliable data, which should, instead, have been immediately expunged as false from history because patently absurd or impossible, once subjected to rational sifting. In fact, a rigid attachment to the past was unsuitable for the development of the discipline.

---

[6]"*Wa al-ḥaqqu lā yuqāwimu sulṭānahu.*" The Arabic term used here is, significantly, "*haqq*," a word that means "truth," but also "justice" or "law" (in this sense, in the *Qur'an*, it is 1 of the 99 names of God), and that, therefore, takes on an important normative nuance. I thank Nora S. Eggen for drawing my attention to this terminological detail.

[7]As Horrut (2006, 28) points out, this belief in rational speculation as the key for accessing Truth has disturbed many traditionalists in the Arab and Muslim world, as it recalls, in some ways, elements of the European Enlightenment: however, in Ibn Khaldūn the search for truth is never placed above religion.

For Ibn Khaldūn therefore, first of all, an initial check on the truthfulness of the information handed down should be carried out. This check should have been free from subjection to the authority of tradition, from the consolidated and stiffened canons of *taqlīd* (conformal repetition), and from blind reverence towards the historians of the past.

This rigour and striving for dispassionate objectivity were not only applied by Ibn Khaldūn in interpreting the decay of "his" Arab civilisation: not even his own family tree, in his autobiography, was exempted from this scrupulous search for objective and correct data.

Because of the importance he attached to this method, Ibn Khaldūn has been effectively compared[8] to another historian, the Greek Thucydides (460–395 B.C.), who also developed, back in his time, in his *History of the Peloponnesian War* (a work also written in exile), a critical approach aimed at using, in understanding the actions of men and historical events, only objective standards. For Thucydides, sources should be collected as much as possible first-hand, and should in any case be subject to strict personal and critical scrutiny (*autopsy*), without submitting to a counterfactual reverence for tradition and supernatural explanations.[9]

Similarly, before tackling his work, Ibn Khaldūn endeavoured to obtain not only a solid knowledge of previous historical and political works, but also a profound, direct acquaintance with the political dynamics unfolding in the different Mediterranean countries. That is why, initially, he had planned to restrict the scope of his investigation to the Maghreb[10] alone, since—as he wrote—it was only about that region that he possessed first-hand data, and his research could not be based on second-hand information. It was only afterwards, when he had personally collected concrete data on the history of the peoples settled further east during his pilgrimage

---

[8]Goodman (1972). See also Horrut (2006: 150), according to which Ibn Khaldūn's circularity inserts Arab domination and Islam, like all other civilisations, in a river of inexorable temporality. According to Horrut, this partly secular historical relativism would bring Ibn Khaldūn closer to the writings of Aristotle and Thucydides and to Roman historiography (for example, Cicero, Titus Livy, Tacitus, Polybius).

[9]See, for example, Thucydides' commentary on the factors underlying the outbreak of the Trojan War, in which not only the mythological explanations, but also the aura of epic grandeur of the event, are subject to the severe scrutiny of the author's critical thinking: "But through want of money not only they were weak matters, all that preceded this enterprise, but also this [the Trojan War, (author's note)], which is of greater name than any before it, appeareth to be in fact beneath the fame and report which, by means of the poets, now goeth of it" (1989: I, 11). Thucydides, however, can be likened to Ibn Khaldūn also in other respects: like Ibn Khaldūn with his "instructive examples," for example, Thucydides proposes a vision of history conceived as a "perennial possession" (κτῆμα ἐς αἰεί). Since the drives that move human actions (such as fear, desire for honour, utility) are always the same, history is thus conceived by both as a possible basis for the instruction of rulers.

[10]*Muqaddima*, The Introduction. Ibn Khaldūn (1958, Vol. I: 65). Ibn Khaldūn ([1967] 2005: 30): "my intention to restrict myself in this work to the Maghreb, the circumstances of its races and nations, and its subjects and dynasties, to the exclusion of any other region. (This restriction is necessitated) by my lack of knowledge of conditions in the East and among its nations, and by the fact that second-hand information would not give the essential facts I am after."

to Mecca at a mature age, that he decided to broaden his work so as to include these too, for the sake of the critical and comparative advantages that such a greater widening of perspective[11] would bring to his work.

As Ibn Khaldūn (*Muqaddima*, Preliminary Remarks) analytically explained, the main factors that can impair the reliability of information handed down, and of its reading, are:

1. Partisanship for given opinions or schools of thought
2. Reliance upon transmitters[12]
3. Unawareness of the purpose of events, sometimes transmitted without knowing their real significance
4. Unfounded assumptions as to the truth of things
5. Ignorance about how conditions conform with reality
6. The tendency to approach great and high-ranking persons with praise and encomia
7. More importantly, ignorance of the nature of the various conditions arising in a civilisation

In relation to the first point, in particular, Ibn Khaldūn pointed out how easily partisanship leads to acceptance, without hesitation, and in a prejudicial manner, of information that reinforces the supported thesis, or group. This element must, therefore, be kept under control if one wants to avoid perceiving events according to what one would like them to say.[13] Therefore, a strong political solidarity (what he will call *'aṣabiyya*) on the part of the historian turns out, in reality, to be an enemy of truth and accuracy of the historical record.

The importance of this requirement of objectivity, which could perhaps only be brought into focus by a scholar coming, as he did, from a political path free of fixed references, is reflected in the second and third points of his list: in considering the writings of previous historians it is also necessary, Ibn Khaldūn said, to take into account the influence exercised on their vision of events by their awareness of the specific audience which would read and judge their writings. In fact, those historians were, in general, at the service of rulers interested in emphasising political details favourable to them, but which would then become, perhaps, irrelevant in later times:

---

[11]*Muqaddima*, Foreword. Ibn Khaldūn (1958, Vol. I: 12). Ibn Khaldūn ([1967] 2005: 80. In fact, as Talbi (1973, 113–114) points out, in his ambition to make his analysis as universal as possible, Ibn Khaldūn has shown a singular openness to the consideration of all the civilisations—previous and contemporary—that were accessible to him, reaching, in this overview, even China and India, as in *Muqaddima* IV, 22, or V, 10.

[12]Clearly, in an Islamic context, this question brings us back, by analogy, to the typical problems of the discipline aimed at determining the reliability of the testimonies handed down concerning the sayings and actions of the Prophet, on the basis, in particular, of the evaluation of the personality of the witnesses of tradition (the science of *aḥadīṯ*).

[13]In relation to this, Megherbi (1971: 77) mentions some modern studies on the involuntary alteration of reality (in situations similar to the well-known game of Chinese whispers, and studies on "rumours and hearsay") referring, for example, to an experimental study cited in van Gennep ([1910] 1920, book V).

not to take into account the influence of the *intentions* cast on their historical accounts when they were written could, then, easily bring about interpretative distortions.

The fourth and fifth points are aimed at criticising the "traditional" method mostly followed by historians: operating as mere imitators (*muqallid*) of the past, devoid of any spirit of research and stuck to a rigid and immobilised view of tradition, they could provide nothing more than a work consisting in sheer "form devoid of substance"—if not, even worse, in "ignorance dangerously passed off as knowledge."[14]

While other historians, by analogy with the method used in the science of *aḥadīṯ*, took care to consider the probity of the transmitters, and hence their social reputation, as a central proof of the truthfulness of what had been transmitted, Ibn Khaldūn, as far as the historical *ḫabar* is concerned, detached himself from that tradition, no longer hinging his analysis on the authority of the transmitters, but on the objectivity of facts themselves.

In fact, for the purposes of scientific historical research, it was necessary—argued Ibn Khaldūn—to get rid of this "tradition of sleepy complacency" (*Muqaddima*, Foreword; Ibn Khaldūn 1958, Vol. I: 10; Ibn Khaldūn [1967] 2005: 7), in the name of a rational and careful approach, aimed at capturing the data of reality and at speculatively extrapolating from it the causes of events.

In the same way, the points that follow in his list mark crucial defects that a scientific treatment of history should carefully avoid. Only if conceived and elaborated as an intellectual science—as a "branch of philosophy" (*Muqaddima*, Foreword; Ibn Khaldūn 1958, Vol. I: 6; Ibn Khaldūn [1967] 2005: 5)—in full awareness of the need to discard such obstacles from its path, could such a discipline provide, on the basis of verified and selected facts, that subtle and profound *interpretation* of the causes and origins of past and present events, which was Ibn Khaldūn's ambitious goal.

2.3 The Cognitive and Moral Requisites of the New Way of Understanding History

The premise of the *Muqaddima* is the *muqaddima* (the use of the lower case distinguishes it from the overall first volume of *Kitāb*), which was the fruit of mature consideration, as it was written in the period in which he lived and worked in Cairo after 1388. In the *muqaddima* the first need expressed was that of a reformulation of history that could raise it from its "superficial" (*ẓāhir*) status of mere "information on the facts of the past," often misinterpreted because not understood, in order to grasp

[14]*Muqaddima*, Foreword. Ibn Khaldūn (1958, Vol. I: 9). Ibn Khaldūn ([1967] 2005: 7): "they presented historical information [...] as mere forms without substance, blades without scabbards; as knowledge that must be considered ignorance [...]."

instead, by way of interpretation, its "inner meaning" (*bāṭin*[15]), obtained thanks to a deeper understanding of the natural dynamics of social and political reality, and endowed, thus, with practical, instructive added value.

So, distancing himself from the prevailing concept that framed history as an uncritical and fabulous branch of literature, Ibn Khaldūn openly set out rationally to extrapolate the true meaning of reported events, objectively considering them beyond the level of a blind theological redundancy. Only thus was it possible to connect and coordinate the abundance of apparently juxtaposed historical data in a whole, endowed with its own logic, arising from the intersection of events and the dynamic modification of the characteristics assumed by social organisation in different times and places. The "inner meaning" of history to which Ibn Khaldūn aspired was not an immediately visible one, but the fruit of a rational interpretative effort, conducted with the same kind of rigour that scientific enterprises require.

So, the first condition to obtain a deep knowledge of the reasons and conditions of each event[16] requires, according to Ibn Khaldūn, that data be sifted, in order to discern, as has been seen, the genuine from the spurious (Ibn Khaldūn, like Thucydides, points out that "it would be important to personally check one's own sources"[17]).

In the second place, the method adopted for the *interpretation* of the historical data thus obtained should also be carefully considered. A first essential condition for a profound historical understanding, according to Ibn Khaldūn, consists in the interpreter's possession of a *good speculative mentality*, to be applied, in general, to the principles of politics, and to the understanding of the true nature of existing things. Only this could make it possible to grasp and appreciate all the subtle but important peculiar qualities differently characterising the various societies, such as

[15]*Muqaddima*, Foreword. Ibn Khaldūn (1958, Vol. I: 6). Ibn Khaldūn ([1967] 2005: 5): "the inner meaning of history." By the way, one cannot fail to notice that, in the Islamic religion, *ẓāhir* and *bāṭin* are, respectively, the 75th and 76th names of God, mentioned in the *Sura Iron* (*Qur'an* 57, 3) (Haleem 2004: 359).

[16]*Muqaddima*, The Introduction. Ibn Khaldūn (1958, Vol. I: 55–56). Ibn Khaldūn ([1967] 2005: 24): "Today, the scholar in this field needs to know the principles of politics, the (true) nature of existent things, and the differences among nations, places, and periods with regard to ways of life, character qualities, customs, sects, schools, and everything else. He further needs a comprehensive knowledge of present conditions in all these respects. He must compare similarities or differences between the present and the past (or distantly located) conditions. He must know the causes of the similarities in certain cases and of the differences in others. He must be aware of the differing origins and beginnings of (different) dynasties and religious groups, as well as of the reasons and incentives that brought them into being and the circumstances and history of the persons who supported them. His goal must be to have complete knowledge of the reasons for every happening, and to be acquainted with the origin of every event. Then, he must check transmitted information with the basic principles he knows. If it fulfils their requirements, it is sound. Otherwise, the historian must consider it as spurious and dispense with it."

[17]*Muqaddima* III, 16. Ibn Khaldūn (1958, Vol. I: 371). Ibn Khaldūn ([1967] 2005: 146): "It often happens that people are (incredulous) with regard to historical information, just as it also happens that they are tempted to exaggerate certain information, in order to be able to report something remarkable. [...] Therefore, a person should look at his sources and rely upon himself."

those linking nations, places, and periods with lifestyles, qualities of character, customs, religious sects, schools, and many other things. And again, only thanks to a speculative, rigorous mindset could it be possible to understand the origins of the different forms of power and of religious groups, and to see the reasons and driving forces lying behind their emergence.

Moreover, the scholar in this discipline should also have a general knowledge of the *present* conditions of all these things—this being an essential basis for making comparisons and for grasping and understanding the similarities and differences between present and past conditions and between near and far places.

In the same way, this speculative lucidity would also keep the historian safe from the opposite error: that of too easily rejecting events and data witnessed and reported by others, qualifying them as impossible simply because they were unusual and uncommon for the present time and place (as happened, in his time, to the accounts of the unusual facts and customs reported by Ibn Baṭṭūṭa,[18] returned from his travels in India). Ibn Khaldūn's criticism of any censorship based on the commonplace, and of obtuseness towards what is unusual and new, is rigorous and punctilious:

> A person who looks at these (data) [...] should not reject (data) for which he finds no observable parallels in his own time. Otherwise, many things that are possible would (be considered impossible by him and) escape his attention. Many excellent men, hearing stories of this kind about past dynasties, have not believed them. This is not right. Conditions in the world and in civilisation are not (always) the same. He who knows a low or medium (level of civilisation) does not know all of them.[19]

As an example of this, Ibn Khaldūn cites a paradigmatic story: the dialogue between a prisoner and his son. Having lived all his life in prison, the son, hearing his father praising the taste of mutton, cannot help imagining it in terms of the only meat that he knew in prison: rat meat. As this example shows, it is easy to fall into interpretative fallacies of this kind, and therefore it is important, says Ibn Khaldūn, that the historian takes great care to avoid them:

> It often happens that people are (incredulous) with regard to historical information, just as it also happens that they are tempted to exaggerate certain information, in order to be able to report something remarkable.

Yet, as Ibn Khaldūn points out:

> With a clear mind and straightforward, natural (common sense), he should distinguish between the nature of the possible and the impossible. Everything within the sphere of the

---

[18]Ibn Khaldūn, in *Muqaddima* III, 16, speaks about the "incredible" stories reported by Ibn Baṭṭūṭa, back from his travels, about the disbelief they aroused, but also about the importance of not excluding a priori the truthfulness of what is not yet known only because, precisely, new, recommending instead the use of an "empirical" method.

[19]*Muqaddima*, III, 16. Ibn Khaldūn (1958, Vol. I: 368–369). Ibn Khaldūn ([1967] 2005: 144). Ibn Khaldūn acknowledges that he himself has received, in this sense, an important "lesson of rigour" from Fāris Ibn Wadrār, vizier of Sultan Abū 'Inān, who, in reference to the stories of Ibn Baṭṭūṭa, recommended to him: "Be careful not to reject such information about the condition of dynasties, because you have not seen such things yourself" (*Muqaddima* III, 16; Ibn Khaldūn 1958, Vol. I: 371; Ibn Khaldūn [1967] 2005: 145).

possible should be accepted, and everything outside it should be rejected. (*Muqaddima* III, 16; Ibn Khaldūn 1958, Vol. I: 371; Ibn Khaldūn [1967] 2005: 146).

A good speculative mentality, applied to the understanding of the main factors influencing the social world, is not the only important skill of the historian, however. A second element, this time not cognitive but moral, is topical too: *integrity*.

In fact, as Ibn Khaldūn sharply points out, sometimes the wrongness of reported information is not so much due to a lack of understanding, but rather to the human taste for what we could call malicious "gossip." This is why, as a rule, many untrue stories abound in the work of historians. Attracted by the secret pleasure one feels in questioning and sullying the reputation of others, they "often appear very eager for such information and are alert to find it when they go through the pages of published work" (*Muqaddima*, The Introduction; Ibn Khaldūn 1958, Vol. I: 40; Ibn Khaldūn [1967] 2005: 23)—an aside, moreover, that articulates Ibn Khaldūn's warning about the influence of partisanship in the misrepresentation of data.

This is still not enough, however. A third factor must also be considered, which is also decisive in ensuring or undermining the rigour and explanatory power of the discipline: awareness and attention (neglected, unfortunately, by many previous historians of his world) towards the phenomenon of *change* that constantly moves history. This is a transformative motion that is certain and constant, says Ibn Khaldūn, but which is, at the same time, slow and subtle, and, therefore, rarely perceived in its unfolding:

Change is a sore affliction and is deeply hidden, becoming noticeable only after a long time, so that rarely do more than a few individuals become aware of it. (*Muqaddima*, The Introduction; Ibn Khaldūn 1958, Vol. I: 56–57; Ibn Khaldūn [1967] 2005: 24).

While, on the one hand, the nature of things entails constant background elements and patterns, on the other hand its multiple and changing phenomenological conditions do not permanently maintain the same aspect:[20]

The condition of the world and of nations, their customs and sects, does not persist in the same form or in a constant manner. There are differences according to days and periods, and changes from one condition to another. Such is the case with individuals, times, and cities, and it likewise happens in connection with regions and districts, periods and dynasties. (*Muqaddima*, The Introduction; Ibn Khaldūn 1958, Vol. I: 57; Ibn Khaldūn [1967] 2005: 25).

[20]*Muqaddima*, Preliminary Remarks. Ibn Khaldūn (1958, Vol. I: 77). Ibn Khaldūn ([1967] 2005: 38): "If this is so, the normative method for distinguishing right from wrong in historical information on the grounds of (inherent) possibility or absurdity, is to investigate human social organisation, which is identical with civilisation. We must distinguish the conditions that attach themselves to the essence of civilisation as required by its very nature; the things that are accidental (to civilisation) and cannot be counted on; and the things that cannot possibly attach themselves to it."

Cultural change takes place gradually, however, through progressive shifts and adjustments that are apparently negligible, in their singularity, and for this reason it is not easily identifiable except to an alert, prepared and attentive eye.

Some changes, of course, can be macroscopic, evident, and traumatic, such as those produced by the great plague, but actually the most powerful action, a transformation that incessantly affects and modifies people, periods, cities, countries, times, and empires, is the one produced by the slow and imperceptible transformations of time and by the passing of days (*Muqaddima*, The Introduction).[21]

The consideration of the persistence over time of the external and rigidified forms of institutions, expressions, even linguistic terms, as opposed to the radical internal change of their substance, is a recurring theme in Ibn Khaldūn's *Muqaddima*. For example, Ibn Khaldūn analyses in chapter III the change that occurred over the centuries to the role of the helper and "doorkeeper" of the sovereign (*Muqaddima* III, 32; Ibn Khaldūn 1958, Vol. II: 6–14; Ibn Khaldūn [1967] 2005: 190–195). Its original function was, as the term itself suggests, essentially to protect the sovereign and to help him maintain a certain detachment from the crowds of his subordinates by keeping the doors of his home locked. However, as Ibn Khaldūn notes, with the great flourishing of Arab civilisation under the reign of the Abbasids, the doorkeeper came to assume the much more important role of the sovereign's delegate, able to wield both pen and sword. This role later developed even further, growing in importance, until it led to the institution of the "*wazir*," totally (and in fact, disdainfully) alien to the original role of the doorkeeper. When, however, power passed into the hands of non-Arab rulers, the title of "*wazir*" declined, as a symbolic reminder of the defeated civilisation: for this reason, to indicate this function, the term was replaced by the different title of "*emir*" or "*sultan*."

In relation to these time shifts in the meaning of things, Ibn Khaldūn dwells at length, perhaps for autobiographical reasons, on the change that had progressively affected the social significance and status of teachers and judges too—showing the slow but profound transformation that, even in such cases, had affected their substance, despite the permanence, over time, of an identical external form.

On the basis of all this, in order to avoid the distorting effects of a surreptitious projection of the categories of the past onto the present, Ibn Khaldūn stresses the importance, for historians, of paying constant attention to change, it being central to the soundness of the interpretative enterprise.

What was lacking in the historians criticised by Ibn Khaldūn—in their disorderly "wandering like nomads through time"[22]—was an actual *theory* of historical change, a theory capable of providing rational interpretive hypotheses. This constituted a danger because, as Ibn Khaldūn observed, given a lack of awareness of the weight and importance of change, and faced with the temptation, rooted in human nature, to

---

[21]As the historian Pomian (2006: 81) says, as far as his vision of history as a cyclical universal pattern of change is concerned, Ibn Khaldūn is a unique not only among the Muslims, but also among the Christians of his time.

[22]Coltman-Brown (1981: 22): "wandering like nomads through time."

judge present facts by analogy with those of the past, even knowledge of the past could turn out to be a source of errors—or rather, using his own expression, of "knowledge that must be considered ignorance." If, without hesitation, categories and dynamics appropriate to past times are applied to the present, such bad analogies, carelessly and negligently elaborated, would eventually lead—and in apparent safety—to very serious errors of evaluation.[23]

Thus, precisely in order to counter all these intrinsic limits of the historical discipline, Ibn Khaldūn set himself the ambitious task of writing a historical work of new concept, methodically organised and "remarkably original" (*Muqaddima*, Foreword; Ibn Khaldūn 1958, Vol. I: 11; Ibn Khaldūn [1967] 2005: 8), which would consider the whole set of factors that, interacting with each other, determine the character of history.

To do that implied analysing, from the philosophical-scientific perspective mentioned above, and in an integrated manner, not only the origins of races and dynasties in their interaction with the earliest civilisations, but also:

> the reasons for change and variation in past periods and within religious groups, concerning dynasties and religious groups, towns and hamlets, strength and humiliation, large numbers and small numbers, sciences and crafts, gains and losses, changing general conditions, nomadic and sedentary life, actual events and future events, all things expected to occur in civilisation. (*Muqaddima*, Foreword; Ibn Khaldūn 1958, Vol. I: 13; Ibn Khaldūn [1967] 2005: 9).

So, not only the exclusion of what was impossible and absurd had to be considered as the first necessary criterion for selecting true historical information from false, and the adoption of a speculative and integral mentality was to be considered as the basic condition for obtaining a profound and careful interpretation of history, but something else had to be considered, too. That is, this interpretation could only be based on a vision of human societies (*al-ijtimā' al-bašarī*) capable of discerning (apart from the properties that cannot belong to them) their essential (*ḏāt*) stable properties, linked to their multiform phenomenologies, from contingent ones (*a'rāḍ*).

---

[23]*Muqaddima*, The Introduction. Ibn Khaldūn (1958, Vol. I: 58). Ibn Khaldūn ([1967] 2005: 26): "Analogical reasoning and comparison are well known to human nature. They are not safe from error. Together with forgetfulness and negligence, they sway man from his purpose and divert him from his goal. Often, someone who has learned a good deal of past history remains unaware of the changes that conditions have undergone. Without a moment's hesitation, he applies his knowledge (of the present) to the historical information and measures the historical information by the things he has observed with his own eyes, although the difference between the two is great. Consequently, he falls into an abyss of error."

2.4 The Premises of a New Science

The fundamental assumption underlying Ibn Khaldūn's work was both revolutionary and simple. It was the idea—only later resumed, after the long historical hiatus produced by the shelving of Ibn Khaldūn's thesis in the Arab world, with the flourishing of the social sciences and the birth of sociology—that human society, together with its dynamics, could intrinsically be regarded as a living and intelligible reality, a part itself of the world of nature. Therefore, reasoning could also be relied upon to recognise the constant dynamics lying behind the many empirical phenomena in which it takes shape.

In fact, after the general introduction (again, the "*muqaddima*," with the lower case), the work opens by reiterating that history—essentially consisting in *information* relative to human organisation[24]—would be for the first time treated, in the *Muqaddima*, as a new and independent science, and studied through the analysis of its "essential" and "accidental" elements (*Muqaddima*, Preliminary Remarks; Ibn Khaldūn 1958, Vol. I: 77; Ibn Khaldūn [1967] 2005: 38). In other words, this work was proposed as both a "container of philosophy" and a "container of historical knowledge."[25]

Not only that: precisely because of the intelligibility and regularity of the mechanisms of history it postulated, this work was understood from the outset as having an educational perspective as well. In fact, as the title of the book itself says, it was meant to provide its readers with important "*'ibar*," or "memorable lessons,"[26] taken from the past with the aim of helping people understand the present and orient the future,[27] as "the past resembles the future more than one drop of water to another" (*Muqaddima*, The Introduction; Ibn Khaldūn 1958, Vol. I: 17; Ibn Khaldūn [1967] 2005: 12).

The project, as Ibn Khaldūn pointed out, was aimed at developing an original science, completely new, different both from rhetoric and politics,[28] and, last but not least, extremely useful, being endowed with a practical purpose. Subjects of the study were

> such conditions affecting the nature of civilisation as, for instance, savagery and sociability, group feelings, and the different ways by which one group of human beings achieves superiority over another. It deals with royal authority and the dynasties that result (in this manner) and with the various ranks that exist within them. (It further deals) with the different

[24]The Arabic *'umrān* has also been translated as "culture" and as "civilisation" (and with the French word "*civilisation,*" which somehow merges society and culture (Vanoli 2004: 140)).

[25]*Muqaddima*, Foreword. Ibn Khaldūn (1958, Vol. I: 12). Ibn Khaldūn ([1967] 2005: 9): "a vessel for philosophy, a receptacle for historical knowledge."

[26]The concept of *'ibar* as a set of lessons is retraced, in this sense, already in the *Qur'an* (e.g., in the sura *The Forceful Chargers* (*Qur'an* 79, 26) (Haleem 2004: 407)).

[27]*Muqaddima*, Foreword. Ibn Khaldūn (1958, Vol. I: 13). Ibn Khaldūn ([1967] 2005: 9): "memorable lessons to be learned from early conditions and from subsequent history."

[28]Described, in *Muqaddima* (I, First preface), as a discipline aimed at administering the masses by pushing them towards behaviour aimed at the preservation of the species.

> kinds of gainful occupations and ways of making a living, with the sciences and crafts that human beings pursue as part of their activities and efforts, and with all the other institutions that originate in civilisation through its very nature.[29]

Furthermore, since, as he wrote in *Muqaddima*, it is the task of those who define a new discipline to be first to indicate its object, chapters, divisions, and the succession of problems that it must deal with (*Muqaddima*, Concluding Remarks), Ibn Khaldūn, before going into the substantial heart of his analysis, took care to provide a sketch of the premises on the basis of which the architecture of his work would be built.

As he stated, man differs from other living beings essentially:

1. Through his ability to develop arts and sciences, which are the product of his ability to think.
2. Through his need to have a strong authority over himself to restrain his aggressiveness, and through his awareness of this: it is true in fact, notes Ibn Khaldūn, that even some animals, such as bees[30] and locusts, in their social organisation, resort to an individual exercising a kind of authority over them all. In their case, however, this is the result of instinct. In man, this derives from prudent reflection.
3. Through the efforts he organises in order to obtain his means of subsistence.
4. Finally, through the social organisation he creates, which can be nomadic (*'umrān badawī*) or sedentary (*'umrān ḥaḍarī*). In order to ensure their survival, men are predisposed for social life, and this usually takes shape in one of these two ways, which are alternative, but dynamically related. In fact, neither of these two types of social organisation (to which lifestyles, social and political systems, and consequent levels of development of sciences and techniques, are linked) is definitive, since both essentially constitute the two poles of oscillation, opposite and complementary, of an underlying cycle of unitary political evolution. Therefore, they should be understood not as successive stages of development, but rather as two constantly coexisting parts of a single ("bipolar," as Cheddadi (2006: 181) defines it) system of civilisation, constantly driven by internal cyclical movements, and governed by such social factors as power, the relationship with resources and group spirit.

On the basis of this scheme, the *Muqaddima* would be naturally divided and organised into six chapters—related to the above points—set out in logical order:

- The first chapter would be devoted to human social organisation in general.
- The second chapter, to non-urbanised social organisation—(*'umrān badawī*)—which, from a logical point of view, precedes the urban and sedentary civilisation which is the *'umrān badawī*'s goal.

[29] *Muqaddima*, Preliminary Remarks. Ibn Khaldūn (1958, Vol. I: 71). Ibn Khaldūn ([1967] 2005: 35). Montesquieu too, centuries later, in the *Ésprit des lois*, took nature and its influences on man as a basis for his work, defined as "*prolem sine matre creatam.*"

[30] See the sura *The Bee*. (*Qur'an* 16) (Haleem 2004: 166–174).

- The third chapter, to the analysis of dynasties, the caliphate, and the royal authority which precede and determine the organisation of the sedentary civilisation of cities and towns.
- The fourth chapter, to the analysis of sedentary civilisation—the *'umrān ḥaḍarī.*
- The fifth chapter, to the arts and crafts developed and used by man as ways to make a living (by natural necessity).
- The sixth and last chapter, finally, to an exhaustive review of the sciences existing at that time, and their current level of development. The sciences are logically treated after the arts and crafts, since the possibility of developing sciences requires that primary needs be already guaranteed, as they represented a luxury compared to these.

All his work is structured around the causal-demonstration nexus for which knowing means grasping the reasons for the different states of things. As can be seen, the centrality of this nexus is replicated also in the overall structure of the work, as much as, in more detail, in the structure of his own, typical, scheme of presentation: in the various paragraphs articulating the book, its elements are laid out in an order of precedence that reflects the order of knowledge, organised through progressive examinations and demonstrations.

In fact, while the word "*Muqaddima*" means "Introduction" in everyday language, it also philosophically defines the axiom or the premise—as well as the first part—of a classic tripartite syllogism, scientifically laid out in a "*more geometrico demonstratum*" structure, according to an Aristotelian scheme. Accordingly, the facts observed in the various paragraphs making up his work are linked in an argumentative method similar to that of a mathematical or geometrical explanation. Each paragraph starts with the enunciation of a thesis and continues with its development, carried out by analysing with personal observations the accounts of past facts reported by others, in successive stages, until the demonstration is complete. By making the historian observe the social world from unprecedented angles, grasping, thus, meanings otherwise destined to remain in the shadows, this method also leads to a different way of looking at the contents which compose the historical picture.

In fact, the inevitable change which affects societies develops through complex causal chains, which cannot be understood by studying only its single components. Thus, Ibn Khaldūn devotes hundreds of pages—displaying a sensitivity that we could define as fully proto-sociological—to revealing the *interdependence* that links a broad range of apparently unrelated events, seeking all the deep connections between all these elements. Examples of this are the connection between pestilence and famine, or the spread of a certain type of diet and the weakening of a group's natural defences; or the influence of an increase in population density on the development of the arts, the prestige of poetry, and the construction of monuments; or the tendency of the law to rigidify in imitation of the past.

Ibn Khaldūn, therefore, interprets society as a complex system, in which multiple factors (economic, political, cultural, religious, familiar, etc.) are dynamically correlated with each other in significant interactions, cooperating to shape the unfolding meaning of history. This view brings about a change in the *ḫabar* itself: in Ibn Khaldūn's work, this acquires a clear, scientific meaning and a new evaluation. In fact, in a world marked by such instability, it was no longer useful solely to conceive a *ḫabar* as a "passing on" of histories from the past, brought about by the stewardship of near-sighted historiographers, not interested in making any intellectual effort to interpret them.

Far from offering a mere record of events, in Ibn Khaldūn's interpretation history is understood as a set of instructive examples (Mahdi 1957: 63–72), marked by an "educative" rationality, drawn from the changeability of the facts unfolding over time. Even more, it is proposed as a discipline through which these facts can be *interpreted*, arriving by inductive reasoning at the general laws governing the functioning of society, in its temporal and evolutionary dynamics, from the study of their causes, starting from an empirical investigation of reality.

Facts, in the *Muqaddima*, are analysed in detail, with an aptitude for the observation of "revealing symptoms" which is exceptional for the time.[31] This is captured in a particularly vivid way, for example, when Ibn Khaldūn explains the correlation between the level of prosperity of a society and the behaviour of the beggars living in it (*Muqaddima* IV, 11), or between the type of animals and parasites present in the city (or, at an even more micro level, in dwellings) and the level of the economic and social differentiation of its inhabitants (*Muqaddima*, IV, 11); or between the state of buildings and their (new or recycled) materials and whether they indicate an upward or downward phase in history (*Muqaddima*, IV, 10).

In fact, Ibn Khaldūn's observations are born out of continuous intersections of different perspectives and registers: while the concrete is distilled into the abstract, in an accurate and virtuous correspondence, the analytical and innovative (especially for its time) use of reason is combined with an attention to empirical detail, and at the same time reconciled with the religious conviction of a sincere believer.[32]

Finally, the same attitude toward historical traditions, critical and far from complacent, invoking a strict and censorious sifting, a speculative approach, and a broad perspective, is also adopted to his own work itself: at the end of the *Muqaddima* he expresses the hope not only that it could be accepted, but also that it could be improved, corrected, integrated, and developed by new and competent

---

[31]Pomian (2006: 191): "Les caractères visibles sont traités comme des signes qui permettent des conclusions sur ce qui ne se dévoile pas au regard. Ils manifestent l'invisible. Mais il ne le manifestent qu'à condition de savoir les repérer, de distinguer, par exemple, le matériau de remploi de celui qui sert pour la première fois. Cela suppose un temps passé à scruter l'extérieur des édifices, à discuter avec des architectes, à comparer les différents bâtiments et les différentes villes. Autant dire, un intérêt soutenu pour la dimension matérielle de la vie urbaine. Et un appareil conceptuel permettant de l'interroger."

[32]It is in this sense that Pomian (2006: 9) describes Ibn Khaldūn as a scholar "qui avait su jouer en virtuose sur une diversité de registres, passer de la métaphysique au reportage, des démonstrations abstraites à des descriptions plastiques, de l'admiration à l'ironie, de la passion d'un croyant au détachement d'un savant."

scholars in the future, since "the capital of knowledge that a single scholar can offer is limited."[33]

Ibn Khaldūn decisively asserted the originality of this new science, centred on the requirements of accuracy, completeness, and integration of its parts, and on the merging of the methods—empirical and deductive—employed in it, and expressly denied being influenced by any predecessor whatsoever. He stressed instead, several times, the "divine" character of his inspiration ("We became aware of these things with God's help and without the instruction of Aristotle or the teaching of the Mobedhan [Zoroastrian priests]"; "We [. . .] were inspired by God. He led us to a science whose truth we ruthlessly set forth. If I have succeeded [. . .] this is due to divine guidance." And even further: "[...] God guides whoever He will to his light"[34]), even while acknowledging the impossibility of excluding that someone, somewhere, may have already organically tackled the subject, perhaps in a work that had been lost. In fact, as he himself pointed out, the amount of knowledge lost in time was expected to be greater than the amount preserved up to then.[35]

On the one hand, thus, Ibn Khaldūn claimed for himself, thanks to the amount of material provided to him by his rich culture and life experience, and with the help of divine inspiration [without which no scholar could be enlightened about what he did not yet know (*Muqaddima* VI, 36)], the original intuition that rational explanatory paradigms could be identified in history, capable of providing it with a meaning and, thus, of innovating and reformulating it as a science.

On the other hand, it was to the scientific community—much more than to the rulers to whom copies of his works were donated—that he entrusted his innovative creation, together with the hope of its future development.

[33]*Muqaddima*, Foreword. Ibn Khaldūn (1958, Vol. I: 14). Ibn Khaldūn ([1967] 2005: 9): "I wish that men of scholarly competence and wide knowledge would look at the book with a critical, rather than a complacent eye, and silently correct and overlook the mistakes they come upon. The capital of knowledge that an individual scholar has to offer is small. Admission (of one's shortcomings) saves from censure. Kindness from colleagues is hoped for. It is God whom I ask to make our deeds acceptable in His sight. He is a good protector."

[34]*Muqaddima*, Preliminary Remarks. Ibn Khaldūn (1958, Vol. I: 82). Ibn Khaldūn ([1967] 2005: 41); *Muqaddima*, Preliminary Remarks. Ibn Khaldūn (1958, Vol. I: 83). Ibn Khaldūn ([1967] 2005: 42). The last statement is a quotation from the sura *Light* (*Qur'an* 24, 35) (Haleem 2004: 223).

[35]*Muqaddima*, Preliminary Remarks. Ibn Khaldūn (1958, Vol. I: 78). Ibn Khaldūn ([1967] 2005: 39): "Where are the sciences of the Persians that 'Umar ordered to be wiped out at the time of the conquest? Where are the sciences of the Chaldaeans, the Syrians, and the Babylonians, and the scholarly products and results that were theirs? Where are the sciences of the Copts, their predecessors? The sciences of only one nation, the Greeks, have come down to us, because they were translated through al-Ma'mūn's efforts, He was successful in his direction because he had many translators at his disposal and spent much money in this connection. Of the sciences of others, nothing has come to our attention."

2.5 An *'Aql-naql* Mind

The study of the essential and accidental elements of different models of social organisation, of their interactions, and of the empirical details that are linked to them, is precisely the aim of the first book of *Kitāb*, the *Muqaddima*. It is here that all this combines to form a new, independent, and rational science—integrated, as the author himself stated, in the field of the intellectual sciences and, specifically, in the philosophy-*ḥikma*.

In a perspective radically different from that of both the apologetic works of the historiographers of his time and the utopian studies of the school of al-Fārābī, Ibn Khaldūn's *Muqaddima* aimed at providing a rigorous, scientific and realistic analysis[36] of facts, endowed with a cognitive and instructive mission. This was intended to provide instructive indications on the "inner meaning" of historical dynamics, even at the cost of overturning taboos and demythologising entrenched cultural clichés.

This was clearly a departure from what still was, for the most part, the dominant historical interpretation of its time. In fact, this was generally formulated on the basis of a theological key of interpretation, which aimed at seeing in history an effort made to achieve, to a greater or lesser extent, the ideal provided for by divine law. This kind of reading was given on the basis of a clear-cut contrast that saw, on the one hand, the good (lifestyles prescribed by *Shari'a*) and, on the other, the evil, inherent in real lifestyles based on custom, essentially wrong because of their inevitable distance from the ideal.

At least until the tenth century, in this cultural context, the only notable exception to this "theological" explanation of historical events which, both in Islam and the Christian West, continued to constitute "normality" (as a logical counterbalance to a total lack of confidence in the powers of limited human reason) had been represented by the interpretation of sacred texts based on the logic and reasoning proposed by the Muʿtazilites. This had paved the way to the rationalisation of culture (Fakhry 1970: 18–22) carried out in the twelfth century by Averroes.

In the wake of their thinking, the rational interpretation of Ibn Khaldūn's history also keeps its distance from this clear-cut contrast, which was the result of the theological-judgmental perspective with which history was read. In his view, instead, immersed in a process of continuous social change, good and evil often turned out to be the two-faceted[37] and transient aspects of a reality endowed with its

[36]As Laroui wrote, that is very relevant because, while the normative datum draws its meaning only from itself, the historical explanation, which has indicative value, draws its meaning from the relation between itself and the external fact that corresponds to it. Laroui (1999: 144 n. 11).

[37]For Ibn Khaldūn the same thing could be good or bad at the same time: for example, if, on the one hand, he praised the Arab nomads' high sense of morality, at the same time he described them as having a wild character; similarly, he also highlighted the good and bad aspects of sedentary civilisation. But even senility and death, in Ibn Khaldūn's conception, are not only negative facts, but rather natural phases in the historical path, regressive but also necessary in order to sweep away corruption and to start again in a renewed cycle, with new, fresh, and vital forces.

own dynamic laws. This reality was not only complex, but also never definitive, moved by continuous change, and understandable only if framed in a broad perspective encompassing its natural developments too. In this framework, social entities too (Dale 2015a: 25) could be seen as having their own natural, physical, or historical trajectory—understandable, and therefore a possible object of study.

However, although Ibn Khaldūn's theory of history needed to start from rationally interpreting collected data on the basis of a logical scheme linked to the nature of the social group, rather than imposing a preconceived theologisation of every remarkable event in history, the ultimate value of the theological tradition remained still undisputed in the background of Ibn Khaldūn's thought. In fact, his serious and sincere religiosity could not but find a place—as a "prologue in heaven"—in his political thought.

For Ibn Khaldūn, God is always present; yet He is transcendent, placed in another dimension—the deepest, theological one and, certainly and ultimately, the most truly important one. However, in this world of every event under the sun, it is not theology but the rational interpretation of reality which can provide the constitutive elements necessary for a study aimed at understanding the "inner meaning" of the historical trajectory unfolding below the surface of events. Thus, it is within this dynamic and multifaceted reality, constantly repeating its cycle and yet, from time to time, spatio-temporally determined in a unique and particular way (due to the many influences determined by environment, climate, food, economy, and many other variables, and to the particular temporal positioning of culture and civilisation within their own parable of historical development), that divine precepts must necessarily be understood.

Ibn Khaldūn's aim, in his study, was not so much that of evaluating, judging, and framing historical events as right or wrong, but rather to understand them, in their causes, their effects, and their intersections and transmutations, reading the articulations of history through empirical observation and logical reconstructions. Yet, all this presupposed not a contraposition, but a full convergence between what was revealed by scientific analysis, and what Islam, in religious terms, had already expressed.

This general framework, within which this harmonious coexistence—in their respective fields—of rationality and religious afflatus, of scientific spirit and respect for the true sense of tradition, was inscribed, can be traced back to that particular type of "hybrid" mentality adopted by Ibn Khaldūn which is defined, in Arabic, *'aql-naql*. This is an approach (perhaps difficult to understand for modern Western science, mostly based on the intrinsic incompatibility of the two things) capable, by definition, of combining intellectual (*'aql*) and revealed (*naql*) knowledge. It is the distinction between, and complementarity of, these two areas, that allows Ibn Khaldūn neatly to separate the world of science from that of religion, without bringing them into contradiction[38] or diminishing either one relative to the other (Hamès 1999).

Before Ibn Khaldūn, the theme of the combination of reason and religion had been addressed by many other authors. For example, the legitimacy of this combination had been strongly defended, and in fact recommended, by the important Arab religious scholar Ibn Taymmiyya (1263–1328) in his "*The Prevention of Contradictions Between* ʿAql *and* Naql" (1981), as well as by Averroes, who supported the thesis of the compatibility of the two in his "*Decisive Treatise,*" although the methodological priority he gave to philosophy and to its logical method led him, in the end, to give it pre-eminence over theology (Fakhry 1970; Campanini 2017).

Ibn Khaldūn—probably also pulled in this direction by his education, having been trained both in religious and intellectual sciences—directly addresses, at various points of his work, the question of the priority between the two. In these passages, he supports the idea of the cognitive inadequacy of philosophy in relation to the knowledge of divine things (and, therefore, to metaphysics and theology), where revealed religion is the unique reference, but judges instead the use of rationality and logic, and the analysis of tangible elements, to be absolutely essential in the study of history, society, and politics.

In fact, Ibn Khaldūn believes that the causes of historical events, and the variables of social conditions, are subject to the same scientific-explicative potential that characterises the events and variables of the physical world, as they are part of the realm of nature too: therefore, these can and must be rationally investigated. On the other hand, he admits that reason alone cannot understand the causes operating at the metaphysical level. If everything in this world of existing things, be it essence or animal or human act, depends on a previous cause that brings it into the world according to the use[39] from which its existence derives, then, wrote Ibn Khaldūn, these causes, gradually rising up to the Creator, multiply to the point beyond which intelligence is no longer able to understand them. Therefore, the human endeavour of understanding must stop at that point, on pain of being deceived by inevitably defective knowledge.

In short, while Ibn Khaldūn's vision of the "nature of things" is rational (although not in an Enlightenment vein (Triki 1986: 335)), the scope within which reality can be explained through rationality encounters, according to his view, set boundaries: beyond these, only religion is entitled to speak.

Thus, in the "*ʿaql-naql*" mode of relationship with reality (scientific and religious), Ibn Khaldūn finds a formula that allows the two dimensions to coexist and

[38]Dhaouadi (2005). See also Mohamed Talbi (1973), for whom Ibn Khaldūn's philosophical vision on the two perspectives recalls, in its background, precisely the *sunnat Allāh*, as it implements the fusion of the philosophical and ethical-religious elements placed at the basis of Averroes' philosophy. Also Ahmed Abdesselem (1983) argues that Ibn Khaldūn has combined in a balanced way the traditional Arabic heritage with a rational wisdom free from religious conventions.

[39]The *divine* use, Monteil points out, in brackets, in his translation.

intimately to relate to each other: a formula certainly rooted in the preceding cultural tradition, but still completely new, at the time, as far as history was concerned.[40]

Framed within this polarisation between the sphere of traditional knowledge (*naql*), and the sphere of intellectual knowledge (*'aql*), Ibn Khaldūn's history, conceived as an interpretative examination aimed at understanding the deep rationality of history, and alert to the complexity of reality and to its changing dynamics, could in no way ever be included in the *naql* sphere of tradition, examined solely on the basis of the methodological canons of the religious science of *aḥadīṯ*. Rather, by its very logic and essence, it fell within the *'aql* sphere of intellectual science, whose rigorous methodology and internal logic it shares.

This displacement of history, however, positioned in this way within the field of the intellectual sciences, could not but imply a sort of "epistemological fracture" with the past. Due to this change of perspective, history—no longer reduced to a setting for necessarily and rhetorically edifying examples—became the material for rational reflections, while the future—no longer the domain of unknown and unpredictable divine designs—came to be conceived as causally produced by the past itself, intelligible (at least in part), and essentially predictable, at least as far as its deep structure was concerned.

Thus, while, in the past, the unravelling of traumatic events and disasters used to be essentially ascribed to the divine will (beyond the classic references to the prophetic biblical literature, one can see, for example, the causal reference to divine wrath still underlined in the *Indicolus luminosus* of the Andalusian Paulus Alvarus of Cordoba (ninth century)), in Ibn Khaldūn's picture it was instead to the logic of existence, and to its internal laws—to be systematically analysed and understood—that all these events had to be linked. And yet, this would not diminish the value, which was also religious, of these rationally produced conclusions.

For example, this is why, after having argued, on the basis of examples and rational arguments, that power would be best exercised by a single sovereign (otherwise, people would be led to diverge from one another and that this fragmentation would eventually ruin the social order[41]), Ibn Khaldūn does not neglect also to legitimise his reasoning through a religious analogy,[42] invoking the *Qur'an*: "If there had been in the heavens or earth any gods but Him, both heavens and earth would be in ruins."[43]

---

[40]The rationalism of the great thinkers who had preceded Ibn Khaldūn, such as Maimonides and Averroes, was in fact directed above all towards metaphysics, theology and the natural sciences, while in the historiography of his time—much closer, as we have seen, to literature than to science—the principle of the authority of tradition was essentially in force.

[41]*Muqaddima* III, 10. Ibn Khaldūn (1958, Vol. I: 337). Ibn Khaldūn ([1967] 2005: 132): "[...] politics requires that only one person exercise control. Were various persons, liable to differ among each other, to exercise it, destruction on the whole would result."

[42]*Muqaddima* III, 10. Ibn Khaldūn (1958, Vol. I: 337). This passage is not included in the abridged edition of [1967] 2005.

[43]This passage is taken from the sura *The Prophets*: (*Qur'an* 21, 22) (Haleem 2004: 204).

Therefore, while, for Ibn Khaldūn, earthly history unfolds under the aegis of divine law (when concluding his explanations, he frequently refers to divine will, in expressions such as "This is how God proceeds with His creatures" (*Muqaddima* III, 7; Ibn Khaldūn 1958, Vol. I: 330; Ibn Khaldūn [1967] 2005: 129)), his analysis puts its own dynamics into focus, and grasps, behind the multiplicity of events, their underlying scheme. This is done with the ultimate purpose of allowing a better social organisation and a better government, and of giving man the possibility of reaching higher levels in the realisation of the social ideal.

It is precisely in this tension between the real and the ideal that the whole dynamic theory of civilisation of Ibn Khaldūn unravels. It is precisely thanks to this "partition of the spheres" that the history of the continuous and inevitable changes accompanying human civilisation (and so, also the history of events such as wars, pestilences, internal conflicts, and famine) can find a rational explanation. Thanks to this separation, history can be ultimately placed, in Ibn Khaldūn's view, within the more reassuring framework of a "new science," capable of overcoming the limits of a "literary" narrative, and, thus, of delivering (albeit within certain limits) the instructive knowledge which could enable man, caught in the ebb and flow of events, at least to grasp the actual "inner meaning" whose uncovering defines the new mission of historical inquiry itself.

2.6 Methodological Empiricism and Theoretical Rationalism: The Backdrops of History

Let us reassemble the whole picture. According to the historian Toynbee, struck by the rational scheme proposed by the great Arab thinker, his work should be best defined as a "philosophy" of history. However, not all critics and readers of Ibn Khaldūn have agreed with this classification: on the contrary, there has been a lively debate among critics on the question of the predominantly sociological, philosophical, historical, or even theological character (Pomian 2006) to be attributed to this new science. In any case, all these different opinions always ended in reducing the author, respectively, to one or the other of these exclusive disciplinary areas.

However, the question is badly framed, for his investigation spans *all* of these areas, and is in fact complex and multi-layered, working on all these levels at once. We know that, in painting, it took centuries to transition from the flat, two-dimensional figures of Egyptian, Byzantine, and early European art to the first, laborious, repeated endeavours of Paulo Uccello to model perspective—not to mention that this, too, was happening in this very critical fourteenth century. It can safely be said that, in this period, the same shift was happening with Ibn Khaldūn's *Muqaddima*, which introduced the idea of perspective into the study of history and civilisations.

In fact, Ibn Khaldūn's *Muqaddima* is a theory of depth and perspective, and it would be a mistake to pigeonhole him into any single category, only highlighting the useful historical and empirical data he gathered (thus, classifying him under a historico-sociological label[44]) or his philosophical bent,[45] expressed in his cyclical view of the life of civilisations (in a scheme that many consider para-Aristotelian[46]). In such a way we would, indeed, fail to appreciate the richness and depth achieved by virtue of the mutual cross-fertilisation among all these dimensions.

The *Muqaddima* has a multifaceted significance. Not only do all these dimensions intertwine with each other, but they also interact with its third great profile—its being a *historical* investigation, in which history is understood in modern terms as a study of civilisations conceived as a cultural unit, and where society, as never before, emerges as a *sui generis* object of study, characterised by its own dynamics.

Far from being a work that we can box into any single discipline, then, the architecture of the *Muqaddima*, like a theatrical stage—and here is where its extraordinary interest lies—presents several levels of depth and focal planes. In other words, it offers a true multi-dimensional stage.

On one plane, under the spotlights of its meticulous consideration of empirical and concrete factors (often observable "with one's own eyes"), the stage of history is filled with meticulously *empirical* observations on the dynamics governing the interrelations among *concrete* actors, such as kings and chieftains, but also characters one would encounter in one's everyday experience: beggars, merchants, teachers, fashioned into proper "ideal-types."

Yet on a deeper plane, in the background, we can find the *environment* and *culture* in which these characters are steeped—a background that exerts a shaping and determinant (although not deterministic) influence on humans and their activities. For example, Ibn Khaldūn shows how the climate affects human character and predispositions.[47] He does this brilliantly by anticipating Montesquieu's intuitions and combining observations from the *Book of Roger* by al-Idrīsī[48] and geographical work of Ptolemy ([II century BC. C.] 1940) with Galen's theories on the equilibrium of moods and temperament, according to which, for example, heat is associated with expansion and cheerfulness, and cold with contraction and sadness. Moreover, the conclusions and observations he draws from this are consciously and decisively emphasised in an antiracist perspective.

However, Ibn Khaldūn's "climatic determinism" is constrained by the convergence of other factors too, as he adds many other sociological-empirical tiles to his mosaic of the many influences affecting the character of different types of civilisations. Thus, for him, the importance of climate intersects with the influences of other

---

[44]See, for example, Megherbi (1971), Baali (1988), Hassan (2006: 1–23), Dhaouadi (2011: 1–5), Soyer and Gilbert (2012), Soyer (2010), Alatas (2014).

[45]See Hussein (1918), Bouthoul (1930), Mahdi (1957), Dale (2015a), among many others.

[46]Cfr. Bouthoul (1930), Mahdi (1957), Turroni (2002), Cheddadi (2006), Pomian (2006), Dale (2015a), among many others.

[47]The observations of Ibn Khaldūn on how climatic influence can explain the characteristic traits, for example, of African populations, were proposed by the author himself in an antiracist perspective, and in this sense they were used in the 1930s by Gaston Bouthoul (1930).

[48]Written in 1154 for Roger II (1129–1154), Norman King of Sicily (al-Idrīsī 2008).

elements, such as the characteristics of the natural environment where a population lives, or the dietary custom of that population—which, in turn, derives from the characteristics of the environment as well.

Again on the basis of Galen's theories,[49] Ibn Khaldūn also elaborates on the influence exerted by a more or less abundant and refined diet on the characteristics of individuals: excess in food "intoxicates" and strips individuals—as well as animals, after all—of the tone in their bodies, as shown by the fact that the hungriest people are also the healthiest, most belligerent, intelligent, and pious. Ibn Khaldūn does not fail to emphasise that this difference can be noticed, for example, also between the appearance and temperament of animals living in the wild where food is scarce, such as gazelles, oxen, ostriches, giraffes, asses, and buffaloes, and that of their domestic counterparts who can rely on safe pastures, such as goats, camels, donkeys, and cattle: the first, and not the second, are the best in physical appearance, health, intelligence, and sharpness of perceptions. Similarly, city people, used to consuming refined and abundant meals, eventually become as delicate as their food and, thus, more vulnerable.

Even the very fact of living in more or less dense or more or less isolated social groups is a factor analysed by Ibn Khaldūn, and so are many other apparently eccentric or contingent elements: for example, the influence of one's coaching in a certain art or science on the "colouring" (we might say, here, the *habitus*) which is impressed on one's cognitive and temperamental character (*Muqaddima* VI, 45); or the way young people are influenced by their education, whether rigid and aimed at instilling a sense of submission and a uniformity of behaviour, or liberal and aimed at maximising "fortitude"; or the correlation between the fluency acquired in another language and the resulting opportunity of access to particular concepts.[50] All such factors, for Ibn Khaldūn, combine collectively to co-characterise human groups.

In turn, even this second background plane, in Ibn Khaldūn's theory, is encapsulated within a third plane, placed, in our theatrical metaphor, between the wings and backstage. This is the plane of the dynamic laws identified by Ibn Khaldūn, which are not absolute, to be sure, but are nonetheless sufficiently constant so as to indicate the regular, preset trajectories that the course of human history will predictably follow.[51]

[49]Ibn Khaldūn explained this by saying that not only does the consumption of refined food prevent the vitality of basic food from being absorbed, but that, in addition, the moisture of food such as meat, spices, and refined flour, produces superfluous corrupting matter in the body, which, eventually, reaches up to the brain.

[50]The concepts are, for Ibn Khaldūn, "nets with which one goes hunting for the (desired) objective with the help of one's natural ability to think and entrusting oneself to the mercy and generosity of God": *Muqaddima* VI, 36. Ibn Khaldūn (1958, Vol. III: 296–297). Ibn Khaldūn ([1967] 2005: 419). As Wittgenstein will later say, the limits of our language also determine the limits of our world: see Wittgenstein ([1921] 1989: prop. 5.6).

[51]See, for example, *Muqaddima* III, 12, where the life cycle of a "dynasty" is described by comparison with the life cycle of a person.

In this scheme, history's various interacting factors do in fact generate changes in the real world, but these are predictable, and the variations they admit follow determined patterns, circular but not repetitive, almost like modifications in a musical canon. Incidentally, in the musical field in his own time, in "his" Iberian peninsula, similar patterns were germinating in a primitive form such as the (antiphrastic) *Follies of Spain* (Lombardi 1997), which would soon take over Europe and its "high" music, with their reiteration of codified and predictable, reassuring, almost trancelike variations set against a background based on a fixed common scheme.

As this identification of cyclical orbits in history represents what can be described as the more "philosophical" plane of Ibn Khaldūn's inquiry, this philosophy, understood as a rational attempt to understand the world, already relies, as sociology does, on the scientific method. The laws governing the cyclical progression of history are not moral laws (even if an understanding of such natural laws, influencing human awareness, cannot but eventually have normative-prudential consequences), but are essentially framed like the physical laws of nature. In fact, according to Ibn Khaldūn, social facts are much like physical facts, in that their elements can be interpreted by the light of an "instructive" scientific inquiry providing indications (this is the parabolic sense of the *'ibar* that gives his overall work its name) that could allow us to be more aware of the next cycle. In fact, simultaneously new and old elements will reappear in the cyclical dynamics of the development of civilisations. Provided that the macroscopic mistakes one is liable to make, by reading history through preconceived paradigms, are avoided, history is the source that provides the constitutive elements for such an inquiry.

Finally, there is one more dimension to consider. Moving even further behind the scenes in this multi-dimensional construction, we find the final backdrop. It consists of the empty space that contains all these narrations and their logic, but which extends immensely beyond them. This is the space of the transcendent and divine dimension, a realm that Ibn Khaldūn, a proto-sociologist but at the same time a man of deep and sincere faith (a barely conceivable combination to a Western mentality, used to linking the birth of social sciences to the Enlightenment's influence on secular thought), acknowledged to be—apart from what had been religiously revealed—beyond his grasp (*Muqaddima* VI, 30).

2.7 A Spiral-Shaped Cycle

Even time, in Ibn Khaldūn's approach, takes on a particular depth. In fact, the present is no longer merely understood as the outcome of the contingencies of the day, a simple *event* to be anecdotally reported, but is rather set in a process of constant and cyclical but directional change: it becomes a constitutive element in a wider and more complex scenario.

Specifically, time is understood as the product of the influences of the past, but, by the same token, it is also the causal antechamber of the events which are yet to come, in a chain-sequence developing on an increasing number of levels. Precisely on account of this complexity, history's rationale seems elusive; yet, Ibn Khaldūn manages to bring it into focus thanks to an unprecedented profusion of details making up a true sociological picture.

In Ibn Khaldūn's concept of history, previous events and cycles affect the positioning of current events. To reach a proper understanding of current history, then, it is necessary to locate its position within its own cyclical scheme. The logico-causal scheme in the background (the third level in our theatrical metaphor), in other words, makes it possible to confer on history a rationality that allows a certain predictability.

As Rosenthal wrote, the peculiar richness of Ibn Khaldūn's work would be lost were its meaning reduced to the internal framework of his structure, as this would do no justice to the light projected by the many meticulous, empirical details fixed in his work.[52] On the other hand, this structure is required, to understand these interconnections: no detail of this "history" can be explained without taking into account what has happened before. For Ibn Khaldūn the past is what lays the groundwork for the developments we can observe today—and, so, also for the decisions that will advance the development of history: these decisions, then, in line with the idea that history is to serve an educating function, will accordingly have to be taken bearing in mind what their future effects are likely to be in the long run.

It is in view of this prudent training, therefore, that Ibn Khaldūn has handed down to us, in his work, theses on the dynamics of political history aimed at reconstructing the complex game of intersecting political forces that by turns come to power in accordance with a predetermined scheme. Looking at this, we can try to infer general (and, in this sense, universalisable) laws on the functioning of civilisation.[53]

Ibn Khaldūn's scheme is centred on the axial pivot given by *'aṣabiyya*, a cohesive and social solidarity force made necessary by the individual man's inability to provide for his own subsistence. This aggregating force—found at the highest level in yet-to-be urbanised, economically deprived, and segmented societies, where it assumes the primordial form of family ties, alliances, and clientage—is then diluted in the comforts of city life. This progressive weakening (parallel and contrary to the growth of the sense of security and abundance afforded by urban life) will eventually result in gradually draining the group and its civilisation from within of its "fortitude," exposing it to be overtaken by other stronger social groups originating from the more cohesive *badāwa*, in a self-feeding circularity.

This "pendulum swing"[54] trend is presented as the inevitable product of the nature of the forces involved, and is framed within a cyclical scheme determined

---

[52] Rosenthal (1958: lxxi): "Much of its value lies in the light it sheds upon details in Ibn Khaldūn's political, sociological, economic, and philosophic thinking."

[53] Here "civilisation" is interpreted as a broader and more complex entity than society, encompassing not only the population but also its symbolic and cultural universe.

[54] Reference is spontaneously made to Ernest Gellner's (1981) thesis on Islam's "pendulum swing" between urban formal and literal tradition, and rural informal and mystical tradition—a thesis born out of the juxtaposition of Ibn Khaldūn's thought with David Hume's theory ([1779] 1976) on the

by the dialectic between *'aṣabiyya* on the one hand, and, on the other hand, the individualising and disruptive dynamics of city life, which constitute at one and the same time the aim and goal of *'aṣabiyya* itself, and the cause of its failure. As a result, new cycles and new *'aṣabiyyāt*, in order to eliminate from the social organism that entropic disruptive drive that Ibn Khaldūn calls "senility," will periodically bypass each other so as to start again in a new upward thrust.

Essentially, Ibn Khaldūn's cycle proceeds along a course set in an ever-renewing scheme broken down into predetermined phases:

- The starting point is a specific "backward" environment at the margins of civilisation—an environment that, in the time and place in which Ibn Khaldūn was writing, was defined by the *'umrān badawī*,[55] an ideal-typical context[56] related not only, as in the specific case of North Africa, to the desert, but to all areas politically and economically marginal. In this environment, social groups that live in a subsistence economy, and whose culture is comparatively unrefined, begin to form. Even so, the members of these groups share a strong sense of cohesion and pride; they are proud and do not perceive themselves to be (nor are they) subject to the rule of a sovereign. Rather, they feel bound by the pride they take in supporting a natural leader, someone chosen from their own ranks whom they elevate to the status of first among equals (*primus inter pares*), one who is seen as a "champion" of their group as he embodies the virtues and values it cherishes.

---

oscillatory development of religion. In opposition to the thesis of the unilateral development of religion from polytheism to monotheism, David Hume had proposed the thesis of a continuous oscillation between the two poles, given by flow and reflux movements determined by the competitiveness of human beings in worshipping and "making their own" one particular deity or another, "affiliating themselves to it," until they arrive, through successive affiliations, at the cult of a unique divinity endowed with absolute power. This path would be exemplified by biblical history, in which God, initially defined as the specific divinity of Abraham, Isaac, and Jacob, and their descendants, ends up being conceived as the creator of the whole world. But when the divinity comes to be conceived of as being unique and universal, it also becomes distant and inaccessible, thereby producing the need to interpose other more approachable intermediate divinities, capable of mediating between man and the universal God. From here, the path of universalisation would then begin again, following a pendulum-like pattern. However, as Gellner notes, Hume's explanation is psychologistic and lacks any reference to social dynamics. These elements can be precisely given by its integration with Ibn Khaldūn's thesis, which identifies in the urban situation the typical terrain on which the oscillation towards monotheism develops, and in the nomadic one, characterised by tribal *'aṣabiyya*, low division of labour, and social segmentariness, the phase that can be linked to the development of "hierarchical" polytheism. See also Ahmed (2005).

[55]The term derives from a three-letter root (*ba*, *dal*, *waw*) which indicates the desert and its inhabitants—the Bedouins, in fact.

[56]Many Khaldunian concepts can be considered as true ideal-types, in the Weberian sense: among them, the *badāwa*, *ḥaḍāra*, power (*mulk*) in its natural (*ṭabī'ī*) and political (*siyāsī*) modes, the caliphate, the different types of *'aṣabiyya*, the different types of government (*siyāsa 'aqliyya*, i.e., rational government, and *siyāsa dīniyya*, religious government), etc. See Cheddadi (2006: 469–470).

- Having built up "fortitude" and cohesion—a concept referred to as *'aṣabiyya*,[57] that plays a key role in Ibn Khaldūn's theory—and having, thus, become predisposed to pursue individual glory as well as the glory of the group, even at the cost of sacrificing oneself (all virtues nurtured in the harsh desert environment), a close-knit group manages to bring down the previous dynasty and to conquer and re-build the city. In the urban area (*ḥaḍāra*) that has been taken over, power is consolidated into the hands of a leader; at the same time, the arts and sciences find the ground in which they can gradually flourish.
- In the last phase, however—by virtue of a number of factors that include the individualistic atomism attendant on urbanisation, the mutual dependence resulting from an increased division of labour, the inevitably corrupting effect of power (as evidenced by an unreasonable increase in taxes, which in any event cannot sustain the level of public spending), an accustomisation to luxury that becomes compulsive (*Muqaddima* IV, 11; IV, 12) and, above all, a progressive, albeit predictable, detachment from the group's own foundational values—the social group as a collective entity becomes depleted of vitality and loses control over its internal functioning. As Ibn Khaldūn effectively wrote: "Time feasts on them, as their energy is exhausted by well-being and their vigour drained by the nature of luxury." (*Muqaddima* II, 20; Ibn Khaldūn 1958, Vol. I: 297; Ibn Khaldūn [1967] 2005: 114–115).
- This, in turn, will set the scene for conquest by other social groups, newer and more cohesive, again emerging out of the *'umrān badawī*.

  In this phase, the social group's civilisation falls into senility—a debilitating condition where once-strong cohesion comes apart and pristine virtues are lost—thus paving the way for emergent groups to sweep in, propelled by the poverty of the *badāwa* and eager to establish a place for themselves in the comfort and security of the *ḥaḍāra*.
- However, history will repeat itself once more along the same lines because the nascent power—having found strength and common cause in the very privations from which it emerged, and prompted by that same condition to seek power and comfort—will itself become corrupted in its own *'aṣabiyya* (the true engine of Ibn Khaldūn's history) once its objective is achieved. For that reason, it will be doomed to succumb and fall in its turn.

In this way, the *'aṣabiyya*—although so impalpable as to almost appear "metaphysical" (Kalin 2016)—acts, in its cyclical growing and fracturing, as the main engine of historical change, and as a necessary condition for the well-being of society as a whole.

The key element in sustaining the moral and material well-being of a society lies, therefore, in its cohesion, or solidarity. *Mutatis mutandis*, when that same central factor which enables the group to protect itself against the aggressions of the outside world (and, therefore, to survive in history) is no longer nourished by an upward

[57]In relation to the word "*'aṣabiyya*," in Arabic the three-letter root "*'ayin, sad, ba*" is related to concepts that revolve around the idea of "bonding."

perspective (concurrently with the achievement of social peace and a flourishing urban culture), it becomes corrupted. This will strip citizens of their "fortitude" and pride from within and weaken them just as they are losing that sense of cohesion that had allowed them to advance and reach civilisation.

It may be that the insight that led Ibn Khaldūn to identify this dynamic came to him, or was reinforced in him, by the Quran, and in particular by sura 8,[58] which, at verse 46 (a passage certainly known to such a great expert of tradition as Ibn Khaldūn), says: "Obey God and His Messenger, and do not quarrel with one another, or you may lose heart and your spirit may desert you. Be steadfast: God is with the steadfast."

In Ibn Khaldūn's perspective, in fact, everything revolves around the stimulating, aggregative, and organisational strength of *'aṣabiyya* and its natural tendency to head towards *ḥaḍāra*, up to the limits of its sustainability and final withdrawal, when a new cycle replaces the previous one.

During this continuous change, only culture acts as a glue between the cycle of the dying civilisation and that of the nascent civilisation, by virtue of its own transmissibility and the drive for the mimetic acquisition of the "highest" and most advanced cultural models, that it typically inspires in the new winners of the political game (Turroni 2014). Culture, in fact, has the potential to impress on the cyclical unfolding of history an underlying sense of continuity and direction: and in fact, it is thanks to this element that the successive cycles of civilisation will almost never start anew from scratch—a circumstance that emancipates Ibn Khaldūn's cyclicality from the closure of a circularity of phases always identical to themselves, deprived of any possible evolution. On the contrary, as pointed out by Talbi (1973: 93–98), precisely the *fil-rouge* represented by the tendency to permanence and transferability, from one cycle to another, of the cultural factor—the ultimate fruit of civilisation—, working as a bridge among civilisations, endows time with an evolutionary direction, and allows each new cycle to start again from a more advanced stage than the one before.

In fact, Ibn Khaldūn wrote:

> When politically ambitious men overcome the ruling dynasty and seize power, they inevitably have recourse to the customs of their predecessors and adopt most of them. At the same time, they do not neglect the customs of their own race. This leads to some discrepancies between customs of the new ruling dynasty and the customs of the old race. The new power, in turn, is taken over by another dynasty, and customs are further mixed with those of the new dynasty. More discrepancies come in, so that the contrast between the new dynasty and the first one is much greater than that between the second and the first one. Gradual increase in the degree of discrepancies continues. The eventual result is an altogether distinct (set of customs and institutions). (*Muqaddima*, The Introduction; Ibn Khaldūn 1958, Vol. I: 58; Ibn Khaldūn [1967] 2005: 25).

If, therefore, civilisations do decline, culture will not necessarily do so as well: as a "booty of war," handed down from winner to winner in successive cycles, it will remain, as a sort of common thread, in the continuous change of the social groups.

---

[58]Sura *Battle Gains*, (*Qur'an* 8, 46) (Haleem 2004: 113).

Precisely the transmissibility of culture, affording the possibility of always restarting from a "higher" level, implies that Ibn Khaldūn's scheme of history should not be construed as a perfect circle, in which the course of events is inescapably locked in a loop of repetition (as deplored by various exegetes who have descried in it Ibn Khaldūn's alleged "pessimism" (Bouthoul 1930; Gautier [1927] 1952: 112; Irwin 2018; Campanini 2019: 45)). Such a model of the anacyclosis of history, incidentally, had been previously envisioned in Plato's *Republic* ([390–360 B.C.] 2007: VIII e IX), in the 40 books of Polybius's *Histories* ([144 B.C.] 2001–2006), and, even before that, in some of the *Bible*'s Wisdom Books—most notably in *Kohelet*.

Rather, Ibn Khaldūn's scheme of history should be described as spiralling upward, in a mixed model, at once cyclical and directional. Unlike the closed loop model, this scheme significantly makes it possible, for those who are instructed in the "inner meaning of history" (even though the timescale on which to reason in this way about history may be long), to recognise with keener awareness situations from the past so as to move forward in facing the events of the present, advancing to a higher level.

In fact, while the idea of the looping evokes a view of a past endlessly and ineluctably repeating itself in the manner suggested in *Kohelet* (in keeping with the old saying that there is nothing new under the sun: *ein chadash tachat hashemesh*), the spiral-shaped model opens up the possibility of new iterations building on the cultural legacy of the previous ones. This offers a vantage point from which to observe and supersede the past by learning from its "instructive examples," thus moving into the new cycle with the benefit of the knowledge and understanding gained from an awareness of what has gone on before.

After all, in the *Qur'an* there is a verse, based on the sura *The Throngs*, that seems to suggest, in turn, a similarly cyclical image of the unravelling of time:

> He created the heavens and earth for a true purpose; He wraps the night around the day and the day around the night; He has subjected the sun and moon to run their courses for an appointed time. He is truly the Mighty, the Forgiving.[59]

In this image, night and day incessantly settle into each other until the end of time as they wind up what has been described as "the immense scroll of time," (Piccardo 1994: 399) in which the present endlessly coils around the past, repeating its trajectory across a wider radius, and providing, in its turn, the basis for the future.

One can imagine that this spiralling *Qur'anic* image of time and its progressive cycling—an image that Ibn Khaldūn was certainly familiar with—, may, perhaps, have also poetically inspired his reconstruction of the complex parables of political forces taking turns in government, in line with a similarly "spiralling" circular scheme.

For Ibn Khaldūn history is, therefore, a continuous mutation and a continuous beginning—a succession, as Horrut (2006: 30) wrote, of waves, "which gives

[59]Sura *The Throngs* (*Qur'an* 39, 5) (Haleem 2004: 295).

universal history the feeling of a continuous *deja vu*." But while it is true that in Ibn Khaldūn's scheme the curve drawn by the trajectory of history will continue to force a rotation and spin modelled on the past, and will continue to do so even in the present, when the same curve reaches the start of a new and higher cycle, it will still have the possibility of adjusting its course, advancing, and evolving. The possibility of bringing about this corrective adjustment and evolution will depend precisely on historical consciousness, and hence, ultimately, on the awareness handed down from the historical past.

Precisely to this end, history is analysed by Ibn Khaldūn (with a commitment and an urgency stimulated by the particular criticality and instability of his period) with the declared aim of redeeming it from the many fallacies that, in his time, undermined its reliability.

2.8 Destiny and the Possibility of Control

As has been noted, Ibn Khaldūn was a man of both thought and action, and these two aspects of his life cannot be separated: this can be well appreciated from his autobiography, but it is also a feature of his thought and of the very science to which he devoted himself.

In fact, it is not difficult to grasp the practical and political import of his reflection on the spiral-shaped structure within which the development of society and culture is framed. For what Ibn Khaldūn gives us, is a conceptual and interpretive toolkit through which the complex history of the changing forms of civilisation makes sense, and can be made intelligible and understood, in the light of the rational causality it seems subject to. And this rationalisation makes it possible, and requires, that political action be steered with the wisest possible insight, thereby indirectly urging reflection and caution in governing society—an attitude that proved all the more necessary in Ibn Khaldūn's own time, in the light of the many profound changes, destructions, and reconstructions then taking place.

On the one hand, a linear concept of time would have made it possible for the ruler to avoid accounting himself responsible for the future course of events—allowing him to think of it as something placed beyond his ken, and therefore unpredictable. On the other hand, a circular concept stuck in the *ouroboros* of an eternal return would have presented as pointless any endeavour, on his side, to control and change destiny. Ibn Khaldūn's spiral instead, as we have seen, implies, on the contrary, the possibility (and the responsibility) to be wiser and more cognisant in seizing the opportunities and averting the dangers that come along in the present. In fact, since the same dangers and opportunities already encountered in the past will continue to crop up in the future, it will be possible to foresee them precisely thanks to the clear vision—handed down culturally from the past—that the knowledge of history and its twists and turns can provide.

Inevitably, then, the possibility to anticipate the direction of social development, drawing it from the objective data of reality placed against the backdrop of a cyclical—and hence intelligible—iterative scheme, will imply the possibility—and, therefore, the necessity—that the key practical and normative actions and decisions that are to be taken in such important spheres of social life as politics and the economy, be controlled and regulated. Within such a scheme, today's actions will be charged with a causative value for the future.

Furthermore, since Ibn Khaldūn identifies in social cohesion, in the form of the *'aṣabiyya*, the keystone on which the survival of civilisation rests, the whole philosophico-historico-sociological architecture he designs seems to suggest, especially to those in positions of power, that this is precisely the basis on which to steer social policy. Society can thrive only so long as it rests on moral, legal, and political principles predicated on the need constantly to maximise the intensity and duration of its own cohesion, in order to counteract the inherently destructive force that seems always to be looming on the horizon: the entropy that naturally tends to break it up.

In reality, we have even more ancient examples in which history has been read "admonishingly," as a ragbag of events tied together by a design—that is to say, by a running thread represented by the annihilating power of corruption and by the causal link between the loss of collective moral values (exemplified in individualism, the loss of moral cohesion, the unleashing and diversification of desires) and the downfall (both political and salvific) of the social unit.

Consider the books of the Biblical prophets such as Jeremiah, Isaiah, Jonah, and Zechariah, dating from the eighth to the fourth century B.C. (and going back even further is the work of the oral prophets, who did not leave behind any written scripture, such as Samuel, Nathan, Elijah, and Elisha). In those books, the loss of coherence in collective values and the break-up of social solidarity (corruption, a lack of solidarity with orphans and widows, mutual iniquities) are connected with a "rightful" salvific decadence as well as with political decadence (also associated, as in Jeremiah 1:15–16, with political conquest by other peoples).

This foresight should not come as a surprise since Biblical culture represents one of the basic references on which the *Qur'an* draws—however unsystematically—for its narrative, and, through these, it resurfaces constantly, if unmethodically and in a "phreatic" way (like the desert *wadi*), from the deep undercurrents of Islamic culture. It would, therefore, not be far-fetched to think that these themes could also have influenced Ibn Khaldūn, all the more so as he made explicit reference to the prophetic books (as in *Muqaddima* III, 31), demonstrating that he is quite conversant with them.[60]

However, what in biblical narratives[61] is still a "theological" personification of a logic of corruption and decadence, takes on new and revolutionary traits within the scope of Ibn Khaldūn's "new science," simultaneously rational and empirical.

---

[60]Not only that: according to some scholars he may also have been acquainted with the interpretations of the same themes proposed, a century earlier, by Maimonides in his *The Guide for the perplexed*: cf. Pines (1970: 265–274). Maimonides ([1180–1190] 2000).

[61]But, again, this can be found also in works closer in time to Ibn Khaldūn, such as the already mentioned *Indiculus luminosus* by Paulo Alvaro of Cordoba, dating from the ninth century.

A practical effect follows from this rationalising re-reading of history that does away with the alibi of fatalism, and which, in its place, brings in the idea of a historical and political intelligibility. Once we are trained to see the dynamics of this rationalised history, we implicitly commit ourselves to a consequence that, previously, the concept of history as an unpredictable flow of events did not impose: we commit ourselves to the task of pondering, evaluating, and assessing, in a "scientific" way, the decisions that will shape the course of history as a function of the "hold" of the social *'aṣabiyya*.

This is a "formula" that will re-emerge centuries later, passing through Durkheim (reader of Ibn Khaldūn and teacher of a generation of jurists attentive to sociology), and re-defined as the famous "general rule" of conduct emphasised by Léon Duguit[62] (2003: 91), according to which "nothing must be done that diminishes social solidarity by similarity and social solidarity by division of labour, while everything must be done to increase social solidarity in its various forms."

There is something of the tragic here: as in the earlier idea of the palpable, and tragic, consequences of knowledge—the "*pathei mathos*" of the ancient Greek tragedies—, in Ibn Khaldūn, with the foresight gained by knowledge of the "inner meaning" of history, there inevitably comes a sense of (eventually, tragic) responsibility. And it is this element that ends in applying a transformative force to the historical account itself. Instead of being conceived as a registration of self-enclosed events, paratactically set next to others, this is made a conceptually understandable temporal syntax, rationally linking chains of events, making it intrinsically possible, thus, to assess the wisdom and advisability of political and legal action on the basis of its effectiveness in feeding aggregative forces and driving senility away.

But perhaps, in relation to this very "warning" function, it was the other side of the coin that prevailed and blighted Ibn Khaldūn's work in the centuries immediately following: it is perhaps not going too far to speculate that the hard legacy entrusted by Ibn Khaldūn's history to political leaders might have been an important factor in explaining why, for such a long time, his concept failed to find favour with the very rulers of North Africa to whom Ibn Khaldūn had devoted and entrusted his "totally new" science.

References

(A) Ibn Khaldūn's Works

Ibn Khaldūn. 1958. *The Muqaddimah: An Introduction to History* (ed. Franz Rosenthal). 3 Voll. New Jersey: Princeton University Press.

[62]For Léon Duguit, a jurist strongly inspired by the sociology of Durkheim, the "natural" right par excellence synthetically consists in favouring everything that increases solidarity. See, in particular, the first chapter of his *L'État, le droit objectif et la loi positive* (2003).

———. [1967] 2005. *The Muqaddimah: An Introduction to History* (ed. Franz Rosenthal), abridged edition. Princeton: Princeton University Press.

(B) Other Works

Abdesselem, Ahmed. 1983. *Ibn Khaldūn et ses lecteurs*. Paris: Presses Universitaires de France.

Ahmed, Akbar S. 2005. Ibn Khaldūn and Anthropology: The Failure of Methodology in the Post 9/11 World. *Contemporary Sociology. Essays on Ibn Khaldūn* 34 (6): 591–596.

Alatas, Syed Farid. 2014. *Applying Ibn Khaldūn. The Recovery of a Lost Tradition in Sociology*. London: Routledge.

Alvarus of Córdova, Paulus. [IX century]1844–1855. Indiculus luminosus. In *Patrologia Latina*, Vol. 121, sez. 35, ed. Jaques Paul Migne, 513–556. Paris: Garnier.

al-Idrīsī, Muḥammad. [1154] 2008. *Il libro di Ruggero*. Palermo: Flaccovio.

al-Mas'ūdī, Abū al-Hasan 'Alì. [X century]1861–1877. *Muruj al-Dhahab,* 9 Voll. (eds. Charles Barbier de Meynard e Abel Pavet de Courteille). Parigi: Imprimerie Imperiale.

Baali, Fuad. 1988. *Society, State, and Urbanism: Ibn Khaldūn's Sociological Thought*. Lanham: University Press of America.

Boulakia, Jean David C. 1971. Ibn Khaldūn: A Fourteenth-Century Economist. *The Journal of Political Economy* 79 (5): 1105–1118.

Bouthoul, Gaston. 1930. *Ibn-Khaldoun. Sa philosophie sociale*. Librairie Orientaliste Paul Geuthner: Paris.

Campanini, Massimo. 2005b. *Ibn Khaldūn: la Muqaddima, la storia, la civiltà, il potere*. In *Studies on Ibn Khaldūn*, ed. Massimo Campanini, 9–48. Milano: Polimetrica.

———. 2017. *Averroes. The Decisive Treatise*. Piscataway, NJ: Gorgias Press.

———. 2019. *Ibn Khaldūn. Passato e futuro del mondo arabo*. La Vela: Viareggio.

Cheddadi, Abdesselam. 2006. *Ibn Khaldūn. L'homme et le théoricien de la civilisation*. Paris: Gallimard.

Coltman Brown, Irene. 1981. Ibn Khaldūn and the Revelation from the Desert. *History Today* 31: 19–25.

Dale, Stephen Frederic. 2015a. *The Orange Trees of Marrakesh. Ibn Khaldūn and the Science of Man*. Cambridge, MA: Harvard University Press.

Dhaouadi, Mahmoud. 2005. The 'Ibar: Lessons of Ibn Khaldūn's 'Umrān Mind. *Contemporary Sociology,* 34/6: *Essays on Ibn Khaldūn*: 585–589.

———. 2011. Ibn Khaldoun, sociologue avant la lettre. *Sciences Humaines* 15 (6): 1–5.

Duguit, Léon. [1901] 2003. *L'État, le droit objectif et la loi positive*. Paris: Dalloz.

Fakhry, Majid. 1970. *A History of Islamic Philosophy*. New York: Columbia University Press.

Gautier, Émile Félix. [1927] 1952. *Le Passé de l'Afrique du Nord*. Paris: Payot.

Gellner, Ernest. 1981. *Cohesion and Identity: the Maghreb from Ibn Khaldūn to Émile Durkheim*. In *Muslim Society*, ed. Ernest Gellner. Cambridge: Cambridge University Press.

Goodman, Lenn Evan. 1972. Ibn Khaldūn and Thucydides. *Journal of the American Oriental Society* 92 (2): 250–270.

Haleem, M.A.S. Abdel (trans.). 2004. *The Qur'an*. Oxford University Press.

Hamès, Constant. 1999. Islam et Sociologie: Une rencontre qui n'a pas eu lieu? In *Sociology and Religions. An Ambiguous Relationship*, eds. Liliane Voyé and Jaak Billiet, 171–182. Leuven: Leuven University Press.

Hassan, Faridah Hj. 2006. Ibn Khaldūn and Jane Addams: The Real Father of Sociology and The Mother of Social Works. *Congreso Ibn Khaldūn*, November 3–5, Madrid. http://www.docsford.com/document/6091263. Accessed 17 Sept 2020.

Horrut, Claude. 2006. *Ibn Khaldūn, un Islam des "Lumières"*. Paris: Les Éditions Complexes.

Hume, David. [1779] 1976. *The Natural History of Religion*. Oxford: Oxford University Press.

Hussein, Taha. 1918. *Étude analitique et critique de la philosophie sociale d'Ibn Khaldoun*. Paris: Pedone.
Ibn Taymmiyya. 1981. *Dar' ta'āruḍ al-'aql wa-l-naql*. Cairo: Dār al-Kutub.
Irwin, Robert. 2018. *Ibn Khaldūn. An Intellectual Biography*. Princeton: Princeton University Press.
Kalin, Ibrahim. 2016, December 10. Ibn Khaldūn has a Message for Us. *Daily Sabah Columns*. https://www.dailysabah.com/columns/ibrahim-kalin/2016/12/10/ibn-khaldun-has-a-message-for-us. Accessed 17 Sept 2020.
Lambton, Ann K.S. [1954] 1980. *Theory and Practice in Medieval Persian Government*. London: Ashgate.
Laroui, Abdallah. 1999. *Islam et Histoire*. Paris: Flammarion.
Lombardi, Marco. 1997. Le follie di Spagna. In *Percorsi europei*, ed. Maria Grazia Profeti, 167–192. Firenze: Alinea.
Mahdi, Muhsin. 1957. *Ibn Khaldūn's Philosophy of History*. Chicago: University of Chicago Press.
Maimonides, Moses. [1180–1190] 2000. *The Guide for the Perplexed*. New York: Dover.
Megherbi, Abdelghani. 1971. *La pensée sociologique d'Ibn Khaldoun*. SNED: Alger.
Piccardo, Hamza (ed.). 1994. *Il Corano*. Roma: Newton & Compton.
Pines, Shlomo. 1970. Ibn Khaldūn and Maimonides, a Comparison between Two Texts. *Studia Islamica* 32: 265–274.
Plato. [390–360 a.C.]2007. *La Repubblica*. Milano: BUR.
Polybius. [144 a.C.]2001–2006. *Storie*, Vol. 1–8. Milano: BUR.
Pomian, Krzysztof. 2006. *Ibn Khaldūn au prisme de l'Occident*. Paris: Gallimard.
Ptolemy. [II century B.C.]1940. *Tetrabiblos (Quadripartitum)* (ed. Frank E. Robbins). Cambridge, MA: Loeb.
Rosenthal, Franz. 1958. *Preface to Ibn Khaldūn*. In Ibn Khaldūn, *The Muqaddimah: An Introduction to History* (ed. Franz Rosenthal). Vol. I, xxix–cxv. Princeton: Princeton University Press.
Soyer, Mehmet. 2010. *Examining the Origins of Sociology: Continuities and Divergencies between Ibn Khaldūn, Giambattista Vico, August Comte, Ludwig Gumplowicz, and Emile Durkheim*. Master Thesis. Denton: University of North Texas.
Soyer, Mehmet, and Paul Gilbert. 2012. Debating the Origins of Sociology: Ibn Khaldūn as a Founding Father of Sociology. *International Journal of Sociological Research* 5: 13–30.
Spragens, Thomas A. 1976. *Understanding Political Theory*. New York: St. Martin's Press.
Talbi, Mohamed. 1973. *Ibn Ḫaldūn et l'histoire*. Tunis: Maison Tunisienne de l'Édition.
Thucydides. [IV century B.C.]1989. *The Peloponnesian War* (trans. Thomas Hobbes). Chicago: The University of Chicago Press.
Triki, Fathi. 1986. *L'Esprit historien dans la civilisation arabe et islamique*. Tunis: Maison Tunisienne de l'Édition.
Turroni, Giuliana. 2002. *Il mondo della storia secondo Ibn Khaldūn*. Roma: Jouvence.
———. 2014. 'Umrān. La civilisation dans la théorie khaldûnienne. In *Encyclopédie de l'humanisme méditerranéen*, ed. Houari Youati, encyclopedie-humanisme.com/?Umran. Accessed 17 Sept 2020.
Van Gennep, Arnold. [1910] 1920. *La formation des légendes*. Paris: Flammarion.
Vanoli, Alessandro. 2004. Recensione di G. Turroni. *Filosofia politica* 1: 139–141.
Wittgenstein, Ludwig. [1921] 1989. *Tractatus logico-philosophicus*. Torino: Einaudi.

Chapter 3
Inside the *Muqaddima*: Sociocultural Compactness and Social Transformations

Abstract This chapter goes to the heart of the *Muqaddima* to analyse the general framework within which Ibn Khaldūn explains the dynamics of historical changeability.

Ibn Khaldūn starts from a series of premises explaining, in general terms, the need for social organisation and the diversity of its different forms, which are strongly influenced by the variety of the environment. Despite this variety, however, a constant oscillation operates, according to Ibn Khaldūn, between two modes of social organisation: that of the margins and the urbanised one. While the former is characterised by poverty, but also by the solidary and strengthening union of its members (*'aṣabiyya*), which gives it a transformative impulse towards urbanisation, the latter is characterised by forms of material luxury and intellectual wealth, but also by a disruptive trend that, following precise historical phases, determines its decadence.

The *'aṣabiyya*, therefore, is for Ibn Khaldūn the primary key element governing the change of forms of civilisation over time. This factor is analysed, in the chapter, both in relation to its specific nature, and in relation to the dynamics that can allow its "permanence" even when the political community hosts a plurality of other minor solidarity groups within it. The second key element in defining political and social dynamics, for Ibn Khaldūn, is leadership and power. This, too, is examined in relation to the factors that determine its origin, the qualities that characterise it, and the changes that it encounters in the course of historical development.

3.1 Six Premises on Human Social Organisation in General

As we have seen, in Ibn Khaldūn's new science even the order in which the issues are addressed acquires a logical value. In the first chapter of *Muqaddima*, before elaborating his theses, Ibn Khaldūn articulates the premises underlying all his work in six preambles. The following books of *Muqaddima*, then, would be devoted to

A. Verza, *Ibn Khaldūn and the Arab Origins of the Sociology of Civilisation and Power*, https://doi.org/10.1007/978-3-030-70339-4_3

analysing the essential points of these premises, presenting them sequentially, in the subsequent paragraphs, as "propositions."

According to Ibn Khaldūn the foundation of the political behaviour of men and their history is to be found in the material basis of civilisation[1] first and foremost—that is, in the climate, the environment, nutrition, and the way problems related to the necessities of life are resolved. The differences that distinguish human beings, who are born everywhere with identical basic capacities and potential, result precisely from the influence exerted on humans by these background factors. The environment, in particular, exerts a particularly strong influence, at a basic level, on both the moral characteristics of human beings and the level of social solidarity binding them.[2] However, this occurs only at a ground level: in fact, although it is conceived as a baseline, Ibn Khaldūn's thesis of the influence of the environment on human character does not lead to a rigid, abstract, and dogmatic determinism: as the environment combines with the many other complex factors at stake, and with their reciprocal interactions, many variations emerge that can be captured by an empirical observation of reality.

As set out in the first premise, on the basis of the geographical theories of the time Ibn Khaldūn begins by describing the Earth as divided into different climate zones: basically, the influence of each climate zone is exerted on the social groups populating it, to which it transmits specific characteristics.[3] Then, all individuals within these groups also acquire peculiar traits, on the basis of their specific intelligence, which is formed by a combination of their different types of "soul," and which is distinct for everyone, as is underlined in the seventh premise.

In his consideration of the diversity of human civilisations, described in their variety (even while recognising the uniqueness of the fundamental structure which propels them forward in common cyclical trajectories), Ibn Khaldūn, as Pomian (2006: 144) observes, sets himself apart from the theories of human development proposed by the Christianity of his time. In fact, although works such as Marco Polo's *Il Milione* had already described the great variety of human civilisations in detail, the tendency of Western Christian culture at the time was to inscribe human development within a unitary line of temporal development. In this, the six phases of a man's evolution (*infantia*, *pueritia*, *adolescentia*, *iuventus*, *gravitas*, *senectus*)

---

[1]Various authors, such as Yves Lacoste ([1996] 1998), would consider this method, putting material factors, such as the environment and survival strategies, at the basis of the theory, as a "materialism" comparable to the approach subsequently developed by Marx and Engels.

[2]These Khaldunian premises recall themes separately developed, much later, by Montesquieu, who, in the *Ésprit des lois*, took nature as the basis of his research, and claimed to have derived his principles on the relations between men and their forms of government and laws "from the nature of things" (1748: xliii). Montesquieu stressed that human life is governed by many factors, such as climate, religion, laws, maxims of government, past examples and customs, and that the interaction between all these produces a general "spirit" which must be recognised by the law.

[3]The idea that man depends on his physical environment and that this also influences his character and customs, had already been expressed in Greek culture by Ptolemy's geography ([first century BC] 1940: 120 f. ii 2), which was well known in the Muslim world.

were transposed, by analogy, to the phases marking, in an ideal line, the development of humanity, from its fall from Heaven (*Gen. 3*) up to the end of the world, according to the subdivision in epochs set out by St Augustine ([413–462] 2011: XXII, xxx, 5).

In Ibn Khaldūn's eyes, instead, empirical observation showed a much more complex picture, diversified in a variety of forms of development that primarily resulted from the specific influence of the environment on the culture developed within it. By affecting the psychic make-up of the individuals immersed in it, in fact, the environment imprints on them common characteristics that will then constitute a sort of basic common "character" for their group.

3.1.1 First Preface: The Necessity of Social Life and Power

Ibn Khaldūn immediately focuses his analysis: he sets out to devote his attention directly to the organisation of man's social life, instead of concentrating on the individual (less relevant to his purposes, individuality being, to a large extent, the final product of environment and education).

His study, far from centering on an ideal and utopian view, focuses on analysing the conditions where civilisation might exist, starting not only from the assumption of the impossibility of man surviving as a single individual, but also from the impossibility of social groups surviving in anarchy.

First and foremost, human social organisation is viewed by Ibn Khaldūn as something necessary, for the simple reason that man understands that, as an individual, he cannot provide for his own subsistence. The logical procedure followed here by Ibn Khaldūn is a hypothetical-deductive one: in fact—he argues—even if men were able to obtain on their own enough food to ensure their survival, they would still need tools and utensils both to obtain and to prepare it; in turn, then, manufacturing these tools would require the cooperation of other people, experts in their respective arts:

> Thus, he cannot do without a combination of many powers from among his fellow beings [. . .]. Through co-operation, the needs of a number of persons, many times greater than their own number, can be satisfied (*Muqaddima*, I, First Prefatory Discussion. Ibn Khaldūn 1958, Vol. I: 89–90. Ibn Khaldūn [1967] 2005: 45).

Moreover, each individual would also need the help of his peers in order to ensure his own defence: while wild animals naturally have claws, teeth, or armour to attack others and defend themselves, man needs to use weapons and tools for this purpose, and to do so he will need to rely on a social organisation that will allow him access to the contribution of others, masters of the art of making all these things.

Therefore, if man lives in society, this is not due to any gregarious instincts,[4] but to the fact that, being endowed with intelligence, he understands that being in society is the best possible way to ensure his survival.

But then, in turn, a simple gathering of peers does not, in itself, constitute a stable or peaceful form of society. Man's faculty of thought also demonstrates to him that social organisation, in order not to disintegrate, needs to identify, within itself, some form of power capable of limiting its members' natural tendency to mutual aggression.[5]

Therefore, an element indispensable to the existence of society is the natural human quality given by the attitude and desire for command, which is the source of political power: the *mulk*. The concept of *mulk*—namely, power—in Ibn Khaldūn takes on a "factual" connotation, realistically independent of religion,[6] which manifests itself, as we shall see, along the spectrum of a whole variety of (Weberian) "ideal-types," ranging from natural leadership to traditional authority (*Muqaddima* III, 2), and rational legal authority (such as, for example the caliph's).

3.1.2 Second Preface: Civilisations and Regions of the Earth

On the basis of Ptolemy's *Geography* ([first century BC] 1940), and al-Idrīsī's *Kitāb Rujār*[7] (*Book of Roger*) ([1154] 2008), Ibn Khaldūn describes the earth as a sphere, half of which emerges from water, which is held together by the attraction of its centre. Most importantly, the earth is described as being divided, starting from the equator, into seven climate zones (*aqālīm*), in which civilisation (*'umrān*) does not flourish homogeneously.

In such a vision, the centre of civilisation lies in the fourth, middle zone, the most temperate, where the climate is more benevolent. The third and fifth zones are also favourable, although slightly less. On the contrary, in the other zones civilisation struggles to develop—especially in the most extreme areas from a climatic point of view: in the first and seventh zones, in fact, due to the environment's unfavourable

[4]Ibn Khaldūn observes (*Muqaddima*, Preliminary Remarks) that even social animals such as bees and locusts submit to a chief, which is also, generally, somatically different, and, therefore, easily identifiable. Yet, in their case, this is due to instinct, while for humans—who are similar to each other, since no individual is physically marked to perform such functions—the need to submit to a leader is due to a rational understanding.

[5]The idea that, if left to himself, man would be too aggressive, had already been exposed in two works by Avicenna: the *Kitāb al-Šifā* and its reduced version, the *Kitāb al-Najā*.

[6]The predisposition to an objective observation of the reality shown by this clarification should be emphasised, as this was, in the North African context, one of the points on which most criticism directed against the author focused.

[7]On the relationship between the map included in the *Muqaddima* and al-Idrīsī's world map, see Kahlaoui (2008).

influence, human beings are doomed to live in a state closer to that of animals than to that of rational beings.

3.1.3 Third Preface: The Temperate Regions

Just as the fourth, the third, and fifth zones have a temperate climate, so everything that grows and is produced there—such as the sciences, arts, buildings, clothes, food, fruit, animals, and likewise the bodies, colours, and characters of people—also tend to have temperate characteristics and harmonious proportions.[8] For the sake of objectivity,[9] Ibn Khaldūn emphasises that this advantage applies to the full extent to the temperate zones, whether or not they fall under the rule of Islamic law. On the contrary, unless the climate is somehow corrected (as a result of the influence of sea currents, for example), the character of the inhabitants of the non-temperate zones is affected by this imbalance. Ibn Khaldūn constructs the first brick of his theory of civilisation out of these physical-geographical premises, together with the consequences attached to them.

More to the point, commenting on the fact that, in reality, there are lands where people live in a way that is similar to that of animals, Ibn Khaldūn argues that the blame for this is not to be attributed to their "history" of poor evolution,[10] nor to their race, but to the environment that hosts them. For this reason, he criticises those who explain this phenomenon exclusively by genealogy, as if it were the sole cause of the differences between nations.[11] Having failed to consider the influence of geographical conditions, customs, and other environmental factors, as well as the importance of the change that also affects these elements, they have actually proposed a spurious explanation which, neglecting a fundamental factor, is inevitably fallacious.

It is on this basis that Ibn Khaldūn (exhibiting, once again, his singular capacity for detachment from the commonplaces of his time, no matter how undisputed and

---

[8]The same term—*mu'tadil*—is used by Ibn Khaldūn to indicate the characteristic of moderation, both in climate and temperament.

[9]This statement, which applies an Islamic-centric vision only to the field of faith (*'aql-naql*, precisely), imposing rigour and objectivity in all other areas, is far from obvious, when compared to the Eurocentrism expressed by the thought of anthropologists such as James Frazer (1890), or Lewis Henry Morgan (1877).

[10]See the vision of African culture expressed by Cornelius de Paw (1774). See also Hegel ([1837] 1902).

[11]In short, as Pišev (2019: 5) observes, for Ibn Khaldūn "the concept of human primitivity, futility and backwardness had nothing to do with skin colour or ethnic origins." In 1930 Gaston Bouthoul used precisely these observations by Ibn Khaldūn (1930: 42) to refute the racial essentialism expressed by theses such as those of Joseph Arthur, Count of Gobineau (1853–1855): "Ibn Khaldoun, quoique d'origine arabe, montre qu'il penche vers une théorie plutôt égalitaire puisqu'elle rattache le caractère et la noblesse au genre de vie plutôt qu'a la seule origine. Et il justifie sa position en la fondant sur une de ces théories positives qui sont par essence dissolvantes de tous les prestiges."

rooted), explicitly denies, for example, the popular thesis that attributed black people's lesser development to the curse cast by Noah on his son Ham.

Ibn Khaldūn pointed out that this allegation, apparently supported by a (superficial) interpretation of a biblical passage (which actually says nothing in relation to skin colour), totally neglected the importance of environmental factors. In fact, he wrote, the lifestyle of these populations is essentially determined by the influence exerted by the atmosphere, and in particular by the sun and the "composition of the air" specific to the area, on creatures living within it. This, he adds, is demonstrated by the fact that the colour of the skin of the populations gradually changes from south to north: in fact, if the northern populations tend to have increasingly whiter skin, less and lighter hair, and blue eyes, this is due to the progressive prevalence of cold climate and darkness, as one moves north. Yet—Ibn Khaldūn sharply noted—"white" people do not define themselves on the basis of their colour, almost as if this were not also a particular characteristic. This is, because:

> the people who established the conventional meaning of words were themselves white. Thus, whiteness was something usual and common to them, and they did not see anything sufficiently remarkable in it to cause them to use it as a specific term (*Muqaddima* I, Third Prefatory Discussion. Ibn Khaldūn 1958, Vol. I: 172. Ibn Khaldūn [1967] 2005: 60–61).

3.1.4 Fourth Preface: The Climate and the Environment's Background Influence on the Character of People

The issue of the different character of the populations living in different climatic zones is further investigated by Ibn Khaldūn on the basis of Galen's theses, adopted in Arabic medicine, which linked the balance of moods, temperament, and other factors, to the opposites hot/cold and dry/humid characteristics of the climate. On the basis of these theses, associating heat with expansion and joy, and cold with contraction and sadness, Ibn Khaldūn explains the character traits most commonly associated with the temperament of the different populations.

For example, the fact that black people appear as characterised by lightness, excitability, emotionality, and a penchant for dancing, is in no way related (as al-Mas'ūdī had assumed) to any supposed weakness of their intellect, but it is essentially the result of the expansion of their vital spirit generated by heat. Moreover, similar effects on character, due to the reflection of the sun on the water, are also produced in the temperate zones' coastal countries.

By the same token, on the contrary, sadness and seriousness are characteristics linked to the contraction and concentration induced by cold. In Ibn Khaldūn's view, an example of this can be provided by the inhabitants of Fez, who are surrounded by cold mountains and characterised by almost constant sadness and by worries about hoarding food, almost as if they had to stave off impending shortages.

This relationship between climate and mood, Ibn Khaldūn wrote, can also be observed in everyone's personal experience if we consider the typical effects of drunkenness, which induces joy and lightness because of the warming and expansion of the spirit caused by wine, or, more simply, if we observe how even a hot bath often produces an effect of this kind—that is, a raising of the mood, frequently expressed in people's desire to sing.

To be sure, the thesis of the environmental influence on man was not a new one: not only had Aristotle, in his *Politics* (a book which Ibn Khaldūn did not know, as we have seen), already attributed the moderation of Greek institutions to the climate, but Hippocrates (460–370 BC) had also emphasised the effects exerted on humans by the seasons, winds, geographical situation, and climate. Ibn Khaldūn's merit, however, lies not only in his consideration of such paradigms, used in order to explain and dismantle commonplaces, but also in his ability to integrate them into a more complex and organic thesis.

3.1.5 Fifth Preface: The Influence of Food Abundance and Scarcity

By observing the different social groups, Ibn Khaldūn said, we can see that the quantity and quality of resources taken from the environment for one's sustenance—and therefore, in the first place, food—also influences the character of men: in fact,

> The desert people who lack grain and seasonings are found to be healthier in body and better in character than the hill people who have plenty of everything. Their complexions are clearer, their bodies cleaner, their figures more perfect, their character less intemperate, and their minds keener as far as knowledge and perception are concerned (*Muqaddima* I, Fifth Prefatory Discussion. Ibn Khaldūn 1958, Vol. I: 177–178. Ibn Khaldūn [1967] 2005: 65).[12]

Ibn Khaldūn suggests that the reason for this diversification, even within the same climate (as we shall see, this is, in fact, one of the main differential traits between *badāwa* and *ḥaḍāra*), may lie in the fact that the excessive amount of food and moisture available generates unnecessary matter, harmful to the body and mind. Therefore, the poorer and simpler diet of the desert, rich in milk and meat (*sic!*), is preferable to the city's, refined and rich in cereal and fruit.

As an example of this, he suggests observing and comparing the health, strength, and temperament of wild animals with domestic ones: gazelles with goats, giraffes with camels and wild asses, and oxen with domesticated ones. Just as animals living in the wild, where food is to be hunted on a daily basis, are stronger and more intelligent than those bred on fertile plains, so, by the same token, men living in abundance have more delicate constitutions than those living in areas that demand frugality and simple living. This is not all: they also succumb earlier to famine or

[12]When Montesquieu, in his *Esprit des lois*, described the influence exerted on the qualities of man by a non-fertile land (which he linked to courageous, sober and combative people) or by a fertile land (which he linked to men who are essentially concerned with their own survival), he seems, in fact, to follow Ibn Khaldūn's distinction.

drought, victims not so much of scarcity itself, but of their having formerly been used to a condition of continuous plenty.[13]

Moreover, abundance or shortage also affect religiosity, because frugal life, and being accustomed to hunger and abstinence, better dispose people to religious devotion than luxury and abundance do, both individually and collectively.

3.1.6 Sixth Preface: Continuity Among the Stages of Creation

As Ibn Khaldūn explains, the world of creation begins with minerals and progresses in a gradual evolutionary process: the last stage of minerals is connected to the first of plants, the last of plants to the first of animals (represented, for example, by snails) and, after that, the animal world branches off. This, finally, reaches man from a branch inhabited by monkeys, sagacious and perceptive. Intermediate between them and the angels, man is distinguished by his ability to think.

This is the level of the physical world, but complexity and hierarchical order also inform the other levels of existence. Ibn Khaldūn follows al-Fārābī (the "Second Teacher," from whom he gets his idea that causes are linked together up to unity with the divine) in positing that, besides bodily substance, a different substance follows, too—the soul, which perceives and causes movement—, and that, above this, the realm of angelic intelligences unfolds. The three worlds—the physical, that of the soul and thought, and the angelic/spiritual world—are in contact with each other: it is within this general theory that Ibn Khaldūn incorporates his view of prophecy. According to Ibn Khaldūn, by virtue of the body we all belong to the animal world, and because of our thinking capacity we can all gain access to the world of the soul, but the highest realm, remote and invisible, is accessible only, and rarely, to a few men.

The powers of sensory perception (here Ibn Khaldūn relies on Avicenna and Galen) are also hierarchically graded, up to the peak of rational thought. It is in this direction that the soul heads, in a continuous wandering caused by its "constitutive" and natural desire to think and to blend with the angelic stage. The powers that, together, compose the faculty of "thought," analytically connected to different parts of the brain, are "common sense"—i.e., the ability to synthesise the perceptions that simultaneously come from the senses—, imagination—which moves towards abstraction from sensory perceptions—, evaluation, and memory.

As for man's souls, these can be of three kinds: the first, characteristic of men of wisdom, scholars, and scientists, is too weak to reach spiritual perception, and limits itself to processing sensory information in a way that both perceives it and is aware of the act of perception. On the contrary the second, characteristic of mystics and saints, is able to intuitively reach further, towards inner observation. Finally, the

[13] In this, as well as in the whole basic structure of his thesis, Ibn Khaldūn captures particularly acutely the paradox of the vulnerability that arises from an excess of protection and preventive care.

third, very rare, encompasses the potential completely to transform human nature into the nature of angels.

By divine gift, the third soul is possessed only by prophets. They are closer to the realm of angelic entities and have the natural gift of being able to understand the words of the universal soul and the divine discourse. This happens in the flash of a moment, in a sudden exit from time characterised by pain and a sense of suffocation caused by the transcendental passage itself.

Ibn Khaldūn deals, then, in this paragraph and also in later parts of the *Muqaddima* (Chapter VI), with other phenomena such as divination, dream visions, astrology, geomancy, and numerology, which he describes as minor and imperfect forms of the relationship with the supernatural, which do, however, also respond to a natural disposition of man.

As Talbi (1973: 99–104) comments, the thesis of universal evolutionism—the pathway from minerals to plants, animals, man, and, finally, angels—had actually long been inscribed in Islamic thought. This constant tension in the search for man's place in the cosmos had gradually been developed from the thought of al-Jāḥiẓ (781–869), subsequently arriving at Avicenna's Aristotelian conceptualism by way of the Pythagorean speculation of Iẖwān al-ṣafā' (expressed in their *Rasā'il*) and the empirical observations of al-Bīrūnī (973–1048).

According to Talbi (1973: 100–101), the author who most influenced Ibn Khaldūn on this point (although he does not quote him directly), is Miskawayh (932–1030), the author of a theodicy where the world is seen as a single being composed—as if it were a unique necklace of precious stones—of infinitely diversified parts, and different realms, connected through progressive transitions. Among them lies the realm of human beings themselves—reaching a different stage of development according to the areas they inhabit—which culminates in the class of prophets.

It is therefore not possible, considering the above theoretical precedents, fully to share Megherbi's thesis (1971: 111) that sees in Ibn Khaldūn the true father of "evolutionism"—even though it certainly cannot be denied that his integration of such ideas into the coherent whole of his theory does indeed represent an original and important contribution. This thesis especially cannot be shared to the extent to which the evolutionism of which Megherbi speaks is understood in the fully secular sense the term has today. In fact, it is no coincidence that Ibn Khaldūn maintains his *'aql-naql* balance in this section, and premises his discussion with an explicit religious reference to the knowledge contained in the *Qur'an*, "the greatest, noblest, and clearest miracle," thus taking care always to keep his discourse on paths compatible with religion.

If we effectively find, therefore, in his sixth premise the thesis of the existence of a *continuum* that unites all creatures, it is a kind of "evolutionism" that nevertheless lies under the wing of religion and, in fact, tends towards it, to the point of placing those men who are endowed with the capacity of reaching the divine (the prophets) at the highest level among earthly creatures.

On the other hand, however, neither can we share Cheddadi's opposite thesis (2006: 266), according to which this gradual path should be seen simply as depicting a hierarchy of value that puts created beings in order, and not as tracing, in its unfolding, a true evolutionary line. On the contrary, Ibn Khaldūn explicitly writes that every element in this "ascension" has the potential to transform itself into the next one in the chain (which is always more refined than the previous one), or, on the contrary, to regress and resume its previous characteristics—and that, sometimes, this transformation actually occurs. This framework, therefore, is intended to describe a real, continuous link connecting the elements of creation within an ascensional process, directed towards an ever-greater complexity (and refinement) of the creatures that belong to it, and not merely a hierarchical arrangement between them, structured in that way for simple, scientific-narrative purposes.

3.2 The Unit of Analysis and Its Intrinsic Changeability: The *'Umrān* and Its Forms

In Ibn Khaldūn's "new science" men are always contextualised in their social, as well as physical, environment. In fact, from the very first pages of *Muqaddima,* individuals are defined as beings who are necessarily social: not because of their nature, but rather because of their rational understanding that their need to survive, flourish and express their cultural and creative potential can only be realised in associative terms. It is this understanding that leads them to realise themselves as *social* beings. In the same way, it is yet another rational cause—that is, their understanding of their need to find a centre of power capable of restricting (*wāzi'*) their innate aggressiveness towards each other and organising their living together—which leads them to become *political* beings as well.

Ibn Khaldūn concentrates his analysis on the two models—real ideal-types (Baeck 1994: 115; Patriarca 2009)—of socio-political structure that, in his thesis, constitute the two alternative modes of social organisation that follow each other in a continuous cycle of alternations. This cycle, analysed in the many empirical micro-details in which the pure and intermediate stages of these forms of organisation are expressed, is framed within a general scheme which also outlines the rise and decline of civilisations within the framework of this alternation between non-urbanised and urbanised forms of life.

Even the very structure of the *Muqaddima* is developed precisely on the basis of this scheme: it is by following this that Ibn Khaldūn firstly analyses the idea and conditions of social organisation in general, and then, more specifically, presents its two basic expressions. The analysis of the two is then enriched by a reflection on the transforming action of the ruling power, which is called upon to restrain antisocial instincts (on the assumption that "dynasty and royal authority have the same relationship to civilisation as form has to matter"[14]). Finally, a description of the

[14]That is, they constitute the external shape which, because of its specific qualities, preserves its existence (*Muqaddima* IV, 19; Ibn Khaldūn 1958, Vol. II: 300; Ibn Khaldūn [1967] 2005: 291).

material forms that characterise civilisation, and a review of the traditional and intellectual sciences developed there, are offered.

In order to define the organisation of society in a broad sense, Ibn Khaldūn significantly prefers the more dynamic and "living" term "*'umrān*"—which he redefines, however, in such a rich and complex way that it ends up constituting a sort of neologism (Talbi 1973: 59)—to the more common, but more static, term "*ijtimā,*"[15] used essentially to define the broader *genus* of social organisation.

In fact, the term "*'umrān*" comes from the root *'ayn*, *mim*, *ra*, which designates such concepts as the fact of visiting people, of living in a place or at home, of cultivating land, of being frequented, of making prosperous. It therefore conveys the ideas of populating a place, bearing fruit, cultivating, and enhancing.

In Ibn Khaldūn's picture, however—as in the etymology of Romance languages, too—the concept of "cultivating" extends well beyond its most natural and immediate sense to include human "cultivation" of the highest "level," that is, "culture"—the sciences, arts, and crafts—which "colours" a group and endows it with its own, typical characteristics. This concept therefore—an "operative concept," in Megherbi's reading—extends as an umbrella ideally to include all components of the social dimension. These range from the morphological element, mainly related to demography (a fact fraught with consequences for Ibn Khaldūn since, as we shall see, it determines the production of qualitative changes in the social structure in the face of quantitative increases), to the economic and "superstructural" ones, and up to values—the least immediately evident element, but also the most decisive in determining whether any given social group will head up or down in the vectorial orientation of its cycle of existence.

In fact, in Ibn Khaldūn's framework, the system that defines social organisation and civilisation is not only configured as complex because of its various components, but also as dynamically alive—*'umrān*, precisely (Amri 2008): while, externally, it appears to be essentially stable, it is actually internally crisscrossed by a double movement, which constantly modifies it according to two different trends.

On the one hand, there is a straight line (involving the sciences and the arts), which conforms to the tendency of all organic things to follow a pattern of development leading from simplicity to complexity—a line that would recall the principle of the passage from power to action, if we were to apply the Aristotelian scheme.

On the other hand, there is another trend in operation (involving individuals, cities and states, and civilisation as a whole) that follows the biological trajectory that goes through the phases of birth, growth, senility, and death, and is conversely characterised by a cyclical direction. According to the hypotheses of scholars such as Cheddadi (2006: 475), Pomian (2006), Dale (2015a), and others, this trend may suggest the different Aristotelian scheme that describes the cycle of generation and corruption, governing the nature of all living beings populating the earth. In fact, Ibn

[15]Thus, Turroni in Campanini (2005a: 135–136). *Ijtimā'* is the term also chosen by Al-Fārābī to translate the Greek word *koinonia*. The term *tamaddun* (from the root from which the word "*medina*" comes) more specifically indicates civilisation.

Khaldūn starts his analysis precisely from the definition of the nature of each social group (owing part of its essence to its environment and to the material conditions that characterise it) on the assumption that its specific nature will generate typical institutions and activities, and predictable historical trajectories.

His idea is, therefore, that society should be thought of not only as a natural object (in a naturalistic view—embedded, anyway, within a theocentric vision of the world). It is also a "living" subject, endowed with its own history, and characterised by regular dynamics of development (elements of its essence, defined by the ways in which its members join together in the environmental space they inhabit), as well as by distinctive internal and external characteristics (accidents) which also determine its developmental rhythm.

3.3 Two Ideal-Typical Conditions, Two Transformative Factors: An Alternate Cycle in the Background

3.3.1 Man Is the Offspring of Custom: "Fortitude" and Dependence, Autonomy and Heteronomy

The two essential models of *'umrān*—of society—, always transmuting into each other and defined by Ibn Khaldūn as "natural groups," are described in the *Muqaddima* according to structural dichotomies: on the one hand the countryside, on the other the city; on the one hand nomadic, on the other sedentary society; on the one hand a strong group solidarity (*'aṣabiyya*), on the other the explosion of individualistic selfishness (Baeck 1994: 115). The characteristics of these models are determined by the way of life adopted by the social groups: the man who grows and develops inside them is, in short, essentially forged by the life habits that he assumes there.

As Ibn Khaldūn writes at the beginning of his work:

> It should be known that differences of condition among people are the result of the different ways in which they make their living. Social organisation enables them to co-operate toward that end and to start with the simple necessities of life, before they get to conveniences and luxuries (*Muqaddima* II, 1. Ibn Khaldūn 1958, Vol. I: 249. Ibn Khaldūn [1967] 2005: 91).

Living together produces customs, specific traits, and habits (a habit—*malaka*—is defined by Ibn Khaldūn as a quality acquired by repeating an action or activity several times, until it is firmly established (*Muqaddima* III, 17)) which cooperate in determining the character of man:

> Man is a child of the customs and the things he has become used to. He is not the product of his natural disposition and temperament. The conditions to which he has become accustomed, until they have become for him a quality of character and matters of habit and

custom, have replaced his natural disposition (*Muqaddima* II, 5; Ibn Khaldūn 1958, Vol. I: 258; Ibn Khaldūn [1967] 2005: 95).[16]

Ibn Khaldūn corrects many stereotypes and clichés of his time from this perspective. For example, on this basis he denies the commonplace that attributed negative character traits to Jewish people:[17] these characteristics—he explains—are far from being attributable to a pre-existing and inherent nature of such a group. On the contrary, they are the product of his adaptation to continuous precarious political conditions of insecurity and, often, of oppression, in which Jewish people had to survive. In other words, the principle of social influence on human character traits explains slavery and persecution as being the cause, and certainly not the effect, of those traits.[18]

More specifically, the two basic models of society analysed by him are the *badāwa* and the *ḥaḍāra*. The first (from the root *ba*, *dal*, *waw*, linked to the word "bedouin," indicating an outdoor life) includes different typologies of non-urbanised social organisation, comprising both a nomadic type of life and that of rural sedentary communities located far from large urban centres. Within this typology, groups may have different characteristics: Ibn Khaldūn points out, for example, that among all types of nomads the camel drivers, forced to venture deep into the desert by the needs of their animals, are the wildest human beings that exist. By the same token, he writes, while nomads tend to be destroyers, farmers tend to be weak because of their dependence on urban organisation.

However, all the subtypes of *badāwa* have in common the fact of being based on a minimal political organisation, associated with an economically deprived and segmented lifestyle.

---

[16]In this affirmation of the importance of the social environment in defining the identity of its inhabitants, Baali (1988: 39) sees an anticipation of ideas subsequently developed, for example, in Cooley's theory ([1902] 1962: 152) of the "looking-glass self," according to which everyone tends to see himself as he believes others do. Also Mead's thesis (1934: 152–164) on the "generalised other" and on the abstraction of social expectations, factors that profoundly influence the thought of individuals, structured as it is as a conversation with these "others," is anticipated by Ibn Khaldūn's theory. Another author that Baali links to this is Charles Wright Mills, who stated (1939: 673) that it is on the basis of such socially constituted points of view that individuals approve or disapprove of given arguments as valid or invalid, logical or illogical.

[17]*Muqaddima* II, 18. Ibn Khaldūn (1958, Vol. I: 287). Ibn Khaldūn ([1967] 2005: 110): "The reason for this is that meekness and docility break the vigour and strength of group feeling. The (very fact) that people are meek and docile shows that (their group feeling) is lost. They do not become fond of meekness until they are too weak to defend themselves. Those who are too weak to defend themselves are all the more weak when it comes to withstanding their enemies and pressing their claims. The Israelites are a good example." See also *Muqaddima* VI, 39, where he attributes the bad character ascribed to Jewish people precisely to the defensive dispositions of character generated by the oppression historically exerted on them. See also Bernard Lewis ([1986] 1999: 129–30).

[18]*Muqaddima* II, 18; VI, 39. These observations have by far anticipated explanations that only from the eighteenth century onwards have been advanced to counter the political and social discrimination of Jewish people: Fischel (1958: 162–163).

The second model of society—defined as *ḥaḍāra* (*ḥa*, *ḍad*, *ra* is a root indicating the fence)—is the urban one,[19] marked, on the contrary, by a high division of labour and the presence of organised and institutionalised forms of power.

These two models, which constitute the poles between which the continuous oscillation of the cycle of political evolution moves, are both characterised by their own lifestyle, by a corresponding social and political system, and by a particular level of development of science and technology. The two main types of social aggregation, in fact, have *a'rāḍ*—that is, particular accidental attributes[20]—which are different and, in many ways, opposite and complementary. However, an infinite number of possibilities are allowed between the two extremes: far from constituting static and successive stages of development, they rather form, in their constant mutual recalling, a unique system of civilisation, simultaneously static and inwardly animated by cyclical movements governed by factors such as ambition, the feeling of group solidarity, and the corrupting effects of power.

In fact, civilisation is built by Ibn Khaldūn as a "bipolar" phenomenon (Cheddadi 2006: 476–477), stretching in the tension between the two models (one economically based on the minimum needed to survive, and one characterised by the search for luxury and the superfluous) which are conceived as recurring but never stable paradigms, alternating in a dynamic oscillation,[21] where the two opposite extremes never cease, in reality, to exercise their polarising function. In other words, the historical succession implied by the evolution cycle does not refer to the models themselves, but only to their historical realisations.

The history of the groups of peoples in these models—driven by laws endowed with a specific force, which are as constant as the laws governing the natural world—follows its own natural tendential direction, which can be captured beyond the apparent randomness of individual events. This, schematically, involves the rhythmic succession of precise phases in an unstoppable cycle.

Of the two poles, the one considered logically to come first is that of *badāwa*—the natural group that exists by necessity.[22] The reasons given by Ibn Khaldūn for this are mainly psychological. Actually, the inhabitants of the "natural group" of *badāwa*, immersed as they are in a frugal and natural lifestyle based on agriculture and pastoralism, and marked by the continuous risk of deprivation, are the only

---

[19]The life model of *ḥaḍāra*, however, also includes agricultural activity, and for this reason, as Franz Rosenthal (1958: lxxvii) notes, the two types of society can be said to be qualitatively diversified essentially on the basis of a quantitative gradation, moving from simple to complex.

[20]Here the term is used according to the meaning used by Aristotle, Avicenna, Averroes and St. Thomas Aquinas, identifying a secondary characteristic of an entity.

[21]While the linear progression—which is used here to describe the different stages of creation—can be seen as proto-Darwinian, West (2015) observes that the continuous and never resolved oscillation between the two poles typical of the dynamics involving *badāwa* and *ḥaḍāra* seems, instead, to be closer to the model of the evolutionary tendency towards "regression toward the mean" theorised by Darwin's cousin, Francis Galton.

[22]Aristotle in his *Politics* stated (1252b30), instead, that the city—the *polis*—exists by necessity. See also Stuurman (2015: 49).

peoples placed in the condition of aspiring to gain the comforts of *ḥaḍāra*. The opposite never happens.

This observation, both logical and empirical in character, imprints a primary dynamic movement on Ibn Khaldūn's scheme by identifying the unambiguous trend of the vector, driven by natural human aspirations, which moves socio-political transformations, in the ambition to move upwards towards the *ḥaḍāra*. "Urbanisation is found to be the goal to which the Bedouin aspires," (*Muqaddima* II, 3; Ibn Khaldūn 1958, Vol. I: 252; Ibn Khaldūn [1967] 2005: 93) and, thus, it is in this sense that political and social development moves forward. The inverse movement, although inevitable according to Ibn Khaldūn, is, therefore, configured only as a physically unavoidable undertow of the previous movement, never as the goal of a specific social intention.

Ibn Khaldūn describes the *badāwa* by looking at the way in which the principal human needs are met, starting with food. Given the characteristic lifestyle of the people of *badāwa*, food is necessarily limited to what is strictly necessary. In fact, the food consumed by the people of *badāwa* is hardly ever refined, their clothing is simple and their dwelling is functionally conceived, essentially, merely as a shelter.

In turn, in the nomadic situation this absence of a fixed dwelling determines the establishing of other features typical of this status, such as a minimalistic organisation of the human habitat, aimed at merely finding the bare means of subsistence, and the custom of common ownership of land.

The harshness and deprivations which make such a lifestyle unattractive, consequently also strengthen the group's members' tendency to marry only among their own people, and this explains, consequently, other characteristics given great importance in *badāwa*: first of all, the social and moral centrality accorded to lineage and family, understood as a system of kinship extended to the various nuclei of cousins often destined to marry among themselves; and also, in connection with this, purity of lineage, which is seen as the source, in this context, of the concept of "nobility."

Lifestyle, as we have seen, also has profound implications for the character and behaviour of people. Ibn Khaldūn says that the *badāwa* peoples (despite the diversity grouped under this ideal type) are not spoiled by indulgence in worldly pleasures, and are destined to develop a more upright character compared to urbanised people. The importance they attach to honour and loyalty is not undermined by attention to luxuries and comforts, as long as they keep within this lifestyle.

The conditions of their lives, characterised by a very low level of political organisation, prompt them to be autonomous, accustomed to being ever alert, and ready to fight in defence of themselves and their loved ones. In this context they develop the qualities of courage, pride, and, thus, "fortitude"[23] (a virtue particularly crucial in Ibn Khaldūn's framework of sociological explanation) emerges in them.

In fact, this virtue, generated by living as self-reliant people, often isolated, without guards or walls as protection, is not only fundamental in determining the

---

[23] *Muqaddima* II, 5. Ibn Khaldūn (1958, Vol. I: 258). Ibn Khaldūn ([1967] 2005: 95): "Fortitude has become a character quality of theirs, and courage their nature."

success of the transformative project set in motion under the guidance of a leader with the goal of conquering *ḥaḍāra*. It also plays a decisive role in determining and perpetuating the properties of the social organisation typical of *badāwa*.

This "fortitude" leads everyone, in the entire social group "coloured" by it, to compete with each other on an egalitarian basis and resist impositions from others.[24] In this context, the members of the group are not disposed to follow any heteronymous directives, unless on the basis of a proper and spontaneous decision driven by sincere admiration for a leader's personal qualities, and provided that mutual respect is guaranteed. In other words, the concept of sovereign power (*mulk*) cannot flourish in this context, where it is, instead, replaced by a strongly cohesive sociality where only a subject freely recognised and acclaimed as the very best, according to the values shared by the group, will be able to stand out—and, in any case, only as long as he continues to attract such a consensus. According to the logic of such a social formation, as soon as he shows signs of weakness, competition inevitably restarts.

Starting from these assumptions, two factors are the driving forces that set in motion the movement from *badāwa* towards civilisation and culture. First, an aspiration that pulls in this direction is needed, arising from a desire for luxury and an easier life. In the second place, an opportunity has to arise: the effective emerging of a recognised leader capable of attracting to himself the admiration and identification of his group and, thus, of combining it under his guide in order to realise its ambition for domination.

On the other hand, the lifestyle of the urbanised inhabitants of *ḥaḍāra*, a civilisation characterised by a division and specialisation of functions that grows in line with the size of a city's population, is characterised by a well-being which extends far beyond basic needs. Furthermore, the well-being produced by this cooperative system involves the gradual development of an increasingly compulsive habituation to comforts and luxury goods (*taraf*).

But, as if it were a historical counterbalance, the function of luxury in *ḥaḍāra* is ambiguous: an attractive end to be desired on the one hand, on the other it is also a vector of corruption, and it performs as such, until the inhabitants are completely stripped of their "fortitude" and find themselves laden with vain objects of consumption, but at the same time weakened, unarmed, and dependent on others "like women and children" (*Muqaddima* II, 5), even for the very defence of their lives.

In fact, this dependence and fragility constitute the negative backlash of the seemingly positive process, intentionally pursued to maximise well-being and security.

The habituation to comfort and well-being into which the *ḥaḍāra*'s inhabitants sink, together with their reliance on external elements such as the walls that surround

[24]As West observes (2015: ch. 2) in commenting on this characteristic of *badāwa*, it is perhaps not by chance, as evidence of a link still active between inhabited but not urbanised territory and the moral characteristics that it encourages, that even today, in some Maghreb countries such as Morocco, some lands remote from the centre, traditionally populated by nomadic groups, are usually defined as "lands of insolence," i.e., places where insubordination prevails.

them and the guards appointed by the government to defend their lives and their property, as well as the torpor brought about by their calmly predictable lives, regulated by laws organising and rationalising their existence, inevitably lead, once a certain point of equilibrium has been crossed, to the downward reversal of the cycle.

As a result, the very characters of the inhabitants of *ḥaḍāra* undergo a profound transformation, compared to their original state in the *badāwa*: corrupted by luxury and softness, nurtured by an individualism unleashed by the pursuit of increasingly fancy goods, they now acquire (they get their "colouring," Ibn Khaldūn says) those attitudes that, from a social point of view, are among the worst of defects,[25] such as lying and selfishness. At the same time—as one of the "propositions" at the beginning of one of his paragraphs says—because of their trust in authority, they lose their courage, together with those very qualities that determined their rise from *badāwa*: "The reliance of sedentary people upon laws destroys their fortitude and power of resistance" (*Muqaddima* II, 6; Ibn Khaldūn 1958, Vol. I: 258; Ibn Khaldūn [1967] 2005: 95).

Moreover, this corruption of character and spirit can be worsened by the specific defects of the form of power characteristic of an urbanised group. Since, as a rule, hardly anyone can avoid being hierarchically dominated by someone else in this social context, this situation progressively undermines the self-confidence and courage of the dominated people, producing an effect which is all the greater whenever power is exercised in a more *unjust* and *oppressive* way. In fact, an oppressive and intimidating domination, implemented by laws imposed through punishments inflicted on people who cannot defend themselves, ends up humiliating them by completely breaking their "fortitude," depriving them of their capacity to resist, and engendering inertia and resignation in their oppressed hearts.

Incidentally, this interesting observation on the interweaving of "fortitude" and the tendency to autonomy on the one hand, and degeneration and heteronomy on the other, is also re-proposed by Ibn Khaldūn in other more specific contexts in which this same dynamic takes place—producing, proportionally, the same results.

For example, in Chapter Six, Ibn Khaldūn warns that one has to be very careful about using oppressive and humiliating approaches in the education of students (being himself a charismatic and enlightened teacher, he might have derived his view from his own experience), and, even more so, in the education of children—both of them unequal and hierarchically ordered contexts *par excellence*.

In fact, an unrestrained use of power produces indirect negative effects arising, at both individual and collective levels, from the flawed construction of character that inevitably emerges as a consequence in the medium to long term. For this reason, Ibn Khaldūn—with arguments (Cheddadi 1994: 8) that are extremely innovative compared with his time's vision of teaching and education—vehemently urges the most sparing use possible of any oppressive discipline enforced, without patience, through

[25] *Muqaddima* II, 4. Ibn Khaldūn (1958, Vol. I: 254). Ibn Khaldūn ([1967] 2005: 94): "Their souls are coloured with all kinds of blameworthy and evil qualities."

punishments. In fact, this system, if we look to its long-term consequences, produces major systemic repercussions in the development of character, alongside its immediate effect of forcibly inculcating rules or ideas (an effect whose achievement is by no means certain). The humiliation and fear instilled in people who feel powerless to react impels them to defend themselves with lies and other such behaviours, until they become accustomed to them—as the effects of habits are "colourings" of the character that, after a while, become indelible.

Finally, this negative effect can be found at work, even from a much broader historical perspective, when a society moves on from autonomy to a rigid heteronomy, because of the social importance of the psychological effects of such a change. Ibn Khaldūn follows this causal pattern when he comments on the difference between the experience of Islam in its early and later stages. In its early stages, religious rules were not perceived by the faithful as imposed by external authority, but as intimately their own—something that had fed Muslim "fortitude" at the highest level. In its later stages, once religious enthusiasm had decreased and the rules ended up as rigid, external impositions, an important qualitative change in the relationship between believers and their own religion had occurred.[26]

3.3.2 **ʿAṣabiyya** *and Its Genesis in the* **Badāwa**

It is possible that some of the intuitions behind Ibn Khaldūn's acute analysis of the solidal concept of *'aṣabiyya* owed something to the very horizon on which the Maghrebin thinker's eyes fell, as he wrote in 1377. Immersed in the tribal and "segmented" reality of the desert in the Berber stronghold of Qal'at Ibn Salāma, Ibn Khaldūn managed to bring into focus the centrality of a factor of social aggregation whose radical importance has long escaped European thought. In fact, the latter has concentrated too much on (and for a long time had been imprisoned by) the classic legal-naturalist dichotomy according to which, from Hobbes ([1651] 1985) onwards, only a binary alternative was given between a totally abstract and disaggregated state of nature on the one hand, and, on the other, an associated state of life governed by a form of power justified because voluntarily conferred upon the sovereign, by virtue of the benefits that such a state of affairs brought to his rational subjects. Beyond these two extremes, *tertium non dabatur*.

Ibn Khaldūn, instead, not only theorises, but directly *observes* that political *power* (*mulk* in his terminology), which is typical of *ḥaḍāra*, does not at all exhaust the sources of social cohesion. In fact, the "imperative" phase of the *mulk* is dialectically produced by the mutation and development of the "attractive" form of aggregation of

[26] *Muqaddima* II, 6. See also, for example, the passage in which Ibn Khaldūn criticises the attachment to tradition when it is so blind as to incapacitate the production of an independent judgement, considering it an obstructive defect for an *imām*: *Muqaddima* III, 24. Ibn Khaldūn (1958, Vol. I: 395). Ibn Khaldūn ([1967] 2005: 158): "[The *imām*'s] knowledge is satisfactory only if he is able to make independent decisions. Blind acceptance of tradition is a shortcoming."

the *badāwa*, which does not amount to an imaginary state of asocial nature. On the contrary, it constitutes a very powerful form of sociality: one which has the power to stimulate a feeling of union, among its members, which is, in reality, even much stronger than the one which the State, governed by political power (conceptualised by Ibn Khaldūn in the contextualised sense of the *dawla*[27]), can stimulate.

As cited above, Ibn Khaldūn starts from the assumption, based on the *Qur'an* (90, 10; 91, 8), that, insofar as it is inherent to man,[28] the tendency towards injustice and mutual aggression cannot be eliminated unless restrained by religion or power.

In the situation of the *badāwa* all subjects have to rely on themselves for their defence, in the absence of any government or authority to take on the task of protecting them. However, "Their defence and protection are successful only if they are a closely knit group" (*Muqaddima* II, 7; Ibn Khaldūn 1958, Vol. I: 263; Ibn Khaldūn [1967] 2005: 97): the defensive strength provided by a united group not only protects the individual much more effectively, but it also plays a preventive function, as it deters external elements from offending. When the individually nourished "fortitude" of all these subjects takes the form of a reciprocal network of help and protections, not only is an effective defence provided, but fear and preventive respect are also stimulated. In short, in this context, the presence of the bond (the group spirit, or the sense of unity, impelling members to protect one another) constitutes almost the only real guarantee of survival for the individual.

This "concrete" and homogeneous sense of unity is *'aṣabiyya*. Organised according to a hierarchy of nobility and virtue—derived not from coercive power but from the internalisation of the values and the common identity of the group itself—it constitutes, compared with Hobbes' binary alternative, the "third possible form" of social structure, an alternative both to anarchy and to institutionalised power.

The cohesive *'aṣabiyya* of the *badāwa* binds together individuals relating with each other as "equals," proud of being its members, all equally participants in the collective enterprise.[29] Its members, linked by the common sensation of constituting a whole, are united not by fear or a disjointed calculation of rational self-interest, but by an emotionally founded, affective inner feeling, and by reasons which are to a large extent irrational (Francesco Gabrieli ([1930] 1984: 214) speaks here of a "suggestion of connection"), although their consequences are no less productive and real.

---

[27]The meaning of the term "*dawla*," generally translated as "dynasty" (today, it could be extensively brought back to the government of the "State," or more generally to "political unity"), refers to rotation and alternation from an unfortunate condition to a happy one (it is the same term used in Arabic to indicate the revolution of the stars).

[28]Ibn Khaldūn quotes, in this regard, a poem of his time that said that "if you find a moral man, there is some reason why he is not unjust" (*Muqaddima* II, 7. Ibn Khaldūn 1958, Vol. I: 262. Ibn Khaldūn [1967] 2005: 97).

[29]In this sense, Jon Anderson ([1983] 1984: 120), who defines *'aṣabiyya* as "a concept of relation by sameness, opposed both to the state (*dawla*) based on relations of difference or complementarity, and to religion (*din*), which alone supercedes it," grasps the transversality of the notion well.

The term comes from an Arabic root (*'ayn, ṣad, ba*) which indicates a pre-Islamic concept radically linked to the idea of bonding (and being bound), of connecting, of tightening and grouping together, and to an image of protective surrounding.[30] In order, therefore, to indicate the eminently socio-psychological phenomenon that he defines as "*'aṣabiyya*,"[31] Ibn Khaldūn has to evoke, and also enrich and "redefine," the Arabic term.

Differently translated by several critics in the sense adopted by him as "esprit de corps," "group feeling" or even, in a clearly anachronistic way, as "patriotism," Ibn Khaldūn's dynamic and propulsive *'aṣabiyya* constitutes the true "cornerstone" of his theory in relation to the changes that propel history forward.

The centrality attributed to union and togetherness throughout Ibn Khaldūn's theoretical construction confronts the reader from the very first lines of his work. In fact, Ibn Khaldūn emphasises the paramount importance of social compactness as early as his ritual dedication of the work to God and the Prophet, following whom the faithful "found unity while their enemies were weakened through dispersion" (*Muqaddima*, Invocation. Ibn Khaldūn 1958, Vol. I: 5. Ibn Khaldūn [1967] 2005: 3).[32]

It is precisely because of its importance in the construction of the sense of equal dignity and "fortitude" of its members that, in the *badāwa*, the *'aṣabiyya* can assume different degrees of intensity: in fact, it is much stronger among independent nomadic groups than among rural peasant populations, which are frequently subjected to the city and, consequently, weakened in spirit.

A corresponding scepticism about the moral stance of the peasant populations was also expressed in a *ḥadīṯ* attributed to Bukhārī (n. 2321), according to which the Prophet is reported to have said, in front of a plough: "There is no house in which this equipment enters except that Allāh will cause humiliation to enter it" (Gardet [1977] 2002: 148).

[30]This root is common to verbs indicating binding, bandaging, belting, putting oneself with, supporting someone, being fanatical about, cheering; to terms that can be translated as nerve, tendon, league, association, nervousness, camaraderie, group spirit (*'aṣabiyya*, precisely), bandage, gang, zeal, fanaticism, intolerance; and to adjectives that can be translated as neurotic, intolerant, fanatical, partisan. See Baldissera (2006). Other terms, drawn from the same root, indicate putting somebody at the head of a party (*'aṣaba*), waving a flag, being fanatical (*ta'aṣṣaba*), hardening (*in'aṣaba*); furthermore, nouns indicating a troop of men (*'iṣāba*), the élite of a group or the nerve holding a muscle together (*'aṣab*), a leader (*mu'aṣab*), and so on, are constructed from this root (Megherbi 1971: 159–160).

[31]Ibn Khaldūn's concept of *'aṣabiyya* has been regarded by many people as a clear forerunner not only of Durkheim's concept of "solidarity" (Durkheim after all, as already seen, was well acquainted with the work of Ibn Khaldūn), but also, in part—by virtue of its internal connotations—, as a forerunner of the concept of "social capital" which was first defined in 1916 by the sociologist Lyda Judson Hanifan, and then developed by Pierre Bourdieu, James Coleman and Robert Putnam, and which was also intuited by Alexis de Tocqueville (1835: ch. 4) when he wrote his first pivotal texts on liberal and democratic constitutionalism.

[32]Here, however, although the meaning is appreciably similar, the term used by Ibn Khaldūn is not "*'aṣabiyya*."

"Only tribes held together by group feeling can live in a desert," says one of the *Muqaddima*'s titles: in fact, this is precisely the factor[33] which, all things being equal, determines the success of the most united groups in the struggle for survival that takes place in the unfavourable environment of the *badāwa*—an environment which, Ibn Khaldūn says, is the source of its inhabitants' courage, pride and, eventually, "fortitude," precisely because of the hard challenges with which it continually presents them.

3.3.3 **ʿAṣabiyya** *as a Natural Force*

Ibn Khaldūn describes *'aṣabiyya* as the cohesive factor, linked primarily to the solidarity binding the family group, which creates the group and keeps it united, raising it to a dimension that transcends the individual. This is a primary social dimension that at the same time nourishes, and, in turn, produces, a unity of interests and a uniformity of behaviour that exponentially increases its members' strength. In this sense, *'aṣabiyya* as a social structuring factor determines both the unity of the group and the separation of its internal "we"-identity from what lies outside the group's boundaries.

The basis of the typically stimulating and propulsive action of *'aṣabiyya* (the "engine" of historical dynamics) is therefore, as Franz Rosenthal[34] wrote, the human need to belong to a group.[35]

The concept was essentially associated, in its common pre-Islamic use, with the particular and fragmentary logic of the familiar-tribal *'aṣabiyya*, and, therefore, it referred to the idea of "making common cause with one's own relatives."[36] As Ibn Khaldūn points out, however, although the primary meaning of the concept was linked to the tribal characteristics of social groups, it extended beyond the family dimension to include other types of social ties, also characterised by a feeling of sharing, such as relations with neighbours and relationships involving protection—in particular, alliance (*ḥilf*) and patronage (*walā'*).

---

[33]A fine definition of *'aṣabiyya* is given by Talbi (1973: 44): "L'asabiya est donc à la fois la force cohésive du groupe, la conscience qu'il a de sa specificité et de ses aspirations collectives, et la tension qui l'anime et la projette nécessarirement, sans qu'il ait la liberté du choix, par degrés vers la conquète du pouvoir. À sa base on trouve ainsi l'instinct de domination, et des phénomènes de foule." Talbi also defines it as (1973: 44) "un élan vital, ou comme une forme de lutte pour la vie se développant à l'echelle du groupe."

[34]F. Rosenthal (1987: 566): "Man's innate psychological need to belong and give political support to a group dominated by one or more leading personalities."

[35]In fact, pre-Islamic society was (and in part still is) characterised precisely by its being structured as a set of groups, more than as a set of individuals (Montgomery Watt 1961a: 6).

[36]A support essentially given, literally, "by party taken," that is, regardless of the justice of the cause in question. In this sense, the *'aṣabiyya* uniting clans and families may be compared to Banfield's (1958) concept of "amoral familism."

The reason for this is that, just like family relationships, these relationships also succeed in producing that psychological feeling of close belonging which prompts common defence and undisputed support for one's own group, as well as the sense of wounded pride and impulse to a defensive-offensive reaction[37] that arises when one of the group's associates is unjustly humiliated, attacked, and betrayed.

This is essential in the *badāwa*: in fact, in the absence of any institutionalised power, effective protection from other people's aggression is based not so much on moral principles, but rather on the immediate right of revenge that an attack on an individual arouses in the group to which the attacked person belongs. The loyalty of the group to its member must be balanced, at the same time, by the loyalty of the member to his own group (Montgomery Watt 1961b: 150–151).

This original form of *'aṣabiyya*, as an impulse blindly to support one's own group (even to the detriment of the wider collective social interest), is often associated, however, with forms of tribal misoneism, that is, with an orientation to view anything exogenous to the group hostilely. That is why it had been expressly condemned by early Islam. In fact, the Prophet himself, after initially escaping assassination by his own relatives, firmly condemned the antagonisms and the competitive tribal-type fragmentation encouraged by this primary form of *'aṣabiyya* (that Megherbi (1971: 165) defines, with reference to its family-clan dimension, "*'aṣabiyya-nasab*"): in a *ḥadīṯ* of Abū Da'wud, Muhammad is reported to have said: "He is not one of us who calls for *'aṣabiyya*, or who fights for *'aṣabiyya* or who dies for *'aṣabiyya*."[38]

Islam had intervened with all its super-cohesive force to counter tribalism by uniting different tribes on the basis of a superior identity bestowed by the principles of faith, and by bringing this sense of unity to encompass society as a whole. The transcendental dimension of Islam had, therefore, succeeded in elevating instances of tribal sociality, typical of nomadic culture, to the higher level of the entire *Umma* of the faithful. By projecting them to a dimension of ethical transcendence it gathered all its believers under its umbrella, thus outsourcing beyond the *Umma*, in a clear divide between Moslems and infidels (Coltman-Brown 1981: 19), all residual and ineradicable drives to conflict and the submission of others.

As Ibn Khaldūn explains (*Muqaddima* III, 26), the objective of the Prophet's condemnation[39] was not the spirit of solidarity per se, but the contrasting and competitive aspect of *'aṣabiyya*—the element, in fact, that prevented the different

[37]Bouthoul (1930: 45–46) writes that in this explanation one can sense the influence of his specifically North African experience. In relation to this, the founder of polemology argues that the particular passion of the austere Berber societies for individual or collective revenge, together with the culture of hatred and the taste for violence and revenge, is also liable to be interpreted as an outlet for the monotony of an existence which, in such a socio-environmental context, does not allow people to invest their energies and ambitions in other types of objectives (such as wealth gathering, study, art or travel).

[38]Quoted in Ahmad (2003: 114).

[39]This is the sura *The Private rooms*. In verse 13 it is written: "in God's eyes, the most honoured of you are the ones most mindful of Him" (*Qur'an* 49, 13) (Haleem 2004: 339).

clans composing the Arab society of his time from coalescing into a single community that could unite their hearts, and make them ready to die for each other. Muhammad's aim was, therefore, not to censor *'aṣabiyya* in itself, but to direct it towards virtuous purposes.

In the sense in which Ibn Khaldūn uses this term, however, it simply refers to the centripetal force that holds a group together, and as such it is not judged, but rather scientifically studied—just as a physical law could be—as the real, fundamental and ineradicable component of social dynamics.

Beyond any partisanship and ideology, *'aṣabiyya* is analysed by Ibn Khaldūn as a "natural force" and as such is literally described, with references explicitly taken from the world of physics: as when, for example, Ibn Khaldūn explains that its force is more powerful at its centre than at its edges, and that for this reason an attack on the "*medina*" (the vital centre of the kingdom) is comparable to an attack on the beating heart (*qalb*) from which a person's vital spirit emanates (*rūḥ*), and has, thus, more deadly effects for the dynasty than a peripheral attack; or as when he reflects on the fact that when the group's sense of cohesion builds up to the maximum possible, it eventually weakens and—like a soap bubble, we might say—loses restraining force.

By the same token, says Ibn Khaldūn, when the dynasty enters the stage of senility, it is precisely from its edges or borders that the process of weakening quietly begins, until it finally gets to its heart. Conversely, if it is struck directly in its centre—in the heart—, it immediately dies at its edges too. Even more examples proposed by Ibn Khaldūn, always referring to the natural world, suggest the deep similarity that links this sociological phenomenon to parallel physical phenomena. One more example is the comparison he suggests with rays of light, which fade away as they expand from their centre, or another that compares the strength of the cohesive group to ripples in water, which lose definition as they expand until they disappear.

Similarly, just as, in general, "the life of everything that comes into existence depends on the strength of its character,"[40] it is numerical force that proportionally determines the strength of *'aṣabiyya* in its three physical dimensions: the *power* of the dynasty built on it, the extent of the *space* over which it is exercised, and its duration in *time*.[41]

---

[40]*Muqaddima* III, 8. Ibn Khaldūn (1958, Vol. I: 331). Ibn Khaldūn ([1967] 2005: 130): "The life of anything that comes into being depends upon the strength of its temper."

[41]This is the initial proposition of *Muqaddima* III, 8. Ibn Khaldūn (1958, Vol. I: 330). Ibn Khaldūn ([1967] 2005: 129): "The strength of a dynasty, the extent of its territory, and the length of its duration depend upon the numerical strength of its supporters."

3.3.4 ʿAṣabiyya *Is Rooted in Imagination*

In the harsh and impoverished environment of the *badāwa*, the *'aṣabiyya*, perceived there as vital, is stimulated to its utmost and reaches its peak.

As we saw, the first among the factors capable of producing *'aṣabiyya* is blood ties. This factor is reinforced by the fact that endogamy, especially in nomadic groups, is almost inevitable. Incidentally, precisely the primary role it plays in the construction of *'aṣabiyya* explains the enormous importance attributed to genealogy in nomadic societies such as the Arab—but think also of the genealogies minutely listed in the Bible.

Even if family should be understood philologically, here, in a properly agnatic sense (since, originally, the term precisely indicated kinship along the male line), this peculiarity, stemming from essentially historical-social reasons (i.e., the patriarchy of such groups), is not a necessary part of Ibn Khaldūn's definition.

As Megherbi has pointed out, this was not only because the family clan united by *'aṣabiyya* existed, and was relevant, along both agnatic and cognatic lines,[42] but above all because, beyond the limits of blood, *'aṣabiyya* also grouped within its own gravitational field individuals, such as clients or allies, linked by relationships other than family (see, today, Haidt 2012: chaps. 9 and 10).

The decisive factor, then, had to be something that was well beyond the parental line and even *beyond* the family, seen simply as the most immediate and natural example of relationship. The unifying element lying behind all kinds of *'aṣabiyyāt* should be identified, for Ibn Khaldūn, in a psychological and imaginative factor: an *idea* of connection (*Muqaddima* III, 18).

Without the activation of imagination, not even family succeeds in creating the sense of the group—while, on the other hand, imagination is capable of creating bonds of empathic sympathy even among people who would otherwise be strangers to each other, when activated by the impact of "narratives" that establish imaginative bonds and then build upon them. For example, a kinship between distant cousins unknown to each other, although real and proven on paper, would, in the end, have no force at all without their underlying imaginative aspects, and their relative capacity to arouse empathy. Therefore, when the sense of communion normally produced in families by daily custom is missing, it can be compensated for by that key element which comes not so much from the genetic link itself (since, as Ibn Khaldūn writes, "a pedigree is something imaginary and devoid of reality" (*Muqaddima* II, 8; Ibn Khaldūn 1958, Vol. I: 264–265; Ibn Khaldūn [1967] 2005: 99)), but, precisely, from the imagination aroused by the idea of the common bond.[43]

---

[42]The tribe or clan united by *'aṣabiyya* in the North African context can be seen, taking up a definition by Germaine Tillion (1966: 11), as a "republic of cousins."

[43]*Muqaddima* III, 18. Ibn Khaldūn (1958, Vol. I: 374). Ibn Khaldūn ([1967] 2005: 148): "The consequences of common descent, though natural, still are something imaginary. The real thing to bring about the feeling of close contact is social intercourse, friendly association, long familiarity, and the companionship that results from growing up together, having the same wet nurse, and

In short, the cohesive bond basically works on an imaginary and evocative level, and lies in the ideal, empathic identification with the other, prompted by the fact that this other person is considered as being part of one's own *'aṣabiyya* of mutual help.

It is, therefore, precisely because of its inability to actually move the imagination and arouse unifying emotions, that even a real kinship, when too distant in time or space, becomes practically ineffective (*Muqaddima* II, 8; III, 18), whereas a "living" relationship of alliance or patronage—capable of triggering a sense of connection (*al-iltiḥām*: *Muqaddima* II, 8; Ibn Khaldūn 1958, Vol. I: 264; Ibn Khaldūn [1967] 2005: 98) and identification in a more essential way—, can easily produce that psychological and imaginative drive that is the essence of *'aṣabiyya*.[44]

In short, behind its genealogical "grounding," the true essence of *'aṣabiyya* lies in the sense of common identity that can be produced in people's conscience by stimuli related to the identity of their interests, aspirations, and destiny and, in general, by a wide variety of other possible brotherhood-building conditions. Even more explicitly, Ibn Khaldūn writes that

> When the things resulting from common descent are there, it is as if (common descent) itself were there, because the only meaning of belonging to one or another group is that one is subject to its laws and conditions, as if one had come into close contact with it (*Muqaddima* II, 10; Ibn Khaldūn 1958, Vol. I: 267; Ibn Khaldūn [1967] 2005: 100).

It is important to understand its nature because, particularly in situations of environmental disadvantage and deprivation, the aggregating factor given by *'aṣabiyya* is not only the original generator of the creation and maintenance of the strength of the social group, but its strength or weakness also determines, more than any other element, the success (even military) of the ascending ambition of groups coming from the margins of civilisation.

Despite the fact that these groups may be materially worse equipped, the force produced by this factor leads them to prevail over groups already immersed in well-being and, thus, corrupted by materialistic individualism, and destined to crumble and submit to more cohesive social forces.

This is so, because *'aṣabiyya* produces a strong drive to fight in defence of the group: union and combativeness go together, as *'aṣabiyya* urges putting the collective interests of one's own group before the atomistic interests of the individual, and leads its members to see death for the sake of the group as the most glorious and honourable thing. This total solidarity is decisive in the face of the sacrifices required by the struggle for survival[45] in the difficult, ever potentially warlike environment of the *badāwa*.

---

sharing the other circumstances of death and life. Observation of people shows this to be so." The same dynamic applies to the relationship with clients and allies.

[44]In a recent work, Lilian Abou-Tabickh (2019) supports the idea of the voluntary, "manifactured" nature of such bonds, instead.

[45]As West points out (2015: ch. 3), Darwin (1871) too, in *The Descent of Man*, observed that the probability of winning battles is strongly unbalanced in favour of groups highly bound by

So, in the push towards *ḥaḍāra*, willingness to sacrifice, conviction, and immersion in the common objective of groups determined to fight "for themselves" and the glory of their own communities, are infinitely greater than those of the groups which, crushed at the lowest levels of a hierarchicalised and institutionalised structure (as is typically the case in *ḥaḍāra*), have to fight out of duty, fear of punishment, or the need for reward, as in the case of a mercenary armed force.

3.4 Super-*'Aṣabiyya*, and Super-Cohesive Factors

For an *'aṣabiyya* feeling to be produced, first of all, a sufficient level of value conformity and cultural unity is required, expressed in the awareness of the group's specific common values and "norms" (*Muqaddima* II, 10): it is on this basis[46] that the identity of the group itself is built and defined.

Important consequences follow from this. Ibn Khaldūn writes, for example, that a dynasty is rarely able to settle safely on lands inhabited by many different groups and "tribes,"[47] because this situation leads to a plurality of opinions and an attachment to different goals. Where there is a separate *'aṣabiyya* to guard every group and its aspiration,[48] such "pluralism" is an obstacle to the construction of a stable civilisation.

The logic of the cohesive force, in fact, implies important corollaries, including those which relate to the overlapping or opposition that occurs among different group loyalties coexisting within a larger and composite social group. The presence of this variety of solidarities may depend both on external factors (such as the conquest of already socially organised lands) and internal factors. As the *'aṣabiyyāt* of the conquered groups annexed to the main one help to expand the social whole, and as this society gradually organises itself to produce a life of well-being, it becomes more and more internally differentiated; at the same time the alliance system (*ḥilf*) sets in motion a process which immerses allied groups simultaneously in two *'aṣabiyyāt*—their own, and also the stronger one of the dominant group which they join and strengthen further.

patriotism, loyalty, obedience, courage, and empathy, where members are ready to help and sacrifice for each other. He classified it as a mechanism of natural selection.

[46]See, in the twentieth century, Talcott Parsons (1951).

[47]It is precisely for this reason, Ibn Khaldūn says, that in places characterised by a minor presence of the tribal phenomenon, such as Andalusia, Egypt or Syria, it is much easier to found a lasting dynasty. Riots are rare, and consequently the upper classes are able to maintain themselves more easily over time.

[48]*Muqaddima* III, 9. Ibn Khaldūn (1958, Vol. I: 332). Ibn Khaldūn ([1967] 2005: 130): "A dynasty rarely establishes itself firmly in lands with many different tribes and groups. This is because of differences in opinions and desires. Behind each opinion and desire, there is a group feeling defending it."

The key to the success of a governing force in such a situation rests precisely with its capacity firmly to guarantee, in the face of all these minor "*'aṣabiyyāt*," a preponderant role for its own larger *'aṣabiyya*, which needs to remain the strongest one (we could define it a super-*'aṣabiyya*), in order to be able to contain and, eventually, unify all the others. As Ibn Khaldūn observes, in fact, reinforcing his thesis with analogies taken from physics:

> When the elements are combined in equal proportions, no mixing can take place. One (element) must be superior to the others, and when (it exercises) its superiority over them, mixing occurs. In the same way, one of the various [...] group feelings must be superior to all, in order to be able to bring them together, to unite them, and to weld them into one group feeling comprising all the various groups (*Muqaddima* III, 10; Ibn Khaldūn 1958, Vol. I: 336–337; Ibn Khaldūn [1967] 2005: 132).

In order to avoid divisions, dissent and clashes and, in the end, inevitable disintegration, it is, therefore, necessary to identify a superior *'aṣabiyya*—a "super-*'aṣabiyya*"—which can operate as a common framework and reference in which all the others can combine to form a wider cohesive unity.[49] If different groups are to coexist in harmony, or even to amalgamate, they need, in short, to be united under the protection of one of them—the strongest of all,[50] the central *'aṣabiyya*, source of power and civilisation.

All the groups joined together in this super-*'aṣabiyya* contribute, in this way, to develop the identity of the composite, unified group. In this process—provided that the super-*'aṣabiyya* maintains its dominant role—the annexed groups, in fact, increase the strength of the dominant one and, thus, its capacity for conquest.

Different factors come together to maintain a position of strength for the central *'aṣabiyya*. First of all, one of the key elements lies in a real disparity of forces in favour of the majority *'aṣabiyya*, compared to that of the other groups. As Mahdi (1957: 197) comments, composite groups "cannot form a harmonious whole except when arranged hierarchically with an undisputed leader at the top."

The *'aṣabiyya* of the strongest group—and, even more so, of the "super-*'aṣabiyya*" produced precisely by this enlargement and strengthening—then, tends, in turn, to incorporate neighbouring *'aṣabiyyāt* unless they are equally powerful: this state of affairs continues until the senility of the group. As Ibn Khaldūn observes, in fact, because of the submissive character that this domination induces, the resulting submissive group, forced to pay taxes to another group, can never produce, or maintain within itself, any royal authority powerful enough to compete with that of the majority.

---

[49] *Muqaddima* II, 16. Ibn Khaldūn (1958, Vol. I: 284–285). Ibn Khaldūn ([1967] 2005: 108): "Even if an individual tribe has different 'houses' and many diverse group feelings, still, there must exist a group feeling that is stronger than all the other group feelings combined, that is superior to them all and makes them subservient, and in which all the diverse group feelings coalesce, as it were, to become one greater group feeling. Otherwise, splits would occur and lead to dissension and strife."

[50] *Muqaddima* III, 10. Ibn Khaldūn (1958, Vol. I: 336). Ibn Khaldūn ([1967] 2005: 132): "Group feeling [...] is something composite that results from (amalgamating) many groups, one of which is stronger than all the others."

> Man is a natural leader by virtue of the fact that he has been made a representative (of God on earth). When a leader is deprived of his leadership and prevented from exercising all his powers, he becomes apathetic, even down to such matters as food and drink (*Muqaddima* II, 23; Ibn Khaldūn 1958, Vol. I: 301; Ibn Khaldūn [1967] 2005: 117).

In fact, whoever loses control over their life and knows that all chances of controlling it are over, because they have become an instrument of others, heads towards their own ruin. Such is the nature of man, and not only man: the same orientation can also be seen in the behaviour of wild animals, which, once captured, undergo a transformation (a subtle symptom of the same process) even in their basic habits, such as eating and drinking (*Muqaddima* II, 23).

Similarly, the same apathy that takes hold of those who lose control over their own affairs, becoming dependent on others, causes a nation, once beaten and fallen under the domination of another, to perish quickly and even lose its own identity: in such a situation, the frustration of the ascensional perspectives and desire to emerge drives the group to withdraw into itself. In fact, while solidal unity can be produced on the basis of free submission to a leader and spontaneous consent, as is the case in the *'aṣabiyya* emerging from the *badāwa*, it is very difficult for it to develop in a situation of forced submission.

This situation will also negatively influence the rate of population growth in the group, as the propensity to grow also depends on the presence of strong hope and future perspectives—elements that, in turn, generate energy in people's animal strength, influencing their reproduction rate. But if this is lacking, the drive to reproduction will also diminish.

The loss of any possible ameliorating perspective, however, is not the only factor weakening the *'aṣabiyya* of groups subject to forms of domination. A further important sociological factor identified by Ibn Khaldūn—an attractive element, this time—plays a role in this direction: the fact that weaker groups will normally endeavour to imitate the dominant one. This social trend presides over the harmonisation and unification of *'aṣabiyyāt* in a higher framework, and is determined, Ibn Khaldūn says (with words that seem to anticipate René Girard's theory[51] of mimetic desire), by the tendency of the "defeated" to imitate the customs of the group that has come to power, out of attraction towards the strong winning model (see García Lizana 2006).

As Ibn Khaldūn writes, "The vanquished always want to imitate the victor in his distinctive characteristics, his dress, his occupation, and all his other conditions and

[51] According to René Girard's ([1961] 2002) theory of mimetic desire, desire for an object is based not so much on its intrinsic value, but rather on the fact that a prestigious Other possesses such an object. For this reason desire, which, in itself, is amorphous and never satiated, is projected onto that object (cf. Verza 2015a, b). Girard also applied his theory of mimetic desire to the cultural clash taking place today between Islam and the West. In the light of his intuition, today's Islamic terrorism, in order to be correctly understood, should not be framed on the basis of the categories of difference, but on the basis of the concept of competition against a model—precisely the object of mimetic desire. In fact, those fighters seem to adopt both the values and ideals of personal success of the West against which they fight, together with its expressive styles, models of consumption and technological idiosyncrasies.

customs" (*Muqaddima* II, 22; Ibn Khaldūn 1958, Vol. I: 229; Ibn Khaldūn [1967] 2005: 116). This happens, he explains, because the soul yearns for the perfection of the person appearing superior—either because of the respect due to them, or because it mistakenly thinks that their superiority is due not to their victory, but to their greater degree of refinement. A similar process can be observed in children's imitation of their father, or in the fashion for military clothing raging in the historical phases when populations are openly governed by militias.

Once this erroneous conviction settles in the soul, it becomes a firm belief, and this will make the defeated subject feel inclined to adopt all the customs of the victor, and conform to his habits—so much so, that an intelligent observer will be able to deduce the external domain from the imitated customs and clothes.[52]

Finally, even religion itself, Ibn Khaldūn says, can exert a super-cohesive and important unifying influence on society: in fact, as Madhi (1957: 201) writes, religion

> creates new loyalty, absolute belief in, and obedience to, the demands of Law and the religious leader. [...] Second to natural solidarity and based on it, religion is the most powerful force in the creation of civilisation, and it commands the most effective instrument for preserving it.

However, this can only happen provided that religion relies on a pre-existing, basic *'aṣabiyya*:[53] in this sense, religion is only "additional" (*Muqaddima* III, 5) to natural solidarity. The altruism that the logic of *'aṣabiyya* generates is itself conceived, in fact, not as universal but, on the contrary, as "parochial," tribal and coupled with moral indifference towards those who are not part of the reference group.

Therefore, while it is certainly true that the most powerful dynasties often base and found their values and legitimacy in religion, nevertheless, as Ibn Khaldūn objectively points out, religious propaganda cannot produce its effects in the absence of an underlying, prior and necessary "natural" *'aṣabiyya*,[54] produced by the sense of commonality of the group's members, and which is all the more powerful the more numerous the group itself is.

---

[52]In Ibn Khaldūn's theory there are two mimetic processes involved, which proceed in opposite directions: on the one hand, in relation to the *'aṣabiyya* of afference, the defeated always want to imitate the victor in his distinctive characteristics, his dress, his occupation and all his other conditions and customs. On the other hand, in relation to culture, which is normally more developed in the conquered sedentary civilisation than in the group coming from *badāwa*, the victor appropriates the culture of the conquered civilization (as if it were "spoils of war"): see *Muqaddima* III, 13. The expression "spoils of war" to describe the legacy acquired by the new victors, used by French-speaking novelist Kateb Yacine, is quoted in Bozarslan (2014: 46).

[53]Ibn Khaldūn cites the Jewish people as an example of a group to which God Himself has promised the attainment of royal authority through the consecration of His *'aṣabiyya* (*Muqaddima* II, 12).

[54]"[...] profecy, the establishment of royal authority, or propaganda. Nothing can be achieved in these matters without fighting for it, since man has the natural urge to offer resistance. And for fighting one cannot do without group feeling [...]" (Muqaddima II, 7; Ibn Khaldūn 1958, Vol. I: 263; Ibn Khaldūn [1967] 2005: 98).

In sum, the need for a particular *'aṣabiyya* on which to found the sense of common religious identity responds to psycho-social needs. To avoid the disintegration of the sense of collective identity and of the relative group loyalty, perceivable (and therefore, by necessity, not too extensive) boundaries, within which to define the "us"-identity, are necessary. The existence of a different element from oneself, beyond these boundaries, on which to channel aggressive tension diverting it from the internal domain, also effectively counteracts the tendency to return to atomism. Only once this basis—inevitably non-universal—is laid, is it possible to widen the extent of loyalty.

When this basic *'aṣabiyya* is joined by the religious factor (which, by virtue of its universal scope, is able to connect its members above their particular affiliations), it acquires considerable additional strength.[55] One of the "secrets" of this union lies in the fact that the idealistic and "high" projection determined by the religious afflatus, together with the quality (the "colouring") that it imprints on the human soul, manages to lead individual hearts and desires to harmony. In fact, a powerful aggregator such as religion can succeed in making many individuals feel as one, and can, consequently, motivate them to act in unison, even in relation to their own objectives. It does so by sweeping away the separations and jealousies which, on the contrary, with their disruptive function, tend to prevail when the heart turns to worldly goals succumbing to "false desires," oppositional and never definitely fulfilled (*Muqaddima* III, 4).

Whereas other groups, not united by such strength, are humble, divided, frightened by death and weakened by the false and counterproductive pursuit of earthly goods, religiously-inspired groups, thanks to their convergence on a common transcendental purpose, form a formidable, strong unit, made up of individuals readily willing to die for the good of the community.[56]

In this sense, religions (Ibn Khaldūn analysed Islam in particular) have had—and have—a particular catalysing capacity, being capable of repressing individualism in favour of a brotherhood extended in space (in relation to its borders, expanded far beyond what is determined by direct social ties[57]), and in time (beyond the natural duration of the cohesive force of a natural *'aṣabiyya*).

---

[55] *Muqaddima* III, 5. Ibn Khaldūn (1958, Vol. I: 320). Ibn Khaldūn ([1967] 2005: 126): "Religious propaganda gives a dynasty at its beginning another power in addition to that of the group feeling it possessed as the result of the number of its supporters."

[56] The same concept underlies Ara Norenzayan's study ([2013] 2015), where it is claimed that the great religions, precisely because of their capacity to suppress individual selfishness in favour of the group, have been decisive for the transition from *Gemeinschaft* to *Gesellschaft*, and for the latter's endurance over time.

[57] A similar logic was adopted—albeit on a political level—in Greek history when Cleisthenes, in 508–507 B.C., understood that the clan structure had to be forcibly disrupted in order to enlarge the boundaries of group loyalties beyond the natural primary dimension of the family, and, thus, bring about a democracy. Thus, he reorganised the four dominant groups into ten new groups, based on 30 political regions that were, in turn, also broken up, and eliminated patronymics, replacing them with demonyms.

As a demonstration of this, Ibn Khaldūn recalls (*Muqaddima* III, 5) how, at the beginning of the history of Islam, in al-Qādisiyya, an army of only 30,000 Muslims managed to defeat first a Persian army of 120,000 units and then 400,000 Byzantine soldiers. Ibn Khaldūn also shows how they were able to hold on to these conquests, thanks to the fact that the group, precisely because of the cohesive force of religion, was able to remain compact even after the death of the charismatic leader who had initially united them.

As a matter of fact, however, *'aṣabiyya* does not depend on its religious "colouring": this is only one of its possible qualities, since *'aṣabiyya* is basically a form of natural power, which is generated, operates and mutates on the basis of its own laws, which are as natural as the laws of physics. Precisely for this reason, in its political development, it is also subject to the cyclical process that involves the corruption—ineluctable because it is natural—of every kind of organism (collective and otherwise), thus following the nature of the basic *'aṣabiyyāt* with which it merges and unites.

3.5 *'Aṣabiyya* and Leadership as Catalysts of Political Dynamics

3.5.1 The Origins of Leadership in the Badāwa

The basis that makes the birth of royal authority, and thus of power, possible, as Ibn Khaldūn clearly explains, is determined by the "upstream" existence of a cohesive group, strengthened by the sense of its own identity and by *'aṣabiyya*, a feeling of mutual affection and willingness to fight and die for each other.[58] Especially in rural societies, where no institutionalised forms of power exist (even the elders' authority is based on respect and not on fear or coercion), and where defence is delegated to the members of the group themselves, both the aggressive and defensive forces of such a group depend on the prior existence of this organisational and catalysing factor.

But while *'aṣabiyya* is essential, as it makes protection, mutual defence, and social activities in general possible, allowing individuals to assert their claims, thanks to the support and backing of the group, yet on its own it is not sufficient to guarantee the safety of its members. As we have already seen, a tendency towards aggression is, in fact, intrinsic to man: for this reason, the group tends to identify a leader within its borders—the subject most capable of emanating, evoking, and channelling this cohesive force—so that he can exert a restraining influence and mediate among the members of the group, preventing men from fighting each other. Therefore, in this situation, the leader performs his function not only by ensuring the

[58] *Muqaddima* III, 1. Ibn Khaldūn (1958, Vol. I: 313). Ibn Khaldūn ([1967] 2005: 123): "*'aṣabiyya* which means affection and willingness to fight and die for each other."

protection of his community from potential aggressions coming from outside, but also from within the community itself, where tendencies towards mutual aggression need to be curbed.

The characteristics of the *'aṣabiyya*-based sociality, typical of *badāwa*, also affect the nature of the relationship existing between the leader and his group.

Unlike what happens in urban societies, in the situation of the *badāwa*, where the *'aṣabiyya* essentially unites "peer" and autonomous subjects, the respect paid to a leader endowed with charisma is not based on constraint, but is produced naturally, thanks to the leader's qualities, in the intrinsically competitive situation of a group of equals. The leader is the one most effectively able to concentrate the group's sense of belonging around himself, thus generating and reinforcing a sort of "internal point of view"[59] in relation to his authority. In short, the one who, against the background of a form of social union based on *'aṣabiyya*, succeeds in emerging as a leader, is only able to be so by consensus, not by force.

For this reason, where Ibn Khaldūn emphasises the personal qualities of a leader,[60] he stresses the importance of his natural authority in particular—a concept that was unthinkable at the time in the West, where power was thought to be conferred by God's will, but plausible in Islam, where even the *imām* was supposed to be "the best" of all by definition (Ben Salem 1972: 300).

Being not only respected, but also admired and feared, such a leader needs, above all, to be endowed with a natural ability[61] to evoke the state of emotional fusion with the group—with the "collective self" that absorbs the individual self—in which the *'aṣabiyya* consists, so as to make the spontaneous loyalties of its members converge there (since, in this phase, its "strength" can be based only on these).

Therefore, in this phase (Rabi' 1967: 134–135) the internal hierarchy (which, in the *ḥaḍāra*, is based on strength) is only germinal, and, above all, is formed naturally and based on free consent. Only the groups endowed with a leader with such characteristics will be able to catalyse and organise their forces effectively, so as to realise their ambition, naturally aimed at the conquest of *ḥaḍāra* and the foundation of their own dynasty.

Ibn Khaldūn does not miss the impalpable and a-rational essence of the quality of "leadership"—similar to that which, in Weber's vocabulary (derived, not surprisingly, from religious language), would be later defined as "charismatic." In this regard, he comments that the ability to gain control of the group is a quality bestowed by God—something that, in its essence, is not related to rational factors such as, for example, the "rightness" of a leader's ideas. Without that "divine gift" (charisma, in fact), it is not possible to lead a group successfully: for this reason, those who try and undertake political enterprises without being endowed with the gift of "divine call,"

---

[59]In Herbert L.A. Hart's sense (1961).

[60]*Muqaddima*, II, 19. Ibn Khaldūn (1958, Vol. I: 291). Ibn Khaldūn ([1967] 2005: 111): "A sign of royal authority is a person's eager desire to acquire praiseworthy qualities, and vice versa."

[61]Ibn Khaldūn's frequent expression describing a leader as the one who "possesses" the superior *'aṣabiyya* should be understood in this sense (e.g., *Muqaddima*, II, 11).

bestowed by their capacity for leadership, make a serious error of judgement. That is why they are inevitably punished by history with ridicule and are described as "madmen," if not worse.

To sum up, Ibn Khaldūn concludes, the legitimation of power lies in its very success:[62] political endeavours must be undertaken only when there is an effective possibility of bringing them to a successful conclusion (*Muqaddima* III, 6), which is confirmed by the effectiveness of the "gift" of leadership.

However, religious factors can also contribute to nourish the *'aṣabiyya* and, therefore, the "grip" and prestige (*jah*) of a leader (Megherbi 1971: ch. 6): for example, it is not infrequent for a leader, in order to galvanise the masses, to express his charisma in a religious fashion, going as far as substituting himself for the Prophet. Even more frequent is the case of leaders who use religion genealogically, claiming descent from the Prophet or from his companions[63] in order to increase their reputation.

Incidentally, this custom also partly explains the characteristics of pre-Khaldunian Arab historiography, especially that of the Maghreb, to the extent (Megherbi 1971: 175–176) that Ibn Khaldūn[64] notes with amazement the very unusual attitude of Yaġamrāsan b. Zayyān when he said of himself: "We gained worldly power and royal authority with our sword, not through (noble) family connections. The usefulness of (our royal authority for us) in the next world depends on God."

3.5.2 *Change of Leadership in the* Ḥaḍāra

Once the *ḥaḍāra* stage has been reached, leadership is transformed into power (*mulk*). When the goal of the conquest of *ḥaḍāra* is achieved, the new goal of the group is the creation of a more solid and stable condition, more capable of resisting uncertainty. As Ibn Khaldūn says, the aims of a leader, at that stage, are directed to secure royal power, glory, peace, and a more comfortable lifestyle. In fact, just as the assurance of sustenance granted by abundance is the natural aim of a group emerging from a condition of deprivation, similarly, also the transition to royal authority—that is to say, to a consolidation of whatever ensures a certain and safe leadership—is the ultimate goal towards which a leader (who initially became such in a context of instability where his "grip" on the group was linked to the precariousness of consensus) naturally aims.

[62]The phenomenon does not necessarily require a religious basis, since, as Ibn Khaldūn points out, it also occurs among pagans.

[63]This is not too difficult, since tradition reports (Megherbi 1971: 175) that there were about 100,000 of them.

[64]*Muqaddima* II, 11. Ibn Khaldūn (1958, Vol. I: 272). In Ibn Khaldūn ([1967] 2005) the episode is not reported.

A leader, who was initially followed for "attractive" reasons, by virtue of his ability to better engender cohesion and a sense of unity in his group, and certainly not by imposition on others and force, does not want to be liable to lose his role. Thus, he transforms the quality of his "grip" on his group: his power, initially conquered by feeding the *'aṣabiyya* in such a way as to make his group gain superiority over others, is transformed from an attractively founded authoritativeness into a form of command and control based on the royal power to impose obedience.

In this transformative process, habit plays a major role: once firmly established, leadership no longer needs a direct connection with the *'aṣabiyya* that generated it, because it is sustained by habit,[65] and is no longer subject to discussion (*Muqaddima* III, 2). This change, however, leads to the atrophy of *'aṣabiyya* itself, since the latter, previously determined by the necessities of life in the *badāwa*, is no longer fed and nurtured in the urban context,[66] where opposite dynamics of obedience, functional to a consolidation of strength and power, come into play.

On the contrary: after a while, the very enlargement of the group, due to its success, inevitably leads the original *'aṣabiyya* to break up and disperse into fragmented and mixed lineages, losing the relational compactness of the early days, as it progressively incorporates new and different *'aṣabiyyāt* in a cultural osmosis pushed to the limits of its possibility. This contributes to its weakening and to the progressive fading of the reciprocity and empathy that initially nourished it.

In this sense, then, the civilisation of the *ḥaḍāra* turns out to be essentially based on an intrinsically dialectical construction that already possesses within itself the seed of its own corruption. Whereas the emergence of a higher and more powerful *'aṣabiyya* is necessary to unify and keep together all the others in a unitary group under its influence, *mutatis mutandis* this affirmative, "direct flurry" of the wave produces the "inverse flurry" of its contradictions. As a matter of fact, the new position of a leader of the whole "super-*'aṣabiyya*" brings him to detach himself from the rest of the group because of his increased and even more vertical superiority, and pushes him, following an innate human tendency, to become haughty, proud and distant from the group that initially supported him.

Thus, as he no longer wishes to share his glory with others, he finally develops the character—also innately human—of egotism—the opposite of the sense of group and, indeed, one of the factors which, by shifting the ground on which he stands, paves the way to his fall.

---

[65] As Celarent writes (2013: 901), this argument seems to anticipate Weber's argument of the "routinisation of charisma," in detail, and half a millennium before Weber.

[66] Quoting Gurvitch, this passage can be seen as a shift from the *'aṣabiyya*-communion situation of *badāwa* to the much more feeble *'aṣabiyya*-community situation of *ḥaḍāra*.

3.6 The Virtues of Command, the Justice of Power, and the Influence of the Laws

According to Ibn Khaldūn, power, which is essentially aimed at ensuring the survival of the community by protecting it from internal dissent and from external attacks, does not exist *ad maiorem Dei gloriam*, but for the protection of men (Erwin Rosenthal 1932: 60). It does not constitute a gift granted "a priori" by God to a ruler, but a functional necessity of the governed subjects themselves.

In this sense, according to Ibn Khaldūn, royal authority represents a natural institution for mankind. In fact, while only through social organisation and mutual cooperation can material needs, such as nourishment, be satisfied, unless a sovereign authority is present society is unable to keep balance,[67] since "Each one will stretch out his hand for whatever he needs and (try simply) to take it, since injustice and aggressiveness are in the animal nature."[68]

A consequence of this, Ibn Khaldūn explains, would be the reactive onset, in the group, of anger and irritation—strong human reactions that normally occur when property is threatened—which, in turn, would lead to hostility and then to problems, bloodshed, and death—in a crescendo that, if generalised, could lead to the destruction of the species.

The problem would arise not only on a material level, but also on the wider level of the culture of reference—which is a fundamental cohesive element. In fact, one of the inevitable consequences of the enlargement of social organisation is the increase in the plurality of the values supported in the social sphere, and in the relative pressure exerted by them. In the absence of a dominant subject capable of exerting a restrictive influence, the consequent disagreement, if generalised, would lead to the destruction of any society and, therefore, of humanity itself[69]—something which is contrary to divine will.

For all these reasons, a political group cannot remain in a state of anarchy. It needs a subject endowed with power and capable of restraining its people:

> Now, the human species is one of the things the Creator has especially (enjoined us) to preserve.[70] People, thus, cannot persist in a state of anarchy and without a ruler who keeps

---

[67]As Lilia Ben Salem (1972: 294–295) observes, this idea that power serves to preserve the "balance" of society sounds typically modern and functionalist.

[68]*Muqaddima* III, 21. Ibn Khaldūn (1958, Vol. I: 380–381). Ibn Khaldūn ([1967] 2005: 151–152): "The others, in turn, will try to prevent him from taking it, motivated by wrathfulness and spite and the strong human reaction when one's property is menaced. This causes dissension, which leads to hostilities, and hostilities lead to trouble and bloodshed and loss of life, which lead to the destruction of the species."

[69]*Muqaddima* III, 24. Ibn Khaldūn (1958, Vol. I: 389–390). Ibn Khaldūn ([1967] 2005: 156): "One of the necessary consequences of social organisation is disagreement, because of the pressure of cross-purposes. As long as there is no ruler who exercises a restraining influence, this leads to trouble which, in turn, may lead to the destruction and uprooting of mankind."

[70]*Muqaddima* III, 24. Ibn Khaldūn (1958, Vol. I: 390). Ibn Khaldūn ([1967] 2005: 156): "Now, the preservation of the species is one of the necessary intentions of the religious law."

> them apart. Therefore, they need a person to restrain them. He is their ruler. As is required by human nature, he must be a forceful ruler, one who exercises authority.[71]

As Ibn Khaldūn (*Muqaddima* III, 21) points out, according to the generally accepted use of the term, governmental authority belongs to those who dominate subjects, collect taxes, send out (military) expeditions, protect frontier regions, and have no one stronger than they are over them. If one of these elements is missing, it is defective.

For it to constitute a "good" government, however, the further presence of certain elements, and especially of certain qualities and attitudes in the sovereign, is necessary. In fact, while power exists to protect men, nevertheless—and this is an important contradiction—at the same time it oppresses by vocation: as Ibn Khaldūn observes, inside each man lurks a latent aggressor who, as Talbi (1973: 40) writes, "is awakened by the scent of power." Furthermore, as Ibn Khaldūn underlines, injustice is another important disruptive factor (*Muqaddima* III, 41).

It is equally important, for this reason, to examine the limits and barriers that may be able to counteract this trend: in relation to this, Ibn Khaldūn considers a series of heterogeneous elements (from personal virtues to the use of general rules as instruments of government) potentially capable of steering a leader's rule.

First of all, Ibn Khaldūn explains that meekness and a protective attitude towards the ruler's subjects are crucial: these are necessary to gain the love and trust of the people who will be asked to sacrifice themselves for the sovereign's cause. In fact, government is as good as it is meek: a good sovereign has to know how to be generous and must be able to manage his own strength. Therefore, the apparent one-sidedness of the ruler's power is, in reality, an illusion: rulers can maintain the solidarity of the governed only by cultivating empathy with their needs and emotions (Gierer 2001: 95–96).

The true meaning of royal authority is only realised when the ruler defends his subordinates. Haughty detachment and excessive harshness on his part are highly counterproductive and, in most cases, cause the destruction of his authority,[72] insofar as they undermine the subjects' sense of unity and identification with the *'aṣabiyya* represented by the sovereign. In other words, the feeling of identification that keeps alive the "correlative" relationship binding a ruler exercising his functions, and the subjects under his government, has mainly *relational roots*:[73] the interest that the

[71] *Muqaddima* III, 21. Ibn Khaldūn (1958, Vol. I: 381). Ibn Khaldūn ([1967] 2005: 152). Here, evident similarities emerge with some aspects of Hobbes' thought.

[72] *Muqaddima* III, 22. Ibn Khaldūn (1958, Vol. I: 382). Ibn Khaldūn ([1967] 2005: 152): "Exaggerated harshness is harmful to royal authority and in most cases causes its destruction."

[73] *Muqaddima* III, 22. Ibn Khaldūn (1958, Vol. I: 382–384). Ibn Khaldūn ([1967] 2005: 152–153): "The interest subjects have in their ruler lies in his relation to them [...] The concomitants of good rulership are kindness to, and protection of, one's subjects [...] To be kind and beneficent toward them is part of being mild to them and showing an interest in the way they live."

subjects have in their ruler lies essentially in the quality of the relationship that he establishes with them.[74]

When those in government punish people harshly and mercilessly, publicly exposing their shortcomings, they act in a manner which is incompatible with the logic of *'aṣabiyya*, and those under their rule will react accordingly. In fact, a downtrodden and frightened people learn to defend themselves with the expedients typical of a spoiled character—such as lies, cunning, and deceit—until these behaviours become a habit, an aspect of their character that permanently affects their mind and temperament.

On the other hand, however, if those in government approach their subjects with mildness and forgive their faults by behaving kindly and charitably and showing an interest in their lives, they trust their sovereign and seek protection from him, truly love him, and are willing to die for him in battle against his enemies.[75]

Ibn Khaldūn adds, though—in a clarification that clearly marks his great distance from Platonic political conceptions,[76] and his affinity, instead, to the Aristotelian ideal of *aurea mediocritas*—that this attitude is also related to specific character traits: very seldom, in fact, is meekness found in very alert and shrewd people. On the contrary, says Ibn Khaldūn, referring to a *ḥadīṯ* according to which Muhammad said: "Follow the step of the weakest among you" (*Muqaddima* III, 22; Ibn Khaldūn 1958, Vol. I: 384; Ibn Khaldūn [1967] 2005: 153), it is in less anxious and more carefree people that this virtue flourishes the most.

On the one hand, a stupid person is too rigid in his thinking. On the other, someone much more intelligent and careful than most may go too far the other way: for example, by imposing on his subordinates tasks that exceed their abilities and whose purpose and meaning only he, thanks to his intelligence, can understand.[77] In short, behind the popular saying that defines the particularly intelligent person as "a devil," Ibn Khaldūn warns, there is some element of truth: the extremes of all human qualities (such as generosity and avarice, courage and cowardice) are problematic.[78]

---

[74]As Lilia Ben Salem (1972: 301) observes, even the idea that power does not depend only on the individual personality of those who exercise it, but that it implies an element of reciprocity as well, is very modern, and has only really been understood as a result of some experimental studies on small groups carried out since the 1930s. Lilia Ben Salem cites, in this regard, J. Gaudemet (1962) and Bertrand de Jouvenel (1945).

[75]*Muqaddima* III, 22. Ibn Khaldūn (1958, Vol. I: 383). Ibn Khaldūn ([1967] 2005: 153): "If the ruler is mild and overlooks the bad sides of his subjects, they will trust him and take refuge with him. They love him heartily and are willing to die for him in battle against his enemies."

[76]Plato, as is well-known, favoured the attribution of power to the *aristoi*, the "best ones."

[77]*Muqaddima* III, 22. Ibn Khaldūn (1958, Vol. I: 384). Ibn Khaldūn ([1967] 2005: 153): "The least (of the many drawbacks) of alertness (in a ruler) is that he imposes tasks upon his subjects that are beyond their ability, because he is aware of things they do not perceive and, through his genius, foresees the outcome of things at the start. (The ruler's excessive demands) may lead to his subjects' ruin. Muḥammad said: 'Follow the pace of the weakest among you'."

[78]In his treatise on Sufism (2017: 37), by the way, Ibn Khaldūn also argues that human traits are not to be stifled, as each natural human disposition "is created for a purpose: if the appetite in man were

Consequently, a good political leader should neither be too stupid nor too clever, since in both circumstances he is hindered in understanding normal people and in making himself understood by them, and in establishing, therefore, a sense of commonality with his people.

Furthermore, royal authority, by its very nature, demands superiority and strength, qualities indicative of the "fury" in animals and man. If not tempered, these same qualities normally lead rulers' decisions to deviate from the just: for this reason, they have to be balanced (following the model of the Persians and other great civilisations) by making use of laws accepted by the masses to which they submit.

As far as the foundation behind such a body of rules is concerned, it is possible to distinguish, according to Ibn Khaldūn, three possible types of government. One is based simply on its own brute force and superiority or on the power of anger (*al-mulk al-ṭabīʿī*), which is tantamount to *tyranny* and injustice—characteristics condemned by both religious law and political wisdom.[79]

The second type is government exercised through the use of thoughtful rules worked out through rational reasoning by the members of the ruling dynasty (*al-mulk al-siyāsī*). The result is a political institution oriented towards wisdom and endowed with a *rational* intellectual basis, albeit still defective in the long run, because it lacks divine enlightenment.

Finally, if it is laws commanded by God that the legislator enforces (as was done by the Prophet and his successors, the first caliphs), the result is a religiously founded political institution (the *ḫilāfa*—the caliphal institution[80]): inasmuch as it is aimed at pursuing the people's happiness not only in this life, but also in the next, this type is superior to all the others.[81] Yet, this was only realised—Ibn Khaldūn says—in the early days of Islam, in the period of the first "well-guided" caliphs (Abū Bakr, ʿUmar, ʿUṯmān and ʿAlī, the first successors of the Prophet). In fact, Muhammad himself, Ibn Khaldūn says, predicted that only 30 years of caliphate would be needed

---

suppressed, the human race would either die out from hunger, or become extinct out of abstinence. If anger were extirpated, man would perish due to being unable to defend himself against the oppressor."

[79] *Muqaddima* III, 23. Ibn Khaldūn (1958, Vol. I: 386–387). Ibn Khaldūn ([1967] 2005: 154–155): "Anything (done by royal authority) that is dictated by force, superiority, or the free play of the power of wrathfulness, is tyranny and injustice and considered reprehensible by (the religious law), as it is also considered reprehensible by the requirements of political wisdom."

[80] In this regime the caliph is neither the ultimate sovereign nor the source of law and, therefore, is subject himself to the religious laws, almost as if in an embryonic form of scripturalist *rule of law*.

[81] *Muqaddima* III, 23. Ibn Khaldūn (1958, Vol. I: 386). Ibn Khaldūn ([1967] 2005: 154): "If these norms are ordained by the intelligent and leading personalities and minds of the dynasty, the result will be a political (institution) with an intellectual (rational) basis. If they are ordained by God through a lawgiver who establishes them as (religious) laws, the result will be a political (institution) with a religious basis, which will be useful for life in both this and the other world. [...] This entire world is trifling and futile. It ends up in death and annihilation."

after his death for the royal authority to change its nature and turn tyrannical (*Muqaddima* IV, 16).[82]

Therefore, exercising a natural royal authority means governing the masses on the basis of one's own power and one's own desires and objectives; exercising a rational political royal authority means governing them as required by intellectual understanding and reasoning in order to find the best means to favour the interests of the people and to avoid anything that can harm them;[83] exercising caliphal authority, instead, means governing the masses as required by religious law, thus pursuing both their worldly interests and those relative to the world to come.[84]

To be sure, Ibn Khaldūn, disproving as contrary to the fact an idea that was common in his time, objectively points out that the restraining influence on the social group, which is necessary in order to dispel internal disagreements and avoid its disintegration, is essentially the natural result of the strength and power of royal authority, and that, therefore, it applies even in the absence of a revealed religious law, and regardless of prophecy itself. In this regard, he cites examples taken from many other great civilisations, pagan or prior to Islamic revelation.

According to Ibn Khaldūn, the very observance of religious laws requires a context furnished by a pre-existing sense of group, an *'aṣabiyya*, as a basis for establishing royal authority. It is, therefore, in the *'aṣabiyya* itself that the fundamental, self-sufficient factor that determines the strength of a group lies: the *'aṣabiyya* is "the secret divine agent," operating as its nature dictates, that keeps people from dividing and opposing each other—the source of unity and agreement, and the element that also guarantees the very laws of Islam.[85]

On the other hand, while *'aṣabiyya* is sufficient to maintain institutions, these should be inspired, in order to reach the highest level of perfection, by religious laws, which can enable them to see beyond the reach of human reason (reason in the metaphysical field, as we have seen, lacks any real cognitive means). It is also in this

[82]Therefore, not even the Islamic political community has historically been spared from falling within the law of the inevitable corruption of things, established in the order of creation. As written in the sura *The joint forces*: "You will find no change in God's practices" (*Qur'an* 33, 62) (Haleem 2004: 271). This verse is recalled twice in Ibn Khaldūn's work: in *Muqaddima* I, Third preliminary discussion (at the end), and in *Muqaddima* III, 48.

[83]*Muqaddima* III, 31. Ibn Khaldūn (1958, Vol. I: 473). Ibn Khaldūn ([1967] 2005: 183): "[...] the human species must have a person who will cause them to act in accordance with what is good for them and who will prevent them by force from doing things harmful to them. Such a person is the one who is called a ruler."

[84]*Muqaddima* III, 23. Ibn Khaldūn (1958, Vol. I: 387). Ibn Khaldūn ([1967] 2005: 155): "(To exercise) natural royal authority means to cause the masses to act as required by purpose and desire. (To exercise) political (royal authority) means to cause the masses to act as required by intellectual (rational) insight into the means of furthering their worldly interests and avoiding anything that is harmful in that respect. (To exercise) the caliphate means to cause the masses to act as required by religious insight into their interests in the other world as well as in this world."

[85]*Muqaddima* III, 28. Ibn Khaldūn (1958, Vol. I: 438). Ibn Khaldūn ([1967] 2005: 170): "(Group feeling is) the secret divine (factor that) restrains people from splitting up and abandoning each other. It is the source of unity and agreement, and the guarantor of the intentions and laws of Islam."

sense that his argument should be understood on the need for human beings to have a leader who impels them to act in accordance with what is good for them, and who forces them to refrain from doing things that are harmful to them—in a claim of legal paternalism, entrusted to those who assume governmental functions, aimed, in particular, at guaranteeing the pursuit of what is defined as "good" in the sphere of Muslim law.[86]

The pursuit of this idea of good, however, also requires intelligence and rational judgement. It is true, for example, that the first requirement of the *imām*—guide and interpreter of religious laws—lies in his knowledge of these laws, but this requirement can only be said to be truly satisfied when—far from imposing an application of the laws based on blind and rigid acceptance of tradition—he is capable of understanding their inner meaning. Only in this case can he apply them and take new, independent decisions (*Muqaddima* III, 25) truly faithful to that meaning's spirit.

3.7 The Psychology of Power

The holder of political power must be able to exercise many functions: for example, he must be able to keep people subject to his power, but at the same time defend them; guide people to act in their own best interests; apply laws so as to avoid hostilities and threats to property; take care of road safety; supervise weights and measures so as to avoid cheating; supervise the mint. These functions have an

[86]For example, it is in the Muslim community, explains Ibn Khaldūn, that holy war, because of the universalism of the Islamic mission, is considered as a religious duty. In other religious groups there are no such political implications (here Ibn Khaldūn, perhaps, forgets to consider the history of the Crusades): in the Gospels, for example, very few laws are stated. At this point of the discussion, Ibn Khaldūn expresses himself with very strong and—to say the least—controversial and contemptuous expressions, quite unusual compared to the tone used in the rest of the text, particularly about Christians. In fact, he writes (*Muqaddima* III, 31. Ibn Khaldūn 1958, Vol. I: 480. Ibn Khaldūn [1967] 2005: 188): "We do not think that we should blacken the pages of this book with discussion of their dogmas of unbelief. In general, they are well-known. All of them are unbelief. This is clearly stated in the noble *Qur'ān*. To discuss or argue those things with them is not for us. It is (for them to choose between) conversion to Islam, payment of the poll tax, or death." Rather, Ibn Khaldūn points out that, as predicted in a book that was widely popular in his time, the "*Book of Predictions*," Muslims are still bound, in the future, to conquer European lands, arriving "through the sea": *Muqaddima* III, 32. Ibn Khaldūn (1958, Vol. II: 46). Ibn Khaldūn ([1967] 2005: 213). The disconcerting contrast between the general, admirably objective, rational, and detached tone of his work, and this specific passage (which, among other things, seems to recall controversial contemporary issues in its reference to a conquest through the sea) seems to prompt us here to give credence to Mahdi's thesis of his "cryptophilosophy," as the only comprehensible possible explanation of this discrepancy, at least with reference to these strident notes. However, a second reference to the (literal) "repulsion" he felt towards Christianity is also found in his autobiography, when he describes, in relation to his visit to Jerusalem, the feeling which the church, built on the place where the Cross had been placed, aroused in him (Ibn Khaldūn 2002: 222).

important practical utility. However, the subtle *psychological* implications of the sovereign's actions are also relevant. In fact, the management of power requires—as he claims—exceptional ability and attention to a large array of details.

There are many elements that can produce a strong psychological impact and are, therefore, needed, to consolidate and strengthen the sovereign's "grip" on his subordinates; these elements are analysed by Ibn Khaldūn with great lucidity.

In this regard, Ibn Khaldūn highlights outward signs designed to instill a sense and fear of authority such as, for example, the sovereign's use of larger tents or more sumptuous palaces compared to the dwellings of his subordinates. Similarly, he instances the setting up of a throne, aimed at placing the sovereign higher than others; the use of original seals in the minting of coins, or in the "official" validation of correspondence; the use, finally, of royal coats of arms embroidered on robes (a custom often adopted also by officers of lower rank, who are certain to increase their prestige, in this way, by virtue of that same mechanism of imitation of the winning model cited above). Even the splendour of the banquets offered in a society, or the type and magnificence of a dynasty's monuments, are eloquent facts. Denying the reliability of some "fantastic"[87] accounts popular at the time (he refers to the widespread belief according to which ancient monuments were very large because of the greater stature of men of the past), Ibn Khaldūn states that from the proportions and majesty of the monuments erected by a given dynasty it is possible to draw clear symptomatic information on the level of the underlying social organisation.

Just as the different details of a patient's appearance can be interpreted by a doctor in their deep and complex meaning, by the same token the external data of a civilisation acquires, in Ibn Khaldūn's new science, the value of symptomatic clinical signs.

When observed from such a perspective, therefore, even monuments, beyond their aesthetic, artistic, and functional aspects, appear as symptoms, signs to be interpreted: one of Ibn Khaldūn's axiomatic propositions reads: "The monuments of a given dynasty are proportionate to its original power." (*Muqaddima* III, 16; Ibn Khaldūn 1958, Vol. I: 356; Ibn Khaldūn [1967] 2005: 143).

Even the importance attached to the various secular functions is determined by the political situation of the moment and reflects its historical and social conditions. No function, in fact, has a permanent status, as is shown, for example, by the direct association linking the privilege and the importance attributed to military forces, or to men of letters or finance, to the relative historical circumstances of peace or war. Ibn Khaldūn shows how, even within the same category and the same function, time gradually produces slippages of meaning and social value, as demonstrated, for example, by the change over time in the role, and especially in the power, of the doorkeeper (*Muqaddima* III, 32): even the changes that affect the different functions of those who surround the sovereign may be useful, therefore, as a yardstick for understanding the level of *mulk* development.

---

[87]Ibn Khaldūn reports, in this regard, the story of Og, son of Anak, which he judges to be preposterous (*Muqaddima* III, 16).

In general, for example, the importance of the "sword" prevails over that of the "pen" both at the beginning of a dynasty and towards the end of its trajectory (when its *'aṣabiyya* is weakened, and the population decreases due to senility); in the intermediate period, however, it is the administration and collection of taxes that are the most important activities.

Ibn Khaldūn focuses also on the analysis of the psychological impact, on both individuals and groups in war and battle, of the deployment of different symbols of sovereignty, ranging from flags and royal emblems to the traditional custom of going into battle to the sound of drums and horns.

He explains, for example, how flags, with their vivid colours and their size, help to inspire terror in an adversary, which is why they have always been used in war.

On the other hand, with regard to the custom of playing drums and blowing trumpets and horns in war, Ibn Khaldūn goes beyond the explanation (also supported in the pseudo-Aristotelian *Politics* circulating in his time) based on the fact that they would frighten enemies. He stresses, instead, the importance of another kind of effect that is produced in the soul by sounds—especially when they are harmoniously arranged, as is the case with music. More precisely, he refers to the important intoxicating effect they have of making soldiers euphoric, which is fundamental in order to prepare their souls to offer their own lives in battle. The euphoria produced by music in the soul, just like drunkenness, leads to courage.[88] Thus, Ibn Khaldūn writes, anticipating Durkheim's observations (Durkheim 1912) on the effects of the state of "collective effervescence" produced by the emotional rituals with which group solidarity is cemented,

> the truth is that listening to music and sounds no doubt causes pleasure and emotion in the soul. The spiritual temper of man is thereby affected by a kind of elation, which causes him to make light of difficulties and to be willing to die in the very condition in which he finds himself.[89]

As a further proof of this, he stresses how such an effect is also produced in animals, however far they are from the level of human intelligence: camels and horses, for example, "as everyone knows," are influenced by their master's spurs to action, but above all by his whistles and cries.

War is seen as an inevitable natural phenomenon, common to all races and nations, and is explained by Ibn Khaldūn with reference to the unleashing of passions such as jealousy, envy, hostility, zeal in the name of religion or royal authority, or the desire to found a kingdom.

---

[88] *Muqaddima* III, 34. Ibn Khaldūn (1958, Vol. II: 49). Ibn Khaldūn ([1967] 2005: 214): "The origin of it all is the cheerfulness created in the soul (through music). It leads to bravery, just as drunkness does, as the result of the cheerfulness which it produces."

[89] *Muqaddima* III, 34. Ibn Khaldūn (1958, Vol. II: 48–49). Ibn Khaldūn ([1967] 2005: 214). And again: "Singers with instruments [...] move the soul of brave men emotionally and cause them to be willing to die."

Ibn Khaldūn lists four types of war,[90] distinguishing those that are unjust—that is, those motivated by greed or competition, or moved by the desire to attack others—from the just, which are the holy, religiously motivated war, and also the war waged by the sovereign against rebels and dissidents in his kingdom.

Even the very manner in which the battle is waged is subject to analysis and interpretation: Ibn Khaldūn compares, for example, the Arab system of fighting, based on the alternation of attack and retreat by the various combatants, with the non-Arab system, based on the attack launched in a compact formation—more powerful, rational and close fought, but also more difficult to coordinate and, therefore, requiring greater discipline and organisation. In relation to this, and on a more general level, he stresses how the whole solidarity of the army, its *'aṣabiyya*, plays an essential role in the events and logic of war.

Ibn Khaldūn emphasises, for example, how the battle dynamics change when fighting is carried out by a cohesive group of subjects, familiar to each other and, therefore, able to form a force united by *'aṣabiyya*, compared to the situation that occurs when a dynasty, once in possession of vast territories, is called upon to coordinate a much larger but heterogeneous and less manageable number of soldiers. In such a case, there is a risk that they may even attack each other—unless some sense of group is reconstructed by dividing them into smaller and more compact units where they can recognise each other and coalesce (*Muqaddima* III, 35). In fact, "it is proven," writes Ibn Khaldūn, that in battle, all forces being equal on the field, it is the *'aṣabiyya* that constitutes the determining factor of superiority (*Muqaddima* III, 35).

Different expedients are designed and used in different situations to encourage and strengthen the sense of *'aṣabiyya*, and to fortify the soldiers' psychology. The Persians, for example, used to place wooden towers on the back of elephants, marshalled in orderly lines like fortresses behind the fighters to provide them with a sense of strength and protection. With the same aim in mind, Byzantine and Goth rulers used to sit on a throne in the middle of battle, surrounded by soldiers, so that their presence and observation of the fighting might stimulate them to feel the desire heroically to sacrifice their lives.

Ibn Khaldūn observes that such a function was also served by the custom (motivated, at the time, by necessity) of the first Arabs, at the time still living in tents, of bringing their whole families into the army camp—a situation that led them to find, in the need to protect their lives, an additional stimulus to fight to the best of their ability, even to death. This encouragement disappeared when, thanks to

[90] *Muqaddima* III, 35. Ibn Khaldūn (1958, Vol. II: 74). Ibn Khaldūn ([1967] 2005: 224). This distinction is also taken up today by Khaled Abu El Fadl (2001: 31), who uses Ibn Khaldūn's quadripartition to define "Islamic" extremism and these groups as "*ḥirābī*" (from Arabic *ḥarb*, war) or *muḥāribūn*, i.e., practitioners of immoral and illegal unjust war, distinguishing them from those who practice *jihād*. Cfr. Hillenbrand (2016: 279; 258) and Albarrán (2019).

increasing affluence, fighters began to leave their families safe in other dwellings and take only their animals with them to the tents in the camp.[91]

In any case, Ibn Khaldūn concludes, the outcome of war is always difficult to predict even in the face of disproportionate deployments of men and means, if only the superficial and "visible" elements are observed. In fact, the causes determining the superiority of one group or another derive from a combination of different factors; and while the most external and visible (such as the number of soldiers, the type and number of weapons, the use of correct and astute tactics, etc.) certainly do count, the effects of other factors—sometimes hidden, such as, for example, the use of cunning—must be added and balanced with these. We should not underestimate, for example, the results of such tactics as spreading alarm in order to cause defections: in fact, terror itself can lead to defeat even more than other more visible external and material factors.

For Ibn Khaldūn even the events that led Muslims to the progressive conquest of other lands, at the beginning of the history of Islam, are explicable on the basis of this very factor—the "secret," lying in

> the willingness of the Muslims to die in the holy war against their enemies because of their feeling that they had the right religious insight, and in the corresponding fear and defeatism that God put into the hearts of their enemies (*Muqaddima* III, 48; Ibn Khaldūn 1958, Vol. II: 134–135; Ibn Khaldūn [1967] 2005: 255).

Finally, we must also give due weight to the effects of factors deriving not from man's actions, but from imponderable "heavenly reasons"—schemes and programmes written in the depths of time (among which we can also include the very cyclicality of the historical-political fortunes of every civilisation)—which are also liable to produce powerful, albeit hidden, psychological influences.

All in all, as Ibn Khaldūn writes, "Victory in war as a rule is the result of imaginary psychological factors" (*Muqaddima* III, 48; Ibn Khaldūn 1958, Vol. II: 130; Ibn Khaldūn [1967] 2005: 253). The very factors that are not visible, such as those determined by the stage a certain civilisation has reached within its life cycle, and, thus, by its remoteness or proximity to the stage of its senility—often weigh more than external factors in determining superiority and victory in war.

Similar concepts were also expressed centuries later by Montesquieu ([1734] 1876, 273) who, in his work *Considérations sur les causes de la grandeur des Romains et de leur décadence*,[92] wrote:

---

[91]*Muqaddima* III, 35. Ibn Khaldūn (1958, Vol. II: 80). Ibn Khaldūn ([1967] 2005: 227): "These things, unlike one's own family and property, do not inspire any willingness to die."

[92]Montesquieu (1876: 273): "Ce n'est pas la Fortune qui domine le monde. On peut le demander aux Romains, qui eurent une suite continuelle de prospérités quand ils se gouvernèrent sur un certain plan, et une suite non interrompue de revers lorsqu'ils se conduisirent sur un autre. Il y a des causes générales, soit morales, soit physiques, qui agissent dans chaque monarchie, l'élèvent, la maintiennent, ou la précipitent; tous les accidents sont soumis à ces causes, et, si le hasard d'une bataille, c'est-à-dire une cause particulière, a ruiné un État, il y avait une cause générale qui faisait que cet État devait périr par une seule bataille. En un mot, l'allure principale entraîne avec elle tous les accidents particuliers."

Fate does not dominate the world. The Romans are witnesses to this, who had a continuous succession of prosperity when they governed according to a certain plan, and an uninterrupted succession of adversity when they behaved according to another. There are general causes, both moral and physical, which act in every monarchy, whether they raise it up, maintain it, or overthrow it; all accidents are subordinate to these causes; and if ever the outcome of a battle, that is, a particular cause, ruined a state, then there was a general cause according to which that state had to perish because of one battle. In a word, the general cause carries all the particular accidents along with it.

References

(A) Ibn Khaldūn's Works

Ibn Khaldūn. 1958. *The Muqaddimah: An Introduction to History* (ed. Franz Rosenthal). 3 Voll. New Jersey: Princeton University Press.

———. 2002. *Le Livre des Exemples. I. Autobiographie, Muqaddima* (ed. Abdesselam Cheddadi). Paris: Gallimard.

———. [1967] 2005. *The Muqaddimah: An Introduction to History* (ed. Franz Rosenthal), abridged edition. Princeton: Princeton University Press.

———. 2017. *Ibn Khaldūn on Sufism. Remedy for the Questioner in Search of Answers* (trans. Yumna Ozer). Cambridge: The Islamic Texts Society.

(B) Other Works

Abou-Tabickh, Lilian. 2019. *Al-'aṣabiyya in Context. Choice and Historical Continuity in Al-Muqaddima of Ibn Khaldūn*. Toronto: Ph.D. Thesis, Department of Political Science.

Ahmad, Zaid. 2003. *The Epistemology of Ibn Khaldūn*. London: RoutledgeCurzon.

Albarrán, Javier. 2019. Holy War in Ibn Khaldūn. A Transcultural Concept? *Journal of Medieval Worlds* 1 (1): 55–78.

al-Idrīsī, Muḥammad. [1154] 2008. *Il libro di Ruggero*. Palermo: Flaccovio.

Amri, Laroussi. 2008. The Concept of 'Umran: The Heuristic Knot in Ibn Khaldūn. *The Journal of North African Studies* 13 (3): 345–355.

Anderson, Jon W. [1983] 1984. Conjuring with Ibn Khaldūn. In *Ibn Khaldūn and Islamic Ideology*, ed. Bruce B. Lawrence, 111–121. Leiden: Brill.

Augustin of Hippo. [413–426] 2011. *La città di Dio*. Milano: Mondadori.

Baali, Fuad. 1988. *Society, State, and Urbanism: Ibn Khaldūn's Sociological Thought*. Lanham: University Press of America.

Baeck, Louis. 1994. *The Mediterranean Tradition in Economic Thought*. London: Routledge.

Baldissera, Eros (ed.). 2006. *Dizionario compatto italiano arabo e arabo-italiano*. Bologna: Zanichelli.

Banfield, Edward C. 1958. *The Moral Basis of a Backward Society*. Glencoe, Ill.: Free Press.

Ben Salem, Lilia. 1972. La notion de pouvoir dans l'oeuvre d'Ibn Khaldūn. *Cahier Internationaux de Sociologie*: 293–314.

Bouthoul, Gaston. 1930. *Ibn-Khaldoun. Sa philosophie sociale*. Librairie Orientaliste Paul Geuthner: Paris.

Bozarslan, Hamit. 2014. *Le luxe et la violence. Domination et contestation chez Ibn Khaldūn*. CNRS Éditions: Paris.

Campanini, Massimo. 2005a. *Studies on Ibn Khaldūn*. Milano: Polimetrica.

Celarent, Barbara. 2013. Taha Hussein, La philosophie sociale d'Ibn Khaldoun. *American Journal of Sociology* 119: 894–902.

Cheddadi, Abdesselam. 1994. Ibn Khaldūn. *Prospects: The Quarterly Review of Comparative Education* 24 (1–2): 7–19.

———. 2006. *Ibn Khaldūn. L'homme et le théoricien de la civilisation*. Paris: Gallimard.

Coltman Brown, Irene. 1981. Ibn Khaldūn and the Revelation from the Desert. *History Today* 31: 19–25.

Cooley, Charles H. [1902] 1962. *Human Nature and the Social Order*. New York: Charles Scribner's Sons.

Dale, Stephen Frederic. 2015a. *The Orange Trees of Marrakesh. Ibn Khaldūn and the Science of Man*. Cambridge, MA: Harvard University Press.

Darwin, Charles. 1871. *The Descent of Man*. London: Murray.

de Jouvenel, Bertrand. 1945. *Du pouvoir, histoire naturelle de sa croissance*. Genève: C. Bourquin.

de Paw, Cornelius. 1774. *Recherches philosophiques sur les Américains ou Mémoires intéressants pour servir à l'histoire de l'espèce humaine*. Berlin: Georges Jacques Decker.

de Tocqueville, Alexis. 1835. *De la démocratie en Amérique*. Paris: Charles Gosselin.

Durkheim, Émile. 1912. *Les formes élémentaires de la vie religiouse*. Paris: Alcan.

El Fadl, Khaled Abu. 2001. Islam and the Theology of Power. *Middle East Report* 221: 28–33.

Fischel, Walter J. 1958. Ibn Khaldūn on the Bible, Judaism and the Jews. In *Goldziher Memorial Volume*. Part II, eds. Samuel Lowinger et al. Jerusalem: Rubin Mass.

Frazer, James. 1890. *The Golden Bough*. London: Macmillan.

Gabrieli, Francesco. [1930] 1984. Il concetto di 'aṣabiyya' nel pensiero storico di Ibn Khaldūn. In *L'Islam nella storia*, ed. Francesco Gabrieli, 211–252. Bari: Dedalo.

García Lizana, Antonio. 2006. Tradición y progreso: las claves del futuro. *Cuadernos de CC.EE. y EE.* 50–51: 159–176.

Gardet, Louis. [1977] 2002. *Gli uomini dell'Islam*. Milano: Jaca Book.

Gaudemet, Jean. 1962. Esquisse d'une sociologie historique du pouvoir. *Politique* 19–20: 195–234.

Gierer, Alfred. 2001. Ibn Khaldūn on Solidarity ("Asabiyah")–Modern Science on Cooperativeness and Empathy: A Comparison. *Philosophia Naturalis* 38: 91–104.

Girard, René. [1961] 2002. *Menzogna romantica e verità romanzata*. Milano: Bompiani.

Gobineau, Joseph Arthur, comte de. 1853–1855. *Essai sur l'inégalité des races humaines*. Paris: Firmin Didot Frères.

Haidt, Jonathan. 2012. *The Righteous Mind*. New York: Vintage Books.

Haleem, M.A.S. Abdel (trans.). 2004. *The Qur'an*. Oxford University Press.

Hart, Herbert L.A. 1961. *The Concept of Law*. Oxford: Oxford University Press.

Hegel, Georg Wilhelm Friedrich. [1837] 1902. *Lectures on the Philosophy of History*. London: Bell and Sons.

Hillenbrand, Carole. 2016. *Islam. Una nuova introduzione storica*. Giulio Einaudi: Torino.

Hobbes, Thomas. [1651] 1985. *Leviathan*. London: Penguin.

Kahlaoui, Tarek. 2008. Towards Reconstructing the *Muqaddimah* Following Ibn Khaldun's Reading of the Idrisian Text and Maps. *The Journal of North African Studies* 13 (3): 293–306.

Lacoste, Yves. [1966] 1998. *Ibn Khaldoun, Naissance de l'Histoire, passé du Tiers Monde*. Paris: La Decouverte.

Lewis, Bernard. [1986] 1999. *Semites and Anti-Semites: An Inquiry into Conflict and Prejudice*. New York: Norton.

Mahdi, Muhsin. 1957. *Ibn Khaldūn's Philosophy of History*. Chicago: University of Chicago Press.

Mead, George Herbert. 1934. *Mind, Self and Society*. Chicago: University of Chicago Press.

Megherbi, Abdelghani. 1971. *La pensée sociologique d'Ibn Khaldoun*. SNED: Alger.

Montesquieu, Charles-Luis de Secondat, baron de. 1748. *De l'ésprit des lois*. Amsterdam: Chatelain.

Montesquieu, Charles-Luis de Secondat, baron de. [1734] 1876. *Considérations sur les causes de la grandeur des Romains et de leur décadence*. Paris: Garnier Frères.

Montgomery Watt, William. 1961a. *Muḥammad*. Oxford: Oxford University Press.
———. 1961b. *Islam and the Integration of Society*. Bristol: The Burleigh Press.
Morgan, Lewis Henry. 1877. *Ancient Society*. New York: Holt.
Norenzayan, Ara. [2013] 2015. *Big Gods. How Religion Transformed Cooperation and Conflict*. Princeton: Princeton University Press.
Parsons, Talcott. 1951. *The Social System*. London: Routledge.
Patriarca, Giovanni. 2009, December 20. Il prologo della modernità. Filosofia della storia e scienze sociali in Ibn Khaldūn. *Dialegesthai*. https://mondodomani.org/dialegesthai/gpa02.htm. Accessed 17 Sept 2020.
Pišev, Marko. 2019. Anthropological Aspects of Ibn Khaldūn's Muqaddimah: A Critical Examination. In *Bérose–Encyclopédie internationale des histoires de l'anthropologie,* 1–21. Paris: Bérose. http://www.berose.fr/article1777.html?lang=fr. Accessed 17 Sept 2020.
Pomian, Krzysztof. 2006. *Ibn Khaldūn au prisme de l'Occident*. Paris: Gallimard.
Ptolemy. [II century B.C.]1940. *Tetrabiblos (Quadripartitum)* (ed. Frank E. Robbins). Cambridge, MA: Loeb.
Rabi', Muḥammad Mahmoud. 1967. *The Political Theory of Ibn Khaldūn*. Leiden: Brill.
Rosenthal, Erwin. 1932. *Ibn Khaldūns Gedanken über den Staat. Ein Beitrag zur Geschichte der mittelalterlichen Staatlehre*. Oldenbourg: Munich.
Rosenthal, Franz. 1958. *Preface to Ibn Khaldūn*. In Ibn Khaldūn, *The Muqaddimah: An Introduction to History* (ed. Franz Rosenthal). Vol. I, xxix–cxv. Princeton: Princeton University Press.
———. 1987. Ibn Khaldūn. In *Encyclopedia of Religion*, ed. Mircea Eliade, 565–567. New York: Macmilllan.
Stuurman, Siep. 2015. Common Humanity and Cultural Difference in the Sedentary-Nomadic Frontier: Herodotus, Sima Qian, and Ibn Khaldūn. In *Global Intellectual History*, eds. Samuel Moyn and Andrew Sartori, 33–58. New York: Columbia University Press.
Talbi, Mohamed. 1973. *Ibn Ḫaldūn et l'histoire*. Tunis: Maison Tunisienne de l'Édition.
Tillion, Germaine. 1966. *Le Harem et les Cousins*. Paris: Seuil.
Verza, Annalisa. 2015a. "Quest" identitaria mediata dal web, (cyber)bullismo e stratificazione sociale alla luce di un singolare caso di "devianza" di massa. *Studi sulla questione criminale* 2–3: 129–150.
———. 2015b. Ansia panottica e "treadmill effect" nell'utopia eudaimonistica delle nuove tecnologie. In *Filosofia del diritto e nuove tecnologie*, eds. Raffaella Brighi and Silvia Zullo, 89–103. Roma: Aracne.
West, Ed. 2015. *Asabiya, What Ibn Khaldūn, the Islamic father of social science, can teach us about the world today*, e-book. https://www.amazon.co.uk/*Asabiyya*h-Khaldun-Islamic-father-science-ebook/dp/B0133Y2XSG/ref=sr_1_1?ie=UTF8&qid=1438364083&sr=8-1&keywords=*Asabiyya*h. Accessed 17 Sept 2020.
Wright Mills, Charles. 1939. Language, Logic and Culture. *American Sociological Review* 4: 670–680.

Chapter 4
The Internal Forces of the Crisis and the "Colouring" of Civilisation

Abstract This chapter focuses on Ibn Khaldūn's analysis of urbanised civilisation: it highlights both its cultural products and the economic well-being it produces, as well as the disruptive transformative movements that, in due course, inevitably lead it towards decadence and conquest by other social groups.

Of the main corruptive principles that come into play in this phase, particular attention is paid, in addition to the economic factor, to the change that characterises the form of power typical of urban civilisation (*mulk*), to social density and its effects on the break-up of family clans, as well as to the disruptive and weakening effect and vulnerability produced by the habit of luxury and by the obligatory reliance on others for protection. At a certain point, all these factors converge in determining the downward phase of the sociodynamic cycle that Ibn Khaldūn calls "senility."

Moreover, Ibn Khaldūn's analysis of the different crafts and ways in which man earns his livelihood, together with the temperamental characteristics that each of them encourages in those who exercise it, is retraced and commented on.

Finally, Ibn Khaldūn's analysis of the sciences and arts, and of education, that allow the handing down of culture to subsequent generations, is addressed as the ultimate fruit of the economic well-being deriving from the prosperity of an urbanised civilisation.

4.1 Metamorphoses of Politico-Legal Power: The Undertow of History

The final part of the second chapter, and especially the entire third chapter of the *Muqaddima*, are devoted to themes related to the nature of sovereign power and to the typical phenomena accompanying it. From the beginning, Ibn Khaldūn sets out to investigate these themes not in an ideal and religious perspective, but by framing them, in a path articulated through "basic and additional propositions," as

A. Verza, *Ibn Khaldūn and the Arab Origins of the Sociology of Civilisation and Power*, https://doi.org/10.1007/978-3-030-70339-4_4

phenomena that are necessarily determined by the nature of civilisation and human existence.[1]

As we have seen, in the seventh century the fragmentation resulting from the subdivision of the Arab world into different clans and tribes had been overcome, at a higher level, by the impact of Islam. Religious solidarity had the important effect of suppressing the disintegrating factors (aggressiveness, envy, jealousy, egoism) linked to the particular *'aṣabiyyāt*, in the name of a higher fusion, with the aim of providing a common orientation and objective that would make believers willing to put aside any selfishness, to the point of sacrificing their own lives for it.

In that exceptional moment, religion had also played an important role in reconciling the structures of nomadic life with those of city life (Islam was born essentially as an "urban" and, thus, also political religion, and its settlement in Medina was an essential stage in this process[2]): while the deeply moral afflatus of nomadic culture—given by its sense of loyalty, belonging, religion, and honour—had been called upon to correct the city's commercial corruption, civilisation—typical of urban culture—was brought to enrich the nomadic spirit (Abun-Nasr 1975: 12).

At the time of Ibn Khaldūn, however, the cohesive spirit of Islam no longer exerted the same force as in early days: on the contrary, the social landscape was fragmented by antagonisms juxtaposing the different tribal groups both with each other, and with the cities—which, in turn, were even more internally fragmented (Abun-Nasr 1975: 131–136). Moreover, the deep structural contradiction existing between the *ḥaḍāra*'s *mulk* and the *badāwa*'s *'aṣabiyya* was still very visible. While urban culture, on the one hand, developed social order, security, and civilisation, the wild character of *badāwa*, implying freedom from the authority and (because of the simple lifestyle it implied) little demand for functional cooperation between people, appeared antithetic to civilisation[3] and to a submission to external power.

In fact, as Ibn Khaldūn's analysis showed, the people forged by *badāwa* are inclined to be leaders themselves, to the extent that their actual leader, who can only be such by consensus, is forced to cultivate his popularity prudently, and to always be careful to act with kindness and to avoid causing antagonisms.

Only in *badāwa*, however, could true social cohesion be produced: in *ḥaḍāra* the *'aṣabiyya* is, without exception, subjected to the fate of an inevitable and

[1] *Muqaddima* III, 32. Ibn Khaldūn (1958, Vol. II: 5). Ibn Khaldūn ([1967] 2005: 190): "to discuss royal and governmental positions [...] as something required by the nature of civilisation and human existence [...] and not under the aspect of particular religious laws."

[2] Moreover, the Islamic religion, unlike the Jewish and Christian religions, flourished precisely at the time of its greatest military and political glory—and, perhaps for this reason, from the very beginning (in particular, since the "descent" of the Medina suras) it aimed at identifying the religious with the political field, and vice versa.

[3] *Muqaddima* II, 25. Ibn Khaldūn (1958, Vol. I: 304). Ibn Khaldūn ([1967] 2005: 119): "It is noteworthy how civilisation always collapsed in places the Bedouins took over and conquered, and how such settlements were depopulated and laid in ruin." The original 1958 edition (like the French translation by De Slane and the subsequent translation by Cheddadi) literally translated into "Arabs," but the translation of the 1967 edition has been preferred here, motivated by an interpretation more consistent with the plausible sense of the discourse: "Bedouins."

physiological crumbling. In the social model of the *ḥaḍāra*'s urbanised life, which is rich and rationally predefined by its rulers, the *'aṣabiyya* of the group is destined to weaken progressively, starting from the most peripheral areas, commensurately with the growth of its dimensions and with the consequent dilution of its internal sense of unity.

At the same time, the leader—supported, in the previous phase, by the *'aṣabiyya* of his peers—after consolidating his position by transforming and hardening his natural leadership in power (*mulk*), also gets determined, following a natural human tendency, to concentrate all this upon himself, and to want more and more of it—thus, putting distance and disagreements between himself and his former companions.

Moreover, his natural tendency to try to rationalise and, therefore, simplify his control over his people, leads him to turn the previously internally shared rules and values of the group into coercive obligations, thus producing a clear change in the way they are perceived.

In fact, because of its original function of maximising the self-defence of the group, *'aṣabiyya* is essentially egalitarian in nature; even though it allows minimal social differentiation based on nobility and genealogy, or glory, this is more a differentiation aimed at reaffirming the shared values, and based on those, than a real hierarchy of power. In the *badāwa*, a chief cannot force the other members of the tribe to do anything: in order to have influence over them, he must obtain their consent by embodying common values or pursuing common goals.

On the contrary, the operating principle of the *mulk* is power: a force exercised, at best, on the basis of known and knowable laws, but which still retains a coercive character. Even positive laws, in this sense, imply and produce submission and a moral weakening of people.

The original force of religion, which in the previous centuries had exercised a strengthening influence on men as they obeyed its rules out of conviction, had changed deeply, once institutionalised in *ḥaḍāra*, codified in coercive laws, and inculcated at the school level.

In short, once the government turns coercive—becoming the *mulk*—it transforms from within the motivations and the mental and affective coordinates that direct the behaviour of the group, inevitably ending in suffocating the *'aṣabiyya*, which can only survive on the basis of free feeling, and not coercive power. This process continues to the point where the authority of the new political leader, who came to power thanks to *'aṣabiyya*, opposes *'aṣabiyya* itself, just as any power, necessarily asymmetrical by its nature, is logically opposed to shared feelings.

In parallel, factors of economic and demographic crisis increase as synchronic symptoms of this phase of senility, as the central power, immersed in its own "*libido dominandi*" and the cult of its own image, clashes with other claims to power coming from the margins of its domain.

4.1.1 Solve et Coagula*: Change in a Leader's Political Qualities*

"As each of us can see with his own eyes," everything that belongs to the world of the elements is subject to a dynamic of ascent, corruption, and fall, according to Ibn Khaldūn. This same law does not spare things created by man: therefore, not even the prestige (*jah*) of the leader, an element that is essential to unite the group around him, inasmuch as it is intrinsically unstable, can escape this destiny. This inevitable cycle is depicted by Ibn Khaldūn according to a schematisation that is re-proposed several times in the work, to articulate the process of disintegration, respectively, of the sovereign's prestige, of the character of the group's members, and of the rulers' character.

In presenting the first of these schematisations (*Muqaddima* II, 14), Ibn Khaldūn shows that prestige, in a process that takes at most four generations, is at its maximum intensity in the founder of a dynasty (the "builder"). Having emerged from the *badāwa*, he is the one who is fully aware of the efforts he had to make and the qualities he necessarily had to develop to conquer the *ḥaḍāra*.

The prestige of the son ("the one who has had contact with his father") is lesser, although, in his actions, he can still rely on the examples personally offered by his father.

Prestige decreases even more with the grandson ("the one who follows the tradition"), who limits himself to "traditionally" following in his grandfather's footsteps: "a person who relies upon tradition is inferior to a person who exercises independent judgement" (*Muqaddima* II, 14; Ibn Khaldūn 1958, Vol. I: 279; Ibn Khaldūn [1967] 2005: 105).

Finally, it reaches its lowest point in the fourth generation: in this case, the sovereign ("the destroyer"), considering his own status and privileged position as being his birthright, does not feel obliged to cultivate the necessary virtues of humility and respect. On the contrary: considering himself superior by birth to the group he is in charge of, he does not take care to nurture its *'aṣabiyya* (which is linked, as we have seen, to dynamics of group identification) and, thus, brings about a clear separation between himself and others.

With the disappearance of *'aṣabiyya*, therefore, the leader's nobility and prestige also disappear. Such attributes, in fact, exist only to the extent that they are conferred by the opinion of the group.

This cycle of rise, corruption, and fall can be observed even if we analyse the changes that, as a whole, affect the groups that get from *badāwa* to *ḥaḍāra*. Ibn Khaldūn writes that the more "wild" groups, precisely because they are tempered by a life of deprivation, are at first more easily capable of gaining superiority over other groups. Yet later, because of the affluence they achieve, they end up losing their courage and their ability to fight in the same way that wild animals—such as gazelles, buffaloes, and donkeys—, once domesticated, undergo changes in temperament that can even be seen in the colour of their fur and the elegance of their movements.

Ibn Khaldūn summarises that the reason for this is the fact that "familiar customs determine human nature and character" (*Muqaddima* II, 15; Ibn Khaldūn 1958, Vol. I: 283; Ibn Khaldūn [1967] 2005: 107): it is the habit of well-being, developed in such circumstances, that drains the energies of the group that came to power, triggering the process—irreversible, from a certain point onwards—of senility.[4]

As the group, once elevated[5] thanks to the strong *'aṣabiyya* exalted by its leader, devotes itself in the shadow of the ruling dynasty to the enjoyment, at last, of the riches it has obtained, it shifts its competitiveness and desire to prevail into outward signs of superiority, such as the beauty of its clothing or the splendour of its houses, until its *'aṣabiyya* is completely exhausted. At this point, the group, no longer able to defend itself, invites its own destruction. As it is confronted with new groups from the reserve of virgin forces of the *badāwa*, tightly bonded and morally superior, the wheel of history spins, assigning the emerging, rejuvenating, and regenerating young force to *ḥaḍāra*, and the old one back to marginalisation.

In the *ḥaḍāra*, this atrophy of *'aṣabiyya*—previously a powerful vector of political power and a pole of moral value and social strength—also implies, in due time, the atrophy of society and the dynasty it supported.

This fall in the spirit of *'aṣabiyya* is also reflected in the development of a defenceless, mild attitude towards people outside the group. It is, in fact, fallacious to interpret docility and meekness towards people outside the group (in opposition to the old spirit of conquest) as one of the causal factors behind the fall of the *'aṣabiyya*. Ibn Khaldūn emphasises, in fact, that the relationship between cause and effect is reversed: the human character of meekness, itself produced by the circumstances of life, only develops when a group, internally disintegrating, is already too weakened and fearful even to be able to imagine that it can defend itself. That is the situation, precisely, of *ḥaḍāra*, in which members of the group, unable to protect themselves, consciously become a burden upon the state, "like women and children who need to be defended." (*Muqaddima* III, 12; Ibn Khaldūn 1958, Vol. I: 345; Ibn Khaldūn [1967] 2005: 137).

Ibn Khaldūn presents, as a clear example of this process, the biblical story of the Israelites[6] who, having escaped slavery in Egypt, were forced by God to remain in the desert for 40 years before they could access a new *ḥaḍāra* in the promised land. This period in the desert *badāwa* was necessary to complete the total replacement of the generation of exiled, weak slaves (crushed in their *'aṣabiyya* and fortitude by the forced docility, humiliation, and oppression from which they had escaped) with a

---

[4]*Muqaddima* II, 21. Ibn Khaldūn (1958, Vol. I: 297–298). Ibn Khaldūn ([1967] 2005: 114–115): "Time feasts on them, as their energy is exhausted by well-being and their vigour drained by the nature of luxury." "That is how God proceeds with regard to life in this world." "Luxury wears out royal authority and overthrows it."

[5]*Muqaddima* II, 20. Ibn Khaldūn (1958, Vol. I: 295). Ibn Khaldūn ([1967] 2005: 114): "[Savage people] do not stop at the borders of their horizon."

[6]As Pines (1970) wrote, it is plausible that, in relation to this example, Ibn Khaldūn might have been inspired by Maimonides' *The Guide for the Perplexed* ([1180–1190] 2000), which was certainly known, for example, to Ibn Taymmiyya, and which he might also have known.

strong, cohesive generation that had grown up without laws (apart from divine ones), oppression, and the stigma of meekness.

Only a new generation, with a character sufficiently tempered by the harsh conditions of the desert and never humiliated by superior powers, could develop its own, new *'aṣabiyya*, and be endowed with the necessary drive to defend itself, fight, and assert its claims.

Ibn Khaldūn's vision of *'aṣabiyya*, conceived as the pivot and engine of history's cycles of progress, and causally linking the decadence of cultures and civilisations to a process of universal and inevitable corruption that sooner or later strikes at the cohesive heart of each group, implies, as Campanini wrote (2005b: 23), that every civilisation—without distinction of ethnicity or race—"will end up devouring itself," causing "an inversion of the vector sense of history," following the development of a cyclical logical process in which "the end is entirely contained in its beginning" (al-Azmeh 1982: 55).

Of course, not even Islam could escape such a process—Ibn Khaldūn reluctantly admits—once the initial moment of its flourishing glory, in the period of the four *Rashidun* ("well guided") caliphs, had passed (what Weber would later describe as a period of charismatic leadership (Weber 1978, II: 1120)[7]). In fact, at the end of the "state of exceptionality"[8] characterised by the incredible unifying force of Islam's first days and its great conquests, the physical and social laws of *'aṣabiyya* intervened in the Islamic context too, together with the inevitable process of involution decreed by the nature of things, implying a gradual decline in social unity, courage, and moral standing, in a descending curve eventually leading to the decadence that Ibn Khaldūn saw as topical (Dale 2015a: 14–16).

Ibn Khaldūn observes, moreover, that, in parallel with the transformation that led from the caliphate to the *mulk*, this degeneration took place (Dale 2015a: 297) in the religious spirit too: initially vital, authentic, and simple, this dried up and became distorted in the complex and rigid textualism of the law scholars of later times—themselves a manifestation of a comfortable and sedentary way of life—who were far from understanding the logic of *'aṣabiyya*.

---

[7] Alatas (2013: 126–127) believes, instead, that Ibn Khaldūn describes the period of caliphal authority following the death of the Prophet as a period of legal-rational authority: not, therefore, traditional (as obedience was not due), nor charismatic (as not related to the exceptional character of the caliphs).

[8] Pomian (2006: 73). Pomian (2006: 74–77) further observes that, similarly, the emphasis was also placed at that time in Christianity on the regression of the Church from an exceptional state of initial morality, poverty, and spirituality, to a rigid spiritual hierarchy, accompanied by the hoarding of wealth and the lust for temporal power. This shift was harshly condemned, for example by the "*fraticelli*," but also by Marsilio of Padua (1275–1342) in his *Defensor Pacis*, in the writings of William of Occam (1285–1347), in the campaigns against the wealth of the Church led by John Wyclif (1330–1384), and in the choice of preaching in the vernacular language made by Jan Hus (1369–1415) in Bohemia. But unlike in Islam, where, with Ibn Khaldūn, all this had been framed within a broad and consistent sociological vision, in Christianity this vision of the Church's regression was framed as heretical and ferociously repressed.

Noteworthy, in this sense, is the fact that Ibn Khaldūn refused to adopt, even when dealing with the full decadence of his own civilisation, both the utopian perspective of the jurists, still tied to the unrealisable political model of the caliphate, and that of the philosophers, focused on the identification of the "virtuous city." On the contrary, he held on to his project of scientific objectivity. His awareness of the advanced ankylosis and senility of Muslim civilisation appears so lucid in his writings, to the extent that he comments with ill-concealed bitterness on the fact that, at that time, the new world was perhaps in gestation on other shores (*Muqaddima* VI, 18; Talbi 1973: 115).

In such a realistic reading of his time (a reading that brought him much criticism), Ibn Khaldūn remained, above all, consistent with the scientific principles of a non-apologetic history he enunciated at the beginning of his path, indicating in the "physical" or "physiological" cycle of *'aṣabiyya* the profound reason for such changes, far from the blind dogmatism that had led the historiography of his time to even legitimise behaviours that were quite distant from the original model (*Muqaddima*, The Introduction).

4.1.2 The Main Operating Principles of Corruption

While *'aṣabiyya* represents, in Ibn Khaldūn's cycle, the essential, decisive factor supporting and decreeing the success of any collective human enterprise, the paradox is that the achievement of its goals—which at the political level, says Ibn Khaldūn, are control and power (*mulk*)—can only produce its disintegration.

Ibn Khaldūn devoted many richly detailed pages to illustrating what Talbi (1973: 79–86) called "the etiology of decline." In fact, the third and fourth chapters of the *Muqaddima* are aimed at explaining in every aspect how the success of the political enterprise and the achievement of control over the coveted urban civilisation, *ḥaḍāra*, by its very nature ultimately lead to its corrosion. It does so by unleashing individual desires, atomising the social whole, and reducing the sense of interdependence and mutual responsibility of the members of the group (which is the basis of its aggregative drive, itself all the greater the more the environment challenges individuals).

In analysing the process of internal corruption that leads from the success of leadership to its senile involution, Ibn Khaldūn follows a path full of sociological-psychological observations aimed at analysing the relationship that links the growth of the sovereign's proud egotism, the disconnection in his relations with his people, and his need to flaunt pomp and luxury, to the corresponding development of meekness, individualism, and consumerist frenzy in his subjects.

There are many intertwining factors at this stage, but at least five main ones.

4.1.2.1 Power Does Not Tolerate Being Shared

A first important element determining the fall towards senility consists, for Ibn Khaldūn, in the passage from the intimate sense of unity that in *badāwa* binds the leader to the group he represents, to an increasingly evident disconnection between the two, that leads to a relationship more and more inclined to domination and less and less to belonging. At the beginning of the process, in fact, when the glory of victory is shared by the group, triumph represents the personal priority for all the members who, united in *'aṣabiyya*, are willing to prefer death and glory to the loss of (their own) pride.

It is thanks to the support of all members that the new leader—the embodiment of his group's *'aṣabiyya*—succeeds in taking power. Once placed in charge of his group, however, he is faced with the possibility—and then, the desire—of keeping all the power and glory (intrinsically unequal factors) for himself, which ends up shattering the identification between him and the members of the group.

Power, according to Ibn Khaldūn, is indispensable to avoid a situation in which people with similar resources continue attacking each other. On the one hand, therefore, it responds to a collective need. On the other hand, it is an object of competition, as it also satisfies a selfish desire (Cheddadi 2006: 298). It is precisely because of its duplicity that it always remains unstable, oscillating between the general interest and that of the sovereign.

In addition, even the principle according to which power is to be handled by a single person is challenged, in practice, by the contradictory tensions produced by the very evolution of the system of power. As the boundaries of the *ḥaḍāra* widen further, more peripheral centres of power inevitably emerge, and this exposes the central power to the risk of being overturned by them (that is, from within the political formation itself). So, awareness of the fact that the "peers" in his own group—the men who yesterday were his essential support—could now turn into a threat by becoming less subservient, leads the sovereign, eager to protect himself from potential internal aggression, to reject his former supporters and replace them with others, coming from outside the group and more controllable.[9]

The relationship between the leader and his new collaborators, therefore, is transformed from one of unity and support to one of hierarchical control which has the aim, and effect, of humbling the people belonging to his original group, and lowering their competitive spirit and ambition until they fully adapt to their condition of subordination.

When the natural tendency of the royal authority to claim all glory for itself, to acquire and flaunt luxury, and to run society peacefully is established, the dynasty approaches senility. In this state of mind, weakness and fear prevail in the group over

---

[9]This dynamic is also found in Pareto's theory ([1917] 1988: ch. XIII) of the "circulation of the élites," which describes how the progressive concentration of authority, passing from the collegiality of heroic times to the cult of the sovereign's personality, progressively determines the restriction of the base that sustains it (cf. Talbi 1973: 48). See also Charles Wright Mills (1956).

its members' feeling of belonging. Consequently, people's willingness to sacrifice their lives for a group with which they feel increasingly less identified fades away:

> The feeling of the people of a dynasty become diseased as a result of the contempt in which they are held and the hostility of the ruler (*Muqaddima* III, 17; Ibn Khaldūn 1958, Vol. I: 373; Ibn Khaldūn [1967] 2005: 147).

A particular expression of this dynamic, for example, is the fact that the group's members are relieved of the burden of (but, on the other hand, also prohibited from) defending themselves. This is replaced by dependence on a specific police corps and army—the only subjects to whom the task of protecting the group is delegated (with the consequent exemption of all others). This exemption, and the passivity it inculcates, contribute, according to Ibn Khaldūn, to changing the spirit of the members of the group, leading them to prize meekness and servitude (*Muqaddima* III, 11). This factor, then, also contributes to the weakening of the moral and vital strength and courage of society as a whole.

4.1.2.2 The Urban Context Breaks up the Unity of the *Badāwa*'s Familial Bonds

The original cohesive force behind the group's strength and power—its *'aṣabiyya*, which in *badāwa* is linked, in the first place, to the loyalty arising from the perception of a common identity—also gets crushed and shattered in the highly urbanised context of the city, because the inevitably high number of exogenous marriages, in situations of high demographic concentration, leads to a dispersion of family lines that, eventually, breaks the unity of the original large parental groups.

For this reason, therefore, in *ḥaḍāra* the *'aṣabiyya* also gets diluted and citizens find themselves de-tribalised by the incidence of mixed marriages. The incidence of extended families progressively reduces, until the same relations of hostility occur among these increasingly small and fragmented units, that normally separate tribes and families linked to different *'aṣabiyyāt* (*Muqaddima* IV, 21). The danger posed by this type of opposition and fragmentation had already been clearly noted since the early days of Islam. It was precisely for this reason, for example, that caliph 'Umar had forbidden non-Arab peoples living under Islamic rule to use—divisively—their native idioms (*Muqaddima* IV, 22).

"But when the group feeling is lost and replaced by another group feeling," concludes Ibn Khaldūn, "a great disintegration sets in" (*Muqaddima* IV, 19; Ibn Khaldūn 1958, Vol. II: 301; Ibn Khaldūn [1967] 2005: 291). This change also leads to an atomistic disintegration of the social fabric and a progressive individualistic isolation, also reflected in the values that are socially supported and take the place of common cohesion.

A further factor of destruction, linked to the previous one, is the decline in the birth rate. At first, in fact, luxurious conditions of life give additional strength to a dynasty and prolong it with a greater birth rate and by attracting new alliances. With the onset of the stage of senility, however, "when the roots are gone, the branches cannot be strong on their own, but disappear completely, and the dynasty no longer retains its former strength" (*Muqaddima* III, 14; Ibn Khaldūn 1958, Vol. I: 352; Ibn Khaldūn [1967] 2005: 140).[10]

4.1.2.3 Prosperity and Luxury Weaken the Group's Strength, Courage, and Unity

The desire to obtain more and more new luxury goods, progressively perceived as real needs, also contribute to driving decadence forward (Mahdi 1957: 176 ff.; Ibraham 1988: 51–7). In relation to this, Ibn Khaldūn's empirical observations are corroborated by a *Qur'anic* quote, which reads: "When We decide to destroy a town, We command those corrupted by wealth [to reform], but they [persist in their] disobedience; Our sentence is passed and We destroy them utterly."[11]

As Ibn Khaldūn observes, although the advantage gained from the first victories almost always opens up immediate opportunities to the group for greater well-being (normally, as we have seen, once the sedentary stage is reached, people immediately copy the most refined customs from the previous dynasty[12]), these new standards of living are soon abandoned in favour of higher and higher standards. As Ibn Khaldūn points out, people soon "get used" (*Muqaddima* III, 10) to their comfortable lifestyles and, therefore, they aspire to ever more luxury, in food, fashion, and furnishings, not only for immediate purposes—i.e., to obtain satisfaction—but also for indirect goals, that is to say, to satisfy their intrinsically comparative and competitive social pride.

In fact, in the phase of *ḥaḍāra* the production of increasingly diversified commodities and luxury goods triggers dynamics of desire and competition. These dynamics set in motion the mechanism of *jah*, the "system of prestige"[13]—a dynamic of rivalry in the hoarding of resources, which are felt as indispensable mainly because of their social value, rooted in a competitive feeling which is

---

[10] A similar metaphor will be used by Rudolf von Jhering to describe the process of desuetude of the laws.

[11] Sura *The Night Journey*: (*Qur'an* 17, 16) (Haleem 2004: 176). With this reference, Ibn Khaldūn harmonises the religious and metaphysical plan with his empirical economic-psychological arguments (Talbi 1973: 84).

[12] *Muqaddima* III, 13. Ibn Khaldūn (1958, Vol. I: 347). Ibn Khaldūn ([1967] 2005: 138): "They come to adopt the customs and (enjoy) the conditions of their predecessors."

[13] Abdesselam Cheddadi (1980: 536–7) observes that the consideration given in the *Muqaddima* to the element of *jah*, that is, to the external elements of social prestige, clearly refers to the sociocultural context of Islamic society, in which wealth is seen as an essential attribute and tangible sign of authority, and where the law, even divine one, also needs to be accompanied by something more primitive and more rooted in human nature in order to impose itself: the attraction for power and the aura of fascination that accompanies it.

radically opposed to the cooperative elation of *'aṣabiyya*, and which leads to the corrosion of social links and of material and spiritual resources.[14]

Luxury, therefore, multiplies its range of offerings by no longer mainly pursuing functionality—in diet, as well as in fashion, architecture, and so on—but rather hedonism and position. Thus, a dynamic is triggered similar (Megherbi 1971: 209–210) to that which, in the 1960s, Henri Lefebvre (1965) defined as a "frenzy of needs," fuelled not only by the proliferation of consumer goods, but also by anomie (that is, by the disappearance of social norms capable of effectively controlling individual drives and aspirations).

This process increasingly intensifies: "From the necessities of life and a life of austerity, they progress to the luxuries and a life of comfort and beauty" (*Muqaddima* III, 10; Ibn Khaldūn 1958, Vol. I: 338; Ibn Khaldūn [1967] 2005: 133), so that each new generation overtakes the previous one in a rush to luxury which increasingly becomes fanciful, addictive and, therefore, weakening. But the more pressure is exerted by the dynamic of prestige, the scarcer these resources become, in their progress towards the downward phase of the cycle. Therefore, especially in the more advanced stages of this process, a progressive gap opens up between men's desires and their ability to satisfy them.

In the pursuit of the satisfaction of increasingly diversified needs, the inhabitants of *ḥaḍāra* end up spending more than they gain. This has, eventually, harmful consequences, not only on a material level, but also in the domain of values, as the extolling of moral rigour is drowned out by the extolling of cunningness, i.e., of the ability to circumvent laws and sanctions, with the aim of satisfying personal interest only and ranking as high as possible in the collective competition for outward prestige.

4.1.2.4 Not Even the Cohesive Force of Religion Can Escape the Corruptive Process

Ibn Khaldūn was a fervent believer, and his severity as a charismatic judge, unwilling to accept compromises and "arranged" judgments—an attitude he maintained in spite of all the problems he encountered in Cairo—represents a tangible proof of this. However, this did not prevent him from observing that not even divine law is exempted, as far as its earthly application is concerned, from paying its toll to the dynamics of corruption.

[14]As Raffaele Alberto Ventura (2020a, 2020b, Chap. 6) writes, Western philosophy and contemporary sociology tried various approaches to understand the social phenomena subsumed by Ibn Khaldūn under the concept of *jah*. Ventura quotes Thorstein Veblen's (1899) view of "conspicuous consumption," Max Weber's ([1922] 1978) concept of "Stände," Pierre Bourdieu's (1984) idea of "symbolic capital," Charles Taylor's (1992) concept of "recognition," Philip Pettit and Geoffrey Brennan's (2006) concept of "kudonomy" (economy of esteem), Marcel Mauss's (2006) idea of "prestige," and Francis Fukuyama's (2018) idea of "dignity," among others.

On the contrary, he was already seeing the effects of the corruptive process in that view of *Shari'a* law, "lifeless" and disconnected both from its own original inspirations and from any understanding of historical change, which was deplorably taught and applied by many religious judges and teachers of his time, and was gradually transforming even religious belief into a faith of complex legal texts, devoid of its original spiritual energy.[15]

In this analysis, in the final part of the *Muqaddima* devoted to the sciences, the criticism directed against the teachers of his time also converges: according to Ibn Khaldūn, they were, for the most part, lacking any critical capacity of independent judgment. Such qualities were now lost, and replaced by the mere memorisation of myriads of texts—what is more, learned according to a conservative textual tradition (simply based on quotations from tradition, without further discussion)—which, in his time, was also affecting the Malikite school to which he belonged (*Muqaddima* VI, 13; Dale 2015a: 214–215).

4.1.2.5 The Search for Comfort and Tranquility Weakens Society

This same "frenetic" search for well-being also, and in fact especially, affects the sovereign's efforts. These start with water being piped to the homes, having gardens and castles as beautiful and spectacular as possible, and end up with accumulating luxury goods: this tendency is passed on to his successors, who, in turn, are not exempt from this addictive habit. All this entails high costs that, amongst other things, require the political power to raise more and more taxes, in a counterproductive and unjust way which causes more injustice. These, in turn, cause further social evils—impoverishment, low incomes, and decrease in military power—with a predictable chain of negative effects since, as Ibn Khaldūn writes, "injustice brings about the ruin of civilisation" (*Muqaddima* III, 41; Ibn Khaldūn 1958, Vol. II: 103; Ibn Khaldūn [1967] 2005: 238).

Even the social stability pursued by the royal authority gradually turns into a habit and, as such, "colours" the nature of the people subjected to it—as happens, Ibn Khaldūn emphasises, with everything one gets used to. As a matter of fact, after conquering power, the sovereign, following his natural instincts, tries to contrast the uncertainty of history and rationalise it, preparing for the future a system capable of structuring life in a preordained, "quiet," and safe way, pursuing an ideal of stability that allows the enjoyment of this new situation. Even this reassuring rationalisation, however, produces weakening effects, by removing any "fortitude" and urge to advance from the inhabitants of *ḥaḍāra*. So, since the generations which have grown up in peace do not have a warrior's vigour, the last descendants in this process are destined, in the end, to be overwhelmed by other groups.

[15]See below Ibn Khaldūn's critique directed at the system used, in his time, to teach the sciences (first of all traditional, i.e., Qur'anic sciences), based on the mnemonic learning of texts that were mostly summarised and scarcely understood in their essence (*Muqaddima* VI, 34–37).

While luxury, therefore, operates its slow and constant effect of corrupting character, at the same time the peaceful attitude that political stability induces also leads the group to sink more and more into the sedentary culture of tranquility and softness, in all its manifestations.

These two factors—the development of a weak nature linked to the construction of a "protected" state of tranquility, and attachment to luxuries—also intersect with each other, producing further, and even worse, synergies: the fact that luxury goods, becoming habits, are increasingly perceived as a need, rather than as fanciful options, brings about an increase in the cost of living and this creates poverty, which, in turn, makes it difficult to subsidise wars out of taxes. The subjects unable to pay taxes are eventually punished with expropriation, thus becoming even poorer, until, in the end, this poverty backfires against the ruler, who, in the face of lower income, experiences difficulties in paying the soldiers on whom the defence of the kingdom relies.

For example, Ibn Khaldūn shows how, as the phase of senility approaches, corruption, and abuse of public office, aimed at extorting goods and money by illicit means for personal gain, also increase (being a judge and government official himself, he had often been sent to collect taxes, thereby gaining great personal experience of all these matters). So, also in terms of security, this has negative repercussions for the sovereign as well—both on the material level and in terms of values—which are parallel to those which affect his subordinates, and for the same reasons.

In this case too, luxury and desire, together with the dynamics they set in motion, are put in close correlation with the corruption that arises from them—a corruption that is seen not only in the quality of the acts perpetrated, but also, and above all, in the quality of the character produced by the development of a sedentary life (Alatas 1986: 9). As Ibn Khaldūn (always careful to reconcile the reasons of nature—including social nature—with divine will) points out, this process evolves "until God permits His command to be executed" (*Muqaddima* III, 10; Ibn Khaldūn 1958, Vol. I: 339; Ibn Khaldūn [1967] 2005: 133).

4.1.3 Metamorphosis of the Group, Metamorphosis of Power

The same division of history into phases from rise to decline, which has been already illustrated with reference to the political prestige of rulers, recurs if one considers the influence of the material conditions of life on the characteristics of civilisations. In fact, these, too, by their very nature, go through predictable phases in the passage from *badāwa* to *ḥaḍāra*, and from there to the destruction of their cycle,[16] linked to the change of generations.

[16]Ibn Khaldūn (*Muqaddima* III, 12) refers to an analogy between a person's life span (measured according to the 120-year term, called by astrologers a "lunar year")—and that of the dynasties,

1. The first generation—corresponding to the government of the leader (the "builder") propelled to taking power—is still endowed with the characteristics of the *badāwa*: its members—accustomed to deprivation, brave, wild, and strong, willing to share their glory, cunning and capable of inspiring fear and respect—are still linked to each other by a strong *'aṣabiyya*. Even the power of the leader (*Muqaddima* III, 14), in this phase, proves exemplary: still *primus inter pares*, an expression of the virtues supported by the group, the object of a shared pride and reference point, he feels organically linked to the group supporting him, without which he would have never gained power.

   On the economic front, the qualities that "colour" the leader in this first generation are magnanimity towards his people, moderation in expenses, respect for the property of others, and sobriety: at this stage, therefore, no high taxes are imposed on his subjects, not least because there is scarcely any need for ostentation.
2. The second generation (the one governed by the "son who had contact with his father") maintains some vestige of the previous virtues (thanks to the human and personal contact the sovereign had with the leader of the first generation), but begins to be affected by a series of mutations, due to the well-being and power achieved: from the sharing of success, the group experiences its monopoly by a single individual; from consuming only essential goods, the inhabitants transition to a more refined lifestyle; from being willing to die for glory, they transition to laziness and indifference towards it; from proud superiority, they adapt to humble submission.

   All this begins to break the group's vigour, even if this generation still retains a memory of its old "fortitude." At this stage, the sovereign is busy excluding from authority those who had helped him to achieve it in the first place, putting an ever-greater distance between himself and his people. In this phase, as power flourishes and expands, the sovereign begins to invest in luxury, and this involves greater expense both for him and his people, who are inclined to imitate the customs of those who govern them.

   The reigning power, therefore, devotes itself to collecting taxes, erecting monuments, and subsidising public spending and the splendours of the court. It is in this context that the various outward signs of power we have already seen—apparently marginal, but, in reality, essential to transmit a suggestive and incisive psychological impression of force—become decisively important instruments of government. In battle, the influence on the human soul of drums, trumpets, and horns to arouse a kind of euphoria similar to drunkenness, so as to stimulate courage and lead soldiers to minimise difficulties and, eventually, sacrifice their lives—or the use of flags to create fear and, therefore, stimulate greater

---

which, apart from variations given by different circumstances, normally lasts three generations. In turn, he assigns to a generation a duration of 40 years, necessary to reach maturity—as shown by the already cited example of the 40 years spent by the Israelites in the desert before their new generation was allowed to reach the promised land.

aggressiveness—prove to be particularly crucial and suggestive, as solidarity's motivation to fight begins to fade away.

3. During the third generation (the one ruled by the "grandson who follows the tradition"), as luxury reaches its peak, *'aṣabiyya* fades away completely into individualism and indifference and the people, dependent on others for their protection, lose the ability to assert and defend themselves, until they are reduced to depend on the dynasty "as women and children who need to be defended." This third generation also completely loses the memory of the desert's harshness and "fortitude": it is as if these things never existed.

   Dominated by force, but also brought up (as will be shown below) in such a way as to break its pride and "fortitude," this generation loses its desire for glory and the sense of the group *'aṣabiyya*; on the other hand, it greatly develops its propensity for consumerism and its craving for luxury, up to the point at which it can no longer do without it, even if this entails living above one's means.

   At this stage, the sovereign enjoys a peaceful reign and the rewards of his power, and he follows the tradition of his predecessors. However, incipient senility makes his soldiers dangerous. He, therefore, ingratiates them with gifts. In order to meet their cost, the people are burdened even more with taxes; in parallel, the habit of luxury stimulates the drive to acquire ever more consumer goods, although they are never enough to satisfy this need.

   People become accustomed to the most refined activities, while agricultural work is heavily taxed and socially discouraged (*Muqaddima* III, 49); on a general level, thus, knowledge of agricultural techniques—and, with it, the art of providing for one's own subsistence—is also forgotten. It is for this reason that this phase frequently involves the outbreak of ferocious famines too. These, in turn, weaken the population and facilitate the spread of pestilence and other epidemics, given the very high density of the population, often concentrated in damp, decaying areas lacking fresh air.

4. With the fourth generation (that of the great-grandson, "the destroyer") prestige is lost and power reaches its senility. It is maintained in this phase by consuming and squandering the reserves and luxury goods accumulated by previous generations.

   All the signs of decadence are present in this phase: from the ostentatious cult of the image to the imposition of taxes which, however high, still prove insufficient to sustain internal expenditure; from demographic collapse to a management of public services based more on the logic of patronage than on competence; and from moral and religious decline to the general inability of people to provide for, and defend, themselves. The *'aṣabiyya* of the leader, long sacrificed to the hunt for power and wealth, eventually crumbles, while the *'aṣabiyya* of the members of the group is replaced by antithetical qualities and habits such as a disposition to deception, lies, and the pursuit of luxury. The independence of the desert and the ability to defend oneself is now long gone in favour of a life of supine submission.

These are the signs of decay that introduce senility (*ḥarām*), a condition of disintegration and weakness. This condition will naturally attract the aggressiveness and ambitions of other groups, until the dynasty is destroyed by new forces—still wild but, for this very reason, still charged with the predatory aggressiveness of *'aṣabiyya*, and with a basic, inner, and necessarily mounting tension caused by their coming "from below," from the *badāwa.*

Security and well-being have the same type of influence, however, on the character traits of the ruler himself, according to a similar cyclical model in five phases[17] (the third proposed by Ibn Khaldūn: *Muqaddima* III, 15). This, marked by the interweaving of overlapping and interacting phenomena (such as politics and economics), determines the transition from the attitude of *badāwa* to the senility of the advanced *ḥaḍāra*, showing how a sovereign's characteristics are influenced by his own position in the dynastic cycle,[18] too.

In the first phase—that of success—the leader acts as a reference model and, precisely because of the solidarity of the group, does not claim all glory for himself but acts as the "champion" of the group. In the second phase, however, after gaining complete power, he detaches himself from his people, excluding them from the honours of his position, until he eventually replaces his old comrades with new clients and allies ranked in a clear hierarchy.

The third phase is the stage of pleasure and peace, in which the central role is played by the administration of the territory and the collection of taxes. This is the last stage in which the sovereign enjoys complete authority and is still capable of independent judgement and decision making, which is a sign of authority. In the fourth phase—that of satisfaction and peace—, rather than personally engaging in a variety of potential political choices and options, the ruler rigidly adopts the traditions of his predecessors, afraid that moving away from them might risk undermining his power, on the assumption that his predecessors knew better than him what had to be done to preserve the glory they had built.

Finally, the fifth phase is the stage of squandering and dissipation, in which the sovereign loses his influence over his clients, who start hating him[19] (because his later followers share none of his glory and are, instead, termed his "servants" (*Muqaddima* III, 18)). In this phase he loses his "grip" on his soldiers, too: this happens both because he can no longer pay them, because of the great waste of

[17]Taha Hussein, in his *Analytical Study* (1918), tried to apply the Comtian sociological architecture to this cycle, describing it as the "law of the three stages."

[18]This scheme seems to anticipate the "*Buddenbrook dynamic*" with which the economist Walt Whitman Rostow (1960) explains his model of economic development.

[19]In fact, Ibn Khaldūn emphasises, it is not uncommon for the *vizier*, or the entourage of a particularly fragile sovereign (as is the case when a king is still a child), to try to assume power (even though they do not possess the "colouring" of the original *'aṣabiyya*) precisely by exploiting the "softening" influence on the sovereign of an education aimed at getting him used to luxury (*Muqaddima* III, 19; Ibn Khaldūn 1958, Vol. I: 377; Ibn Khaldūn [1967] 2005: 150): "He keeps the child away from his people. He accustoms him to the pleasures of a life of luxury and gives him every possible opportunity to indulge in them. He causes him to forget to look at government affairs." The ruler can rarely manage to recover from this situation, since immersion in luxury and prosperity makes him forget the virile attitude of leadership, leaving him to develop a weak soul, depleted of any desire for leadership.

resources invested in luxury goods now perceived as necessary, and because of the (by now, chronic) lack of a personal and direct relationship with them, as he becomes increasingly inaccessible and no longer cares to supervise them directly. Ibn Khaldūn concludes:

> In this stage, the dynasty is seized by senility and the chronic disease from which it can hardly ever rid itself, for which it can find no cure, and, eventually, it is destroyed (*Muqaddima* III, 15; Ibn Khaldūn 1958, Vol. I: 355; Ibn Khaldūn [1967] 2005: 142).

4.1.4 Government and the Economy

The weakening of the fighting group's political-military structure, which results, as we have seen, in the loss of its cohesion, motivation, and sense of identity, is considered by Ibn Khaldūn as one of the two external factors that play a decisive role in the enfeeblement and crumbling of a dynasty, leading it towards irreversible senility. The other factor is economic decline—which is also of the utmost importance in a framework marked by deep interdependence between politics and the economy.

Ibn Khaldūn intimately links three elements in the economic factor: the psychological hold arising from habituation to luxuries, and the ensuing needs this induces; the influence of taxation, progressively increased to meet the demands of a court growing in splendour; and the motivation of the population to put their energies into work.

From the intersection of these three elements, Ibn Khaldūn derives the principle that:

> It should be known that at the beginning of a dynasty, taxation yields a large revenue from small assessments. At the end of the dynasty, taxation yields a small revenue from large assessments (*Muqaddima* III, 36; Ibn Khaldūn 1958, Vol. II: 89; Ibn Khaldūn [1967] 2005: 230).

This principle is known today as "*Laffer's curve*," after the economist Arthur Laffer who, quoting Ibn Khaldūn's *Muqaddima*,[20] brought back these considerations in the 1980s. It states that, at first, taxed subjects and businesses, thanks to the low revenue which allows them to derive satisfaction from the fruits of their work, still maintain the energy and desire to operate which allows them to flourish and, therefore, contribute to the increase in the total revenue of their society. Later, however, the progressive and gradual increase in the amount of taxes raised, due

[20] Laffer (2004) shows, with this principle, that beyond a certain level of tax levy, taxes progressively discourage economic activity: if the tax levy reached 100%, the revenue would be zero. In fact, if the phenomenon is viewed within its social context, it becomes clear that high taxation of economic activity produces tax avoidance, evasion, and outflow of the taxable matter.

to the growing luxury and magnificence, ultimately overwhelms those who are obliged to pay them.[21]

However, as these increases occur gradually, these people do not really realise the extent of their burden (as is often the case when changes occur little by little) and, as a result, continue paying them out of tradition.

Eventually, this disrupts the balance of economic activity: when tax increases go beyond the level of fairness, businesses' interest in staying active simply disappears because the high percentage of earnings that have to be devoted to taxes kills any incentive to continue, thus reducing or nullifying the personal satisfaction and reward people derive from their work. As a result, not only does the psychological incentive to set up culturally valuable businesses disappear—another element, incidentally, which weakens the vitality of the civilisation in question—but the total tax revenue decreases, too.

For this reason, Ibn Khaldūn recommends that the amount of taxes be kept as low as possible, provided that social fairness is ensured, in order to keep alive, in the economically capable and potentially enterprising people, the psychological propensity to engage in such activities.

In addition, as time goes on and senility weakens society further, it also becomes more and more difficult to collect taxes from outlying provinces, and this results in a further decrease in revenue parallelling the increase in the needs typical of this phase. It is necessary, therefore, to impose even more new taxes, in order to be able to remunerate the armed forces needed to defend the political organisation—which hits the economy even harder, and causes more and more people to lose their motivation.

Ibn Khaldūn also studies the effects of public funding on the economic prosperity of a political unit. He states that it would be a big mistake, on the one hand, for the sovereign to undertake a commercial activity in his own name, as this would upset the equilibrium of the market. Conversely, the dynasty, which itself constitutes the "largest market" at the basis of trade,[22] should rather support the economic activity of its subjects—an insight which anticipates Keynes' intuition of the central importance of expenditure by institutions as a determining factor in the economic well-being of society.

---

[21]Some have erroneously interpreted this observation in a neoliberal sense (Gamarra 2015: 452). However, it does not at all imply an invitation to a tax-free society: it is the fact of going beyond the limit of fairness that is seen, here, as a source of entrepreneurial and economic decadence (see also Al-Araki 2014: 97). On the relevance of Ibn Khaldūn's economic theory in the contemporary world, see Rizkiah and Chachi (2020).

[22]*Muqaddima* III; 40. Ibn Khaldūn (1958, Vol. II: 103). Ibn Khaldūn ([1967] 2005: 238): "The dynasty is the greatest market, the mother and base of all trades, the substance of income and expenditure."

Finally, Ibn Khaldūn stresses the importance of another key factor that lies behind the ruin of a civilisation:[23] injustice[24] on the part of the sovereign. Only those in a position of power and authority, in fact—says Ibn Khaldūn incisively—can commit injustice.[25]

As Ibn Khaldūn points out, although over time power has lost the righteousness of the age of the first caliphs, and has returned to the realm of nature and corruption, in line with its cyclical journey, the obligation to follow the rules of good governance and pursue justice remains in force. By virtue of the very dynamics occurring in society, although injustice cannot be prevented by higher rules, the need for a counterbalance to it is nevertheless dictated by its own disruptive effects, inescapably produced according to the "law" of the cycle of civilisation and power.

Ibn Khaldūn emphasises here, in fact, that a full overlap occurs between the commandment, given by the Prophet, to respect people's religion, soul, life, intellect, progeny, and property, and the causal chain which, starting from the injustice of the violation of these values, leads to the destruction of civilisation (and ultimately, if generalised, of the human species itself). For this reason, even though the sovereign enjoys the "freedom" to place himself above what is just, he encounters natural limits: injustice naturally leads to the destruction of civilisation and, therefore, to the ruin of sovereign power itself, and thus carries in itself the very reason why it must be avoided.

By way of example, Ibn Khaldūn enumerates various types of state violence. He lists, first of all, attacks on property by the sovereign, which discourage, as we have already seen, people's propensity to engage in business and production, normally driven by the perspective of making a profit.

Similarly, property confiscation accompanied by little or no compensation also constitutes injustice. By the same token, forced labour (because labour, says Ibn Khaldūn, as part of the elements of capital, is thus extorted), as well as the imposition of duties or taxes that are not actually required by religious laws, or in other ways justified, constitute injustice. Such injustices backfire against the dynasty and civilisation, which are, eventually, ruined by the consequent loss of its subjects' incentive to collaborate in order to keep it strong and vital.

---

[23]*Muqaddima* III, 41. Ibn Khaldūn (1958, Vol. II: 103). Ibn Khaldūn ([1967] 2005: 238): "Injustice brings about the ruin of civilisation." In this passage Ibn Khaldūn combines a directly ethical point of view with his scientific-descriptive considerations. According to Dale (2015a: 249), the moral universe with respect to which the monarch's plundering of property can be seen as unjust, can here only be identified with the Muslim religion.

[24]The term "justice," '*adl*, derives from the Arab root '*ayn dal lam*, which indicates the idea of straightening something.

[25]*Muqaddima* III, 41. Ibn Khaldūn (1958, Vol. II: 107). Ibn Khaldūn ([1967] 2005: 241): "injustice can be committed only by persons who cannot be touched, only by persons who have power and authority."

4.1.5 Senility

"The authority of the dynasty at first expands to its limits and then is narrowed down in successive stages, until the dynasty dissolves and disappears" (*Muqaddima* III, 46; Ibn Khaldūn 1958, Vol. II: 124; Ibn Khaldūn [1967] 2005: 250). With such an axiomatic proposition Ibn Khaldūn, apparently using the metaphor of water, describes the ineluctability of the undertow movement that, after the advance of the expansion of power, is naturally generated, dragging civilisation back again.

As we have seen, the power of royal authority derives from two founding elements: *'aṣabiyya* and economic resources. When these two pillars are weakened and crumble, the irreversible phase of senility intervenes and, with it, the disintegration of the dynasty. "Senility"—Ibn Khaldūn writes—"is a chronic disease that cannot be cured or made to disappear because it is something natural, and natural things do not change" (*Muqaddima* III, 44; Ibn Khaldūn 1958, Vol. II: 117; Ibn Khaldūn [1967] 2005: 245).

Even if the most politically aware people were able to spot its first symptoms and raise the alarm, they would still not be able to prevent its advance, because "customs that have developed prevent him from repairing it. Customs are like a second nature" (*Muqaddima* III, 44; Ibn Khaldūn 1958, Vol. II: 117; Ibn Khaldūn [1967] 2005: 245).

Because of the factors indicated above, such as the progressive detachment of the sovereign from his group[26] and the corruption of people's character brought about by the habit of luxury, the vitality of *'aṣabiyya*—that collective, cohesive force rooted in the feelings of individuals—is drained in the senile phase. Its place is taken, in the minds of men, by such external elements as luxury and pomp, which are visible symptoms and indicators, as we have seen, of the power achieved by the sovereign and the strength of the political unit governed by him.

Ibn Khaldūn explains that it is now, when the level of such ostentation of power and strength falls in parallel with the first signs of crisis, that other ambitious men, ahead of the evidenced weakening of political power, become audacious, sense the possibility of a reversal of power, and might go so far as to challenge and fight it. In fact, explains Ibn Khaldūn, "human beings love very much to gain control over royal authority, especially when the soil is prepared and all the requirements and symptoms [of its weakening] are there" (*Muqaddima* III, 42; Ibn Khaldūn 1958, Vol. II: 113; Ibn Khaldūn [1967] 2005: 244).

This is why, in such a phase, the sovereign feels the need to show off his strength and greatness as much as possible, with costly displays of power aimed at giving the impression that senility is still far away, or that its first signs have regressed. But this is only the dynasty's swan song:

> It lights up brilliantly just before it is extinguished, like a burning wick the flame of which leaps up brilliantly a moment before it goes out, giving the impression it is just starting to

---

[26]The story of the progressive restriction, across generations up to senility, of access to the sovereign, is interesting in this regard (in *Muqaddima* III, 42).

burn, when in fact it is going out (*Muqaddima* III, 44; Ibn Khaldūn 1958, Vol. II: 118; Ibn Khaldūn [1967] 2005: 246).

The dynasty, meanwhile, tries to keep under control its soldiers—who grow more and more arrogant the more they perceive the progressive senility and weakness of the underlying *'aṣabiyya*—with economic handouts. These are only made possible, however, by confiscations and tax increases which, for their part, further bleed society dry. Nevertheless, these donations are necessary because the dynasty really needs its army to maintain its power, and it needs it more than ever in that very situation of constant and continuous threat which characterises the phase of transition between the old and new dynasty.

Meanwhile, in the last years of government of the old dynasty, people are exposed to famine, due to falling cultivation of the land, and to potential plagues in large cities where the growing population (increased because of the sense of security previously provided by the dynasty's protection (Muqaddima III, 49)) has gathered. This situation progressively advances towards its own involution, until, "eventually, God permits the ruling dynasty to end, its life to stop, and disintegration to afflict it from all sides" (*Muqaddima* III, 48; Ibn Khaldūn 1958, Vol. II: 132; Ibn Khaldūn [1967] 2005: 254).

4.2 Urbanisation, Prosperity, and Lifestyles

4.2.1 The Relationship Between Urbanisation, Prosperity, and Lifestyles

After illustrating the process of social and political evolution that characterises the transition from *badāwa* to *ḥaḍāra*, and after showing how this explains the process that led Islamic society from caliphate to monarchy, Ibn Khaldūn sets out to demonstrate how a parallel evolutionary path also occurs on an economic level. This is given by the drive that steers development away from a natural form of economy towards a market economy, and from there to the loss of the individual's dominion and control over things.

In relation to the economy of *ḥaḍāra*, Ibn Khaldūn analyses the multiplier effects of the division of labour with expressions that closely recall those with which Adam Smith (1723–1790) illustrated the same phenomenon in 1776, and which also anticipate the thesis of Frederick Winslow Taylor (1856–1915) on the enormous increase in productivity and wealth produced by specialisation and role division.

In fact, this theme was not entirely new in Ibn Khaldūn's cultural framework, as it had already been at least sketched out, for example, by Al-Fārābī[27] in his *al-Madīna*

[27] Al-Fārābī ([IX-X century] 1998: 229): "In order to preserve himself and to attain his highest perfections every human being is by his very nature in need of many things which he cannot provide all by himself, he is indeed in need of people who each supply him with some particular need of his.

al-fāḍila. Ibn Khaldūn's great and original intuition, however, was to uncouple his economic analysis from any moral superstructure, inserting these observations, instead (and, thus, implicitly confirming them), into a synthetic and "pan-scientific" general framework, so as to link his economic analysis in an inseparable whole to his sociological-psychological reading of society.

To arrive at this, Ibn Khaldūn starts by observing that the construction and inhabiting of urban aggregates necessarily require a condition of peace and luxury that only the protection given by a stable dynasty can offer. Royal authority, therefore, Ibn Khaldūn writes, "calls for urban settlement": "Only strong royal authority is able to construct large cities and high monuments" (*Muqaddima* IV, 2, 3; Ibn Khaldūn 1958, Vol. II: 237, 238; Ibn Khaldūn [1967] 2005: 264, 265).

Cities, which are created for the masses and their protection from enemies, and which require large numbers of people capable of working together in peace, can be seen as secondary products of the serenity offered by the presence of a strong royal authority. In turn, in the shadow of reassuring walls, they lead the inhabitants to seek peace and relaxation. The city walls, in fact, by instilling security, reduce the need to worry, as individuals and as a united group, about one's own defence.

So, while, on the one hand, these arrangements bring the inhabitants to depend on the armed forces organised by the sovereign power for their security, on the other hand they allow the liberation of energies that can be used for the realisation of all those other elements that constitute urban civilisation.

This situation, therefore, favours the cultural development of civilisation, but at the expense of the weakening of the general level of *'aṣabiyya* of the political group. While basic solidarity, deriving mostly from a sense of union and common descent, is very strong in non-urbanised communities, both in its intensity and in its fortifying effect for the individual, the solidarity that develops in the city context, where people become functionally dependent on each other (*Muqaddima* IV, 7), is much weaker.

Returning to some of his initial observations on the influence of climate and environment, Ibn Khaldūn focuses first of all on the importance of the healthiness of the air in the choice of a place to found a city (*Muqaddima* IV, 4): the stagnation of air should be avoided, as it is often the cause of diseases (grossly and erroneously attributed to "curses" and magic spells). He also lists the purity of the water, as well as the proximity of pastures, sources of wood, and, possibly, the sea, as important elements to be taken into account. If attention is not paid to all these factors (as was the case with many cities founded by the Arabs, Ibn Khaldūn points out, who were often recklessly attentive, when choosing a place, only to the presence of water for

---

Everybody finds himself in the same relation to everybody in this respect. Therefore, man cannot attain the perfection, for the sake of which his inborn nature has been given to him, unless many (societies of) people who co-operate come together who each supply everybody else with some particular need of his, so that as a result of the contribution of the whole community all the things are brought together which everybody needs in order to preserve himself and to attain perfection." It is reported by Dale (2015a: 330, no. 53) that, in the third century BC, Chinese philosopher and lawyer Han Fei Tzu (1939, vol. II: 44–45) had already expressed a similar consideration about personal interest and the division of labour: Han Fei Tzu (1939).

their animals, and the proximity of caravan routes), cities can only survive if a thriving political system can supply them with what is necessary for them from outside (*Muqaddima* IV, 9).

After giving due importance to environmental factors, Ibn Khaldūn then focuses on the internal dynamics of sedentary civilisation, stating, first of all, that on principle the main factor in determining the well-being of a city is its numerical magnitude (*Muqaddima* IV, 11).

This is due to the fact that when activities aimed at producing what is needed for life are carried out through a cooperation that involves organising the work of many people—as happens, in fact, in a city—the results of this organisation, as a rule, outweigh what is necessary. Consequently, the resulting surplus labour force can be engaged in pursuing goods that are not strictly necessary—luxury goods, in fact—either by directly producing them or by trading with other cities.

The production of luxury goods requires special skills, however, which have to be developed by people specifically trained for this purpose. As Ibn Khaldūn writes (anticipating a concept that will later play a central role in Durkhem's analysis of the transition between mechanical and organic solidarity), the diffusion of luxury goods requires the development of the customs necessary for their production.[28] It is on this basis, and as an effect of the drive towards the specialisation of work and crafts that is impressed on society, that the characteristic elements of sedentary culture are created:

> Sedentary culture is merely a diversification of luxury and a refined knowledge of the crafts employed for its diverse aspects and ways. This concerns, for instance, food, clothing, building, carpets, utensils, and other household needs. Each one of these things require special interdependent crafts serving to refine and improve it. They increase in number with the variety of pleasures and amusements and ways and means to enjoy the life of luxury the soul desires, and (with the growing number of) different things to which people get used (*Muqaddima* III, 13; Ibn Khaldūn 1958, Vol. I: 347; Ibn Khaldūn [1967] 2005: 138).

This phenomenon expands as the population grows; and so, with the increase of population in the cities, productivity undergoes an ever-increasing rise, resulting in a corresponding rise in new, unrealistic needs. These, in turn, stimulate other productive activities: in short, once basic needs are met, all the additional work is "spent" in the production of ever new luxury goods.

Those in power also play an important role in this type of development: not only do their consumption of, and demand for, consumer and luxury goods, and therefore their investments in this sense, bring prosperity to their people, but this then returns to them in the form of taxes, in a dynamic triggering a ("Keynesian," we would say today) process of progressive development.

That is why the lifestyle and civilisation characteristic of the cities is also qualitatively different from the lifestyle of the villages, where, due to a lower population density, no such surplus is produced. As proof of this, Ibn Khaldūn—

[28] *Muqaddima* III, 10. Ibn Khaldūn (1958, Vol. I: 338). Ibn Khaldūn ([1967] 2005: 133): "Luxuries require the development of the customs necessary to produce them."

faithful to his method of empirical observation, and in search of the latent "inner meaning" behind the most minute, but no less significant, sociological details of reality—considers, for example, the variety of attitudes which characterise the figure of the poor, or the beggar, in different contexts. The result is that while beggars living in centres that are not strongly urbanised (as in the case of Tlemcen or Oran) are usually accustomed to ask for, and receive, only what is strictly necessary for their survival, the typical attitude of beggars living in a big city (such as Fez or Cairo) is different. They find it normal and acceptable also to ask for, and obtain, luxury goods or donations that allow them to offer dignified religious sacrifices too, beyond satisfying their bare survival needs.

So much so—Ibn Khaldūn observes—that this well-known imbalance induces many poor people in the Maghreb to take pains to migrate to these other places, which they imagine inhabited by more generous or richer people, while the truth is that in every city profit and expenditure are in balance: these cities are simply more populous, and this determines their final level of plenty.

The same differences with regard to prosperity and poverty can also be seen when we increase the order of magnitude and compare countries, more or less populated and, therefore, more or less capable—by applying the same formal relationships—of achieving surpluses of production.[29] In fact, although naive observers explain the great wealth of European and Chinese merchants by taking the presence, in their countries, of a greater quantity of wealth or gold mines for granted, the fact is that these, on the contrary, are more abundant close to the Maghreb (especially in Sudan). This shows that wealth is not so much determined by these factors, but rather by other substantial reasons, linked to a higher level of urban organisation.

Another symptom of availability and overabundance of goods—considered, this time, not in relation to cities, but to private dwellings—is the presence of food leftovers that attract animals. The crumbs and leftovers in the houses of the rich are, in fact, proportionally comparable to alms in the cities: only in the houses of the rich, and not in those of the poor (even within the same city), can an abundance of ants, mice, and other animals be found in courtyards and cellars (*Muqaddima* IV, 11).

Within the urban context, however, the prosperity of individuals can also depend on factors linked to the contingent historical moment. For example, one form of enrichment arises from the exploitation of the "fluctuations of the real estate market," deriving from the disparity between the low cost of property in times of crisis (since, in a time of transition from one dynasty to another, property is not guaranteed to hold its value), and the value it later acquires with the growth of the new civilisation (*Muqaddima* IV, 15).

In a similar and opposite way, however, a situation of wealth and prosperity can also suddenly collapse: as a matter of fact wealth, if not accompanied by a capital of high-ranking human relations, is not guaranteed in itself to endure, and it is not uncommon to see owners lacking protection suddenly stripped of everything (even

[29] *Muqaddima* IV, 14. Ibn Khaldūn (1958, Vol. II: 280). Ibn Khaldūn ([1967] 2005: 279): "Differences with regard to prosperity and poverty are the same in countries as in cities."

under legal pretexts: *Muqaddima* IV, 16)—a further demonstration of how intimate and deep is the bond that encapsulates the economic dimension within social logic.

The particular relationship between luxury goods and the urbanised context, compared to the rural scene, is also explored in another sense, considering why in populated cities the cost of basic necessities, such as food, is low and that of luxury goods is high, while in small and poor cities exactly the opposite occurs.

The reason lies in the fact that people accustomed to a life of abundance are not only willing, but also able, to pay very high prices for luxury goods, precisely because they most feel their need:[30] this leads the price of these goods to rise well above their actual value. On the other hand, since basic necessities such as food are scarce in small towns, people are inclined to stockpile them, and this brings about a rise in the price of this kind of goods. Luxury goods, on the other hand, do not have a large market there, and for this reason they tend to cost less.

In both contexts, the amount of time devoted to work is usually influenced by the different types of relationship established with unnecessary goods: in large cities, the habit of enjoying luxury goods—considered, over time, as a real necessity—increases the economic needs of the inhabitants. As a consequence, the working time needed to earn enough money to be able to afford these goods also increases. In the situation of the *badāwa*, on the other hand, needs are still limited to the essential, and hence they require a much smaller amount of work (*Muqaddima* IV, 13)[31] in order to be satisfied.

In short, when a situation of greater demographic concentration arises, the correlative greater quantity of available work potential is employed in the production of greater wealth, in a process that ultimately brings about an increase in production, availability and, in the end, consumption of luxury goods.

This intimate, profound relationship between the strength or weakness of a nation, its numerical magnitude, the size of its cities, and the prosperity that arises from these factors is, in fact, one of the "secrets"—one of the "laws"—that determine the social dynamics making up the "inner meaning" of history, according to Ibn Khaldūn.

4.2.2 *Crisis Is the Product of Civilisation*

As we have seen, a sedentary culture is created thanks to the diversification of labour tasks, a phenomenon which triggers the development of specific and specialised productive activities: after a certain period of time, especially in a highly urbanised

[30]*Muqaddima* IV, 12. Ibn Khaldūn (1958, Vol. II: 277). Ibn Khaldūn ([1967] 2005: 276): "Prosperous people used to luxuries will pay exorbitant prices for them, because they need them more than others."

[31]See the research of anthropologist Marshall Sahlins ([1972] 1980) on the working times of the most primitive populations, drastically shorter than today's averages.

context, and even more so near the centres of power (dynasty and government are, in fact, "the market place of the world," says Ibn Khaldūn), such activities establish themselves as typical and necessary (*Muqaddima* IV, 17).

The sedentariness and pride of citizens, on the other hand, lead them to be more and more alien to the knowledge and skills that naturally enable them to provide for their own maintenance and survival,[32] while the diversification of luxuries extends the ways in which people enjoy the pleasures of food and sex—so much so that they go so far as to contemplate variations that are alien to the logic of nutrition or reproduction of the species.

The influence of habit (which is always a "second nature" for Ibn Khaldūn) in determining the attitude of individuals towards goods that are not strictly necessary may enable these customs to survive even dynastic and political changes. As Ibn Khaldūn writes, when a sedentary civilisation, along with its cultural practices, has been established for a certain period of time, traces of it are then maintained and found, even after drastic dynastic changes, in the customs of later populations (Ibn Khaldūn cites, as an example, the case of Tunisia: *Muqaddima* IV, 17).

Every civilisation for Ibn Khaldūn, however, has its own physiological life—just like every individual, after all—and cannot exceed certain limits. For Ibn Khaldūn—convinced that every state of affairs should be read not in a static way (as stasis does not exist) but by framing it within the dynamic, directionally oriented trajectory to which it belongs—, when the habit of luxury reaches its peak, it transforms itself and takes its toll by inducing in people a kind of "slavery to one's desires."[33] This slavery, moreover, leaves its "colouring" and mark in the human soul, inevitably modifying and damaging it both in relation to its religious dimension and to its worldly well-being, since material goods, regardless of their quantitative or qualitative level, can never fully satisfy man (*Muqaddima* IV, 18).

The pursuit of the pleasure provided by the availability of ever more refined goods, therefore, becomes a factor of crisis and involutionary change, and contributes to the spread of corruption.

In fact, corruption emerges as a result of the efforts made by individuals to satisfy these induced needs, and as a result of the evil qualities acquired satisfying these needs. Finally, it is a product of the damage inflicted on the soul by the habit of their enjoyment and trade: all these things encourage the development of character defects such as a propensity to deception, injustice, perjury, the practice of usury, etc.[34]

---

[32]*Muqaddima* IV, 18. Ibn Khaldūn (1958, Vol. II: 296). Ibn Khaldūn ([1967] 2005: 288): "Man is a man only inasmuch as he is able to procure for himself useful things and to repel harmful things, and inasmuch as his character is suited to making efforts to this effect."

[33]*Muqaddima* IV, 18. Ibn Khaldūn (1958, Vol. II: 292). Ibn Khaldūn ([1967] 2005: 285): "subservience to desires."

[34]Ibn Khaldūn's escalation (as well as those concerning the five phases of development of dynasty and society: cf. *Muqaddima* II, 14; III, 12; III, 15) anticipates a very similar model elaborated, three centuries later, by Gianbattista Vico. Vico ([1725] 1977: para 241–242) described a similar evolutionary process whereby man's nature gets progressively transformed through successive phases—at first crude, then severe, then benign, then refined and, finally, dissolute—that run in

For example, the price of goods certainly goes up in the marketplace thanks to the fact that businessmen inevitably, if given the chance, give into the temptation to grow richer and richer by passing on all their expenses, including personal expenses, and by dumping their tax liabilities, onto the customer. This finds a structural limit, however, within society: beyond a certain point, such a mechanism no longer works, and poverty dominates again (*Muqaddima* IV, 18).

This type of dynamic has a constant bearing. In fact, human beings are all similar in their basic dynamics. If they differ, it is only because, in addition to their character, they acquire virtues and vices: when a person, even one of noble origins, is "coloured" by vices, his character is corrupted.

When luxury goods are diversified and refined beyond a certain measure, therefore, the expansion and blossoming of civilisation, having reached its own peak and limit, invites its own involutive phase and starts its march towards destruction.

A subtle reader is able to deduce that there are some customs that reveal, like symptoms, the achievement of such a phase of extreme diversification. For example, the widespread cultivation in a city of trees such as bitter oranges or oleanders—which require planting and irrigation, but give in return nothing but their beauty, as they produce no edible fruit—is a sign that the city is at least close to the phase when it begins to invite its own ruin, and so its destruction is to be expected (*Muqaddima* IV, 18). The growing custom of public baths is also symptomatic of a highly developed civilisation (*Muqaddima* IV, 20).

---

parallel with the changes in man's economic behaviour. Man is, at first, satisfied with the bare necessities, then he seeks utility, then comfort, then the enjoyment of pleasure, and then, in the search for luxury, he becomes corrupt, until this pursuit overbalances and, eventually, he squanders the goods he owns. For Vico, too, therefore, the degenerative factors underlying such changes flow from habituation to luxury, which makes people slaves and impels them to develop the typical vices of slaves (lying, deceiving, slandering and stealing, and showing cowardice). This will continue until Providence (unlike Ibn Khaldūn, who seeks the causes essentially in the nature of social dynamics, Vico attributes to Providence, to a large extent, the responsibility for these changes) decrees that they truly become slaves, by natural right, of other nations which are better than them. In fact, as Vico comments ([1725] 1977: para 1105), the world is always governed by those who are naturally more capable, and those who do not know how to govern themselves must accept being governed by those who are capable. Cf. Franz Rosenthal (1958: lxxxi, n. 12). See also Rosenthal (1958: lxxxi, footnote 113) who cites, from *Muḫtār al-ḥikam* by al-Mubaššir b. Fātik (an anthology of sayings of ancient sages very popular in Spain in the thirteenth century, and even later), a passage (n. 400) attributed to Plato (Al-Mubashshir ibn Fātik [1048–1049] 1958: 176): "Great dynasties are tough of nature at the beginning, able to cope with realities and obedient to God and civil authority. Later on, towards the end of their course [?], when the security of the people has been assured, the latter begin to participate in the well-being that has been prepared for them. Then, submerged in the life of abundance and ease which the dynasty has made possible, they give themselves over to luxury and no longer come to the support (of the regime when it needs them). They are so affected by this course of events that, eventually, they lack the power to defend themselves against attack. When this has occurred, the power of the dynasty crumbles at the first assault. Dynasties are like fruits: too firm to be eaten at the beginning, they are of middling quality as they grow riper. Once they are fully ripened they taste good, but now they have come as close as fruits can come to rottenness and change."

At these times, the inversion of directionality, in the cycle of civilisation described by Ibn Khaldūn, is at the door: when people's strength, character, and religion are corrupted, despite their refinement and pride, their humanity is also corrupted and it weakens, transforming them, in fact, "into animals."[35]

4.3 Arts and Trades: The Fruits of Civilisation

4.3.1 The Different Ways in Which Man Earns What Is Needed for His Sustenance

Chapter V of the *Muqaddima* is devoted to an analysis of the various ways in which man makes a living. The premise of this discussion is the definition of a theory on the value of goods: this is defined based on the amount of work needed to produce the item. As Ersilia Francesca (2005: 85) writes, this concept which, in its own time, took over from scholastic ideas linked to Aristotle's view of it being a "fair price" proportionate to the usefulness of a product, is rather analogous to the proposal later upheld in Europe by Adam Smith, David Ricardo, and Karl Marx: "profit corresponds to the value of human work."[36]

Within this definition, however—which Ibn Khaldūn presents as a statement of fact—other elements contribute to determine the final price of a product, in a synthetic framework in which the economic phenomenon is strongly intertwined with the social dimension. These elements include the interplay between supply and demand,[37] the crucial factor brought about by the scarcity or lack of an available labour force, the complexity of the product, and the amount of stocks available.

According to Ibn Khaldūn, profit corresponds to the value produced by human work, but it is possible to distinguish in it the part that serves the needs of man—that is, his livelihood—from the rest (the *riyāš*, in Arabic, the reserve), which constitutes wealth, designated to be accumulated.[38]

---

[35]*Muqaddima* IV, 18. Ibn Khaldūn (1958, Vol. II: 297). Ibn Khaldūn ([1967] 2005: 289). The image of animal metamorphosis as a product of the inability to moderate consumption and of slavery to material well-being also featured in the fairytale production of Sinbad's cycle (see his IV voyage), which later became part of the collection of the *Thousand and One Nights* (Denaro 2006), as well as in the Homeric *Odyssey*, in the episode of the sorceress Circe. This image, which passed down the centuries, can nowadays also be found in contemporary frescoes, such as Hayao Miyazaki's *Spirited Away*.

[36]*Muqaddima* V, 1. Ibn Khaldūn (1958, Vol. II: 311). Ibn Khaldūn ([1967] 2005: 297): "Profit is the value realised from human labour."

[37]This had already been mentioned by al-Dimašqi and al-Ġazālī: Hosseini ([1995] 2003: 94, 97).

[38]This concept is translated by Franz Rosenthal as "*capital accumulation*," and can indeed be usefully interpreted in this sense, as long as we remember that, at the time, the concept of capital was not yet understood in the modern sense.

Ibn Khaldūn explains that even though all things that man possesses come from God, work is nevertheless necessary for him to make a profit and accumulate capital[39]—suffice it to say that even natural goods, such as the availability of water from rivers and canals, for example, need work and care, as experience shows, lest they get buried and disappear.

The necessity of work, which is the source of the value of things, is evident when the source of profit consists in work itself, as in the case of artisan work. When, on the other hand, it derives from something else, this may be less evident: however, the value of the profit collected always includes that of the work with which it was obtained, even if this element is hidden.

There are different ways in which man can obtain what he needs for his subsistence. First of all, he can obtain goods from outside: either from other people—through taxes, for example—or from the environment, killing or capturing wild animals or exploiting domestic ones, or through agriculture, a primary and simple activity which does not necessarily require any theoretical knowledge or speculative capacity.

Secondly, man can apply his work to specific materials, as in the case of arts and crafts such as writing, carpentry, tailoring, sewing, etc., or to the environment. He can also apply it to non-specific materials, as is the case with the professions. Arts and crafts are logically secondary to agriculture, and they, therefore, only thrive in sedentary civilisations; moreover, they are composite and require the application of scientific thought and speculative capacity.

The necessities of life can also be obtained through merchandising, either by accumulating goods and then reselling them, taking market fluctuations into account, or reselling them in distant places. Trading is based on the skill of trickery, aimed at profiting from the difference between buying and selling costs. Ibn Khaldūn, always careful to emphasise the qualities that established habits impress on men, forging their character, says it requires (and further develops) cunningness, an ability to deceive, a willingness to enter into disputes, shrewdness, perseverance, and great tenacity.

Consequently, he concludes, those who are fearful and non-aggressive by nature should not engage in trade—all the more so if they also lack the protection of rank, or the support of judges, and do not even think of ingratiating themselves with magistrates through gifts and favours (*Muqaddima* V, 14).

All the qualities developed by trade, "colouring" the soul, affect it in a negative sense by compromising its virtue, sense of honour, and virility (*Muqaddima* V, 13 and 14). Nevertheless, Ibn Khaldūn writes, trade is not comparable to theft, but is allowed by law. This is because those who trade still provide a utility to society in exchange for what they earn, since they satisfy people's perpetual cravings for different things. The tendency to develop varying desires, in fact, makes people

[39]*Muqaddima* V, 1. Ibn Khaldūn (1958, Vol. II: 313). Ibn Khaldūn ([1967] 2005: 298): "Everything comes from God. But human labour is necessary for every profit and capital accumulation."

spend money willingly, and without thinking too much, on things that are not really necessary (*Muqaddima* IV, 11).

There is also another way of making a living: putting oneself at the service of others. Although servitude is not a natural way of making a living,[40] it is implied, for example, by the very logic of power, which requires different types of servants—policemen, soldiers, administrative employees—who are invested with the forms of power related to their calling and are remunerated from the public purse.

The figure of the servant is widespread in society: in fact, servants place themselves at the service of those people who, living in luxury, soon become too proud and also too incompetent to take care of themselves. The expansion of the role of the servant, therefore, is a phenomenon—linked to the increase in social pride and the habit of luxury—which naturally develops, above all, among the noblest, richest, and most powerful families.

Ibn Khaldūn's analysis also reveals, rather disenchantedly, the most regressive and less obvious aspects of a phenomenon such as this, which apparently seems to be advantageous only to those on the "strong" side of the relationship. In fact, as he observes, this type of relationship ends up reserving its most negative effects over time precisely for those who are served: today's luxuries claim a harsh toll in terms of tomorrow's weakness. Ibn Khaldūn writes that entrusting one's own care and business to other people in return for payment, and getting used to leaning on them, instead of personally taking care of one own's security, is an expression of fragility and estrangement from basic human nature.

Ibn Khaldūn stresses that this relationship of dependence is not only a sign of weakness but also, in turn, a source of it. When habit takes root, it ends up becoming second nature in man, capable of determining his character even more than the customs of his (perhaps, noble) ancestors: "Man is a child of customs, not the child of his ancestors."[41]

In Ibn Khaldūn's view, today's developments are to be interpreted in the light of the transformative effect they will have in the future: in this perspective, he argues, the greater weakness entailed by the service relationship is not the most obvious one—that is, that of the servant—but that of those who allow themselves the luxury of being served and, thus, end up indulging in the vice of dependence.

Moreover, Ibn Khaldūn also considers the matter from another point of view: finding perfect servants, both capable and reliable, is actually impossible. Those endowed with both these characteristics, being most in demand and, therefore, in a position to choose, only put themselves at the service of princes and men of government. Those lacking both characteristics are not sought for such work. Consequently, only skilled but untrustworthy servants remain, or (worse still, because even more dangerous) well-meaning but incapable ones.

---

[40] *Muqaddima* V, 3. Ibn Khaldūn (1958, Vol. II: 317). Ibn Khaldūn ([1967] 2005: 300): "Being a servant is not a natural way of making a living."

[41] *Muqaddima* V, 3. Ibn Khaldūn (1958, Vol. II: 318). Ibn Khaldūn ([1967] 2005: 300).

Another category is a result of the changes in character produced by the habit of comfort and loss of the ability to earn a living on one's own. It is made up of those "stupid and deluded persons" (*Muqaddima* V, 4; Ibn Khaldūn 1958, Vol. II: 326; Ibn Khaldūn [1967] 2005: 304) who, trapped in their lazy habits, hope to get rich at once thanks to a stroke of good luck (for example, discovering a treasure thanks to maps they think they can decipher) and, as a consequence, waste their time clinging onto such an illusion. Ibn Khaldūn writes that such a hope is often to be found among the "students" of the Maghreb, or rich inhabitants of Cairo.

The people inclined to put themselves in such a state are those who—having become accustomed to living in a situation of increasing luxury—can no longer adapt to making a living in ordinary ways, as they would consider this irreconcilable with the newly acquired needs they cannot now renounce. An accidental and sudden stroke of fortune, obtained without any effort or trouble, is, therefore, the only possible solution that they envisage for their situation.[42]

On the other hand, a factor apparently unrelated to the economy—possession of a good lineage and the consequent prestige (the *jah*, credit, or social honour[43]) provided by that—, actually does constitute, in itself, a source of subsistence. In relation to this element too, the economic dimension that Ibn Khaldūn depicts is essentially intertwined with the social dimension. This factor—cultural,[44] rather than economic—provides very concrete advantages along with hierarchical privileges.

In fact, not only does this element (a kind of "social capital") protect and guarantee the private property of those who possess it, but it also plays a key role in procuring, for honorary reasons, new wealth to them. This wealth comes from those free gifts and services which are usually reserved for men of rank (seen as potential protectors by aspiring "clients") or men of law and religion (treated in this way by simple people who are convinced they can, thus, pay homage to God). It is in this sense that one can say that the possession of political and social power constitutes, per se, a way of earning a living (*Muqaddima* V, 5; Ibn Khaldūn 1958, Vol. II: 327; Ibn Khaldūn [1967] 2005: 304).

Political power is ultimately necessary for the well-being of society: in fact, although cooperation proves, eventually, beneficial to all, it does not in itself sufficiently motivate individuals to co-operate, since they do not normally have a clear and far-sighted view of their own interests. Consequently, in order to carry out

[42]As Ibn Khaldūn comments, not only are treasure discoveries very rare, but it is not even logical to think that those who decided to hide their possessions would have left maps and formulas lying around to facilitate their finding.

[43]The *jah*, as Horrut (2006: 121) explains, is, in the Arab culture, what "makes one stand upright and the other bow." Horrut (2006: 123) considers the *jah* as important a concept (if not more important), in Ibn Khaldūn's theory, as that of *'aṣabiyya*. In this sense, see also Cheddadi (1999: 130).

[44]As Horrut (2006: 122) explains, the *jah* hierarchy is considered to be divinely based on the grounds of what is written in the sura *Ornaments of Gold* (*Qur'an* 43, 32) (Haleem 2004: 317). This says: "We have raised some of them above others in rank, so that some may take others into service."

God's plan, it is necessary that such cooperation be obtained by force. In this sense, rank is a form of power that enables some to exercise authority and superiority over those who are placed under their control, in order to keep them from harm and enable them to grasp the advantages of social living.

In addition to this, rank and prestige also constitute, for those who possess them, an asset in pursuing their own aims—so much so that often the search for rank becomes an end in itself because of this added advantage. As Ibn Khaldūn observes, "Much good can fully exist only in conjunction with the existence of some little evil, which is the result of matter" (*Muqaddima* V, 6; Ibn Khaldūn 1958, Vol. II: 330; Ibn Khaldūn [1967] 2005: 306). This does not make good disappear: good always comes linked with evil. For Ibn Khaldūn, this is the meaning of the presence of injustice in the world, and if those who wish to obtain the advantages of rank understand the ineluctability of this coexistence, they will realise that they necessarily also have to pay homage to, and flatter, the powerful, if they wish to obtain power and, therefore, wealth and well-being (*Muqaddima* V, 6).

On the contrary, those who are convinced of their own necessity and perfection, and are disdainful and proud towards the powerful—as is often the case with people of noble lineage—do not obtain the desired position of power. They make themselves hated, instead, because human beings rarely agree to attribute to someone else perfection and superiority (qualities which, in any case, cannot be passed down by inheritance) unless obliged to do so by already established social hierarchies.

Thus, because of their pride and habits, these noble people decree their own ruin, since they can no longer earn a living in any other way. In fact, such character traits are often the reason why men of rank in the government, intolerant of these attitudes, choose to detach themselves from their first comrades in favour of new counsellors, more able to flatter and revere them.

As these observations show, a consequence of the burden of prestige, therefore, lies in an apparent inversion of moral values which, once again, reproposes, in relation to this specific element, the circularity advanced by Ibn Khaldūn. Once more, those who rise to the peak of power are the most likely to fall. While the submissive and flatterers achieve success, poverty and isolation are the result of the pride and blind conceit typical of those who, believing themselves to be perfect in their nobility, skill, or wisdom, refuse to bow down to power. All this, however, is simply due to the fact that the former, and not the latter, are in a condition to realistically understand the reality of the rules of human coexistence, the nature of man, power, and the rigid and constrictive character of the system of prestige (*Muqaddima* V, 6; Cheddadi 2006: 389).

Similarly, people in charge of religious offices, such as judges, teachers, *muezzin*, etc., as a rule almost never get rich, because they become too proud by virtue of the noble character of their work, which does not allow them to "prostitute themselves" openly,[45] and their superior occupations which "tax both their mind and body."

[45]*Muqaddima* V, 7. Ibn Khaldūn (1958, Vol. II: 335). Ibn Khaldūn ([1967] 2005: 309): "Indeed, the noble character of the things they have to offer does not permit them to prostitute themselves

In this realism, capable even of recognising a phenomenon "out of tune" with the ideal, yet produced by understandable causes, such as the economic marginalisation of philosophers and religious people, Ibn Khaldūn's vision of society proves, once again, to be realistic and very far from utopian visions such as Al Fārābī's ideal city.

4.3.2 *The Arts and Trades Impart a "Colouring" to the Soul of Man and Society*

For Ibn Khaldūn arts and crafts, and their levels of development, define the "colouring" and specificity of a civilisation in a special way. As a matter of fact, arts and crafts are perfected and refined on the basis of the demand for luxury (which also includes the production of books and culture) which corresponds to the civilisation of each country, and have, therefore, a direct relationship with it.

In their turn, they also influence the customs and characteristics of their civilisation,[46] since they get established as they endure and are repeated. As soon as they are firmly established, giving their "colouring" to the civilisation they belong to, it becomes difficult to wipe them out,[47] because habits become "qualities of the soul"[48] which give it a certain character and, thus, hinder any possible change and the acquisition of a different character.

For this reason, "the person who has gained the habit of a particular craft is rarely able afterwards to master another" (*Muqaddima* V, 21; Ibn Khaldūn 1958, Vol. II: 354; Ibn Khaldūn [1967] 2005: 318), and this also applies to scholars: they too, in fact, acquire disciplinary habits of thought which provide them with specific character traits, and that is why they rarely succeed in developing an equal competence in the practice of different disciplines.

The most ancient among the crafts taken into consideration by Ibn Khaldūn is agriculture. However—striving as ever to grasp the fundamental interrelationship between the economy and society—Ibn Khaldūn points out that agriculture is

openly. As a consequence, they do not become, as a rule, very wealthy." With these observations Ibn Khaldūn reaches the peak of his realism. To find confirmation of this, Ibn Khaldūn, as reported in the same section, made a documentary analysis of the bookkeeping records of al-Ma'mūn's palace, which were, coincidentally, at hand while he was discussing these things with a sceptical colleague.

[46] *Muqaddima* V, 17. Ibn Khaldūn (1958, Vol. II: 349). Ibn Khaldūn ([1967] 2005: 315): "All crafts are customs and colours of civilisation."

[47] *Muqaddima* V, 17. Ibn Khaldūn (1958, Vol. II: 349). Ibn Khaldūn ([1967] 2005: 316): "Once such colouring is firmly established, it is difficult to remove it." Ibn Khaldūn comments that such is, in fact, the situation in Spain at the moment, even if its civilisation is regressing compared to other Mediterranean countries.

[48] *Muqaddima* V, 21. Ibn Khaldūn (1958, Vol. II: 355). Ibn Khaldūn ([1967] 2005: 318): "The reason for this is that habits are qualities of the soul. [...] When the soul has been impressed by a habit, it is no longer in its natural state, and it is less prepared (to master another habit), because it has taken on a certain imprint from that habit."

socially despised: on the one hand, this is so because of its primitive nature, and on the other, because those who practise it are subject to the payment of taxes, and, therefore, to humiliation and misery.

In the specific context of sedentary culture, however, it is architecture that can be described as the most ancient craft, as it presupposes the use of our natural disposition to think, which constitutes the true peculiar characteristic of humanity. This disposition flourishes at varying levels among peoples, and it can actually be seen that people living in temperate and intemperate conditions transfer this difference to the conception of their dwellings as well.

While those living in intemperate zones adapt themselves to caves that are barely sufficient as shelters and feed themselves on raw food, those living in temperate zones think about planning their houses so that they may suit their needs. As a result, and also thanks to the greater protection and comfort they enjoy, they thrive and increase in number until they create groups of houses, and eventually villages or towns—in which, however (for Ibn Khaldūn any increase in comfort and well-being is always accompanied by a reverse effect), after a certain period, they finally end up becoming strangers to each other. Moreover, they surround the cities with walls guarded by the authorities in order to avoid being surprised by night attacks. This sets in motion a circular pattern, as they increasingly require more and more protection—even, in the end, from their fellow citizens, who become more and more strangers to each other in this situation.

Other arts are carpentry, which requires a mastery of geometry and knowledge of measurements and proportions (the great geometricians of antiquity, such as Euclid, Apollonius, Menelaus, and others, were master carpenters, too); the crafts of weaving and tailoring, which especially flourish in sedentary and temperate cultures; the craft of midwifery, a necessary art for the human species, which Ibn Khaldūn describes with surprising competence; and the craft of medicine—described as a branch of physics, having as its object the human body—which preserves health and keeps diseases away from man, and which, unlike midwifery, is not always necessary (i.e., recognised as useful), but precisely becomes so in the *ḥaḍāra*. The reason for this is that in an opulent city the citizens, unlike the inhabitants of *badāwa*, do little exercise; moreover, they live a life of plenty, eating a lot, mixing a variety of foodstuffs and finding it hard to limit themselves, so that they have an excess of food to digest. As it accumulates in the body it festers, with the consequence that this availability of superfluous goods, in cities, corrupts the air, which thus, in turn, de-energises the spirit.

Other arts are calligraphy, which allows written expression and requires specific education (its development, therefore, depends on the level of social organisation, civilisation, and competitive demand for the luxury goods intrinsic to that civilisation); the production of books—and, therefore, also of paper; and, finally, the "aesthetic" arts, such as singing and music. Human beings, in fact, love to unite with what they see as perfect, longing to become one with it, and, for this reason, the search and desire for beauty is intrinsic to the nature of every man (*Muqaddima* V, 31). These, however, are the last arts attained by civilisations, linked as they are to pure pleasure and luxury devoid of other material utility (Lelli 2020). For the same reason, they are also the first to disappear when a civilisation disintegrates. There is, in fact, a necessary link between the level of production of material goods and the attitude to the "cultivation" of the intellect. Just as, on the positive side, it is the excess of available working capacity (compared to the vital needs of a flourishing *ḥaḍāra*) that creates space for the sciences and the arts, by the same token political decadence inevitably strikes, first, the same spirit that had led to their development (and Ibn Khaldūn had to be aware that his own intellectual work, too, was both a product of economic well-being and a sign of decay). The connection of these two things, therefore, merges with the connection that links material factors to intellectual and cultural ones in a single cycle of generation and corruption.

Nevertheless, if, after giving impetus to the development of culture (the peak of the ascensional phase) a civilisation is in fact destined to be swallowed up and replaced by its successor in a new spin of the cycle of history, it is precisely the preservable culture it has developed that makes it possible, even in this cyclical pattern of advances and falls, to maintain some continuity and enable progress to be made over time.

Culture, in fact, does not necessarily die with the society that has fostered it. It can be handed down—and, in fact, is normally absorbed, by a mimetic principle of "imitation" of the most advanced model (*Muqaddima* II, 22)—by those "raw" cultures from the world of *badāwa*, centred on the need for bare survival, which aspire to the power enjoyed by civilisations that have managed to reach the *ḥaḍāra* (*Muqaddima* III, 13). As Ibn Khaldūn states: "When politically ambitious men overcome the ruling dynasty and seize power, they inevitably have recourse to the customs of their predecessors and adopt most of them" (Ibn Khaldūn 1958, The Introduction; Ibn Khaldūn 1958, Vol. I: 58; Ibn Khaldūn [1967] 2005: 25).

While the attitude to the cultivation of culture is, therefore, dragged down with the fall of each civilisation, the products of this culture are nonetheless able to pass through time and move, through the transmission of knowledge, from civilisation to civilisation.[49]

At this point, Ibn Khaldūn's social framework is not yet complete. He has often stressed that all the arts (especially writing and calculation) as well as, in general, all the activities linked to sedentary culture, imply an understanding of the scientific norms behind them, and a habit of disciplined thought that naturally develop the intelligence of those who practice them (*Muqaddima* V, 32). This way, he has laid the foundations for an analysis of the types of intellect, the types of science existing at his time, and the educational methods by which culture and qualities of character are handed down: the subject of the last part of *Muqaddima*.

[49]In the meantime, from the twelfth century onwards, the opinion was emerging in Christianity too that, despite the degradation of humanity, the sciences would continue to progress. Jean de Salisbury (1115–1180) wrote ([1159] 2009: III, 4) that his contemporary Bernard of Chartres maintained that we were "like dwarves on the shoulders of giants," capable of seeing further away, compared to our predecessors, not because of a greater acuity of our eyes, but because of the stature of those on whom we lean (a maxim that later became commonplace, and was repeatedly quoted, especially by Gassendi and Newton) (Pomian 2006: 133–134).

Of course, Ibn Khaldūn hopes that his own "new science" will also be included in the cultural products that could survive, thanks to the reproduction of culture, from the end of the dying cycle into the beginning of the next one. Hence, it is to this perspective of intellectual survival that he entrusts his composite and "multi-layered," rational and empirical structure, suitable for providing an "instructive" interpretation of the "inner meaning" of social dynamics, and bearer of the instructive lessons (*'ibar*) of history, offered as a rational interpretation of the past, a careful observation of the present, and a vehicle for a cautious, instructive projection of the future.

4.4 Sciences and Education as the "Tradition" of Culture

4.4.1 Types and Levels of Intellect

Ibn Khaldūn's theory of knowledge completes the theoretical basis of his science of civilisations, while, at the same time, better delineating his vision of the relationship between religion and philosophy.

As we have already seen, Ibn Khaldūn insists that not only does man's ability to think distinguish him from animals: it also enables him to earn a living, to co-operate with other human beings, and to come closer to the Creator by means of revealed religion.

This ability to think is diversified into different levels (*Muqaddima* VI, 1). The first is the level of the *discerning* intellect, aimed at intellectually perceiving and understanding what exists in the outside world, according to a natural or arbitrary order: it works essentially thanks to man's perceptions, which allow him to distinguish what is useful and avoid what is harmful. This is the type of human thought that can perceive the causal order which, by nature or arbitrary reasons, binds all the things making up the existing world and the actions concerning them. However, the ability to understand this causal order, and, thus, to act on the basis of this understanding, varies in degree: some people come to understand up to two or three levels of causal links; others[50] reach so far as to understand five or six, and their specific humanity, as a consequence, is higher (*Muqaddima* VI, 2).

The second is the level of the *experimental* intellect, which proceeds through judgements obtained on the basis of experience. This type of empirical intelligence is aimed at elaborating the best way of behaving with one's fellow human beings, and of leading them. In fact, in order to live a complete life, man must live in society. Yet, affections or hostility can arise in dealing with his fellows. Experience,

[50] *Muqaddima* VI, 2. Think of chess players, for example (*Muqaddima* VI, 2; Ibn Khaldūn 1958, Vol. II: 416; Ibn Khaldūn [1967] 2005: 336). Ibn Khaldūn, however, admits that this example, while didactically effective, is not fully appropriate because chess is a game, while the knowledge of causal chains is scientific and concerns nature.

especially if it is reiterated, forms the basis of the reasonings elaborated at this level and aimed at establishing what is good and what is bad in relations with others. The habit of acting according to these reasonings, in turn, creates custom, which, accordingly, governs behaviour.

Developing this knowledge on the basis of personal experience alone, however, is something that takes a long time: it is in order to respond to the need to shorten the time needed for this purpose that young people receive education and instruction from parents, teachers, and the elderly, who are entrusted to pass on to new generations the synthesis of the judgments on the rules of good living made by those who preceded them. Ibn Khaldūn quotes, in this regard, an eloquent saying: "He who is not educated by his parents will be educated by time" (*Muqaddima* VI, 3; Ibn Khaldūn 1958, Vol. II: 419; Ibn Khaldūn [1967] 2005: 337).

The third is the level of *speculative* intellect. At this level the ability to think, starting from abstract concepts, elaborates a hypothetical knowledge of the things placed beyond sensorial perceptions, combining perceptions and apperceptions so as to provide further knowledge. These new elements, combined with other material, can then produce further new knowledge. Advancing in this way, thought sets in motion a properly scientific process, supported by a methodology of reasoning that is epistemologically superior to that of the previous levels, based on simple perceptions.[51]

Human beings, in their ambition to reach perfection, tend by nature towards the development of more and more refined forms of intellect. In order to understand the nature of the final ideal to which this aspiration tends—that of becoming pure intellect and perceptive soul—it is necessary also to recall the characteristics that differentiate the three worlds, whose existence man can perceive through a "healthy" intuition (*Muqaddima* VI, 4; *supra*, § 3.1.6).

The first one is the world we encounter through sensorial perception.

Then, our capacity to think presents us with a second distinct world, that of the scientific knowledge of things—which goes beyond the perceptions of the senses. This is the intellectual world of the soul.

Lastly, there is a third world: that of angels and spirits. Its existence can be derived from observation of the influences (e.g., volitions and inclinations) which they exert on us, since from the existence of the effect it is possible to deduce the existence of a cause acting at its origin. Other phenomena also testify to its existence, such as the occurrence of visions, or "real dreams" (which are quite distinct from the confused dreams arising, instead, from sensory images stored in our memory, to which the intellect is applied in a way detached from perception).

While the world of the senses is shared with animals, the intellectual and rational world of the soul, and the spiritual world approached by supernatural perceptions (based on intuition, *wijdān*), are independent of sensorial experience and shared with angels—essences in which intellect, thinker, and the object of thinking are one. It is

[51]These observations recall Comte's law of the three stages.

to the ultimate goal of angelic nature that the soul and intelligence spontaneously aspire.

This drive towards the spiritual world is particularly strong in a special group of people, the prophets: they are subjects capable of understanding divine revelation in an instantaneous escape from time.[52] Their natural predisposition in this sense (a gift from God) allows their soul to leave their humanity, access angelic nature, and then return to humanity in a lightning instant (whence comes the use of the Arabic word *waḥy*—that is, quickness—to describe revelation).

In the world of the angels, the soul grasps angelic revelations and ideas that it is entrusted to transmit to human beings. When prophets swap their humanity to access the nature of angels, they generally experience a physical feeling of exhaustion and choking at the moment when the veil of the supernatural world is lifted, and they mentally reach a clear and direct vision of the truth to be revealed.

Other minor and imperfect forms of relationship with the supernatural, such as magic, divination, etc., also respond to a natural human disposition.

After illustrating man's natural tendency to develop his rationality, Ibn Khaldūn emphasises that man, despite being an animal endowed with intelligence, still proceeds from a basic situation of ignorance; hence, his acquisition of knowledge in any scientific field involves a process that requires habit and practice with its problems and tools (which is different from simple memorisation).[53]

The best way to transmit this habit is the exercise aimed at making the learner acquire the ability to express himself clearly, in discussing and debating scientific problems: this competence requires the stimulus of a scientific education,[54] in order to develop. This encourages students to get involved in the discipline, as opposed to the potential effect of mnemonic and passive study—something that risks making them waste a lifetime of scientific lessons without ever entering the vital heart of the subject.

Scientific education is a craft, too, and it thrives within developed sedentary cultures, like all crafts. As a rule, these follow their own codes and characteristics in everything: from economics to architecture, to the norms of relationships. These determined codes constitute both a limitation and also a characteristic style of culture, which is transmitted from generation to generation, "colouring" the soul, conditioning the intellect in favour of a prompt reception of knowledge, and developing a level of intelligence which, in turn, makes it easier to acquire knowledge of further crafts.

---

[52]*Muqaddima* VI, 5. On prophetic knowledge, see also *Muqaddima* VI, 15, where Ibn Khaldūn also speaks of dreams, and of the awareness of souls in Purgatory.

[53]For this reason, Ibn Khaldūn comments, every scientific authority elaborates its own technical terminology.

[54]Ibn Khaldūn complains bitterly, in this regard, about the disappearance in his time of the scientific tradition in Spain, where it was no longer cultivated, and jurisprudence too had become a shadow of what it used to be. He affirms, however, that although the first cradles of science, such as Baghdad and other cities, were now in ruins, science was still cultivated at least in the East, in large cities such as Cairo: *Muqaddima* VI, 7.

If there are civilisations that are more advanced than others, therefore, the reason for this does not lie in the fact that some of them usually give birth to more intellectually gifted people, but depends on the more or less advanced development of this practice of transmission of knowledge.

4.4.2 Traditional Sciences and Intellectual Sciences

The sciences are divided into two areas (*Muqaddima* VI, 9): on the one hand, there are the traditional sciences—in particular, those to do with the law—and on the other the intellectual sciences, such as the philosophical disciplines, powered by research and use of the speculative intellect.

The traditional sciences have a conventional nature and are based not on the intellect but on the authority of religious law and the study of the Arabic language. Their applications, such as the use of analogy, are also based on tradition, since, in Islam, these sciences have been cultivated in a way that does not allow further developments.[55]

The reason for the use of revelation and tradition in these areas lies in the limits of human understanding. In fact, man is able to understand only the natural and obvious causes of phenomena, and only when they present themselves to his perception in a sufficiently organised and well-ordered manner. On the Cause of Causes, however—which is God—it is necessary for man to give up speculating:

> Therefore, we have been commanded completely to abandon and suppress any speculation about them and to direct ourselves to the Causer of all causes, so that the soul will be firmly coloured with the oneness of God (*Muqaddima* VI, 14; Ibn Khaldūn 1958, Vol. III: 36; Ibn Khaldūn [1967] 2005: 349).[56]

In fact, if man were to rely only and completely on his own perceptions, he would end up with the superficial impression of being able to understand everything on the basis of them: even if he were deaf or blind, he would not perceive what he lacks. Our intellect—which is trustworthy in the field of phenomena within its reach—is fallacious if used to investigate things beyond its capabilities—such as the uniqueness of God, His divine attributes, the truth of prophecy, and all other things connected with the supernatural world—because, with respect to all this, the human intellect is but "one of the atoms of the world of existence which results from God."[57] In fact, the non-recognition of this limit constitutes the great error of metaphysics and speculative theology (*Muqaddima* VI, 14)—termed "philosophy" in a derogatory sense.

---

[55]Paragraphs 12 and 13 of *Muqaddima* VI are especially devoted to analysing the different legal schools and the relationship between the sources of Islamic law.

[56]Cfr. also *Muqaddima* VI, 26.

[57]*Muqaddima* VI, 14. Ibn Khaldūn (1958, Vol. III: 38). Ibn Khaldūn ([1967] 2005: 350). On his criticism of "philosophy" understood in this sense, see *Muqaddima* VI, 30.

The mystical-ascetic science of Sufism (*Muqaddima* VI, 16) also belongs to the sphere of traditional sciences, and is described in great detail by Ibn Khaldūn (as we have seen, he directed a Sufi centre in Cairo, and was buried in a Sufi cemetery) as a kind of Gnostic-initiatory path, featuring several "stations."

Ibn Khaldūn writes, finally, that the science of dream interpretation[58]—developed in Islam in a novel way, independently of the theories expressed on the subject, for example, by previous authors from Greek culture[59]—also belongs to the religious sciences (*Muqaddima* VI, 17). Muhammad himself had addressed the issue, stating that a good dream vision is worth as much as "a forty-sixth of prophecy" (*Muqaddima* VI, 17; Ibn Khaldūn 1958, Vol. III: 107; Ibn Khaldūn [1967] 2005: 367).

The second area of the sciences—the intellectual sciences—constitutes a natural expression of man as a thinking being (*Muqaddima* VI, 18), and they are, therefore, not the privileged prerogative of any specific religious group.

Also known as the "sciences of philosophy" and "of wisdom," they consist of four subclasses: the first is logic, which protects the mind from error in the exercise of deriving unknown data from that which is known. Another is mathematics, divided into four sub-disciplines: arithmetic, geometry, astronomy, and music. Physics, and metaphysics, which refers to spiritual questions, are added to these. Each of these sub-disciplines also includes internal subdivisions: for example, arithmetic deals with calculation, rules on inheritance shares, business sums, etc., while physics also includes medicine.

The intellectual sciences were highly developed by the greatest civilisations—particularly, the Persians and Greeks. Ibn Khaldūn comments, however, that, unfortunately, the sciences of the Persians were lost during the Muslim conquest of Persia when, confronted by the huge number of works to be found in libraries, the second caliph 'Umar al-Ḫaṭṭāb ordered the books to be thrown into the water, taking the view that they could only be either in accordance with religion, and therefore useless, or contrary to it, and therefore harmful (*Muqaddima* VI, 18). Similarly, the sciences of the Chaldeans, the Syrians, and the Copts—who especially cultivated magic, astrology, and the science of talismans—almost disappeared (except for a few practitioners), because they were forbidden by religion.

The first to take an interest in the intellectual sciences of the Greeks was Abū Jafar al-Manṣūr, who had the Byzantine emperor send him Euclid's text on geometry. After him, al-Ma'mūn set in motion an impressively wide-ranging programme of translation,[60] which made many books available to the Arab world. The study of the Greeks strongly stimulated the Arab world from an intellectual point of view: it was

---

[58]Reference is made here to "real" dreams, characterised—Ibn Khaldūn affirms—by an immediate awakening after the dream, and accompanied by an anxious need to return to the senses, and by the fact that the image dreamed of remains imprinted in the memory.

[59]Franz Rosenthal points out, in relation to this (Ibn Khaldūn 1958, Vol. III: 105, note. Ibn Khaldūn [1967] 2005: 367, note), that the work on the interpretation of dreams by Artemidorus, by this time, had already been translated from Greek into Arabic.

[60]On the motivations of al-Ma'mūn, see Cruz Hernández (2003: 70).

on the basis of their philosophical theories that later Muslim thinkers al-Fārābī and Avicenna in the East, and Averroè and Avempace in Spain, "surpassed their predecessors in the intellectual science" (*Muqaddima* VI, 18; Ibn Khaldūn 1958, Vol. III: 116; Ibn Khaldūn [1967] 2005: 374).

By Ibn Khaldūn's time, however, scientific activities had disappeared in the Maghreb and Spain, while the most flourishing sedentary culture was to be found in Cairo, "mother of the world," centre of Islam, and source of the sciences and arts—although Ibn Khaldūn wrote, perhaps incredulously, that, as "we hear," they were still cultivated in the East and the land of Rome, as well as on the adjacent Christian northern shore of the Mediterranean.[61]

The description provided by Ibn Khaldūn of the various sciences is accompanied by interesting observations of a psycho-sociological nature on the effect that the development of each produces on the individual and collective souls, which it "colours."

Ibn Khaldūn says that the science of calculation, for example, as well as geometry, which illuminates the intellect and straightens the mind, trains the cognitive processes to follow a method of clear reasoning based on systematic evidence. This is why it is wise for calculation to be learned early in life: this develops the student's self-discipline and righteousness—qualities that, thus, remain impressed on his soul.

In his encyclopedic enumeration, Ibn Khaldūn ranges from agriculture to physics to land surveying, and approaches metaphysics and even magic[62]—which is read through the observation lens of its effects on the human imagination: he explains, for example, that a person who walks on a tightrope will certainly fall if the idea of falling is strongly present in his imagination (*Muqaddima* VI, 26).

In accordance with his Muslim beliefs,[63] Ibn Khaldūn does not deny the power of the supernatural, which is common to both religion and magic: however, in order to avoid any confusion between the two domains, he tries to indicate the frontiers of the acceptable.

Ibn Khaldūn repeats, however, that in metaphysics the use of philosophical rationality, and therefore also of Aristotelian logic, must stop and give way to traditional science. In fact, in this area philosophy (*falsafa*) is read in a derogatory sense. Once again, it is condemned because of the "well-known obtuseness"

---

[61]*Muqaddima* VI, 18. Ibn Khaldūn (1958, Vol. III: 117). Ibn Khaldūn ([1967] 2005: 375): "We hear that the intellectual sciences are still amply represented among the inhabitants of the East, in particular in the non-Arab 'Iraq and, farther east, in Transoxiana. [...] We further hear now that the philosophical sciences are greatly cultivated in the land of Rome and along the adjacent northern shore of the country of the European Christians. [...] God knows better what exists there." See, in this book, Sect. 1.3.1.

[62]Ibn Khaldūn clearly distinguishes magic from miracles, which are produced for good ends, while magic is moved by evil aims: *Muqaddima* VI, 26. Ibn Khaldūn (ibid.) also distinguishes magic from the "evil eye," the latter being unintentional.

[63]For example, as pointed out by Franz Rosenthal (Ibn Khaldūn [1967] 2005: lxxii), this is mentioned in the Malikite jurisprudence text *Risālah* by Ibn Abī Zayd al-Qayrawānī. For this reason it was assumed that Ibn Khaldūn, in his office as Malikite judge, had certainly had to deal with cases involving magic, the evil eye, and the divinatory power of dreams.

(*Muqaddima* VI, 30; Ibn Khaldūn 1958, Vol. III: 249; Ibn Khaldūn [1967] 2005: 400) of those "intelligent representatives of the human species" (*Muqaddima* VI, 30; Ibn Khaldūn 1958, Vol. III: 246; Ibn Khaldūn [1967] 2005: 398)—the *falāsifa*, including al-Fārābī and Avicenna (*Muqaddima* VI, 30)—who had argued that the use of reason could be a suitable tool to investigate the essences and ultimate conditions of existence, and that it could even be used to assess the correctness of the articles of faith.

"Existence, however, is too wide to be explained by so narrow a view" (*Muqaddima* VI, 30; Ibn Khaldūn 1958, Vol. III: 250; Ibn Khaldūn [1967] 2005: 401), and the duty of Muslims is, therefore, not to pretend to study the divine. In connection with this, Plato (termed, in Ibn Khaldūn's treatise on Sufism (2017: 26), "the greatest Sufi among the ancients") had also stated that through reason[64] it was not intellectually possible to advance anything more than mere conjecture. The divine, placed beyond history, can only be approached mystically—and, in fact, Ibn Khaldūn devotes an important and detailed paragraph of his treatise to the Sufi mystical approach to God.

As a result, logic proves inadequate to achieve the objectives of metaphysical knowledge:

> As far as we know, this science has only a single advantage, namely, it sharpens the mind in the orderly presentation of proofs and arguments, so that the habit of excellent and correct arguing is obtained (*Muqaddima* VI, 30; Ibn Khaldūn 1958, Vol. III: 257; Ibn Khaldūn [1967] 2005: 405).

Logic, in short, teaches a solid and exact method of reasoning, which forces philosophical speculation into the narrow mesh of the most correct norms of argumentation. Ibn Khaldūn admonishes, however, that logic is not only inadequate to investigate theological and metaphysical questions, but it can also be harmful, because it could put those who study it in contact with doctrines and opinions from other civilisations, potentially threatening the firmness of the scholar's religious belief. For this reason, the study of logic should be prohibited before the learner has first been given in-depth study of the *Qur'an* (*Muqaddima* VI, 30).

For a similar reason, the study of astrology (*Muqaddima* VI, 31) should also be prohibited, not only because of its intrinsic weakness (from both religious and scientific points of view: in fact, it attributes earthly effects to causes other than the Creator), but also because of the alarm it can provoke among people—a feeling that, in itself, can encourage riots and political turmoil. As we have seen, Ibn Khaldūn considers terror itself as a cause of weakening and defeat, almost as a sort of self-fulfilling prophecy.

This also shows, incidentally, how, even in discussing these types of sciences, Ibn Khaldūn pays constant attention to framing sciences within their social context, in

---

[64]Ibn Khaldūn stresses that "our perceptions are created and brought into existence. God's creation extends beyond the creation of man. Complete knowledge does not exist (in man). The world of existence is too vast for him. God has comprehension beyond theirs." (*Muqaddima* VI, 14; Ibn Khaldūn 1958, Vol. III: 37–38; Ibn Khaldūn [1967] 2005: 350).

addition to providing comments of an epistemological nature aimed at exposing the underlying principles of the topic (Lakhsassi 1979: 22–23).

4.4.3 The Importance of Method in Teaching and Education

Teaching is the natural extension of scientific activity: in relation to this, Ibn Khaldūn inevitably also speaks from his own experience, having been a teacher himself for many years.

The existence of the practice of education is also explained by Ibn Khaldūn on the basis of natural causality. In fact, he says, when a scientific framework takes shape in someone's mind, it necessarily requires to be communicated to others because only then, through discussion—which requires verbal and linguistic oral or written expression—does it really get clarified in the mind of the person who conceived it, thus confirming its solidity (*Muqaddima* VI, 33).

This gives Ibn Khaldūn the opportunity to provide some clarifications about the conventional nature of language. According to him, no language can be considered as natural, since they are all "constructed,"[65] and the result of convention: "language," in short, "is a technical habit" (*Muqaddima* VI, 45; Ibn Khaldūn 1958, Vol. III: 342; Ibn Khaldūn [1967] 2005: 438). This applies even to the ancient Syrian language and writing, which, because of its antiquity, its deep roots, and the firmly established habit it had produced, is often confusingly regarded as natural (*Muqaddima* VI, 33). In fact, all languages are habits, and, as such, when they "are firmly established and rooted in their proper places appear to be natural and innate in those places" (*Muqaddima* VI, 50; Ibn Khaldūn 1958, Vol. III: 359; Ibn Khaldūn [1967] 2005: 439). The quality of a person's use of language, therefore, depends on the quality of the material that person has learned or memorised.[66]

Language can be used in the form of prose or poetry. With regard to the latter, Ibn Khaldūn states—briefly returning to his criticism of the historiography of his time—that

> the Arabs thought highly of poetry as a form of speech. Therefore, they made it the archive of their sciences and their history, the evidence for what they considered right and wrong, and the principal basis of reference for most of their sciences and wisdom (*Muqaddima* VI, 54; Ibn Khaldūn 1958, Vol. III: 374; Ibn Khaldūn [1967] 2005: 444).

He notes, however, that this way of seeing poetry is not to be understood as universal. As demonstrated by the appreciation expressed, for example, by Aristotle,

---

[65] *Muqaddima* VI, 54. Ibn Khaldūn (1958, Vol. III: 379). Ibn Khaldūn ([1967] 2005: 446): "The author of a spoken utterance is like a builder or weaver."

[66] As Zaid Ahmad (2003: 162) observes, in Ibn Khaldūn's work "Developement in language skill goes in parallel with the process of civilisation. [...] at its lowest level is basically employed as a means of communication, but at its highest level in speech and literary composition it is the manifestation of the embellishment of life."

in his *Logic*, of the (very different) poetry of Homer, every nation cultivates the kind of poetry that suits, and adapts to, its language—and this shows that even art itself can ultimately only be understood when placed within its social context (*Muqaddima* VI, 59).

In any case, the purpose of linguistic discourse can also be primarily aesthetic and expressive, as in the case of discourse aimed at expressing ideas through metaphors and metonymies:

> The moving around causes pleasure to the mind, perhaps even more than the pleasure that results from indicating (the requirements of the situation). All these things mean attainment of a conclusion from the argument used to prove it, and attainment, as one knows, is one of the things that cause pleasure (*Muqaddima* VI, 57; Ibn Khaldūn 1958, Vol. III: 400; Ibn Khaldūn [1967] 2005: 453).

Ibn Khaldūn warns, however, "If no effort is made to convey ideas, speech is like 'dead land' which does not count" (*Muqaddima* VI, 57; Ibn Khaldūn 1958, Vol. III: 398–399; Ibn Khaldūn [1967] 2005: 453).

This relates to the importance of using a teaching methodology capable of involving the student, as Ibn Khaldūn insists. He strongly stresses the importance of the student's active participation in his learning process: the student should indeed be stimulated by the teacher to engage personally with the problems of his discipline. Paradoxically, however, the widespread teaching methodology of the time hindered this involvement in various ways.

First of all, "The great number of scholarly works available is an obstacle on the path to attaining scholarship" (*Muqaddima* VI, 34; Ibn Khaldūn 1958, Vol. III: 288; Ibn Khaldūn [1967] 2005: 414). In fact, planning to teach too many works risks delaying the active moment of the student's direct confrontation with the problems of the discipline, to the point where he loses the stimulus and confidence to be able to do so. A whole life, in fact, could not be enough to know all the existing literature for each discipline, even if one devoted oneself only to that. Ibn Khaldūn recommends, therefore, that the learning process should never go so far as to sacrifice the intellectual identity of the learner to the weight and authority of institutional culture.

At the time, however, this was the most widely practised system of teaching, and since habits become second nature at a certain point, changing it would not be an easy task.

Another obstacle in the education process for Ibn Khaldūn is the large number of manuals devoted to summarising the various scientific topics.[67] Not only do summaries condense the content of their topic to the highest degree—which makes the comprehension of each step more difficult than the understanding obtained through more straightforward language. They also have the effect of confusing the learner by giving him the final results of the discipline long before he is mature enough for

[67] *Muqaddima* VI, 35. Ibn Khaldūn (1958, Vol. III: 290). Ibn Khaldūn ([1967] 2005: 415): "The great number of brief handbooks available on scholarly subjects is detrimental to the process of instruction."

them, thus going against the natural direction of the learning process, and corrupting it.

In the original works, moreover, concepts are repeated over and over again, with a redundance that allows the thorough establishment of knowledge—fundamental, once again, to firmly fix concepts and related reasoning in the soul. The extremely condensed summaries provided by the manuals, on the contrary, do not allow the student to get to the root of problems, exposing him merely to an "impregnation" of the examined concepts sufficient for superficial assimilation.

To be effective, on the contrary, teaching should proceed little by little, in a gradual process marked by a wise use of repetition, in a threefold pattern: at the beginning, the teacher, who has still to observe the potential of the students, should present a summary of the main problems of each area of the discipline; later, he should go into the subject in more detail, providing comments and complete explanations, while also highlighting any different opinions on the topic; finally, the most complicated and deep-rooted issues of the discipline should be dealt with during a third return to the subject (*Muqaddima* VI, 36).

Such a procedure truly enables receptiveness to scientific knowledge to grow gradually, together with its understanding. If, instead, the conclusions of a problem are immediately transmitted and inculcated, the student becomes indolent and reluctant to deal with it. Never stimulated to use and test his own thought, he eventually stops working on it.

It is also important to take care not to interrupt the learning process with overlong intervals between each period of instruction. This causes the student to lose the thread of the subject and forget the connection between different parts of the problem.

For the same reason, it is also advisable not to expose the students to two disciplines (or even more) at the same time, as this requires them to split their attention and, thus, lose concentration. The student is ready to deal with a new discipline only when another has been mastered—and not only that: once that point is reached, he is also interested in the development of his understanding which follows on from the firm acquisition of the previous discipline (*Muqaddima* VI, 36).

The real aim of education, therefore, is to enable the student to master the tools proper to each discipline and its abstract concepts—"nets with which one goes hunting for the (desired) objective with the help of one's natural ability to think and entrusting oneself to the mercy and generosity of God" (*Muqaddima* VI, 36; Ibn Khaldūn 1958, Vol. III: 296–297; Ibn Khaldūn [1967] 2005: 419). This enables him to put his own intelligence to the test, make use of it in such contexts, and not keep it in constant suspension—something that, unfortunately, too often occurs.

Finally, it is also the case that sometimes scientific difficulties can have the effect of blocking thought. From this point of view, it is also important to avoid giving too much space, before reaching the heart of the discipline in question, to the study of its auxiliary sciences (such as, for example, philology, which is auxiliary to religious sciences, or logic, which is auxiliary to philosophy). These should be studied only in order to understand the main sciences that they support. Logic, for example, is only a description of the action of thinking and, in most cases, follows on from it.

The abundance of theories and questions proper to these auxiliary sciences, which are not really necessary to understand the essential sciences, can, in short, lead to badly channelled teaching which often deviates from its ends.[68] It is important, therefore, to keep distinguishing the essential from the accessory, and to avoid losing sight of one's goal, on pain of paradoxically blocking the human act of thinking by the very process of education, wasting the limited time available to each person (*Muqaddima* VI, 37).

On this point, Ibn Khaldūn's exhortation to the student stuck in technicalities is memorable:

> Leave all the technical procedures and take refuge in the realm of the natural ability to think given to you by nature! Let your speculation roam in it and let your mind freely delve in it, according to whatever you desire from it! Set foot in the places where the greatest thinkers before you did! Entrust yourself to God's aid, as in His mercy He aided them and taught them what they did not know! If you do that, God's helpful light will shine upon you and show you the middle term that God made a natural requirement of thinking (*Muqaddima* VI, 36; Ibn Khaldūn 1958, Vol. III: 297; Ibn Khaldūn [1967] 2005: 419).

Finally, a key element in a good method of education, of great importance not only for its effectiveness, but also for its influence on the character of the learner, is the need for teachers (and also parents) to limit their strictness towards students—especially children.[69] In fact, this is precisely one of those factors that most produce bad habits (*Muqaddima* VI, 39; Ibn Khaldūn 1958, Vol. III: 305; Ibn Khaldūn [1967] 2005: 424):

> Students, slaves and servants that are brought up with injustice and tyrannical (force) are overcome by it. It makes them feel oppressed and causes them to lose their energy. It makes them lazy and induces them to lie and be insincere.

Because of the sense of dependence it inculcates, this type of education leads students to lose the very human qualities that are good for civil organisation—

[68]Pomian (2006: 59–60), considering this warning as essentially intended to underline the fundamental nature of the religious sciences, with respect to which other sciences stand as instrumental, stresses the distance of the ideas of the Muslim Ibn Khaldūn from the Christian thought which, based on Genesis and the commentaries of the Fathers of the Church (St. Augustine *in primis*), stated that the study of the visible world could also constitute a path to God. However, it must also be said that, faced with the syntheses of St. Thomas and Duns Scotus, many other thinkers in Christianity, at the time, also rejected this idea, either for philosophical reasons (because of the radical contingency of the created world, according to Occam) or out of the conviction that communication with God could only take place through a mystical experience of imitation of Christ (the *Imitatio Christi* by Thomas à Kempis (1389–1471) was one of the biggest "best-sellers" of Christianity). In any case, this reading of Ibn Khaldūn's affirmation is not entirely acceptable: not only because it contradicts the commitment and pride shown by Ibn Khaldūn himself in the creation of his "new science," but also because this affirmation, placed in this clearly pedagogical-didactic context, seems, instead, to be aimed solely and directly at warning in a general sense against the dispersiveness of those educational programmes in which the hypertrophy of the superfluous ends up stifling the necessary.

[69]*Muqaddima* VI, 39. Ibn Khaldūn (1958, Vol. III: 305). Ibn Khaldūn ([1967] 2005: 424): "Severity to students does harm to them."

namely, the desire and the ability to protect themselves and what belongs to them.[70] Punishment, if anything, has the effect of encouraging cunningness to avoid further punishment, and inculcates such behaviour to the point of preventing the development of the individual's virtues and full human potential.

An unenlightened education can therefore contribute, together with the large number of factors already mapped out, to transform and harm the political characteristics of a civilisation. Ibn Khaldūn adds, in fact, that we can observe the same kind of transformation, in the face of similar factors, if we focus, on a broader political level, on the changes that affect every nation that falls under the yoke of tyranny. Oppression and constraint break the character and oppress the energy of the population, and, in turn, this hinders life in society and human development.

If the child is to be chastised, therefore, this must be done in a moderate manner, ensuring that his personality is respected, and taking care to prevent education, which should be an instrument of elevation, from adversely affecting and killing his spirit.

Ibn Khaldūn's final pedagogical recommendation is to encourage an education based on direct contact between learners and teachers. Ibn Khaldūn—so much of a "pedagogue of example" that he called his entire work "*Book of Examples*"—says that travelling in search of knowledge, and learning through direct contact with teachers, is the best way to learn. This is so because contact creates a personal and emotional impact which, much more than reading books, allows the establishment of a habituation to a discipline (even here, the formation of habit is a central factor) (*Muqaddima* VI, 40).

In his autobiography Ibn Khaldūn takes care to present in detail each and every teacher he has had himself, revealing, thus, a very intimate and deep concept of the didactic relationship, likened to a kind of "epistemological genealogy" which makes the student, in a sense, the "cultural son" of his teacher. Moreover, contact with different teachers—who, supposedly, make use of different terminologies—allows the student to understand science in a more mature and autonomous way, taking him beyond the particularity of personal interpretations.

In any case, says Ibn Khaldūn, the knowledge handed down by scientists and scholars should never be seen as the ultimate and absolute truth, because logic alone can never fully explain all. This, in fact, considered as such,

> cannot be trusted to prevent the commission of errors, because it is too abstract and remote from the *sensibilia*. [...] It is possible that material things contain something that does not admit of logical conclusions and contradicts them (*Muqaddima* VI, 41; Ibn Khaldūn 1958, Vol. III: 310; Ibn Khaldūn [1967] 2005: 428).

[70]*Muqaddima* VI, 39. Ibn Khaldūn (1958, Vol. III: 307). Ibn Khaldūn ([1967] 2005: 426): "Let no hour pass in which you do not seize the opportunity to teach him something useful. But do so without vexing him, which would kill his mind. Do not always be too lenient with him, or he will get to like leisure and become used to it. As much as possible, correct him kindly and gently. If he does not want it that way, you must then use severity and harshness."

Scholars always tend, on the other hand, to try to force reality into the mould of their visions and their way of deducing things, and as a result can make mistakes.

It is precisely because of their habit of relying essentially on theories that, of all people, such scholars—so tied to the abstract, and lacking in attention to the facts of the outside world—turn out to be the least suitable to deal with politics—an activity that demands, instead, an ability to deal with a world in which events are often dictated by obscure and opaque conditions that are hardly amenable to universal formulas.

Maybe not accidentally, Ibn Khaldūn's *Muqaddima* ends with a reflection on the work itself. This ending, placed directly after his criticism of the absolutist blindness of a didactic and philosophical approach over-attentive to general schemes, to the detriment of an empirical, strict, and dispassionate analysis of the real, emphasises the importance of Ibn Khaldūn's complex sociological reconstruction, which is born in direct reaction to such fallacies. The positioning of his "new science" at the end of his exposition of the sciences existing in his time appears, therefore, to underline its important elements of novelty: it is thanks to its sociological attention to concrete data and genuine observation of facts, totally new with respect to the paradigms of the past, that Ibn Khaldūn's science shows itself to be capable of reconciling the deductive abstractionism of the philosophical method with a concrete, inductive, and realistic vision of the world.

References

(A) Ibn Khaldūn's Works

Ibn Khaldūn. 1847–1851. *Histoire des Berbères et des dynasties musulmanes de l'Afrique septentrionale* (ed. William MacGuckin de Slane). 2 Voll. Algers: Imprimerie du Gouvernement.

———. 1958. *The Muqaddimah: An Introduction to History* (ed. Franz Rosenthal). 3 Voll. New Jersey: Princeton University Press.

———. [1967] 2005. *The Muqaddimah: An Introduction to History* (ed. Franz Rosenthal), abridged edition. Princeton: Princeton University Press.

———. 2012. *Le Livre des Exemples, II. Histoire des Arabes et des Berbères du Maghreb* (ed. Abdesselam Cheddadi). Paris: Gallimard.

———. 2017. *Ibn Khaldūn on Sufism. Remedy for the Questioner in Search of Answers* (trans. Yumna Ozer). Cambridge: The Islamic Texts Society.

(B) Other Works

Abun-Nasr, Jamil. 1975. *A History of the Maghrib*. Cambridge: Cambridge University Press.

Ahmad, Zaid. 2003. *The Epistemology of Ibn Khaldūn*. London: RoutledgeCurzon.

Al-Araki, Magid. 2014. *Ibn Khaldūn a Forerunner of Modern Sociology. Method and Concepts of Growth and Development*. Oslo: Høgskolen i Oslo og Akershus.

Alatas, Syed Hussein. 1986. *The Problem of Corruption*. Singapore: Times Books International.
Alatas, Syed Farid. 2013. *Ibn Khaldūn*. Oxford: Oxford Centre for Islamic Studies.
al-Azmeh, Aziz. 1982. *Ibn Khaldūn. An Essay in Reinterpretation*. New York: Routledge.
al-Fārābī, Abū Nasr. [X–XI century] 1998. *On the Perfect State* (trans. Richard Walzer). Chicago: Great Books of the Islamic World.
al-Mubaššir b. Fātik, Abū al-Wafā. [1048–1049] 1958. *Muḫtār al-ḥikam* (ed. Franz Rosenthal). Madrid: Badawi.
Bourdieu, Pierre. 1984. *Distinction: A Social Critic of the Judgement of Taste*. London: Routledge.
Campanini, Massimo. 2005b. *Ibn Khaldūn: la Muqaddima, la storia, la civiltà, il potere*. In *Studies on Ibn Khaldūn*, ed. Massimo Campanini, 9–48. Milano: Polimetrica.
Cheddadi, Abdesselam. 1980. Le système du pouvoir en Islam d'après Ibn Khaldoun. *Annales. Économies, Sociétés, Civilisations* 35: 534–550.
———. 1999. *Ibn Khaldūn revisité*. Rabat: Éditions Toukbal.
———. 2006. *Ibn Khaldūn. L'homme et le théoricien de la civilisation*. Paris: Gallimard.
Cruz Hernández, Miguel. 2003. Siete interrogantes en la historia del pensamiento. *Revista Española de Filosofía Medieval* 10: 69–73.
Dale, Stephen Frederic. 2015a. *The Orange Trees of Marrakesh. Ibn Khaldūn and the Science of Man*. Cambridge, MA: Harvard University Press.
Denaro, Roberta (ed.). 2006. *Le mille e una notte*. Donzelli: Roma.
Fei Tzu, Han. 1939. *The Complete Works of* Han Fei Tzŭ: *A Classic of Chinese Political Science* (trans. Wen-Kuei Liao). London: Probsthain.
Francesca, Ersilia. 2005. Ibn Khaldūn e "la Ricchezza delle Nazioni". Lo sviluppo economico secondo la Muqaddima. In *Studies on Ibn Khaldūn*, ed. Massimo Campanini, 75–99. Milano: Polimetrica.
Fukuyama, Francis. 2018. *Identity: The Demand for Dignity and the Politics of Resentment*. New York: Farrar, Straus and Giroux.
Gamarra, Yolanda. 2015. Ibn Khaldūn (1332–1406): A Precursor of Intercivilizational Discourse. *Leiden Journal of International Law* 28: 441–456.
Haleem, M.A.S. Abdel (trans.). 2004. *The Qur'an*. Oxford University Press.
Horrut, Claude. 2006. *Ibn Khaldūn, un Islam des "Lumières"*. Paris: Les Éditions Complexes.
Hosseini, Hamid. [1995] 2003. Understanding the Market Mechanism before Adam Smith. In *Medieval Islamic Economic Thought*, ed. Shaikh M. Ghazanfar, 88–107. London: Routledge Curzon.
Hussein, Taha. 1918. *Étude analitique et critique de la philosophie sociale d'Ibn Khaldoun*. Paris: Pedone.
Ibraham, Hilmi. 1988. Leisure, Idleness and Ibn Khaldūn. *Leisure Studies* 7: 51–57.
Laffer, Arthur. 2004. The Laffer Curve: Past, Present, and Future. *Executive Summary Backgrounder No. 1765*: 1–18. s3.amazonaws.com/thf_media/2004/pdf/bg1765.pdf. Accessed 17 Sept 2020.
Lakhsassi, Abderrahman. 1979. Ibn Khaldūn and the Classification of the Science. *The Maghreb Review* 4 (1): 21–25.
Lefebvre, Henri. 1965. *Sociologie de Marx*. Paris: Presses Universitaires de France.
Lelli, Giovanna. 2020. *Knowledge and Beauty in Classical Islam: An Aesthetic Reading of the Muqaddima by Ibn Khaldūn*. London: Routledge.
Mahdi, Muhsin. 1957. *Ibn Khaldūn's Philosophy of History*. Chicago: University of Chicago Press.
Maimonides, Moses. [1180–1190] 2000. *The Guide for the Perplexed*. New York: Dover.
Mauss, Marcel. 2006. *Techniques Technology and Civilization*. New York: Berghahn Books.
Megherbi, Abdelghani. 1971. *La pensée sociologique d'Ibn Khaldoun*. SNED: Alger.
Pareto, Vilfredo. [1917] 1988. *Trattato di sociologia generale*. Torino: UTET.
Pettit, Philip, and Geoffrey Brennan. 2006. *The Economy of Esteem*. Oxford: Oxford University Press.
Pines, Shlomo. 1970. Ibn Khaldūn and Maimonides, a Comparison between Two Texts. *Studia Islamica* 32: 265–274.

Pomian, Krzysztof. 2006. *Ibn Khaldūn au prisme de l'Occident*. Paris: Gallimard.
Rizkiah, Kholifatul, and Abdelkader Chachi. 2020. The Relevance of Ibn Khaldūn's Economic Thought in the Contemporary World. *Turkish Journal of Islamic Economics* 7 (2): 70–90.
Rosenthal, Franz. 1958. *Preface to Ibn Khaldūn*. In Ibn Khaldūn, *The Muqaddimah: An Introduction to History* (ed. Franz Rosenthal). Vol. I, xxix–cxv. Princeton: Princeton University Press.
Rosenthal, Franz. [1967] 2005. *The Muqaddimah*. In Ibn Khaldūn, *The Muqaddimah: An Introduction to History* (ed. Franz Rosenthal), abridged edition. Princeton: Princeton University Press.
Rostow, Walt Whitman. 1960. *The Stages of Economic Growth. A Non-Communist Manifesto*. Cambridge: Cambridge University Press.
Sahlins, Marshall. [1972] 1980. *Economia dell'età della pietra*. Milano: Bompiani.
Salisbury, Jean de. [1159] 2009. *Metalogicon* (ed. Daniel McGarry). Philadelphia: Paul Dry Books.
Smith, Adam. [1776] 2008. *An Inquiry into the Nature and Causes of the Wealth of Nations*. Chicago: University of Chicago Press.
Talbi, Mohamed. 1973. *Ibn Ḫaldūn et l'histoire*. Tunis: Maison Tunisienne de l'Édition.
Taylor, Charles. 1992. *Multiculturalism and the Politics of Recognition*. Princeton: Princeton University Press.
Veblen, Thorstein. 1899. *The Theory of the Leisure Class*. New York: Dover Thrift.
Ventura, Raffaele Alberto. 2020a, April 2. Ibn Khaldūn 2020: Medieval Lessons on Social Collapse. *Medium*. https://medium.com/@raffaele.ventura/ibn-khaldun-2020-medieval-lessons-on-social-collapse-bfbd7cacec3c
———. 2020b. *Radical choc. Ascesa e caduta dei competenti*. Torino: Einaudi.
Vico, Giambattista. [1725] 1977. *La scienza nuova*. Milano: BUR.
Weber, Max. [1922] 1978. *Economy and Society: An Outline of Interpretive Sociology*. 2 Voll. Berkley: University of California Press.
Wright Mills, Charles. 1956. *The Power Elite*. New York: Oxford University Press.

Chapter 5
The Topicality of Ibn Khaldūn's Thought: From the *Muqaddima* to Our Society

Abstract This chapter explores the possibility of applying Ibn Khaldūn's historical-socio-philosophical scheme to Western liberal society today, with particular reference to Europe, united by an *'aṣabiyya* of democratic-liberal values expressed in the constitutions of its countries but confronted, from a multicultural perspective—which is the ultimate fruit of those values—with a multiplicity of other *'aṣabiyyāt*, juxtaposed but often very different from the original.

The chapter examines the relationship between them and the *'aṣabiyya* officially called upon to contain them, from Ibn Khaldūn's point of view. It also considers the various transformative factors that Ibn Khaldūn identifies as typical of the urbanised phase of civilization, such as the effect of luxury and individualism, the paradoxical relationship combining the alleged guarantee of security with vulnerability, and the widening of the boundaries of the community. The effect of all these factors on the maintenance of the Western liberal-democratic *'aṣabiyya* is therefore discussed in the light of the paradigms outlined in the *Muqaddima*.

Based on its instructive examples, this analysis aims to understand where our society is presently positioned in its evolutionary arc, and what possible social and political choices could optimise its future prospects from this perspective.

5.1 Applying Ibn Khaldūn Today: The Liberal-Democratic *'Aṣabiyya* and Ibn Khaldūn's Cycle

As our analysis has tried to show, Ibn Khaldūn's theory is a happy synthesis of an early sociological methodology, developed by analysing countless empirical and factual details, with a general theory of civilisation, drawn and inferred from those details. From their variety, the theory is constantly tested and reconfirmed, in an intense dialectic developed between the two dimensions.

A. Verza, *Ibn Khaldūn and the Arab Origins of the Sociology of Civilisation and Power*, https://doi.org/10.1007/978-3-030-70339-4_5

In Ibn Khaldūn's theory, the "accidental"—arising from the contingency of an inevitably different and complex environmental variety and political chronology (Bozarslan 2014: 12)—is constantly reconnected to the "essential," which always returns, and which, as in Aristotle, pertains to the category of universality.

Precisely because it can be universalised, not only is Ibn Khaldūn's theory worthy of attention in a retrospective sense—in relation to the past and in its application to historical study—but it can also prove useful and "instructive" for the analysis of our own time.

The universalistic projection of this theory emerges from the author's own statements—for instance, when he stresses that he has succeeded in transcending historical study in order to arrive at the formulation of a new science (*Muqaddima*, Concluding remarks)—and also from his express wish that some future scholar expand and develop his work, adding possible new elements (ibid).

Yet, the potential of this applicability has been scarcely realised in Khaldunian studies. While, in fact, the "first wave" of studies on Ibn Khaldūn was characterised by an enthusiastic appreciation of the author, seen as a "forerunner" of contents long afterwards elaborated in the West, the "second wave" (which began, more or less, in the 1930s, with analyses such as Benedetto Croce's (1932), and developed further after the "Colloquium" on Ibn Khaldūn organised in Rabat in 1979) was characterised, instead, by a rigid insistence on the need to contextualise his view (Forte 2005: 182–186).[1] However, while certainly understandable in itself, this need has often been interpreted as precluding any new application of the author's thought. In short, most of Ibn Khaldūn's exegetes, in their careful "contextualising" concern, ended up applying a scrupulous philological attention to his discourse which vehemently limited[2] the scope of Khaldunian studies (from Bouthoul's analysis onwards), and, unfortunately, ended up relegating the genius and fertility of the author's ideas to an unresolved sterility. Important exceptions to this are authors such as Alatas (2013, 2014, 2020), Bozarslan (2014), West (2015), Martinez-Gros (2012), and Turchin (2006, 2013).

The last part of this work is inspired by the conviction that Ibn Khaldūn, like all universal thinkers, has offered us precious theoretical insights that may help us understand socio-political dynamics (Bozarslan 2014: 10, 14) beyond his particular space-time context. For this reason, after applying to our examination of his thesis a close-up view focused onto its specific context, we shall now attempt a wide-angled view, in the conviction that his analysis of the dynamics of *'aṣabiyya*, even

---

[1] So much so that, as has been said, the succession of these "historical blocks" of "interpretive trends," functioned "like a mirror." So, it perhaps ended up revealing much more about the cultural needs of the exegetes themselves (see, for example, the inevitable influence of colonial policies, or of the self-validating needs of the West which, in the mid-nineteenth century, was discovering sociology, or of the influence of the Islamisation of education projects promoted by Seyyed Nasri and al-Faruqi (Alatas 2014: 58–62)), than about Ibn Khaldūn, or the intrinsic limits of the applicability of his theses.

[2] This, although every theory of society, being always inevitably formulated in a given context, demands such attention.

discounting all the historical and political *caveats* of the case, can still be sound in its basic principles and can, therefore, still help us understand at least part of today's situation.

In Ibn Khaldūn's fourteenth-century picture of the Maghreb, the *'aṣabiyya* growing out of the desert's *badāwa* described by the author was characterised by its own specific spatio-temporal elements, unrepeatable, in their particular balance, in other contexts. By the same token, the political forces at work had features and names typical of their time and place: caliphates, dynasties, tribes coming from the desert, tribal loyalties, and patronage. However, this does not change the fact that, if we were to look at the deeper dynamic that moves history on, we would find that, as Ibn Khaldūn would say, the past and the future in many ways still resemble each other "more than two drops of water." That is, even if, in the study of different societies, we always find a "substance" specific to their context, the abstract "form" expressed by Ibn Khaldūn's cycle always still appears in the background—although, of course, with the particular name and shapes determined by time and place.

Just as the Almoravid civilisation in Andalusia and the Maghreb was, in its time, overwhelmed by the Berber Almohads, and just as the Islamic world itself, after imposing its rule above powerful empires such as the Persian and over great civilisations such as the Greek, was then, in turn, overwhelmed by Mongolian and Turkish forces, so, too, the Persian, Egyptian, and Roman empires,[3] as well as the ancient and sophisticated Chinese, Indian, and others, have gone through similar parabolas. Their history, therefore, can also be traced in the cyclical perspective which envisages, in a sort of natural law of the political "body," the birth, rise, and final decline of the great empires, brought about by "fresh" and less civilised conquering forces (the "*alius*" of Ibn Khaldūn's nomadic hordes) taking advantage of the weakness of their phases of advanced and torpid well-being, when their bond of identity and solidarity is in full decay.

Although formulated in an inevitably particular context, and more than half a millennium ago, his theory on the mechanisms of *'aṣabiyya*, together with the "*'ibar*" (teachings) that it provides, can still constitute (like all theories that can be universally applied) a useful interpretative tool to assess the dynamic positioning, within Ibn Khaldūn's cycle, of our Western civilisation. It is precisely the "essential" and "macro" aspect of Ibn Khaldūn's theory, and, in particular, the constant cyclical pattern that he distils from the wide and diversified material provided by his sociological work, which constitutes the core that can be universally applied. In short, notwithstanding the inevitable change that has occurred in the appearance, size, and other important characteristics of many key political institutions of today, it is still possible to resort to the "examples" provided by Ibn Khaldūn's "*'ibar*," stripped of their contingent coating and considered in their universal aspect, as possible general interpretative schemes for the decodification of the social dynamics taking place in our times and contexts.

[3]The writings of Gibbon ([1776] 1996) on its fall are very famous.

As we have already seen, long before Durkheim, Ibn Khaldūn, trying to synthesise a concept endowed with a rich polysemic connotation, identified the main cohesive factor in the *'aṣabiyya* existing behind every social formation, i.e., in the solidarity force nourished by the group's sense of identity. The *'aṣabiyya* described by Ibn Khaldūn obviously took its concrete shape in the forms typical of that time and culture. However, the concept should not be confused with its application. As a conceptual core capable of taking substance in different forms, the *'aṣabiyya* cannot, in fact, be reduced to any particular occurrence at a defined time and place, lest it be devitalised and mutilated of any possible further applicability, and the fecundity of Ibn Khaldūn's ideas be unduly penalised.

Ibn Khaldūn's analysis can guide us in such recontextualisation. In fact, it is true that, in the simple and segmentary social forms analysed by Ibn Khaldūn through direct observation of the North African Arab and Muslim world, the *'aṣabiyya* translated, first of all, into the family and clan bond, which indicated and directly sealed the individual's identity. Even in this case, however, as Ibn Khaldūn himself pointed out, the real internal vector of identity was not so much given by the "blood" itself, but rather by the *mental and empathic representation* of being a community produced by the *conviction* of having something in common: in this case, a common bloodline. So much so that such aggregative function could also be produced, in different circumstances and, above all, as the group size changes, by other different cohesive factors—for example, by the feeling of connection produced by treaties, or other conventional factors such as, in the reality of his time, alliances, or the protective relationship that bound a "client" to his patron.

Moving even further away from the relational immediacy of the family and tribe context, Ibn Khaldūn went so far as to consider the broader unifying factor of an aggregating ethno-cultural dimension (for example when he considers the "Arabs," "Berbers," or "Zenatas"): in fact, throughout his work he paid constant attention to the ethnic links and specific "civilisation" of the various subjects in history.

Finally, in dealing with the conquests of Islam in the first centuries after the Hegira, and with the unifying effect produced by their religious afflatus, he came to consider a further and even wider type of cohesive force: the super-ethnic element based on a religious background (in his context, belonging to the Muslim *Umma* of the faithful).

It was certainly unavoidable for a Muslim like Ibn Khaldūn to consider such an expanded dimension of *'aṣabiyya*, as it was inscribed in the very heart of Islam. Born as a religion centred on a revelation "handed down" in Arabic to the Arabs, Islam was, in fact, because of its express vocation towards a universal mission, destined from the beginning to transcend its original ethnic dimension, in favour of a sense of commonality linked to a super-ethnic *'aṣabiyya* rooted in *values and beliefs*—and, therefore, superior and encompassing.

All these ultra-tribal extensions of *'aṣabiyya*, widely discussed by Ibn Khaldūn, can, therefore, guide us when applying his theory to new and even broader contexts, where solidarity is based on the forms of *'aṣabiyya* typical of this time.[4]

Identifying what constitutes today's central *'aṣabiyya*, at the political level, would allow us to bring Ibn Khaldūn's theory back into use. Moreover, this could also allow us to reconsider—at least up to a point—Ibn Khaldūn's inauspicious interpretation (he was deplored for his "pessimism" by many (cf. Bouthoul 1930; Gautier 1952: 112)) of the destiny of quick disintegration that, in his view, seems inevitably to affect the *ḥaḍāra*. In fact, an extension to new, more current forms of *'aṣabiyya* could reveal that, in some measure at least, his vision of the fate of this cohesive force's fast crumbling in the *ḥaḍāra* also depended on the specific context to which he had applied his scheme—namely, on the way *ḥaḍāra* was conceived in its time, and not on the scheme itself.

In Ibn Khaldūn's time, in fact, it was historically inevitable for the cohesive afflatus to cease to exist in the sedentary society, within which the inhabitants were no longer closely linked by their need for survival, and in which political power was gradually evolving into the "right" of a sovereign over his subjects, in a relationship of progressively objectifying detachment which was anything but unifying. This world was not yet capable[5] of conceiving the idea of a democratic foundation of a social pact that would allow participants to be seen not as "subjects,"[6] but as "citizens" called upon to share sovereignty, and linked together by an "associative pact" and by their adherence to a culturally recognised set of values and principles.

This important revolution in conceiving socialised life and sovereignty opens the way to identifying the *'aṣabiyya* that unites today's Western societies in that constitutionally formalised aggregative pact that is, nowadays, called upon to define the identity of Western societies.

As a catalyst of solidarity (certainly more abstract than the previous forms, but nevertheless capable of stirring collective passions, and of acting as a vector of identity recognition), the set of shared political and legal values lying at the basis of the social pact of liberal-democratic countries (essentially, the constitutions' written

---

[4]In fact, as suggested today by evolutionary psychology, the sense of fraternity given by religion, through cohesive narratives and rituals, also reproduces in our brain, through oxytocin (a substance that stimulates "parochial altruism," i.e., a desire to protect those who are close to us, coupled with indifference for those who are not), the same solidarity-building effect of kinship. There are, therefore, no reasons to exclude that this mechanism could also be based on other types of values, such as the secular ones on which the identity of today's Western societies rests. For loyalty and sense of identity to operate, however, group boundaries are required (Haidt 2012).

[5]Even today North Africa tends to maintain a tribalistic aggregative structure: a study by Michael A. Woodley and Edward Bell shows how (2012: 263): "where consanguineous kinship networks are numerically predominant and have been made to share a common statehood, democracy is unlikely to develop."

[6]As Bozarslan writes, in the political context of Ibn Khaldūn's time and world, "subjects had an obligation to accept a kind of power, and a religious or ideological discourse, to which they had not been called to contribute." Bozarslan (2014: 4): "Les assujettis ont l'obligation d'accepter un pouvoir, et un discours religieux ou idéologique qu'ils ne construisent pas eux-mêmes."

or unwritten fundamental principles) represents, when compared to Ibn Khaldūn's universe, a new dimension of solidarity, value-based, yet secular.[7]

For obvious historical reasons, this dimension, placed some half-way between the segmented tribal *'aṣabiyya* and the universalistic *'aṣabiyya* dictated by the religious mission described by Ibn Khaldūn, could not be considered at his time. Nevertheless, it responds to the same cohesive logic:[8] both, on the one hand, as adhering to the aggregating cultural element based on a common abstract identity, "ideal" and therefore, in this sense, also "imaginary," and, on the other hand, as ideally founded on negotiations, like the *'aṣabiyya*-generating alliances described by Ibn Khaldūn (the underpinning reference to the "social contract" is, in fact, culturally intrinsic to it). Therefore, this new aggregating factor is fully consistent with his theory, as it is an application and development of the same "*ratio*" underlying the forms of *'aṣabiyya* historically identified in the *Muqaddima*.

However, the aggregating identity constituting the *'aṣabiyya* of today's Western society is endowed with a new characteristic, compared to the kinds of *'aṣabiyyāt* observed by Ibn Khaldūn. In fact, it is designed to operate, as a basis to maintain a compact group conscious of its common identity, precisely *in the civil and sedentary phase* of social development—a possibility that, for historical reasons, was not contemplated in Ibn Khaldūn's analysis.

This new form of *'aṣabiyya*, in short, is an important cohesive element that works mainly not in the *badāwa*, but at the *ḥaḍāra* stage. That is, it works exactly in the dimension which, for Ibn Khaldūn and on the basis of his political experience, could only bring about the inevitable aggregative void[9] from which he had derived the impossibility (considering the political forms of his time) of maintaining social compactness, and, therefore, the inevitability of a particularly rapid disintegration.

In other words, the citizenship characterising the democratic-liberal political units of the West—a new foundation for the political *'aṣabiyya*, flowing at a moral and cultural level from the set of the constitutionalised values and principles on which the social pact is based—does not only provide a possible conceptualisation of a "modern" *'aṣabiyya* today, compatible with Ibn Khaldūn's framework. It also fosters the hope of a possibly longer cycle (at least, within the limits of the stability of such a civil *'aṣabiyya*). Consequently, its peculiar aggregating modality, precisely based on the phase of *ḥaḍāra,* could perhaps allow the possible avoidance—if not of an ineluctable final outcome—at least of the rapid rhythm of growth and disintegration described by the Maghreb theorist, despite the inevitable occurrence of all the other disruptive factors identified by him.

---

[7]The re-actualising discourse attempted here is deliberately ample and general, not tied to the specificity of a single State, but to the adhesion to that nucleus of common democratic-liberal principles and values which mostly keeps the "Western" societies united.

[8]Kalb 2004: "Universalistic ideologies can be no better than universalistic religions for grounding social order."

[9]As François Furet (1982: 165) wrote: "Un royaume est une propriété, une nation est un contrat."

While, now as in the past, social cohesion and solidarity remain essential to maintaining any society, nevertheless Ibn Khaldūn's lesson also teaches us that, by its very nature, the success of any enterprise aimed at gaining control over a community tends, if internal disintegration is not opposed, to weaken *'aṣabiyya* from the inside, releasing the dynamics of monopolisation of power, proliferation of desire, and individualism. The next paragraphs, therefore, aim not only to analyse the current social framework in the light of Ibn Khaldūn's theoretical scaffolding, and to assess the level of the contemporary liberal, democratic, and constitutionalised *'aṣabiyya*. They also aim to consider to what extent the many symptoms of decadence listed by Ibn Khaldūn are in action today—from consumerism to social and (multi)cultural breakdown, to economic and demographic crises—all factors which, according to his thesis, indicate a clear, potential move towards the sooner or later inevitable stage of senility.

Of course, what may be offered, in the short space of this chapter, is necessarily only an "aerial," general view aimed at broadly testing the outcome of a possible modern application of the concepts and "laws" we can draw from Ibn Khaldūn's work, since a study contextualised in the different nationalities of "Western society" would require further research and greater space.

5.2 The Cultural *'Aṣabiyya* and Multiculturalism

At the beginning of *Muqaddima,* Ibn Khaldūn pointed out that ignorance of the laws that govern the transformations of human society was a principal flaw in the field of historical studies. In particular, it is a big mistake not to consider the importance of identity and solidarity, and to interpret the world by merely applying the logic of the economy, religion, or ideology: in the variety of forms in which we have seen it, *'aṣabiyya* is the most powerful—although, perhaps, not the most visible—force determining the development of history.

Consequently, *mutatis mutandis*, once more it is the interpretative key given by the aggregating force of the "*'aṣabiyya*"—translated, in today's liberal and democratic West, into its secular, modern, and cultural declination—that will allow us to apply Ibn Khaldūn's paradigm to our own world, in order to assess how our civilisation will be able to resist and contrast the fall into the engulfing maelstrom of senility, and verify the trajectory of its next transformations in the twenty-first century.

In fact, if the modern, civil *'aṣabiyya* can be translated (bringing to bear Talcott Parsons's concept of the primacy of *latency* (Parsons 1951)) into the aggregative force of the most important Western democratic-liberal cultural values and criteria, then Ibn Khaldūn's theorisation, precisely because of the crucial importance that it attributes to culture and its values for group identity, could prove a particularly appropriate interpretative tool.

This will allow us to cast a particularly revealing light not only on the condition of the democratic-liberal *'aṣabiyya* which, due to its constitutional status, today plays the "leading" role in the solidarity of Western political groups, but also on the current state of multicultural policy which, widely adopted by Western democratic and liberal states, has also become a source of legitimacy for the minority *'aṣabiyyāt* recognised within these Western communities.

About a quarter of a century has passed since the neutralistic paradigm of justice,[10] aimed at the "impartial" management (cf. Trujillo 2003) of the different conceptions of the good within the same political community, has been replaced by an alternative multiculturalist model, based, instead, on the recognition of equal respect to the various minority cultural traditions living in its territory. In legal-philosophical debate, this model has been promoted on the basis of two fundamental works from the early 1990s (by communitarian scholar Charles Taylor (1992) and liberal scholar Joseph Raz[11]), and has eventually flourished both practically (in liberal countries such as Canada, the USA, and parts of Europe) and theoretically, to the extent it now represents a key area in contemporary political-legal and sociological thought.[12]

Therefore, when considering the state of the central, unifying *'aṣabiyya*, called upon to support the vitality of the group identified with it, we will also have to bear in mind that, in a multicultural framework, this *'aṣabiyya* gathers under its umbrella a number of other *'aṣabiyyāt*. These combine with each other and the central one, in a complex web liable to produce uncertain results. This complex picture can also be usefully analysed with the instruments developed by Ibn Khaldūn to deal with the instability of his time.

The relevance of applying Ibn Khaldūn's thesis to the current Western legal-political situation could, therefore, be important not for one, but for several reasons. First and foremost, it would constitute, in its own right, a *scientifically* multicultural approach to the analysis of social issues. As Ibn Khaldūn teaches us, "partisanship"—that is, in this case, the attachment to culturally proper and self-validating schemes—has no value at all in science: quite the contrary. Yet, the way in which the proudly multicultural study of "other" cultures is mostly understood today is not fully multicultural: other people's culture, in fact, is by and large solely seen as the "object" of a cognitive gaze, which is, however, cast only on the basis of "Western" paradigms and conceptual schemes, the importance of which is never questioned.

---

[10]The reference here, of course, is to John Rawls' theories: both *A Theory of Justice* ([1971] 1999) and *Political Liberalism* (1993). As is well known, many of the criticisms directed at his theories, which helped to open the way for multicultural policies, referred to the fact that neutrality was an emanation of a partial (liberal and democratic) logic (Verza 2000).

[11]Raz (1994); however, the work was presented as early as 1992.

[12]Literature on multiculturalism is very extensive today, and its detailed examination is not one of the aims of this volume. Beyond the works of Taylor and Raz, some of the most interesting works within this debate are: Kymlicka (1995); Okin (1999); Benhabib (2002); Parekh (2000); Phillips (2007); Malik (2015).

However, the act of "seeing" and analysing what is other than oneself is never objective and neutral, but always guided.[13] We see only what we are looking for in order to understand: the eye anticipates and foresees (Arnheim 1974: 18–19). In sociological studies, adopting only our partial and culturally specific point of view is not, therefore, an operation devoid of cognitive consequences.

For this reason, adopting a non-Western perspective (Ibn Khaldūn's Islamic one) as *a point of view* to start an assessment of our own culture and of the multicultural mosaic it supports, would undoubtedly have a merit in itself: overcoming this tendency to interpret multicultural study as an analysis which treats the "other" culture only as the object, and never as the subject, of discourse.

Furthermore, this examination of Ibn Khaldūn's perspective has other advantages: its sociological vision can also prove to be a good cognitive "gateway" to Islam and, thus, a much-needed stimulus towards the knowledge of the cultural structures and values of a conception of the good that is currently one of the main alternatives to the "Western" one, based (Verza 2012) on its own cultural products, and not on an external reformulation of them.

But the most important thing is that the theoretical filters and specific paradigm offered by Ibn Khaldūn may also help us understand the current situation in the mosaic of *'aṣabiyyāt* populating today's Western communities, with particular reference to those which are nowadays more involved in a direct comparison with the majority *'aṣabiyya*.

Islamic civilisation and culture,[14] because of its importance and assertiveness in migratory and macropolitical contexts, represents one of the main "significant others" of Western civilisation—that is, one of the great paradigms against which it is increasingly called upon to measure itself. Among other things, its increasingly larger presence has had the effect of blurring even more the relationship between rule and exception which, in the past and in the Western world, used to distinguish majority and minority on a cultural level. This confrontation takes place on several levels, ranging from the seemingly frivolous matter of appropriate women's clothing,[15] to more

---

[13]With its categories, thought is a fundamental component of perception, in operations such as selection, the ability to grasp the essential, abstraction, analysis and synthesis, active exploration, completion, correction, comparison, problem solving, combination, distinction and contextualisation. This consideration, moreover, was put forward by Plato (2014): in the *Theaetetus* Socrates leads the interlocutor to reflect on the fact that the eyes are not the organ that sees, but that "through which" one sees. Auguste Comte stated (1855, Introduction, ch. I): "If it is true that every theory must be based on observed facts, it is equally true that facts cannot be observed without the guidance of some theory. Without such guidance, our facts would be desultory and fruitless; we could not retain them: for the most part we could not even perceive them."

[14]This does not imply joining the vision of the "clash of civilisations" painted by Huntington (1996).

[15]It is precisely the symbolic issues that more than any other trigger the most heated social debates on the loyalties that it is legitimate or right to show and support, and on their relative religious, political, and cultural implications. While I am writing, for example, the proposed abolition of virginity certificates is splitting France in two.

abstract questions of basic political principles,[16] in a juxtaposition increasingly challenging the validity of many of the most advanced values of the liberal, democratic, and egalitarian culture—from gender equality to ideas of inclusion, tolerance, and neutrality of politics, right up to the culture of respect which, after all, is the basis of multiculturalism itself.

In some cases, these dilemmas of justice have, for some time now, gone far beyond the threshold of the symbolic and of "political correctness," and have reached the law itself. In England, for example, dozens of *Shari'a Councils*, present since 1982, have already sanctioned, in practice, the legitimacy of a sort of (voluntary) substitution of these with respect to the ordinary courts, for controversies concerning family and neighborhood law,[17] while an *Arbitration Act* of 1996 has granted legitimacy to a *Muslim Arbitration Tribunal* to settle matters of a commercial nature (De Angeli 2014: 399–400) on the basis of *Shari'a* rules.

In the meantime, a move towards increasingly greater flexibility of justice, even in criminal law (Monticelli 2003; Basile 2008), has been progressively expressed in the spread and adoption, by the courts of various Western countries, of the practice of invoking excuses, exemptions, and culturally extenuating circumstances—in some cases with paradoxical consequences.[18]

The result of this multicultural juxtaposition of different ethical, political, and cultural traditions is leading today to a profound crisis for even the most traditional "Western" paradigms of justice. The risk therefore exists that this juxtaposition, if not seriously integrated within a unitary framework capable of managing it, may soon lead to a shift from a relatively cohesive and homogeneous social situation (as was the case, recently, in Western liberal countries) towards a situation of fragmentation of the different *'aṣabiyyāt* and their identity and value schemes (much closer to the unstable world scrutinised by Ibn Khaldūn, as James Kalb (2004) writes).

Therefore, our analysis of the degree of resistance of the liberal-democratic, "Western" *'aṣabiyya* to disruptive factors (the spread of luxury, the delegation of security to others, etc.) that are now, as in Ibn Khaldūn's time, impelling it towards crisis, senility, and the completion of its historical cycle, also needs to be placed in the particular context of its combination with the rich constellation of the other *'aṣabiyyāt*, characteristic of our time. For the purposes of this analysis, Ibn

[16]On the deeper level of values, for example, it is common to oppose the Western universalistic concept of human rights to a list of "Islamic" values, differently organised on a non-individualist basis. At the same time, the secular paradigm, fundamental to European liberal tradition, which firstly marked the distinction between law and religion—and, subsequently, between law and morality—as a main feature of the "Western" constitutional systems, is juxtaposed to the Islamic prohibition against separating the two areas. Cf. Verza (2008).

[17]Yet, the situation is not clear, as such "courts" usually define their work as mediation or arbitration (cf. Parolari 2017).

[18]As in Landgericht Bücherburg 14 March 2006, Pusceddu, case KLs 205 Js 4268/05 (107/05), in which a man who had kidnapped and repeatedly raped his ex-girlfriend out of jealousy received a more moderate sentence because of his cultural (Sardinian) origins. See Parisi (2008).

Khaldūn's insights and "warnings" from the history of the past could truly help us to put into focus the greatest risks and the most critical factors threatening the democratic and liberal *'aṣabiyya*, and multiculturalism itself, which is a product of this culture.

The hope is that this might help us to understand how to avoid the risk of a cultural explosion, and the consequent fragmentation of the social structure into a new arena of confrontations between *'aṣabiyyāt* which are not only unintegrated but, more or less, in active opposition to each other.

5.3 Ibn Khaldūn's Transformative Factors in Action

In an article that appeared in *La Repubblica* many years ago—on 9 March 2000—Claude Lévy-Strauss ([2000] 2016: 136–137) offered a series of interesting reflections starting from a singular intuition: the idea that a possible answer to the eternal dilemma on the nature of man—individual and aggressive? or social and cooperative?—could be found, by analogy, in the outcomes of biological studies on one of the simplest forms of life existing on earth: the amoeba.

Such studies proposed a distinctly Khaldunian picture of the cyclically two-faced nature of these creatures. In fact, when amoebas, which feed on bacteria and normally live an independent life without contact with others of their genus, are faced with a scarcity of food, they change their behaviour. They begin to capture, and in turn secrete, a substance which attracts them to each other and leads them to form an aggregate of cells which behaves as a unitary being—internally organised with diversified functions, more combative, and consequently more capable of surviving and reaching its goal: safe places rich in food.

Once this objective is reached, however, the aggregate—just like the elements of society in Ibn Khaldūn's cycle—disperses once again: the individualistic tendency prevails and each amoeba resumes its independent existence.

Another interesting aspect of these studies lies in one detail of the analysis: the substance that brings amoebas to unite with each other is, in fact, precisely the same substance that keeps the cells of each complex together and allows them to communicate—*cyclical adenosine monophosphate* (incidentally, the same substance secreted by the bacteria on which amoebas feed).

As Lévy-Strauss remarks, this example shows how the difference between aggressiveness and sociability appears, after all, to be only a matter of degree: sociability itself seems to constitute nothing more than the "benign modality"—the other side—of aggressiveness.

That is not all: this example also points to the fundamental importance of abundance and security in gradually determining the fluctuations between the prevalence of the individual's reason over group solidarity, or vice versa.

Human beings are obviously more complex than amoebas. In human society, the creation and maintenance of a sense of unity and solidarity is produced not by a substance, but an "imaginary" element, equally viscous and motivating, which is peculiarly human: culture and identity. It is, therefore, important for us to analyse the extent to which this element can make the difference in maintaining solidarity, even in conditions of abundance and security, when the group is expanding.

5.3.1 Luxury and Individualism, Need and Community

As we have seen, for Ibn Khaldūn every consolidation of power inevitably carries with it the seeds—economic, political, psychological, and sociological—of its own downfall, which is produced by them in due course. In particular, of the main disruptive factors highlighted in his analysis, a prominent place is given to the effect produced, within the complex relationship that links urbanisation, prosperity, and lifestyles, by habituation to a progressively increasing use of luxury goods—commodities not strictly necessary for survival, but soon socially perceived as real "needs," due to the widespread habit of relying on them.

This phenomenon is clearly illustrated nowadays by the psychological theories that have identified the "treadmill" effect (cf. Kahneman 2004; Duesenberry 1949) of the consumption of material goods. Yet, Ibn Khaldūn had already lucidly observed how, beyond a certain level, the widespread availability, and therefore use, of economic resources beyond the level of the strictly necessary—which initially constitutes an element of strength—grows at the expense of the soul and "colouring" of the people accustomed to it (in a re-proposal, to a lesser extent, of the circularity that characterises his entire scheme).

In a gradual reversal which is only averted too late (as Ibn Khaldūn insists, change is hardly noticed by those who live through it), the habit of luxury tends to create an effect of addiction and dependence due to the fact that it "colours" the soul, soon becoming an integral part of the nature of man. This process, thus, transforms from within that sense of strength and wealth that was initially produced by abundance, leading to its opposite: slavery dictated by the need for newer and newer goods. This deprives those who rely on material goods of their "fortress," in an inadvertent positional swap that subtly overturns (in a somehow Faustian way) the relationship of strength and control existing between "master" and object.

Not only that: this close relationship that binds individuals and luxury goods nourishes an individualistic drive connected to gratification and social competition (described in *Muqaddima* as the socially competitive dynamic of prestige—the *jah*), and also expresses a profoundly disruptive effect at a social level. Cato the Censor had earlier written: "The city is afflicted by two opposing vices, avarice and luxury, ruinous ailments that have brought down all the great empires."[19] In fact, this system drives everyone to conceive of himself as an individual consumer, and blurs the

[19]"*Diversisque duobus vitiis, avaritia et luxuria, civitatem laborare, quae pestes omnia magna imperia everterunt*": cited in the History of Rome by Titus Livy ([First century AD] 1997: XXXIV, 4).

cooperative solidarity of his relationship with his peers, which is overshadowed and crushed by the unleashing of a fiercely competitive race to hoard the best and most prestigious goods.

From the point of view of this bond, it is poverty—constantly evoked by Ibn Khaldūn as a characteristic of *badāwa*, if not an essential element of it—that works and protects against the effects of the luxury of *ḥaḍāra* and, therefore, fosters social union.

This is not all, however: by necessitating a roughly egalitarian distribution of material resources within the group, due to the lack of a surplus, poverty decisively contributes to the triggering among its members of a symbolic process of mutual recognition, not competitive but egalitarian and empathic. This, in turn, proves to be essential to the solidarity-based union on which, among other things, potentially self-sacrificing armed mobilisation is founded—the enterprise needed to "break through" the protected perimeter of the *ḥaḍāra* (Bozarslan 2014: 174).

Just as Ibn Khaldūn argues, however,[20] individualism and the crumbling of inter-social *'aṣabiyya* also offer significant advantages, at least in the initial stage of the senility process, for simplifying the management and extending the duration of the established power. Often, therefore, these changes are even encouraged by governments themselves, attracted by the positive effects of greater docility and ease of management in an atomised society, where internal conflict is restrained by a sedated people's opportune focus on consumption and the development of individual opportunities, and where the *'aṣabiyya* is kept to the minimum necessary.[21]

As Durkheim later wrote, in fact:[22]

> If the crowd is reduced to passive obedience, it will end up resigning itself to this humiliating role, and little by little it will become as a sort of inert matter, no longer resistant to action, to be forged as one wishes, but from which it will now be impossible to extract the slightest spark of vitality. What makes a people strong, in fact, is the initiative of the citizens, and the activity of the masses.

[20]See *Muqaddima* III, 9: Cf. *Muqaddima* III, 9: although solidarity is necessary to create an organisation of power from below, it is only minimally necessary to keep it stable. Power, in fact, maintains itself thanks to the force of habit (which is fully in line with one of the most central Weberian ideal types). The problem of the lack of *'aṣabiyya* concerns, rather, the resistance of the political organisation to external or internal attacks.

[21]See Goodman (1972: 260): "*'Aṣabiyya* in the broadest sense can never be wholly absent in any group that functions at all differently from a mere collection of individuals. For any such group must somehow command identification [...] of a pragmatically significant number and combination of its members. By the same token, *'aṣabiyya* has a minimum effective level. A group that cannot command allegiance of its members, or [...] bring these feelings to the pitch of action cannot function as a group."

[22]Durkheim (1885: par. IV): "Si l'on réduit la foule à une obéissance passive, elle finira par se résigner a ce rôle humiliant, elle deviendra peu à peu une sorte de matière inerte, qui ne résistera plus à l'action, qu'on pourra façonner à volonté, mais à la quelle il sera désormais impossible d'arracher la moindre énticelle de vie. Or ce qui fait la force d'un peuple, c'est l'initiative des citoyens, c'est l'activité des masses."

As Kalb[23] writes, contemporary consumerism could also be read, in this sense, as an attempt to divert the tension produced by the internal plurality of *'aṣabiyyāt* into individualistic values of personal autonomy, material prosperity, and equality[24]—all factors that make society more easily governable by weakening the sense of group identity to a minimum.

Considering the transformative impact of well-being on our social background, it is possible to see how the individualistic vision of the world stimulated over the last 50 years by a continuous, intoxicating, and insistent drive to adhere to the consumerist model, appears to have shaped a fragmented society of consumers, individually addicted and dependent on a continuous "ratcheting up" of luxury and hedonistic stimuli and desires.[25] Increasingly since the 1960s, in Italy and the so-called Western world in general (initially, perhaps, to exorcise the poverty of the previous years in many parts of that world), the relationship with the things and goods necessary for human subsistence has gradually developed (Parise [1974] 2013) to the extent of producing people firmly accustomed to a hungry, neurotic, and constantly dissatisfied general pursuit of often ephemeral consumer goods.

As consumption has evolved, ending up in a circular and repetitive ritual (Baudrillard [1976] 2010), it has also been correlated to an ever diminishing capacity for appreciation of the goods in question, now largely diverted from direct hedonistic logic and framed, instead, in the logic of a constantly dissatisfied and obsessive search for increasingly newer and more luxurious goods. Such a search, however, because of the various ways in which pleasure can gradually produce addiction and craving (studied, in particular, by Easterlin (1973, 1974, 2001), but earlier suggested in Ibn Khaldūn's analysis of the multiplier effect of the unleashing of desires), can by its very nature never find appeasement and satisfaction.[26]

To this fragmenting and atomising dynamic, must be added the recent crisis of a welfare system which, in Italy as in many other Western countries, has for decades promised that it would take care of everyone—"from the cradle to the grave," as Beveridge said,—in a "top-down" approach which has engendered a strong illusion

---

[23]Kalb (2004): "The modern consumer welfare state can be understood as an attempt to diminish the risk of intergroup struggles by promoting individual opportunity, material prosperity, equality, and (except in relation to ruling bureaucracies) personal autonomy. Such things, Ibn Khaldūn would tell us, weaken group feeling and so make a society more easily governable. Some group feeling would still be needed for government to function, but bureaucratic techniques may reduce the amount necessary, and when force is called for training and weaponry can make up to some degree for loss of the natural group feeling and bravery that distinguished the effective armies of earlier times. The necessary minimum of group feeling might be generated, consistent with fundamental social commitments, through cooperative engagement in the struggle for national prosperity and social justice."

[24]*Ibid*: "Solidarity is based on connections of a sort that prosperity weakens and careerism and equality deny. We feel solidarity with those on whom we durably rely and with whom we share something specific."

[25]On the effect of this ratcheting up of desires, see Verza (2015b).

[26]See, in this regard, the analysis of Risé (2016), which links the luxury of the present day to the greater incidence of diseases which develop from within.

of independence and autonomy (Fineman 2004) in individuals who knew they could count on its "care." This illusion automatically brought about—and the example of the amoeba is paradigmatic here—a reduced need to belong to networks of social and caring solidarity. Today, however, the resources that have so far nurtured this individualistic dream and its consumerist manifestation are greatly reduced, and the consequent crisis in public welfare is putting an end to the "myth of autonomy." Also for this reason, therefore, the conditions that have so far guaranteed a maintenance of the sense of the group kept within the minimum limits for maximum governability, seem to be inevitably doomed to fail.

A renewed, inevitable realisation of people's common basic vulnerability (cf. Goodin 1985; Kittay 1997; Nussbaum 2006; Marian Barnes 2012; MacKenzie et al. 2014), and an awareness of the real state of need and dependence that everyone might feel—in the face of the welfare state and economic crises that are sweeping consumerist habits away—will, therefore, inevitably rekindle a new search for the social and group bond, again felt (or rationally understood, as Ibn Khaldūn would say) as a real human necessity that needs to be satisfied.

So, although, until the 1990s, the predominance of the collective over the personal was mostly considered as a factor linked to the value hierarchies of "other" minority cultures (generally seen as more traditionalist and not yet fully mature in terms of individual rights), today Western individualism seems in perspective to have been nothing more than a parenthesis, a luxury, made possible over the course of a few decades by an exceptional availability of resources. These resources, allowing the continuous replenishment of increasingly greater prosperity and ample individual opportunities, have enabled people to forget for a while the spectre of their dependence on others and, therefore, the need to create social ties. But only for a while.

The consequence of the evident crisis of the individualistic society of welfare and consumption is, today, an increasingly pressing delegation of the care of citizens to families again, and to the charitable and voluntary "second welfare" sector. Apparently, the new bulwark against poverty and vulnerability is being re-identified with a return to an attachment to various forms of community.

As society moves, today, towards such a sudden and renewed need for community bonding, the oscillatory and dynamic nature of the relationship that links the need for community and the value of individuality is confirmed. Just as in Ibn Khaldūn's analysis, and the Lévy-Strauss example, if the unity of a society is the initial condition determining its success and, therefore, the increase in its economic well-being, it is exactly the latter factor which, in turn, inevitably pushes back towards an individualism that stimulates the loosening of close bonds (such as family and community) in favour of increasingly rarefied and "subtle" relational contexts. The resulting relational and identity void is cyclically accompanied, however, by a weakening, a decline in well-being, and a renewed situation of need. These factors are a prelude to a consequent return to the strengthening, albeit on new foundations, of group belonging and forms of solidarity—both ancient, like the family, but also new—in an uninterrupted alternation of solidarity and individualism.

5.3.2 The Circularity That Couples Security with Vulnerability

As we have seen in Ibn Khaldūn's framework, by its very nature the group, while striving to ascend towards *ḥaḍāra*, pursues not only the economic security of luxury (which then goes on to bring about its disintegration), but also another type of security—apparently fortifying, but also destined to destroy it from within. It also seeks protection from external challenges, order, and tranquility—in other words, that rational, predictable, "bureaucratic" and controlled planning of its own world which allows disarmament and relief from the fatigue of self-defence, guaranteeing a perception of security and protection from the unforeseeable events of reality, and bringing about control and mastery over its own environment.

This planning and bureaucratisation of social and daily life (an expression of maximum rationalisation applied to the organisation of the community, according to Weber) goes as far, in contemporary Western societies, as reaching a pervasive, Luhmannian schematisation of existence (Verza 2016). This is aimed at maximising the predictability and rationality of life in all its aspects, and at exchanging the uncertainty intrinsic to exposure to unexpected events (together with the stimuli[27] triggered by this condition) for safety, thus minimising the potentially disorienting impact of encountering untamed life and chance. This striving for security, however, also strongly contributes to the weakening and suffocation of the spirit and "fortress" of the political aggregate, and, thus, also paradoxically, leads to erosion of the connective tissue of Western society.

Just as the dynamic which binds luxury, individuality, and the need for society describes, as we have seen, its own independent circle within Ibn Khaldūn's more general cyclicality, so also the paradox which binds security to vulnerability works out the same circularity traced, in general, by the path described in his theory. As generally happens in complex systems—such as social aggregates (but also personality systems,[28] or even the bodily entities of Parsons' "behavioral organisms"[29])—the strategies put in place to strengthen and protect them normally end up, if pushed too far, causing a particularly strong vulnerability reaction. This reaction is produced by the same effort to deny it and escape it, through the control or denial of its reactive confrontation with the threats that may come from the environment.

The literature on the aetiology of the paradoxical weakening of the social body caused not only by wealth and comfort, but also by protective, top-down social planning (see, for example, Tainter 1957, 1988), is extensive. Along with Ibn Khaldūn, many other great historians, such as Edward Gibbon ([1776] 1996) and Arnold J. Toynbee ([1934] 1962; cf. Kalin 2017b), have strongly emphasised the

[27]It is the concept of "antifragility": see Nassim Nicholas Taleb ([2012] 2013).

[28]On personality, the extremely "fragilising" effect of excessive protection brought about by placing the subject meant to be protected "under a glass dome" is well known.

[29]See in the medical field, for example, the evidence of the iatrogenic effects potentially induced by medicines themselves, denounced, for example, by Austrian philosopher Ivan Illich (1977).

existence, as the largest and most powerful political entities develop, of an important and recurrent causal connection with their eventual weakening. This progressive growth of vulnerability, paradoxical and developed from within,[30] proceeds in parallel with their external strengthening, consolidation of power, and rationalisation of organisational structure (Verza 2017).

For example, Toynbee argued that civilisations—the largest units at the social level—do not develop through placid and linear growth, sheltered from disturbing elements. On the contrary, their progress depends on the stimulus given by challenge and response mechanisms. They, therefore, develop precisely by virtue of their ability to respond creatively to the unpredictable challenges coming from the outside or from within:

> Man achieves civilisation, not as a result of superior biological endowment or geographical environment, but as a response to a challenge in a situation of special difficulty, which rouses him to make a hitherto unprecedented effort [Toynbee [1934] 1962: Argument II. V (1)].

Toynbee also argued that the absence of challenges triggering the group's development, solidarity, and consciousness of identity, hinders the growth of civilisations and leads to the demise of their unused—and thus forgotten—solidarity, until they reach their final stage.

For these authors, too, as for Ibn Khaldūn, just when the strongest societies reach a level of stability capable, in theory, of sheltering them from possible future threats, they are inevitably affected by a sort of "disease of progress" which strips them, both as individual citizens and as a group, of defensive antibodies and, therefore, makes them more vulnerable.

Such mechanisms, like the consumerist process nourishing individualism discussed above, are also produced and favoured by the stabilisation of power, which is undoubtedly interested in encouraging them. In fact, as Ibn Khaldūn observed, those who govern typically put into practice, in order to stay in power, a series of characteristic processes aimed at structuring the profile of a people who are indeed enriched and protected but, at the same time, consigned to a state of dependence.

One of the most revealing and characteristic signs of this process—which, as we have seen, Ibn Khaldūn commented upon at some length—is a deliberate and accentuated disconnection between the members of the group and its protection, brought about by stripping people of this task and, then, of a direct responsibility for their own self-defence, both as individuals and as a group. This task is organically entrusted, in sedentary civilisations (in times gone by as well as today), to special elements, by means of the contextual institution of "professional" armed forces and the construction of static defences, such as walls (manned borders today), put in place to shield the *ḥaḍāra* from the wilder elements at its margins.

[30] As is well known, Toynbee, who had re-elaborated Ibn Khaldūn's theses, claimed that great civilisations disappear because of a weakening from within; the expression attributed to him is famous: "Civilisations die by suicide, not by murder."

This is part of the wider process aimed at bringing the group to "tranquility": the fact of conceiving security as a function delegated to a specific apparatus (often, incidentally, made up of people selected from the more violent *badāwa*) frees individuals from the burden, but also the impulse, of dying for the group—an eventuality not only ever present, but also culturally supported in the *badāwa*.[31] By contrast, in the *ḥaḍāra* this "exemption" constitutes a luxury that releases group members' energies for other activities: in fact, the general duty of subjects is to produce goods and pay taxes. The practice of disarmament is also induced through education, and by inculcating respect for the law.

The transfer of this function—which is, above all, a matter of hard reality—over time also acquires, however, important repercussions on the symbolic plane and on the character of the group, since it makes self-defence no longer even "conceivable" for private individuals, developing in them, instead, the characteristic of "meekness." In Ibn Khaldūn's thought, this characteristic is not the expression of a higher moral attainment (even if individuals might interpret and exalt it in such a way), but is rather seen as the product of living conditions and the psychological attitudes they induce. Meekness, in fact, is the result (and mirror) of a socially dependent and weakened lifestyle: when the habit of protecting oneself and one's group is prevented and lost, meekness inevitably arises as a result of the seeming impossibility of alternative attitudes.

Such a denial, for group members, of the power (but also the right) to defend themselves from the ever present possibility of aggression transforms the group, originally mutually supportive and endowed with its own "fortress" mentality, into a set of subjects made consciously dependent[32] by habit and coercion.[33] Because of the influence of habit on their character, they are also deprived—"like women and children who depend on others for their defence," wrote Ibn Khaldūn—of the sense of being able to rely on themselves for such a purpose.

As we have already seen, for Ibn Khaldūn this loss of control over one's life is followed, according to human (but also animal) nature, by a state of apathetic loss of vitality. In addition, Ibn Khaldūn wrote, rapid demographic effects are often also associated with it. For example, he explained how

> [The population of Ctesiphon] numbered 137,000, including 37,000 heads of families. But when the Persians came under the rule of the Arabs and were subjugated, they lasted only a short while and were wiped out as if they had never been. One should not think that this was

[31]Just think of the frequency, in ancient Greek and Roman literature, of the *topos* according to which "it is beautiful for a young man to die in battle" (from Tyrteus to Horace).

[32]As is well known, Machiavelli also advised the Prince to enrich the poor and impoverish the rich, precisely to create greater docility and more security for the government through a sense of precariousness and dependence.

[33]*Muqaddima* II, 5. Ibn Khaldūn (1958, Vol. I: 258). Ibn Khaldūn ([1967] 2005: 95): "Man is a child of the customs and the things he has become used to. He is not the product of his natural disposition and temperament. The conditions to which he has become accustomed, until they have become for him a quality of character and matters of habit and custom, have replaced his natural disposition."

> the result of some persecution or aggression perpetrated against them. The rule of Islam is known for its justice. Such (disintegration) is in human nature. It happens when people lose control of their own affairs and become the instrument of someone else (*Muqaddima* II, 23; Ibn Khaldūn 1958, Vol. I: 301; Ibn Khaldūn [1967] 2005: 117).

The decline in vitality, linked, in turn, to the birth rate, derives from the deprivation of personal responsibility for one's own destiny and life, and, for Ibn Khaldūn, is one of the "secrets" of the dynamics which govern the incessant transformation of society, as, from the peak of its well-being, it pushes it towards the beginning of its disintegration (*Muqaddima* II, 23).

In other words, if society does not attempt to fend off its vulnerability through active resistance against environmental aggressions,[34] but does so by protectively isolating itself from them and denying the factors that can plunge it into crisis, the risk will be discounted that this protection may cause exactly the same weakness and vulnerability it is intended to prevent. In fact, once the securing action goes beyond a certain limit, instances of unexpected and circular conjunction may appear between the two extremes.

After a while, as Ibn Khaldūn points out when describing the effect of the passage of time on different generations, a further factor intervenes to drain away the group's reactive and self-defence mechanisms: due to the passing of time, even the *memory* of the struggles, risks, and sacrifices of previous generations, which enabled them to achieve what they did, gets lost.

The progressiveness of change—which remains hidden, thanks to its imperceptible slowness, to unobservant eyes—is allied to the power of habit and makes the group lose the memory and the awareness of the role that solidarity and combativeness played in reaching the well-being of the advanced phases of *ḥaḍāra*. The absence of directly addressable challenges—opportunities that would stimulate the awareness of the identity and solidarity that enable the central *'aṣabiyya* holding society together to bear fruit—progressively blurs the group's memory and its attachment to its common identity. The same effect is also produced on the level of imagination, as the very roots of this lost memory are also torn out.

As we have seen, the excess of wealth provokes social disintegration, stimulating an internal competition that gets progressively fiercer the more abundant the resources are. This combines with coercion of the group members into a state of dependence, and their consequent weakening, to corrode the central identity core of *'aṣabiyya*, thus taking away from the *ḥaḍāra* the strong and supportive ground on which it had been built. This can be a serious cause for alarm since, as Ibn Khaldūn wrote, this internal evaporation of *'aṣabiyya* constitutes the most serious sign of an approaching change.[35]

---

[34] See Hashemi (2019: 544), who argues that the deeper dichotomy offered by Ibn Khaldūn in the *Muqaddima*, still relevant today, is that "between the risk-takers and risk-avoiders or between the trained and untrained."

[35] Pareto ([1917] 1988: §1858–1859), an author in some ways comparable to Ibn Khaldūn, had also argued that the societies characterised by the most brilliant civilisation are, conversely, the closest to decline: the aggregates where humanitarianism flourishes to the point of obscuring the sense of self

According to Ibn Khaldūn, therefore, civilisation and culture give the guarantees of a reassuring stabilisation of power, domination over the environment, and then luxury and security; but these very factors, due to their negative, weakening, and disruptive effect on people, then destroy the unifying force that had allowed them to be born—just as, on a biological level, abundance and security end up making Lévy-Strauss' amoebas detach themselves from their unifying formation and return to their individual, separate, and competitive paths.

This process harks back to Saturn/Chronos—the symbol of the golden age of abundance and peace—who, as the myth has come down to us, wraps a scythe around his cloak and eventually, inexorably, eats his own children in the unfolding of time that he himself embodies.

This weakening and meekness, however, could also produce an opposite reaction due to the sudden collapse of the factors supporting them (or the fear of such a collapse). The perception of an outside threat, especially if combined with a perception of ineffectiveness in the "specialised" defence citizens have to rely on,[36] could stimulate the need to return to a defensive aggregation. In this case, the risk is that this would happen not in the name of the open and welcoming *'aṣabiyya* of the *ḥaḍāra*, now perceived as ineffective, but under the banner of more immediate, and above all more violent and combative, forms of unification.

So, just as today's sudden economic crisis is prompting new and needs-driven incentives for people to re-aggregate, so a sudden perception of one's own vulnerability in the face of possible threats could incite forms of reactive re-aggregation[37] developed, perhaps, in the transition to a new generation (as in Ibn Khaldūn's example of the 40 years spent in the desert by the Israelites fleeing Egyptian slavery). Such aggregation would be aimed at replacing the defensive action carried out by the political organisation (perceived as dormant and ineffective) with the action of new *'aṣabiyyāt*, designed so as to be able to involve their members, to lift them out of their status as dependent, and to make them protagonists again, and able to guarantee security in a more tangible way. In this scenario, however, the risk of slipping into potentially violent, politically radicalised, and potentially uncontrollable confrontations, would be very high.

In relation to this trend, several signs of change can already be noticed on a social level, today, in the increasingly widespread search for a return, in different ways, to a private assumption of responsibility for one's own protection—a symptom of individuals' ever-dwindling reliance upon, and identification with, the "top-down" defence organised for them.

---

are those closest to the greatest bloodshed, and the most tolerant élites, by being most remote from any kind of violence, for this reason invoke the revolution that will destroy them (Aron 1967: 474).

[36]The (in)security perceived in today's Western societies, and its political effects, is one of the "hottest" sociological and criminological issues of recent years.

[37]Machiavelli ([1532] 2005: ch. XX) also warned the Prince against the effects of disarming his population, arguing that in this way the sovereign—who would, thus, implicitly offend his subjects by showing that he does not trust them (considering them either cowards or possible traitors)—would end up attracting their hatred and provoking opposition in reaction.

One can interpret in this sense not only the growing trend towards the creation of private bodies for surveillance and street patrols financed by private citizens, no longer confident in the ability of public services to guarantee their security (present in Italy, for example, in Milan, Bologna (Pandolfi 2016) and elsewhere, and also in the USA (Owens 1994: Sec. C, 1)), but also more macroscopic phenomena such as the choice of living in "Gated Communities"—small, modern micro-enclaves increasingly equipped with barrier walls and guards at their entrance, which are built into the fabric of some American cities, and are also beginning to appear in Europe.

While more than 30 million people in the United States, today, live in such "common-interest developments" (CID), often organised so as to provide residents with additional security and control services,[38] the topicality of the security issue is also leading to a spread of the phenomenon in Europe (Ghini 2011).

5.3.3 Dimensions of the Group and the Sense of Belonging

As we have seen, in Ibn Khaldūn's perspective (also embraced by Toynbee and other historians) the collapse of civilisations is not due, in the first place, to an attack from external forces: rather, it is because of their previous internal weakening that external forces are able to penetrate and conquer the *ḥaḍāra*.

In this framework, a further disruptive factor that comes into play in this sense is given by the symbolic (as well as actual) increase in the distance that progressively occurs among the components of the group.

This process reaches its final stage when the idea of collective identity gradually stretches and moves so far away from its original definition as to become completely blurred, thus totally stripping this idea of identity of any meaning—as this concept is linked to the existence of boundaries defining a specific identity of the "group," as compared to the environment. As we have seen, Ibn Khaldūn figuratively described this process of progressive loss of a group centripetal and identity forces through a comparison with ripples in the water: the further away they spread, the more they tend to vanish (*Muqaddima* III, 7; Ibn Khaldūn 1958, Vol. I: 331; Ibn Khaldūn [1967] 2005: 128–129):

[38]Cfr. Kalb (2004): "In the South and West almost all new private residential housing is part of such communities. In aging cities throughout the country existing residential neighbourhoods are forming similar arrangements within municipalities that have shown themselves unable to provide services and protection, closing off streets to discourage outsiders and establishing community crime patrols or hiring private security forces for public safety. Such neighbourhoods are presently organised mostly for such mundane purposes as safety, maintaining property values and administering common facilities, but the Kiryas Joel case [*Board of Education of Kiryas Joel Sch. Dist. v. Grumet*, 114 S. Ct. 2481, 129 L. Ed. 2d 546 (1994)], in which the Satmar Hasidim were able to establish a separate incorporated village in upstate New York and may yet succeed in constituting that village as a separate public school district, suggests the possibility of a far larger role." Cf. also Evan McKenzie (1994) and Timothy Egan (1995).

> A dynasty is stronger at its centre than it is at its border regions. When it has reached its farthest expansion, it becomes too weak and incapable to go any farther. This may be compared to light rays that spread from their centres, or to circles that widen over the surface of the water when something strikes it.

A similar concept was later expressed also by Giacomo Leopardi in his *Zibaldone*:[39]

> universal love by destroying patriotic love does not replace it with any other active passion, and [...] the more the love for one's own group gains in extension, the more it loses in intensity and effectiveness."
>
> In fact, "When the whole world was populated by Roman citizens, Rome no longer had citizens; and when being a Roman citizen was the same as being cosmopolitan, neither Rome nor the world was loved: the patriotic love of Rome became cosmopolitan, it became indifferent, inactive and void: and when Rome was the same as the world, it was no longer anyone's homeland, and the Roman citizens, having the world as their homeland, had no homeland, and they showed it by the way they acted.

In this case, the slide into disintegration is not determined by considerations of the economy or safety, but proceeds precisely from a flaw in the central element of identity.

Within this logic, after the widening of a group identity boundaries, another increase in distance—perhaps, even more paradigmatic and significant for the involution of the *'aṣabiyya*—intervenes between the ruling and ruled in the group.

It is no coincidence that Ibn Khaldūn, on several occasions, describes the institutional and functional changes in the roles of the chamberlain/doorkeeper—who acts as the interface between the sovereign and the other members of the group. As he demonstrates, although the term used to describe these roles has remained unchanged over time, its meaning has progressively changed: initially indicating the

[39]Leopardi, *Zibaldone* ([1989] 2014), 24 December 1820: "l'amore universale distruggendo l'amor patrio non gli sostituisce verun'altra passione attiva, e [...] quanto più l'amor di corpo guadagna in estensione, tanto perde in intensità ed efficacia." Difatti, "Quando tutto il mondo fu cittadino Romano, Roma non ebbe più cittadini; e quando cittadino Romano fu lo stesso che cosmopolita, non si amò né Roma né il mondo: l'amor patrio di Roma divenuto cosmopolita, divenne indifferente, inattivo e nullo: e quando Roma fu lo stesso che il mondo, non fu più patria di nessuno, e i cittadini romani, avendo per patria il mondo, non ebbero nessuna patria, e lo mostrarono col fatto." The text of the *Zibaldone* between the two quotations is as follows: "i primi sintomi della malattia mortale che distrusse la libertà e quindi la grandezza di Roma, furono contemporanei alla cittadinanza data all'Italia dopo la guerra sociale, e alla gran diffusione delle colonie spedite per la prima volta fuori d'Italia per legge di Gracco o di Druso, 30 anni circa dopo l'affare di C. Gracco, e 40 circa dopo quello di Tiberio Gracco, del quale dice Velleio, (II. 3.) *Hoc initium in urbe Roma civilis sanguinis, gladiorumque impunitatis fuit.* col resto, dove viene a considerarlo come il principio del guasto e della decadenza di Roma. Vedilo l. 2. c. 2. c. 6. c. 8. init. et c. 15. et l. 1. c. 15. fine. colle note *Varior.* Le quali colonie portando con sé la cittadinanza Romana, diffondevano Roma per tutta l'Italia, e poi per tutto l'impero. V. in particolare Montesquieu, *Grandeur* etc. ch. 9. p. 99–101. e quivi le note. *Ainsi Rome n'étoit pas proprement une Monarchie ou une République, mais la tête d'un corps formé par tous les peuples du monde... Les peuples... ne faisoient un corps que par une obéissance commune; et sans être compatriotes, ils étoient tous Romains.* (ch. 6. fin. p. 80. dove però egli parla sotto un altro rapporto.)."

original function of doorkeeper, it ended up designating the much higher office of prime minister. The importance of this office—a later development of the previous role—was due precisely to the exceptional position of the chamberlain, who remained, at the end of a certain phase of development, the last and only subject still allowed to be in direct contact with the sovereign.[40]

As emphasised by the recurrence of this reference, for Ibn Khaldūn the passage from the original solidarity between the leader and his group to the hieratic distance between the sovereign and his subjects is not incidental, but (again, as happens with the stupor induced by luxury, and the helpless dependence caused by the disempowerment on self-defense) is intrinsic to, and typical of, political evolution. In a situation where the leadership of *'aṣabiyya* has already evolved in the *mulk*, the chamberlain's role is to maintain and amplify the charisma of the sovereign, who is no longer seen to be the best representative of a well-established and cohesive group, but rather as an individual placed above the group itself. In fact, the very distance of the sovereign from his people also favours, in a sense, his untouchability and sacredness. With that, the sense of contact, mutual responsibility, and, ultimately, recognition of a mutual identity among the members of a political group, fades away.

This increase in distance, because of the disintegrating drift that it induces, also constitutes yet another factor that is not only predictive, but also causative of the exhaustion of the vitality of the political project.

One of the ways in which this detachment manifests itself can be seen in the administration of internal resources (especially taxation) by the central authority. In this phase of incipient senility, the management of the group's economy becomes predatory because the lack of solidarity induces leaders to perceive the masses as other than themselves and, therefore, as a plausible ground for exploitation. As we have seen, Ibn Khaldūn repeatedly points out that one of the most important material roots of the regressive process is injustice, which is also caused by the collection of taxes so excessive that they stifle the economy. This imposition is motivated, on the one hand, by habituation to ever-increasing luxury and, on the other hand, by the setting up of a bureaucratic-administrative machinery and a mercenary army. All these factors, being disproportionate to the productive capacity of the group, eventually drain the economy and send it into crisis.

However, this detachment does not only happen from top to bottom: it also occurs, as we have seen, in a horizontal sense, as the group, because of its blurred boundaries, stops perceiving itself, on an imaginary and emotional level, as a group. In the Western world today, the sense of collective identity that should underlie the common *'aṣabiyya* is becoming increasingly evanescent, due to the extreme lengthening of the chain that should bind together the members of the group, and the total removal from each private individual of responsibility for its administration. In this case, too, economic behaviour is revealing. Loss of the sense of common identity, in

[40]The hiatus produced by such a shift, however, is poorly perceived in the common consciousness—which shows how, sometimes, changes in context, or even in language (Bozarslan 2014: 33), can also impair the memory of the social structures' original meaning.

fact, prompts many people, even if unconsciously, not to see public resources—above all, welfare spending—as something belonging to each person contributing to it (a value, therefore, to be respected and used wisely), but as an "external," "alien," and therefore exploitable element (Bozarslan 2014: 42)—which favours, in turn, a descent into an opportunistic *free-rider*'s logic, mostly without qualms.

Against a context that is so extensive as to obscure, in the eyes of each individual, the link connecting his or her personal agency to the management of public affairs, the perceived significance of everyone's role within society is reduced to the extent of eluding the very sense of his or her belonging and contributing to the group. On the other hand, such reduction is likely to end up triggering the search for other more restrained and perceptible forms of *'aṣabiyya*, as compensation.

The implications of this inversely proportional relationship between the size and organisational rigidity of the group, on the one hand, and the sense of belonging perceived by its parts, on the other, are today also studied and considered as a crucial factor at the sociological "meso" level of corporate organisations. In this field, recent studies have demonstrated that trust and team spirit among a company's internal components—an expression and symptom of *'aṣabiyya*—are key factors for its success.[41]

Here, too, we can see the extent to which the enlargement of the group's boundaries affects *'aṣabiyya*. For example, it is precisely on the basis of the collapse of personal trust, and therefore of the internal *'aṣabiyya*, which follows the enlargement of an enormously successful company, that the apparently paradoxical fate of the demise, about a decade ago, of a company like Nokia was explained by its new manager, Jorma Ollila.[42]

In the same way, some of the most important experts of organisational psychology, such as Richard Hackman (2009), have used Ibn Khaldūn's paradigm to explain why the largest and most varied human groups, endowed with abundant internal resources, instead of being the strongest and most efficient ones, on the contrary, often are more likely to be the most dysfunctional. What is highlighted here is the fact that their increase in scale (and therefore, from this point of view, their strengthening) ends up also increasing (exponentially, as the company grows) the burden of managing the social links between individual and group. This, in turn, hinders the sense of identification between its parts and discourages an individual's ability and freedom to act, and to take risks and responsibilities, when faced with the need to be accountable and to act not in his own name, but in that of the entire group (increasingly felt to be not "one's own"), and with the challenges of coordination and also of motivation which ensue.

[41]In 2015, Zuckerberg himself declared that he considered the *Muqaddima* particularly able to illuminate the present situation: Raffaele Alberto Ventura (2015).

[42]https://nokiapoweruser.com/jorma-ollila-nokias-strategy-with-windows-phones-was-not-succesful-elop-wasnt-the-first-choice-as-ceo/. But the cycle of *'aṣabiyya* can also be observed in the fate of other large companies, which grew with strong corporate values and then collapsed, such as Kodak, General Motors and Yahoo.

The enlargement of the body and, therefore, the mutual estrangement of its parts, brings about a preponderance of the group that crushes the individuals, and often also discourages individual voices from making their potentially innovative contribution[43] to the group. Due to self-censorship, motivated precisely by the idea of lacking control, as individuals, over the whole, these potential contributions are often lost, instead of enriching the group.[44]

In short, even at the "meso" level, an analysis of the effects of the enlargement of the group brings about a corresponding list of costs and disadvantages—a less streamlined approach, the higher costs of communication initiatives, more complex decision-making procedures, and, above all, a proportional tendency to lose the sense of *'aṣabiyya*.

Returning to the political and "macro" dimension, these reflections apply in relation to the moral entropy which follows the spatial extension of the social dimension, too. For example, the remarkable ultra-national enlargement of the boundaries of Western culture involved in the adoption of a common European cultural perspective seems to have ignored and completely neglected the central importance of the dynamics of *'aṣabiyya*.[45] As we shall see, this also applies to the "special" extension of the cultural hospitality required by the contemporary multicultural project. Both directions of this extension, in fact, for the psychological dynamics of *'aṣabiyya*, risk becoming a source of vulnerability and potential weakening.

As Ibn Khaldūn suggests (*Muqaddima* III, 7–8), there is no linear progression leading the *'aṣabiyya* of a wider political context to proportionally increase its strength and intensity. On the contrary: as it grows in size, its bonds gradually lose their restraining force (*Muqaddima* III, 7), and their internal centripetal forces lose tension, in a disintegrating process that risks again favouring a withdrawal into smaller groups that—as surrogates, compared to the larger group—could better guarantee the satisfaction of the individual relational needs in terms of lifestyle, values, and a coherent, clear and reliable culture in which to invest one own's identity.

Thus, considering the three factors examined so far, between the two extremes of an excessively large "European" and internally diverse community at a macro level, and of a sense of loneliness at the micro level of the single individual (confronted with the demise of the liberal myth of autonomy (Fineman 2004), and aware of a vulnerability no longer compensated for by a reliable security system), one can understand the overpowering appeal of the "closer" and more intelligible dimension

[43]An explicitly Khaldunian reflection on the relationship between the group size and its capacity for innovation is also offered by Nobel Prize winner Paul Krugman (2013).

[44]It is not only a problem of communication inhibitions: as Solomon Asch's well-known experiments demonstrated decades ago, the group's "normative" pressure can have limiting effects even at the cognitive level, thus producing distortions in this field.

[45]As West (2015) writes, a country of 500 million people is in no way ten times stronger than a country of 50 million. On the contrary, its expansion, like that of an excessively large soap bubble, ends up putting its stability in crisis.

of the cultural communitarian sub-groups. It is, indeed, a warmer and more tangible *'aṣabiyya* that they propose, capable of providing an individual with greater closeness, values, relationships, and contextual certainties (see also Seligman and Montgomery 2019).

5.3.4 Pandemic, Ecology, and Breakdown

At the beginning of 2020, despite medical advances in the twenty-first century, the Covid-19 pandemic exacted a high toll in terms of human lives and caused a correlated, sudden halt in the normal social and economic-productive routine of the entire world. Should this sudden event also be included in this attempt to reapply Ibn Khaldūn's theory to today's society?

The answer requires careful analysis since, at first glance, a pandemic is of a different nature from the other fall factors already examined. First of all, in fact, the reason for its existence is exogenous to the internal dynamics of social development: it comes from outside and is not generated as a dialectically negative by-product of the objectives of security and well-being achieved by civilisation. Moreover, its impact extends horizontally to all communities, regardless of their position in their development trajectory.

However, comparison of the arrival of the Covid-19 pandemic with the Black Plague which Ibn Khaldūn describes at the beginning of the *Muqaddima,* and which had such a decisive influence on his motivation to undertake his explanatory enterprise, allows us to draw some interesting parallels.

For Ibn Khaldūn, in fact, if the senility of civilisations is not the primary cause of such calamities (the plague arrives to "visit" the lands where it is unleashed, it is not self-generated there), the pandemic's spread is, however, significantly correlated with the density of urbanised civilisation in a way directly related to the extent of such spread.

In fact, in the title of one of his paragraphs (§ 49), Ibn Khaldūn notes that "at the end of dynasties," normally, "an abundant civilisation (large population)" is present, "and pestilences and famines frequently occur then."

Therefore, although pestilence, a highly aggressive and destructive natural factor, does not arise from senility, it is in its eutrophic context that it finds suitable terrain to take root and spread. Also in this aspect, thus, the achievement of the desired urbanisation, and the different social organisation deriving from it, produce risks and weakening factors. Ibn Khaldūn writes:

> The large number of pestilences [..] has its reason in the many disturbances that result from the disintegration of the dynasty. [...]The reason for the growth of putrefaction and evil moistures is invariably a dense and abundant civilization such as exists in the later (years) of a dynasty. [...] This also is the reason why pestilences occur much more frequently in densely settled cities than elsewhere (*Muqaddima* III, 49; Ibn Khaldūn 1958, Vol. II: 136–137; Ibn Khaldūn [1967] 2005: 256).

Despite the prevalence, at the time, of "theological" explanations aimed at identifying in the plagues forms of divine punishment of people's vicious and wicked behaviour, the idea that the epidemic had to do with the excessive density of the population, and that the only way out was to abandon cities and densely inhabited places, full of poisonous miasms ("social distancing," in short[46]), was already outlined by Ibn Khaldūn: "Cities and buildings were laid waste, roads and way signs were obliterated, settlements and mansions became empty, dynasties and tribes grew weak" (*Muqaddima*: The Introduction; Ibn Khaldūn 1958, Vol. I: 64; Ibn Khaldūn [1967] 2005, 30).

In turn, then, social distancing and fear, the "panic" terror of contact with one's fellow man, potentially "guilty" of being an infection spreader (a phenomenon that was also evident during the recent Covid-19 lockdown, with the spread of confused and generalised social blaming), can only have a negative effect on the already declining *'aṣabiyya*, further contributing to its disintegrating process.

Moreover, the apparent uncontrollability of the pandemic also severely affects the confidence placed in the future (Raz 2020), helping to trigger the same dynamics of loss of vitality and solipsistic withdrawal that Ibn Khaldūn so effectively described about human groups and animals, affected in their ability to determine their future.

This relationship between the epidemic and the disintegration of social union has also been highlighted, over time, by other authors who have witnessed periods of plague. For example, Thucydides ([Fourth century B.C.] 1989), who witnessed the plague that swept over Athens around 430 B.C., having contracted the disease and survived, points out (Book II: 51) that:

> But the greatest misery of all was the dejection of mind in such as found themselves beginning to be sick (for they grew presently desperate and gave themselves over without making any resistance), as also their dying thus like sheep, infected by mutual visitation, for the greatest mortality proceeded that way. For if men forebore to visit them for fear, then they died forlorn; [5] whereby many families became empty for want of such as should take care of them. If they forbore not, then they died themselves, and principally the honestest men. For out of shame they would not spare themselves but went in unto their friends, especially after it was come to this pass that even their domestics, wearied with the lamentations of them that died and overcome with the greatness of the calamity, were no longer moved therewith. [6] But those that were recovered had much compassion both on them that died and on them that lay sick, as having both known the misery themselves and now no more subject to the danger.

Lucretius ([First century B.C.] 2004), in his *De Rerum Natura* (6.1241–6.1245), following this passage by Thucydides, also painstakingly stressed the anti-solidal attitudes induced by the plague: "For who forbore to look to their own sick, / O these (too eager of life, of death afeard) / Would then, soon after, slaughtering Neglect /

[46]Ibn al-Khaṭīb, the great scholar from Granada, friend and colleague of Ibn Khaldūn, wrote a treatise on the plague (*The Satisfaction of the Questioner Regarding the Appalling Illness*) which had come even closer to understanding the idea of the spread of the disease by contagion. See Stearns (2007), and Hopley (2016).

Visit with vengeance of evil death and base— / Themselves deserted and forlorn of help."

Francesco Petrarca ([1349] 2009) noted how: "houses were left vacant, cities deserted, the country neglected, the fields too small for the dead and a fearful and universal solitude over the Earth."

Boccaccio, in the introduction to his Decameron ([1353] 1995: 8–9), also writes that:

> It was not merely a question of one citizen avoiding another, and of people almost invariably neglecting their neighbours and rarely or never visiting their relatives, addressing them only from a distance; this scourge had implanted so great a terror in the hearts of men and women that brothers abandoned brothers, uncles their nephews, sisters their brothers, and in many cases wives deserted their husbands. But even worse, and almost incredible was the fact that fathers and mothers refused to nurse and assist their own children, as though they did not belong to them.

Hence, as has been observed, natural phenomena such as pestilence and other pandemics, together with the severe productive-economic crises that follow them, are also part of the typical dynamics that, correlating with the more central ones, particularly unleash themselves onto societies already on their way down, senile and disintegrated, thus also in this respect contributing to their fall.

In the *Muqaddima* the correlation between the two elements is clearly underlined. The great plague:

> overtook dynasties at the time of their senility, when they had reached the limit of their duration. It lessened their power and curtailed their influence. It weakened their authority. Their situation approached the point of annihilation and dissolution. Civilizations decreased with the decrease of mankind. (*Muqaddima*: The Introduction; Ibn Khaldūn 1958, Vol. I: 64; Ibn Khaldūn [1967] 2005, 30)

Within this framework, the relationship linking the two elements is viewed as a form of "ecological" imbalance that is determined in the urbanised environment—a thesis that, once again, anticipates much more recent theories, such as the one developed by historian of epidemiology William McNeill (1976). In fact, as McNeill explains, in agglomerated settlements, anthropogenic changes in the environment, the accumulation of waste, and the presence of too many concentrated organisms (human but also animal), favour destructive contagions and zoonoses,[47] capable of accelerating the process of a collapse that has already begun. This correlation almost seems to express, in Ibn Khaldūn, a para-Malthusian view of the world's self-

[47] As Harper (2020) wrote: "We have learned a lot in the interim about the evolutionary origins of human disease, but the framework is still sound. For example, the reason humans have so many gastrointestinal diseases is because, about 12,000 years ago, we started living in permanent agglomerated settlements and were, therefore, surrounded by our own waste, not to mention the waste of our animals, which are full of pathogens transmitted by the fecal-oral route. The reason humans have so many respiratory diseases is because we have the massive population numbers and sheer density to support pathogens whose strategy is to pass from lung to lung. First in the Old World, and then in the New, early globalization brought different human populations—and their germs—into contact, with often explosive results."

regulation: "It was as if the voice of existence in the world had called out for oblivion and restriction, and the world had responded to its call (ibid.)."

From the Black Plague to the most recent outbreaks of HIV, SARS, Mers, and lastly Covid-19, the transfer from animal to man, and then from man to man, of germs, bacteria, or parasites (a virus is a kind of parasite) carrying pathogenic elements, is therefore related to the characteristics of an environment which has become eutrophic, rich, and fragile, in which even the leaps of diseases between species lend themselves to being interpreted as Khaldunian colonisations, assaulting the well-being of *ḥaḍāra*.

Furthermore, in our time, the ecological imbalance produced by our civilisation has assumed such proportions as to deserve an epochal name for it: Anthropocene[48] is the term used to designate the current geological era, characterised by an environment that has been radically modified on the basis of the human ambition to ensure for itself the highest degree of safety and well-being.[49] This well-being and security, however, have paradoxically also determined, together with the enormous increase in the global population that has resulted, an increase in all the risks related to the consequent social density—including the pandemic (see, on this, also the recent collapsologic approach by Pablo Servigne and Raphaël Stevens (2020)).

Even in this aspect, therefore, Ibn Khaldūn's lesson has something to teach us: not only, after a certain point of equilibrium is passed, does the increase in well-being produce, at various levels, situations that "call," as he writes, for repercussions (not only social, but also natural), capable of bringing the situation back to a level of equilibrium. But these same attacks come to hit an unprepared body, made vulnerable by the same long exorcising of all the risks intrinsic to nature, and by the habit of security and reliance[50] of which it has, in the meantime, taken on the "colouring."

The very organised, dense, and complex contexts, structured to function in a safe and rationalised situation, and relying on such regularity, are, in fact, particularly fragile and vulnerable to the unexpected (see Verza 2018): it is not by chance that a recent interpretation of the work of Ibn Khaldūn (Hashemi 2019) has identified precisely in the ability to remain open and vigilant against the unexpected the main feature that differentiates the *badāwa* of "risk-takers" from *ḥaḍāra*. Such "colouring" and reactivity, however, as Ibn Khaldūn teaches, arise from a specific material environment (and, consequently, a correlated psychic-social structure, corroborated by "fortitude" and social cohesion) in which they mature naturally, and cannot be aroused *ad hoc* by a sudden emergency context.

---

[48]The term was coined in the 1980s by biologist Eugene F. Stoermer and re-launched in 2000 by chemist and Nobel Prize winner Paul Crutzen.

[49]The effect produced by our civilisation on the environment, by the way, was in evidence when the lockdown and the shutdown of transport and production activities, decided upon in the spring of the year 2020, allowed for a blossoming return of nature to urban spaces.

[50]Reliance on specialised elements to grant a society's security, in this case, goes beyond the level of pure military protection that Ibn Khaldūn commented on, extending here to reliance on men of science against disease—a "fideistic" reliance, in fact, as this kind of knowledge has increasingly become too specialised to be understood by the rest of society: see Ventura (2020b: 42).

On the contrary, faced with the disintegrating effect produced by social distancing and fear of the virus, a strong motivation emerges to attribute social stigma to ethnic groups or classes of people[51] (Chinese, Italians, migrants, joggers, plague-spreaders, etc.) considered to be associated with the disease: this is an expression of a vitality eager to survive which, in an involutive way, takes energy from a tribalistic dimension, dividing the social world into sub-groups as if, once more, identity could not help but draw on this element to regain vigour, in an attempt to survive its own collapse.

5.3.5 New and Ancient Solidal Bonds

The perception of the current economic crisis, of an increasingly less protected vulnerability, and of the progressive fading of the *'aṣabiyya*'s borders, also due to exogenous factors, are producing economic, security, and identity pressures for a new, needs-driven search for a sense of community, seen as more reassuring and tangible than the solipsistic dream of the autonomous individual. The present time, using the tools typical of this era, has also already begun to cope with this need for relationships and for an equally important, reassuring collective identity.

On the one hand, new technology is already greatly contributing to stamping this recovery of group feeling with its own original imprint—apparently superficial, perhaps, but actually important, considering its mass dimension. From membership groups to social networks (Verza 2014a), from social streets to communities for the exchange of services, in almost every sphere, web networks are now essential media in the new definition of the sense of belonging to collective identities, which is gradually appearing in a myriad of technologically mediated affiliations. These are also particularly important from an economic point of view, to the extent that a new sector in its own right—the web economy, characterised by a strong spirit of sharing—has arisen (Botsman and Rogers 2010). Yet the particular architecture of the web, with its typical echo-chamber effect, proves to be highly effective in nurturing polarized, violent, fanatic and mutually intolerant group identities too (as shown, e.g., by the whole galaxy of the Manosphere, or by the alt-right phenomenon (Verza 2019, 2020)).

On the other hand, on a different ethnic-cultural level, even the multicultural enhancement of difference, with its prompts to identify oneself with particular sub-groups, responds to this logic of reaffirmation of group identity, and does so with its own dynamics—certainly more enveloping in their traditional richness than those provided by modern forms of community solidarity.

However, the economic, defensive-combatant, identitarian, and safety drives just identified, if not controlled, threaten to bring about aggressive, radical, and violent reactions.

---

[51] On the increase of expressions of xenophobic intolerance related to the pandemic, see Raz (2020).

In fact, in the landscape of the various forms of recovery and reaffirmation of the social solidarity characteristic of our time, the sense of *'aṣabiyya*, together with its strong self-sacrificing implication and its combative tendency, seems to be most intensely found, today, in some religious and violently radicalised sectarian and ideological groups. These—certainly numerically limited, but nonetheless frequently present in the news—often claim to express the "original" spirit (usually, the most conservative and, therefore, the most intransigently "pure") of their traditional cultures. Moreover: precisely because they claim to provide the "authentic interpretation" of these cultures, they sometimes get confused with them (Verza 2015a).

These radicalisations, together with the "effervescent" fanatical magnetism (see Luzzati 2016: ch. I) and the willingness to make individual sacrifices in the name of the group that they inspire, bring together, in a single cohesive phenomenon, different elements: the attractive power of sectarian cultures, with their personalising and enveloping afflatus and the sense of honour that emanates from them;[52] the confirming force of a religious view (or other ideology), in its particular rigid and comforting interpretation;[53] and the diffusive power of technological media. Incidentally, the latter is a key element, today, for the expansion of their message, its reproductive and recruiting capacity, and the colonisation, through the connection with distant cells, of more and more new spaces, where the lack of identity "calls"—as Ibn Khaldūn would say—for its own overcoming.

One of the most recent and remarkable manifestations of this phenomenon lies in the spread of "Islamic radicalization," with the attractiveness that such identity groups also exerts on individuals from the same Western culture—often young, sometimes uneducated or unemployed people, therefore easy to mobilise for radical change. Evidently, as Oliver Leaman (2005) writes, the communitarian and combatant perspective they propose seduces this section of the population, easily attracted to the idea of a fanatical attachment to a community that could encompass them, however violent and self-imposed this may be.

To some extent, the resulting phenomenon evokes some of the dynamics of internal abnegation and misoneism, and also of harshness and fanaticism, characteristics of the tribal groups of the desert *badāwa* described by Ibn Khaldūn in his *Kitāb*. As he said, the effect of a strong *'aṣabiyya*, even more so when religiously

[52]Akbar S. Ahmed (2005: 592) links this phenomenon to the urge for a reformulation—a hyper-oppositional one—of a tribal concept of honour: "based in an exaggerated and even obsessive loyalty to the group, and [...] usually expressed through hostility and often violence toward the other. I call this *hyper-'aṣabiyya*. [...] Simply put, global developments have robbed many people of honor. Rapid global changes are shacking the structures of traditional societies. Groups [...] develop intolerance and express it through anger. No society is immune. Even those societies that economists call "developed" fall back to notions of honor and revenge in times of crisis. By dishonoring others, such people think they are maintaining honor."

[53]Farhad Khosrokhavar ([2002] 2005) maintains that the "foreign fighters" who join the Islamists are moved by a deep need for certainties and identity guarantees: in other words, they seek, above all, the stability of some kind of order and the end of the "liquid" vagueness (Bauman 2003) and of a continuous need for identity negotiation.

supported (because, as Ibn Khaldūn says, religion can only increase the cohesive force of an already existing *'aṣabiyya*), is to eliminate the group's internal divisive factors, in order to concentrate all its tensions on the pursuit of its objectives, resulting in the unification and exaltation of extreme self-sacrifice typical of such groups.

This agglomerating force, as Ibn Khaldūn pointed out, is essentially rooted in the dynamics of empathic imagination, to the extent that it works, as these phenomena demonstrate, even without any real interpenetration in the lives of the members of these groups. As Ed West observes (2015: ch. 3), in such groups Islamic foreign fighters from Sussex are ready to give their lives for the cause together with Chechens and Algerians—people with whom, apart from the militant creed, they have no affinity either by blood or culture. This happens precisely on the basis of the same identity mechanisms that, at the time of the Crusades' religious fighting, could make a crusader say: "When a Breton or a German addressed me, I did not know how to answer him [...] and yet we seemed to form but one people."[54]

On the other hand, although these extreme phenomena represent, perhaps, the most acute aspect of the current aspiration to recover the sense of group identity, they stand out in a culturally different and much broader background, still "coloured," in the West, by its own liberal and democratic culture. This is important because, as Ibn Khaldūn pointed out, the history of civilisations, when possible, follows a spiralling trend. Therefore, if Western society, today, feels the need to re-evaluate group unity and to return to more enveloping forms of communal gatherings, it could still be able to count on the enrichment and awareness of the additional heritage, fixed in principles of constitutional law, achieved in the previous phase. These principles cover, for example, the liberal and democratic vision which led to the definition of human rights, and to the vision of individuals—men and women—as free to define themselves.

The habit of cultivating these values as a basis for identity could, therefore, still impress their "colouring" on the way in which the return to the group dimension is going to be lived, and might, thus, counteract the more violent and tribal drives that could otherwise characterise its development. As Heraclitus said, "one does not bathe twice in the same river": the past and its traces can do nothing but leave their "colouring" on today's experiences, leading them to a fresh renewal. Thus, it is just possible that the vitality of the core of the liberal and democratic principles making up the main Western *'aṣabiyya* might exert its influence, by inducing the new "sense of the group," now approaching at the gates, to remain consistent with its values. The "colouring" of the *'aṣabiyya* which, currently, still supports the associative pact of Western societies, and of the culture it stands on, could, in fact, steer this process towards a new and apparently oxymoronic, but possible, form of "liberal communitarianism."

[54]These are the words of Fulcher of Chartres, a twelfth-century crusader, as reported by West (2015: par. 3), who draws this example from the monumental *Universal History* written by Cesare Cantù (1887).

The phenomenon of the spread and attractiveness of religious radicalisation (incidentally, not the prerogative of the Islamic world alone) could bear out a vision of history such as that theorised by Oswald Spengler ([1918–1923] 2007). In *The Decline of the West*, Spengler had described how the characteristic trajectory followed by the different cultures whose traces history has handed down to us, usually goes through a certain number of phases, starting with their rise, up to the moment when—having lost their desire to exist (again, Ibn Khaldūn's senility)—they head for their fall, generally not without experiencing, before their demise, a final mystical-religious rush.[55]

We do not know, yet, whether the aforementioned phenomenon of the attractiveness of religious radicalisation can be inscribed, in this picture, as a "religious thrill" symbolising a process of disintegration already on the way. Nor do we know how the interplay between the individualistic scope of the basic constitutional values of the Western countries and the renewed hunger for a communal and solidal embrace (two complementary tensions and values destined to coexist without one definitely eliminating the other) will be resolved.

The final outcome of the new community afflatus which, in different ways, is budding in the various dimensions of contemporary reality, remains to be seen. By the same token, it will be necessary to find out how the current urgency of the need to recover the value of community will be reconciled with the need not to betray or forget the legacy of the values which have represented the most advanced achievements, in ethical and political terms, of Western thought. In fact, in the absence of a profound and shared elaboration, in a communitarian key, of such "liberal" values, the regressive, "closer," traditional, fragmented, probably even aggressive forms of communitarian closure could prevail.

To untie this knot, it is crucial to understand whether the liberal and democratic *'aṣabiyya*, absorbed into the constitutional values of freedom, respect for difference, and equality, can continue to be an ultimate horizon of events—as the framework of values and condition of acceptability of the minor *'aṣabiyyāt* included in it—or whether, due to the disaffection produced by the increasingly rarefied sense of identity that it induces today, it will end up shattering and breaking up under the disruptive force of individualism and/or community tribalism.[56]

---

[55]See also what the *praefectus urbi* Rutilius Namatianus, wrote, in the fifth century, at the twilight of Rome's greatness, in his *De Reditu* ([415] 1992). In describing his return to family possessions in Narbonne Gaul—amidst ruins and destroyed bridges, with patricians now demotivated and "lost" in their futile pursuits, while the Goths' incursions raged—he emphasised the rigid and ferocious fanaticism of the new fundamentalist sects of the time, i.e., the "*lucifugi*" Christians, mystically and frantically attached to their exclusive religious identity.

[56]Quoting Bertrand Russell (1996: 9): "Social cohesion is a necessity, and mankind has never yet succeeded in enforcing cohesion by merely rational arguments. Every community is exposed to two opposite dangers, ossification through too much discipline and reverence for tradition, on the one hand; on the other hand, dissolution, or subjection to foreign conquest, through the growth of an individualism and personal independence that makes co-operation impossible."

5.4 One Weak Super-*'Aṣabiyya*, Many Juxtaposed *'Aṣabiyyāt*

To understand the socio-cultural stage a civilisation has reached and, therefore, how far off the critical point it is likely to be in the cycle described by Ibn Khaldūn as a natural process, we must, then, take the *'aṣabiyya* as the benchmark—its strength correlating with the unity and vitality of civilisation. When the *'aṣabiyya*—the unifying reference of a group's cultural and symbolic identity—begins to falter, the danger threshold has been crossed, and there is no turning back.

The *'aṣabiyya* is the main indicator of the vitality of a civilisation. From this point of view, however, Western societies look weakened from within, in their pride and sense of belonging. This may very well be due to the abstractness of their identifying reference points, which are currently barely capable of providing their members with the reassurance of a distinctive "communitarian" embrace and a clear, "close" measure of their own identity.

On the other hand, even at the macro level of the basic attitudes inspiring policies today, a perverse, rupturing effect comes into being. This is the unintended consequence of a multicultural policy born of a noble Kantian ideal of respect for the autonomy of each individual,[57] and yet sown in an ethico-cultural seedbed already in retreat and progressively losing its cohesive force.

The *'aṣabiyya* which works as the "symbolic capital" and unifying cultural glue of the West is, in fact, at the same time, a "special" *'aṣabiyya*, and a unifying *super-'aṣabiyya* that, by virtue of the distinctively open values it embraces through its liberal and democratic model, is developing with the peculiar goal of also accommodating, under its umbrella, a range of other minority *'aṣabiyyāt* grounded in different principles. Although these principles may be sometimes even opposite to its own, still it recognises them, precisely in the name of the specific open, liberal, and democratic nature of its own values. These values are not only enshrined in constitutions, but also put into practice, at the policy level, however imperfectly, in the multicultural space towards which the Western social world is increasingly heading.

Yet, as the liberal-democratic *'aṣabiyya* strives to embrace the culture of "the other," it is probably, in so doing, stretching beyond the point of no return. Whilst supporting the value of respect for other cultures and their *'aṣabiyyāt*, which Western society seeks to catalyse and keep together in a liberal unity, it is apparently at the same time neglecting the need to also nourish its own specific, substantive core ethos and culture. As a consequence, it is now increasingly struggling to ensure consistence in its role as a unifying super-*'aṣabiyya*.

As far as the distinctive values of this form of *'aṣabiyya* are concerned, Western societies seem now to be finding themselves in a profound crisis affecting the sense of their internal identity. As Amartya Sen observed fifteen years ago (Sen 2006a,

[57] I am referring to this ideal specifically as stated in Kant's (1785 (1998)) *Groundwork of the Metaphysics of Morals*.

2006b. See also Touraine 1997; Sartori 2000; Barry 2001; Shachar 2001; Malik 2015), the project of promoting the coexistence of different minority groups within the same political space, where the distinctive cultural identity of each group is recognised and respected, has instead produced, in many cases, a move towards antagonism and confrontation (Malik 2015). This has been the consequence of the dissociation of this project from any serious plan for cultural integration that would also take care of confirming and strengthening the same framework of values that was supposed to support it.

In fact, the attempt to embrace cultural fragmentation through a multicultural policy has gone as far as producing some paradoxical, "perverse" effects through the recognition, and therefore the definition, and even the protection (from change, too), of the different cultural identities taken under its umbrella.

In order to represent all the citizens included within the perimeter delineated by the "minority group" institution, the liberal *'aṣabiyya* has sometimes reached the point of favouring the accreditation of the voice of the often more reactionary, and in any case more powerful, elements within these groups (thus favouring internal hierarchies, in contrast with the liberal spirit: Okin 1999). Moreover, this policy has also ended up producing an additional move towards a progressive identitarian opposition among the minority groups themselves.

This tendency might have been the result of focusing on the distinguishing peculiarities that have been evoked by the trans-ethnic boundaries called upon to fix and define (in a tendentially essentialist and oppositional way,) the identity of each group. In a multicultural framework where differences are exhibited and celebrated, the trans-ethnic boundaries have, by definition, become culturally rigid, thus prompting the groups to discharge their aggressive tensions beyond their boundaries (Malik [2013] 2016).

In fact, while the group's dynamics forge and preserve the minority identities within the multicultural framework, providing assurance and promoting trust within each group,[58] at the same time they set these groups in potential conflict with the broader cultural integrative umbrella that is supposed to support them. The (not totally spontaneous) establishment, in many large Western cities, of urban and suburban districts increasingly distinguished on an ethical basis (almost following

[58]See, in this sense, the idea of trust expounded by Francis Fukuyama (1995), highlighting the essential role that trust plays in society in maintaining cohesive bonds among citizens and fostering social capital, and ultimately in achieving the well-being of society itself. Trust is defined by Fukuyama as "the expectation that arises within a community of regular, honest, and cooperative behavior, based on commonly shared norms, on the part of other members of that community" (ibid., 26), in which connection he speaks of "communities of shared ethical values" (ibid.). In this sense, the norms shared are moral and, if anchored to trust, would enable the community to counteract such practices as patronage, nepotism, tax evasion, absenteeism, lack of respect for speed limits, etc. Only on the basis of such mutual trust, he argues, can people keep complex forms of organisation working.

the model of many Middle Eastern "*medinas*"), seems to represent today, even topographically, this divisive and contrasting trend.[59]

Yet, the unifying background culture should always be able to keep these forces of tension in balance, lest it meet its own demise—with the parallel risk, bringing Ibn Khaldūn's lesson to bear, that the same process could also fuel the rise of other more belligerent and less tolerant forms of *'aṣabiyya*, more cohesive and endowed with greater life force, coming from *badāwa* (to be translated, in today's context, in terms relating to socio-cultural marginalisation).

In short, if an all-embracing *super-'aṣabiyya* is to be able to support a multicultural universe within itself, it needs first and foremost to foster its own strength: the strength of a liberal and welcoming culture, which also needs, however, to keep nourishing a vital and conscious identity of its own, on pain (quoting Toynbee) of its own suicide.

5.5 Liberal Culture and Its Unnoticed Regression

One of the main problems for the *'aṣabiyya* of Western democratic-liberal countries lies, today, in the difficult management of their own multicultural project of relations between groups. Faced with the growing evanescence of what should be society's general all-encompassing "super-*'aṣabiyya*," this project increasingly runs the risks of resulting in the progressive fragmentation of the social fabric.

In fact, without the strong sense of a general and comprehensive *'aṣabiyya*, its most likely outcome is the withdrawal of individuals into smaller groups, more able directly to satisfy the solidal aspiration of everyone and provide them with clear and satisfying symbolic and normative resources.

In this sense, multiculturalism itself, having been mainly implemented in terms of juxtaposition, and not integration, between cultures, has ended up encouraging the communities within the social macro-group to place their loyalties, and their particular cultures, above the common one (Malik [2013] 2016), thus further contributing to dismissing the latter's ethical strength and vitality. Ibn Khaldūn himself, as we have seen, had already observed that the establishment of a safe and healthy government becomes proportionally more difficult and problematic in territories populated by different tribes and social groups (*Muqaddima* II, 9), unless its preponderance and its function as a powerful framework are guaranteed.

However today, to enclose in its ideal embrace the current multiculturally fragmented ethical-cultural landscape, there is an extremely fragile *super-'aṣabiyya*: the tendency to return to intermediate groups, in short, is intersecting with the progressive weakening of the higher-level *'aṣabiyya*—the liberal and, in principle,

[59]Kalb (2004): "Urban and suburban neighbourhoods are beginning institutionally to resemble the separate quarters of a traditional Middle Eastern city."

welcoming democratic culture which is supposed to coordinate and transcend the particular cultures it hosts.

On the other hand, it is also true that Ibn Khaldūn, as mentioned above, accepts that a society can continue to function for some time even without the support of a vital *'aṣabiyya*: this is especially needed in the upward phase, when a civilisation is getting established, but afterwards the force of habit can make up, for a while, for its disappearance. In fact, when the *'aṣabiyya* is less intense, a government can fulfill its functions even more easily (*Muqaddima* II, 9).

However, it is only the calm before the storm—the first phase of senility, which, unnoticed, is the prelude to an inevitable fall.

Apparently, no viable institutional remedy can counteract this: at the moment, politics does not seem to have a force cohesive enough to be able to contrast the ethical-cultural disintegration of our time, nor can a unification brought about under the banner of religion appear plausible, as it is incompatible, in its essence, both with the liberal characteristics of Western cultures and with multiculturalism itself.

Even liberal ethics, especially after the rapid metamorphosis it has undergone over the last 50 years, seem to have somehow lost its strong core values. Today, it seems to have turned into something different—an adjudicative meta-ethics, aimed at continuously mediating between itself and the other conceptions of the good, and at applying the principle of equal respect and neutrality between cultures to the extent of ceasing to support its own liberal values—those which, incidentally, inspired the multicultural approach.

Precisely this relationship, evidently no longer nourished and healthy, between society (as a group of individuals) and the psycho-social "glue" represented by its specific underlying culture—its culturally determined *'aṣabiyya*—constitutes, as Ibn Khaldūn's analysis indicates, the central point, the crucial factor on which the risk of senile involution may depend.

Several voices on today's political stage are pointing to immigration, globalisation, or the crisis of the nation state as the primary culprits of the enfeeblement of the West. However, as Ibn Khaldūn teaches us, the primary reason for the senile decline of the West, if this is the path to be followed, is not to be found in any external factors: neither in the excessively vast European Union's borders, nor in the unpredictable effects of globalisation, nor in terrorism, nor in immigration, nor in epidemics, nor in the well-intentioned mistakes and unintended consequences of the multicultural policies that have been pursued.

According to Ibn Khaldūn, these are all *effects* of, or factors linked to, the crisis, accompanying it like "travelling companions" on a journey whose origin, the root cause of senility, lies in the involution in the *'aṣabiyya* cycle. This involution is given by the *internal* collapse and moral implosion of the liberal culture, caused by Western society losing its moral compass and sense of self and, consequently, its sense of attachment.

Western ethics today, in fact, seems to have become metaethical, in a vague metamorphosis that seems to have realised the old endeavours of its neutralist project to rise to a higher point of view, self-critically impartial and equidistant from all conceptions of the good, "thin" rather than "thick"[60]—an old endeavour that, since the last half of the twentieth century, has never really been put to rest.[61] While the shift to a multicultural discourse seemed to have pushed the neutralist project aside in academia, it actually never subsided and, in fact, it has now become social reality, also dragging along the self-defeating consequences of its *hubris*: its claim to (an impossible) superiority.

This project got underway with John Rawls's 1971 *Theory of Justice* (Rawls 1999). It became the focus of an intense debate that raged throughout the 1980s, until the multiculturalist "revolution" broke out in 1992. Its ambitious idea was that it would be possible to reach a mostly impartial ethical-political viewpoint from which to judge objectively without endorsing any particular moral view—a *view from nowhere*, as it has famously been described (Nagel 1986). This kind of rise, pulled by Kant's universalist view, had been advanced as a unique high ground that could only be reached through the "superior" moral openness of a liberal position (the only one which could supposedly boast the primacy of such high-embracing morality[62]).

Due to the denial of its own content-based perspective, in the pursuit of a rise to a higher, but impossible, neutralist position, liberal culture, having slipped down to a metaethical level now impalpable and lacking substance, is now experiencing the loss of content of its *'aṣabiyya*.

One of the most peculiar features of this "de-nucleation" of liberal culture also lies in the insistence with which severe and often unbalanced criticism is levelled at its "ethnocentrism,"[63] accompanied by the display of sharp sensitivity towards the "other" world views (not balanced, however, by a corresponding primary support for liberal culture itself).

Symptomatic of this appears to be the widespread tendency, especially among the educated élite, which West calls the "*social capital free-riders*"—to belittle, when not ridicule, the (excessively "patriotic"[64]) idea of support for their own Western culture. This is so despite the fact that this feeling is fundamental to its vitalising and unifying function, and, above all, despite the fact that the liberal and democratic *'aṣabiyya* is based on "open" and hospitable values.[65] These values, in fact, include

---

[60]The use of this oppositional pair as a tool to describe moral thinking, whereby "minimalist" (thin) moral principles, which can be applied between cultures and across national boundaries, are opposed to "maximalist" (thick) principles, which can only apply within a given culture, is credited to Michael Walzer (1994).

[61]See my *La neutralità impossibile* (Verza 2000).

[62]We can actually devise in this ambition a new competitive form of search for prestige—the *jah* again—played here on the moral level.

[63]A fundamental and pioneering work in this sense was Edward Said's *Orientalism* (1978).

[64]West (2015): "but a population can only healthily accommodate a certain number of such social capital free-riders; when a large proportion disdain patriotism because to do so signals high status, then it suggests a society deep within the *'aṣabiyya* cycle." See also Scruton (1997).

[65]To exemplify, on the contrary, the idea of concentric circles of trust and loyalty typical of tribal logic, West (2015) quotes the Bedouin maxim: "me and my brother against my cousin; me and my cousin against the world." As this author points out, even today, in the Arab world, *'aṣabiyya*

recognising other cultures, and are potentially capable of providing an extraordinary and, at the same time, stable combination of freedom and democracy.

Moreover, if the liberal and democratic identity can be considered to be the central form of *'aṣabiyya* typical of Western societies, such *'aṣabiyya*, as it is related to the politically organised moment of *ḥaḍāra*, would also be potentially endowed with the peculiar capacity (as long as it is nourished) to remain active and healthy even in such a phase. Therefore, it would also be better able to contrast the descending pressure caused by the inevitable development of the crisis factors already discussed. In this neutralist endeavour, however, what once was mainstream liberal culture ended up neutralising itself, thus dismantling the very basis on which this process was supposed to get underway.

It did so, perhaps, out of conceit,[66] considering itself to be so far above the fray, so strong and superior, that it did not have to defend its own ground. In its ambition to "become superior," overcoming its own partiality in a progressive endeavour to re-calculate its possible content so as to become the "square root" of itself, in an unrelenting attempt to strike an even balance between competing cultures, including its own view in the number, it got caught in a peculiar kind of "slippery slope": not the value-laden descent that entrenches one deeply into a concrete culture, but a value-neutral *ascent* leading to a position so rarefied and unbiased as to gradually, but inevitably, "vaporise" into the abstraction of sheer lack of content.

And yet, it is clear that, in the face of a metaethical claim of equidistance between one's own culture and the non-liberal "other" cultural orientations, the outcome could only go in favour of the latter. In fact, when a theory by definition committed to tolerance and neutrality (such as the liberal one) engages a theory rigidly committed to the binding force of its own content, the latter—for that very reason,[67] being less tolerant and inclusive, and by virtue of the sheer combinatorial logic

---

struggles to reach out to national borders, remaining anchored more to the size of the family clan. This is also due to the widespread practice of marriage between cousins (in Iraq, for example, about half of all marriages are between first or second cousins (Steve Sailer 2003)). In the Arab countries, moreover, as Baali (1988: 111) reminded us, especially in the Gulf area, even the people of the cities still proudly use the name of their native tribe as a nickname, and they know and value its ancient traditions as a sign of identity and distinctiveness. This situation, with the correlative nepotisms and amoral familisms that follow, makes a real establishment of democracy there very difficult in terms of values.

[66] An attitude analogous to the supererogatory stance of the saint, who, apparently considering himself to be living by a higher standard on the way of perfection and justice, refuses as unavailable to himself concessions that he, instead, believes to be perfectly and understandably allowed to others.

[67] To exemplify, consider the "burkini" controversy, raging some years ago, on the extent of a woman's freedom to wear what she chooses. If on one side we have the liberal stance—committed to the idea that women are free to subscribe to any view on the matter, including the view according to which they would be subjected to observe the obligation q to wear a prescribed list of outfits—while on the other side we have the illiberal stance consisting of precisely the obligation q (whose deontic modality, by its very nature, does not allow any option other than itself), it follows that the only practical solution consistent with *both* stances is to recognise q as obligatory, for this is required by the illiberal stance at the same time as it is allowed by the liberal one (see Taleb 2016).

involved—is bound to win out, progressively depriving the former of the content it needs for its own nourishment.

In a confrontation between a principle of freedom and one of obligation, in other words, considered as if they were two deontologically homogeneous attitudes, it is the latter that will almost systematically come out on top. It will do so in virtue of its greater determination—as a result of its being clearer in its content and thick, and bound to the attachment to socially ensconced customs to which concrete cultural meanings are ascribed. Precisely by virtue of these attributes, the obligation will easily overpower the rarefied abstractness that characterises the principle of freedom (a principle whose range of options also allows competing obligations), especially so when this is understood, in its contemporary sense, as an abstract catch-all principle welcoming of all reasonable possibilities, rather than as a first-level value to be supported in its own right.

In sum, unless the structural principles of liberalism itself are protected as tangible reference points of identity, capable, therefore, of nourishing an emotional and imaginary sense of *'aṣabiyya*, the meta-content, or content-neutral, logic of tolerance and liberalism will always, in the face of the need to find rules suitable for all, allow the illiberal stance—the most rigid and demanding one in terms of content—to get the upper hand, in a paradoxical but effective mechanism of "tyranny" of the "minority." If the more flexible culture can, in fact, adapt to follow the more rigid one, the opposite can never apply.

Yet, even freedom and tolerance started out as first-order, content-bearing (or thick) principles, not at all to be taken for granted. They gradually took shape in a long struggle against illiberal systems, and they too, therefore, had to assert themselves as principles of substance against the opposite illiberal principles, before fading into the metaethical hologram into which contemporary liberalism has morphed.

The civil order characteristic of Western societies has, in fact, taken a long time and tortuous historical paths to reach the current set of values enshrined in democratic and liberal constitutions, and its survival is not to be taken for granted, nor will it be granted in the near future, in the absence of the support and loyalty of the group it represents.[68]

This thinning-out process is clearly illustrated, for example, by the way the hard-won freedoms gained by the first- and second-wave women's movements are losing the support of younger generations. In fact, we are now looking at a scenario in which on the one hand, "officially," the advances made in the struggle for gender equality are taken as (apparently) political gains,[69] but, in counterpoint to that development, a "grassroots" (but also academic) post-feminist culture has sprung

[68]Kalb (2004): "It took forty kings to make France, and no less time to grow what Burke once called the British oak; in the parts of Europe subject to invasion from Asia or North Africa nothing similar arose. The gifts of the past may not be ours forever. Common loyalties make a people, and the common culture and history that support a people's identity are needed to make loyalties endure."

[69]Feminism, as well as multiculturalism, seems to have become a default position one is politically expected to subscribe to, at least in academia. However, self-defeatingly, the very dogmatic and

up which complacently shies away from any identification with feminism, and which does not in any way seem intent on asserting and defending equality for men and women,[70] taking this as a matter already settled (cfr. Verza 2014b, 2020).

However, as John Stuart Mill warned:

> even if the received opinion be not only true, but the whole truth; unless it is suffered to be, and actually is, vigorously and earnestly contested, it will, by most of those who receive it, be held in the manner of a prejudice, with little comprehension or feeling of its rational grounds.[71]

Therefore, no longer the object of hard-fought struggles, the gains of the earlier generations have been reduced to the status of "meta-moral" freedoms silhouetted against a background of indifference, and are therefore ready to yield to the much more combative and peremptory demands which contrast with them.

What we have witnessed, in other words, is a shift—which has recently picked up speed—by virtue of which liberalism has ended up undercutting the premises of its own liberal qualities. The strategy of tolerance through which these virtues were initially promoted subtly transitioned to a strategy of impartiality and "impossible neutrality" (see Verza 2000; see also Gozzi 2008), and then to a policy of multicultural openness interpreted in such a way as to swamp and progressively overwhelm the very liberal foundation on which it stood.

In an effort to find a higher lookout point from which impartially to observe the political landscape, multicultural liberalism, hoping to achieve the highest Kantian ambition, went on a quest for the position that Thomas Nagel would have described as a "blind spot," only to find itself in a black hole that circularly sucks in anything trying to reach that view, depriving this view of substance—a condition that seriously hampers society's cohesion. For, as Ibn Khaldūn teaches us, the keystone and existential condition enabling a social group to thrive[72] lies in the cohesive force that unites it under a shared system of values.

Therefore, the equal standing of all cultures included in a diverse society is utopian. The very existence of a pluralistic society necessarily requires the presence of some external framework of general rules and cultural values, which need to be widely accepted by the social group itself,[73] and such rules and values cannot be neutral, but need substantive content.[74]

---

anodyne armour these positions have put on, regardless of whether they prove to be fair on their merits, ends up enervating them.

[70]An eloquent example of this is, among other things, the remarkable spread of movements such as *Waf* (Women against Feminism). See Perra and Ruspini (2015).

[71]John Stuart Mill 1991: ch. II of *On Liberty*.

[72]Or, stated otherwise, with Talcott Parsons, what prevents society from breaking up is, in the first place, its ability to define the boundaries of its own identity—a primal function that Parsons called *latency,* performed by a culture identifying with the whole of its values.

[73]There needs to be a belief in their normativity close to what Hart (1961, ch. 5.2) described as an "internal point of view."

[74]This can be described as a super-utopia. While the utopia criticised by Marx was one of equality among *individuals*, what multiculturalism preaches is the utopia of equality among *groups*.

Yet, on the other hand—as the laws and dynamics of the *'aṣabiyya* show—it is not possible to fill this ethical *vacuum* by coercive means. The solution favoured by a certain line of peremptorily stern political thinking that seeks to *authoritatively* inject and breathe new life into values and cultures through top-down political operations simply cannot work. In fact, as Ibn Khaldūn teaches us, for the *'aṣabiyya* to be real, it needs to be a spontaneous sentiment shared by willing participants.[75] Otherwise, it turns into something else and, thus, vanishes.[76]

As Ibn Khaldūn teaches, the hiatus that distinguishes the *'aṣabiyya*—an internal moral-affective factor—from the external force of coercion—a factor which is central, of course, to the stability of power, but which, on the other hand, makes the bond of solidarity evaporate—is substantial.

However, as Ibn Khaldūn also stressed, the *'aṣabiyya* feeds on imagination too. While the *'aṣabiyya* cannot be *imposed* from the outside, it can always be *nurtured* from the inside, especially if this happens by proposing and relaunching identity contents capable of creating cohesion, consistent and in harmony with those of the tradition that is in danger of waning.

This, after all, is what—in an uptrend running parallel to the downtrend of the Western cycle—is already happening in other parts of the world in relation to values of an entirely different order: *'aṣabiyyāt* conjured back into life from the past (as in the case of Salafism), and "put to market" by appealing to emotion, are gaining much strength also thanks to the stronger identity enticements they exert and to their inevitably ascending directionality, thus gaining devotees ready to even sacrifice their own lives for them. It is particularly significant that such suicidal devotion can also entice the children of the liberal culture itself, "foreign fighters" in search of something that can impart meaning to their lives[77]—such is the power of attraction, the deep sense of identity, belonging, and purpose they can elicit.

---

[75]If the *'aṣabiyya* is coercively enforced by way of obligations, it withers and dies. It does so simply by means of the enfeebling corrupting process that stifles its vitality from within, causing it to collapse.

[76]As Lenn Evan Goodman (1972: 260) wrote: "For when *'aṣabiyya* requires enforcement, it is no longer *'aṣabiyya*. Men continue to identify; they must. They continue to subordinate their atomic interests to those of others. But they no longer identify directly with the other members of the group. Rather they tender such sacrifices as they make in the name of some principle or ideal, the group itself as an abstract, corporate entity, some institution, individual or symbol representative of the group. *'Aṣabiyya* has been sublimated. Its rationale is still at work, and its effects persist, still relating its subject to its object. But both subject and object have greatly changed, and the modalities governing acceptable and unacceptable expressions of identification and alienation *vis-à-vis* the other have been transformed."

[77]Khosrokhavar ([2002] 2005, 49): "Finally, and as we shall see, martyrdom gives individuals who are modern but cannot assert themselves in the way they would like, a formidable ability to assert themselves in death. In the absence of any real individuality or political, economic and cultural autonomy, martyrdom has a remarkable ability to facilitate individuation in death. All the modern aspirations and desires that haunt a disoriented younger generation that is no longer protected by traditional communities and has been abandoned to a purely oneiric modernity can be realised through martyrdom. [...] Whereas tradition made martyrdom an exceptional, and above all painful, phenomenon designed to move believers to pity and to strengthen communitarian bonds in

Clearly, this intersecting run of events, along with its underlying causes, is something that must inevitably be reckoned with, sooner rather than later.

When this devotion and union is strong, it brings about a drive to conquest for the group capable of leading, ascensionally, to victory, even before much greater forces; when, on the other hand, the *'aṣabiyya* is lost, as Ibn Khaldūn reminds us, not even the fear of destruction can give the group the necessary strength to avoid its ruin: the loss of *'aṣabiyya* decrees the end of the cycle.

I would argue that the only feasible resource available to give fresh vigour to the liberal *'aṣabiyya*—thereby re-enlivening the framework of moral values our civilisation needs if it is to overcome the challenges of time and not lapse into the declining phase of its cyclical movement (or at least not yet, even though, according to Ibn Khaldūn's vision, it is "natural" for this to eventually happen)—lies in an educational and cultural effort to achieve integration. Such an effort could only be inspired by the liberal values of tolerance, equal respect, and freedom, that constitute the axiological basis of a multicultural policy. Only in this way, through the gradual, cultural work of fostering such a minimal *super-'aṣabiyya* as the only realistically possible common denominator, will it be possible to legitimise the effort to enhance the unifying, common legacy of the (substantive) liberal principles making up its cultural heritage. Only this would allow it to happen not coercively (for, as noted, that would be alien to the very logic of the *'aṣabiyya*) but by force of attraction. Only this would bring out the morally compelling force of liberalism as a common legacy that we can all turn to as a basis on which to reproduce an *ex-pluribus-unum* dynamic, and set in motion, even among non-liberal groups, the process of *mimesis* which, as Ibn Khaldūn argues, characterises the success of the most *integrated* polities.

However, this means that the liberal values to be supported should not be understood as principles of a superior meta-morality. As we have seen, the presumption of being able to rise above all conceptions of the good in a state of content-independent neutrality is ultimately a self-defeating, self-annihilating expression of metaethical arrogance. On the contrary, liberal values need to be cherished in an open and humbly perfectionistic way as the *content* of a first-order conception of the good—a democratic and liberal conception, to be shared and defended precisely for its substantive import—that is, for its ability compellingly to define a specific community and its values.[78]

This is to say that liberal culture—with the tolerance and freedoms it embraces—should be supported, along with its own roots, not out of a metaethical superiority it may claim to have, but precisely because of its content.

The reasons for the attachment to a liberal culture understood in this way, in other words, are to be found in its commitment to values which have been strenuously fought for, still can stimulate identification, and still need, if they are to remain so, to

symbolic ways, a modernity in which there is no hope of self-realisation generates a type of martyrdom that is readily accessible to any young man who wants it."

[78]Essential reading on the foundational ideas of liberal perfectionism is doubtlessly Raz (1986).

be seen as values of the first degree and, therefore, cultivated and protected. Prominent among these values are the equality of all people, regardless of sex, race, religion, or sexual orientation, the protection of individual liberty, and the flourishing of the individual. The latter, however, is to be interpreted according to a notion of autonomy which is not to be understood as the solipsistic deprivation triggered by the disintegrating consumerism of recent decades, and which does not originate from relational solitude, but which draws on the deep humanistic roots of Western culture. It is these roots that liberal society needs to turn to as the vital source of its own *'aṣabiyya*, if its culture is not to wither away, and the society this culture supports is not to fracture.

As Lenn Evan Goodman (1999: 215) wrote,

> The tragic fact of history, which Ibn Khaldūn insists in bringing before us, is that in politics whatever can be demanded will be demanded: in the nation, as in the tribe, *'aṣabiyya* becomes a matter of willingness to die. [...] Unless individuals are prepared to die for the group, the group itself will die.

Only if the moral kernel of Western liberalism is supported—and not as a point of neutrality among conceptions of the good, but as a substantial ideal itself—can it infuse strength and vigour back into the Western *'aṣabiyya*, enabling it to provide (within the logical limits set by consistence with its principles) a home and habitat for the full range of the other particular, minority *'aṣabiyyāt* included within its sphere, before neutralist liberalism succeeds in completing its self-destruction.

However, as we know, a recovery of this kind—a resurgent pull to embrace the cultural and moral roots of our civilisation—needs to spring from within. Only in this case could it reactivate, within civil society, its desire to be true to itself, finding the strength to assert its own partiality—welcoming, certainly, but within the framework of its own substantive principles. As things stand, however, a revival of this kind seems, at best, a distant utopia.

That is evidence, perhaps, that the senility theorised by Ibn Khaldūn—the point beyond which a civilisation loses its will to fight and, possibly, even to live—may well be at the door, making way, perhaps, for great changes to come.

References

(A) Ibn Khaldūn's Works

Ibn Khaldūn. 1958. *The Muqaddimah: An Introduction to History* (ed. Franz Rosenthal). 3 Voll. New Jersey: Princeton University Press.

———. [1967] 2005. *The Muqaddimah: An Introduction to History* (ed. Franz Rosenthal), abridged edition. Princeton: Princeton University Press.

(B) Other Works

Ahmed, Akbar S. 2005. Ibn Khaldūn and Anthropology: The Failure of Methodology in the Post 9/11 World. *Contemporary Sociology. Essays on Ibn Khaldūn* 34 (6): 591–596.

Alatas, Syed Farid. 2013. *Ibn Khaldūn*. Oxford: Oxford Centre for Islamic Studies.

———. 2014. *Applying Ibn Khaldūn. The Recovery of a Lost Tradition in Sociology*. London: Routledge.

———. 2020. The Contemporary Significance of Ibn Khaldūn for Decolonial Sociology: Methodological and Theoretical Dimensions. *Tajseer. Qatar University Press* 1 (2): 75–98.

Arnheim, Rudolf. 1974. *Arte e percezione visiva*. Milano: Einaudi.

Aron, Raymond. 1967. *Les étapes de la pensée sociologique*. Paris: Gallimard.

Baali, Fuad. 1988. *Society, State, and Urbanism: Ibn Khaldūn's Sociological Thought*. Lanham: University Press of America.

Barnes, Marian. 2012. *Care in Everyday Life: An Ethic of Care in Practice*. Bristol: Polity Press.

Barry, Brian. 2001. *Culture and Equality*. Cambridge: Polity Press.

Basile, Fabio. 2008. *Immigrazione e reati "culturalmente motivati". Il diritto penale nelle società multiculturali*. CUEM: Milano.

Baudrillard, Jean. [1976] 2010. *La società dei consumi*. Bologna: Il Mulino.

Bauman, Zygmunt. [1999] 2003. *Modernità liquida*. Roma-Bari: Laterza.

Benhabib, Seyla. 2002. *The Claims of Culture. Equality and Diversity in the Global Era*. Princeton: Princeton University Press.

Boccaccio, Giovanni. [1353] 1995. *The Decameron* (trans. G. H. McWilliam). 2nd ed. London: Penguin Books.

Botsman, Rachel, and Roo Rogers. 2010. *What's mine is yours. The rise of collaborative consumption*. Harper Business: New York.

Bouthoul, Gaston. 1930. *Ibn-Khaldoun. Sa philosophie sociale*. Librairie Orientaliste Paul Geuthner: Paris.

Bozarslan, Hamit. 2014. *Le luxe et la violence. Domination et contestation chez Ibn Khaldūn*. CNRS Éditions: Paris.

Cantù, Cesare. 1887. *Storia Universale*. Torino: UTET. https://archive.org/stream/storiauniversal07cantgoog/storiauniversal07cantgoog_djvu.txt. Accessed 17 Sept 2020.

Comte, Auguste. 1855. *Positive Philosophy*. New York: Calvin Blanchard.

Croce, Benedetto. 1932. Recensione di M. K. Ayad, *Die Geschichts–und Gesellschaftslehre Ibn Ḫaldūns*, Stuttgart, Berlin, Cotta. *La critica* XXX: 213–214.

De Angelo, Carlo. 2014. Tribunali religiosi e tribunale arbitrale: l'offerta "giudiziaria" islamica in Inghilterra. *Diritto e religioni* 18 (2): 387–410.

Duesenberry, James. 1949. *Income, Saving and the Theory of Consumer Behaviour*. Cambridge, MA: Harvard University Press.

Durkheim, Émile. 1885. Schaeffle, A., Bau und Leben des sozialen Körpers: Erster Band. *Revue Philosophique* 19: 84–101.

Easterlin, Richard A. 1973. Does Money Buy Happiness? *Public Interest* 30: 3–10.

———. 1974. Does Economic Growth Improve Human Lot? Some Empirical Evidence. In *Nation and Households in Economic Growth. Essays in Honour of Moses Abromowitz*, eds. Paul A. Davis and Melvin W. Reder, 89–125. New York and London: Academic Press.

———. 2001. Income and Happiness: Towards a Unified Theory. *The Economic Journal* 11: 465–484.

Egan, Timothy. 1995, September 3. Many Seek Security in Private Communities. *New York Times*: Front Page.

Fineman, Martha. 2004. *The Autonomy Myth. A Theory of Dependency*. New York: The New Press.

Forte, Francesca. 2005. Per una nuova storiografia khalduniana. In *Studies on Ibn Khaldūn*, ed. Massimo Campanini, 181–199. Milano: Polimetrica.

Fukuyama, Francis. 1995. *Trust. The Social Virtues and the Creation of Prosperity*. New York: Free Press.

Furet, François. 1982. *L'atelier de l'historien*. Paris: Flammarion.

Gautier, Émile Félix. [1927] 1952. *Le Passé de l'Afrique du Nord*. Paris: Payot.

Ghini, Agnese. 2011. *Casa, tecnologia, ambiente*. Rimini: Maggioli.

Gibbon, Edward. [1776] 1996. *The History of the Decline and Fall of the Roman Empire*. London: Penguin Classics.

Goodin, Robert E. 1985. *Protecting the Vulnerable. A Reanalysis of Our Social Responsibilities*. Chicago: Chicago University Press.

Goodman, Lenn Evan. 1972. Ibn Khaldūn and Thucydides. *Journal of the American Oriental Society* 92 (2): 250–270.

———. 1999. *Jewish and Islamic Philosophy: Crosspollinations in the Classic Age*. New Brunswick, NJ: Rutgers University Press.

Gozzi, Gustavo. 2008. Neutralità dello stato, libertà religiosa e fondamento dei diritti. In *Diritti umani. Trasformazioni e reazioni*, ed. Silvia Vida, 85–108. Bologna: Bononia University Press.

Hackman, Richard. 2009. Why Teams Don't Work. Interview with Diane Coutu. *Harvard Business Review* 87 (5): 98–105.

Haidt, Jonathan. 2012. *The Righteous Mind*. New York: Vintage Books.

Harper, Kyle. 2020, April 2. The Coronavirus is Accelerating History Past the Breaking Point. *Foreign Policy*. https://foreignpolicy.com/2020/04/06/coronavirus-is-accelerating-history-past-the-breaking-point/

Hart, Herbert L.A. 1961. *The Concept of Law*. Oxford: Oxford University Press.

Hashemi, Morteza. 2019. Bedouins of Silicon Valley: A Neo-Kantian Approach to Sociology of Technology. *The Sociological Review* 67 (3): 536–551.

Hopley, Russell. 2016. Plague, Demographic Upheaval and Civilisational Decline: Ibn Khaldūn and Muḥammad al-Shaqūrī on the Black Death in North Africa and Islamic Spain. *Landscapes* 17 (2): 171–184.

Huntington, Samuel P. 1996. *The Clash of Civilization and the Remaking of World Order*. New York: Simon & Schuster.

Illich, Ivan. 1977. *Nemesi medica. L'espropriazione della salute*. Mondadori: Milano.

Kahneman, Daniel. 2004. Felicità oggettiva. In *Felicità e economia. Quando il benessere è ben vivere*, eds. Luigino Bruni and Pier Luigi Porta, 75–113. Milano: Guerini e associati.

Kalb, James. 2004, February 14. Ibn Khaldūn and Our Age. *Turnabout*. http://antitechnocrat.net/node/23. Accessed 17 Sept 2020.

Kalin, Ibrahim. 2017b, January 21. Remembering Ibn Khaldūn and Toynbee: Challenge and Response. *Daily Sabah Columns*. https://www.dailysabah.com/columns/ibrahim-kalin/2017/01/21/remembering-ibn-khaldun-and-toynbee-challenge-and-response. Accessed 17 Sept 2020.

Kant, Immanuel. [1785] 1998. *Groundwork of the Metaphysics of Morals*. Cambridge University Press.

Khosrokhavar, Farhad. [2002] 2005. *Suicide Bombers: Allah's New Martyrs*, London and Ann Arbr, MI: Pluto Press.

Kittay, Eva F. 1997. Human Dependency and Rawlsian Equality. In *Feminists Rethink the Self*, ed. Diana T. Meyers, 219–266. Boulders, CO: Westview Press.

Krugman, Paul. 2013, August 25. The Decline of E-Empires. *New York Times*. http://www.nytimes.com/2013/08/26/opinion/krugman-the-decline-of-e-empires.html. Accessed 17 Sept 2020.

Kymlicka, Will. 1995. *Multicultural Citizenship. A Liberal Theory of Minority Rights*. Oxford: Clarendon Press.

Leaman, Oliver. 2005. Foreword. In *Studies on Ibn Khaldūn*, ed. Massimo Campanini, 7–8. Milano: Polimetrica.

Leopardi, Giacomo. [1898] 2014. *Zibaldone*. Milano: Mondadori.

Lévy-Strauss, Claude. [2000] 2016. *Corsi e ricorsi: In Vico's Wake*. In *We Are All Cannibals*, ed. Claude Lévy-Strauss, 133–138. New York: Columbia University Press.

Titus Livius. [I century A.D.]1997. *Storia di Roma*. Milano: Newton Compton.

Lucretius. [Ist century B.C.]2004. *On the Nature of Things (De Rerum Natura)*. New York: Dover Publications.

Luzzati, Claudio. 2016. *Del giurista interprete: linguaggio, tecniche e dottrine*. Torino: Giappichelli.
Machiavelli, Niccolò. [1532] 2005. *Il principe*. Torino: Einaudi.
Mackenzie, Catriona, Wendy Rogers, and Susan Dodds, eds. 2014. *Vulnerability: New Essays in Ethics and Feminist Philosophy*. Oxford: OUP.
Malik, Kenan. 2015. The Failure of Multiculturalism: Community versus Society in Europe. *Foreign Affairs* 94 (2): 21–32.
———. [2013] 2016 *Il multiculturalismo e i suoi critici. Ripensare la diversità dopo l'11 settembre*. Roma: Nessun Dogma.
Martinez-Gros, Gabriel. 2012. L'État et ses tribus, ou le devenir tribal du monde, Réflexions à partir d'Ibn Khaldoun. *Esprit* 1: 25–42.
McKenzie, Evan. 1994. *Privatopia: Homeowners' Associations and the Rise of Residential Private Government*. New Haven: Yale University Press.
McNeill, William H. 1976. *Plagues and Peoples*. New York: Anchor Books.
Mill, John Stuart. [1859] 1991. *On Liberty and Other Essays*. Oxford: Oxford University Press.
Monticelli, Luca. 2003. Le "cultural defense" (esimenti culturali) e i reati "culturalmente orientati". Possibili divergenze tra pluralismo culturale e sistema penale. *L'Indice penale* 6: 535–586.
Nagel, Thomas. 1986. *The View from Nowhere*. Oxford: Oxford University Press.
Namatianus, Rutilius. [415] 1992. *Il ritorno*. Torino: Einaudi.
Nussbaum, Martha C. 2006. *Frontiers of Justice: Disabilities, Nationalities, Species Membership*. Cambridge, MA: Harvard University Press.
Okin, Susan Moller. 1999. *Is Multiculturalism Bad for Women?* Princeton, NJ: Princeton University Press.
Owens, Mitchell. 1994, August 25. Saving Neighbourhoods One Gate at a Time. *New York Times*. http://www.nytimes.com/1994/08/25/garden/saving-neighborhoods-one-gate-at-a-time.html?pagewanted=all. Accessed 17 Sept 2020.
Pandolfi, Francesco. 2016, Febbraio 26. Pattuglie in Bolognina: questa è casa nostra e la rivogliamo. *Il resto del Carlino*. http://www.ilrestodelcarlino.it/bologna/cronaca/ronde-bolognina-commercianti-1.1923559. Accessed 17 Sept 2020.
Parekh, Bhikhu. 2000. *Rethinking Multiculturalism. Cultural Diversity and Political Theory*. Cambridge, MA: Harvard University Press.
Pareto, Vilfredo. [1917] 1988. *Trattato di sociologia generale*. Torino: UTET.
Parise, Goffredo. [1974] 2013. Il rimedio è la povertà. In *Dobbiamo disobbedire,* ed. Silvio Perrella, Milano: Adelphi.
Parisi, Francesco. 2008. Colpevolezza attenuata in un caso dubbio di motivazione culturale. *Rivista italiana di diritto e procedura penale* 3: 1447–1456.
Parolari, Paola. 2017. *Sharī'ah* e corti islamiche in Inghilterra tra mito e realtà. Pluralità di ordinamenti giuridici e interlegalità nelle società multireligiose e multiculturali. *Materiali per una storia della cultura giuridica* 1: 157–192.
Parsons, Talcott. 1951. *The Social System*. London: Routledge.
Perra, Margherita Sabrina, and Elisabetta Ruspini. 2015. Femminismi e contro-femminismi? Un tentativo di riflessione a partire dal movimento americano Women against Feminism. *Sociologia Italiana – AIS Journal of Sociology* 5: 97–122.
Petrarca, Francesco. [1349] 2009. *Letters on Familiar Matters (Rerum Familiarum Libri)*. New York: Italica Press.
Phillips, Anne. 2007. *Multiculturalism without Culture*. Princeton: Princeton University Press.
Plato. [390–360 a.C.] 2014. *Theaetetus*. Oxford: Oxford University Press.
Rawls, John. 1993. *Political Liberalism*. New York: Columbia University Press.
———. [1971] 1999 (rev. ed.). *A Theory of Justice*. New York: Oxford University Press.
Raz, Joseph. 1986. *The Morality of Freedom*. Oxford: Clarendon Press.
———. 1994. Multiculturalism. In *Ethics in the Public Domain*, ed. Joseph Raz. Oxford: Clarendon Press.

———. 2020, May 5. Joseph Raz's Response to Covid-19. *Tang Prize*. https://www.tang-prize.org/en/media_detail.php?id=1382. Accessed 17 Sept 2020.

Risé, Claudio. 2016. *Sazi da morire*. Cinisello Balsamo: San Paolo.

Russell, Bertrand. [1946] 1996. *History of Western Philosophy*. London: Routledge.

Said, Edward. 1978. *Orientalism*. London: Penguin.

Sailer, Steve. 2003, January 13. Cousin marriage conundrum. *The Unz Review*. https://www.unz.com/isteve/cousin-marriage-conundrum/. Accessed 17 Sept 2020.

Sartori, Giovanni. 2000. *Pluralismo, multiculturalismo e estranei*. Milano: Rizzoli.

Scruton, Roger. 1997. *Society of Strangers: Education for Citizenship in the Post-Modern World*. London: University of London, Institute of United States Studies.

Seligman, Adam B., and David W. Montgomery. 2019. The Tragedy of Human Rights: Liberalism and the Loss of Belonging. *Society* 56: 203–209.

Sen, Amartya. 2006a, February 27. The Uses and Abuses of Multiculturalism: Chili and Liberty. *The New Republic*. http://www.pierretristam.com/Bobst/library/wf-58.htm. Accessed 17 Sept 2020.

———. 2006b. *Identity and Violence*. London: Penguin.

Servigne, Pablo, and Raphaël Stevens. 2020. *How Everything Can Collapse*. Cambridge: Polity.

Shachar, Ayelet. 2001. Two Critics of Multiculturalism. *Cardozo Law Review* 23: 253–297.

Spengler, Oswald. [1918–1923] 2007. *The Decline of the West*. Oxford: Oxford University Press.

Stearns, Justin. 2007. Contagion in Theology and Law: Ethical Considerations in the Writings of Two 14th Century Scholars of Naṣrid Granada. *Islamic Law and Society* 14 (1): 109–129.

Tainter, Joseph. 1957. The Meaning of 'Political' in Political Decisions. *Political Studies* 5 (3): 225–239.

———. 1988. *The Collapse of Complex Societies*. Cambridge: Cambridge University Press.

Taleb, Nassim Nicholas. [2012] 2013. *Antifragile. Prosperare nel disordine*. Milano: il Saggiatore.

———. 2016. The Most Intolerant Wins: The Dictatorship of the Small Minority. *Medium.com*. https://medium.com/@nntaleb/the-most-intolerant-wins-the-dictatorship-of-the-small-minority-3f1f83ce4e15#.gtww575wa. Accessed 17 Sept 2020.

Taylor, Charles. 1992. *Multiculturalism and the Politics of Recognition*. Princeton: Princeton University Press.

Thucydides. [IV century B.C.]1989. *The Peloponnesian War* (trans. Thomas Hobbes). Chicago: The University of Chicago Press.

Touraine, Alain. 1997. *Pourrons-nous vivre ensemble? Égaux et différents*. Paris: Fayard.

Toynbee, Arnold. [1934] 1962. *A Study of History. Vol. III: The Growths of Civilizations*. New York: Oxford University Press.

Trujillo, Isabel. 2003. *Imparzialità*. Torino: Giappichelli.

Turchin, Peter. 2006. *War and Peace and War: the Rise and Fall of Empires*. New York: Plume.

———. 2013, August 26. Ibn Khaldūn on the Rise and Decline of Corporate Empires. *Clyodinamica. A Blog about the Evolution of Civilizations*. https://evolution-institute.org/blog/ibn-khaldun-on-the-rise-and-decline-of-corporate-empires/. Accessed 17 Sept 2020.

Ventura, Raffaele Alberto. 2015, July 8. Facebook e il declino dell'Occidente. *Prismo*. http://www.prismomag.com/zuckerberg-legge-ibn-khaldun/. Accessed 17 Sept 2020.

———. 2020b. *Radical choc. Ascesa e caduta dei competenti*. Torino: Einaudi.

Verza, Annalisa. 2000. *La neutralità impossibile*. Milano: Giuffrè.

———. 2008. Islam e diritti umani: tra rigidità strutturali e radici interne. In *Diritti umani. Trasformazioni e reazioni*, ed. Silvia Vida, 211–225. Bologna: Bononia University Press.

———. 2012. Lost in Translation: Human Rights Between Western Secularism and Islamic Scripturalism. In *Liber Amicorum René Foqué*, eds. Marie-Claire Foblets, Mireille Hildebrandt, and Jacques Steenbergen, 657–670. Brussels: Larcier.

———. 2014a. Principio di sussidiarietà e universalità dei bisogni: il riaccendersi tecnologico della fiducia. *Notizie di Politeia* 116: 14–35.

———. 2014b. The Rule of Exposure. *From Bentham to Queen Grimhilde's Mirror. ARSP* 4: 450–466.

———. 2015a. "Quest" identitaria mediata dal web, (cyber)bullismo e stratificazione sociale alla luce di un singolare caso di "devianza" di massa. *Studi sulla questione criminale* 2-3: 129–150.

———. 2015b. Ansia panottica e "treadmill effect" nell'utopia eudaimonistica delle nuove tecnologie. In *Filosofia del diritto e nuove tecnologie*, eds. Raffaella Brighi and Silvia Zullo, 89–103. Roma: Aracne.

———. 2016. L'*hikikomori* e il giardino all'inglese. Inquietante irrazionalità e solitudine comune. *Ragion Pratica* 1: 243–257.

———. 2017. La compattezza etico-sociale e il ciclo delle civiltà. Cultura occidentale e multiculturalismo contemporaneo alla luce della lezione di Ibn Khaldūn. *Materiali per una storia della cultura giuridica* 1: 223–247.

———. 2018. Il concetto di vulnerabilità e la sua tensione tra colonizzazioni neoliberali e nuovi paradigmi di giustizia. In *Vulnerabilità. Analisi multidisciplinare di un concetto*, eds. Orsetta Giolo and Baldassare Pastore, 229–251. Roma: Carocci.

———. 2019. Vulnerabilità e forme "altre" di radicalizzazione. L'echo chamber delle comunità online di odio misogino e antifemminista. *Notizie di Politeia* 136: 57–69.

———. 2020. "Mascolinità tossica" sul web: la "cultura" dell'odio antifemminista online. In *Postfemminismo e neoliberalismo*, eds. Annalisa Verza and Silvia Vida, 157–196. Roma: Aracne.

Walzer, Michael. 1994. *Thick and Thin. Moral Argument at Home and Abroad*. Indiana: University of Notre Dame Press.

West, Ed. 2015. *Asabiya, What Ibn Khaldūn, the Islamic father of social science, can teach us about the world today*, e-book. https://www.amazon.co.uk/*Asabiyya*h-Khaldun-Islamic-father-science-ebook/dp/B0133Y2XSG/ref=sr_1_1?ie=UTF8&qid=1438364083&sr=8-1&keywords=*Asabiyya*h. Accessed 17 Sept 2020.

Woodley, Michael A., and Edward Bell. 2012. Consanguinity as a Major Predictor of Levels of Democracy: A Study of 70 Nations. *Journal of Cross-Cultural Psychology* 44 (2): 263–280.

Correction to: Ibn Khaldūn and the Arab Origins of the Sociology of Civilization and Power

Correction to:
A. Verza, *Ibn Khaldūn and the Arab Origins of the Sociology of Civilisation and Power*,
https://doi.org/10.1007/978-3-030-70339-4

The book was inadvertently published with typographical errors in names with special characters. These typographical errors have now been corrected along with certain grammatical errors throughout the book. The names have been corrected in the reference list across all the chapters in the book.

The updated online versions of the book can be found at
https://doi.org/10.1007/978-3-030-70339-4

A. Verza, *Ibn Khaldūn and the Arab Origins of the Sociology of Civilisation and Power*, https://doi.org/10.1007/978-3-030-70339-4_6

References

(A) Ibn Khaldūn's Works

Ibn Khaldūn. 1844. Autobiographie d'Ibn Khaldoun (ed. William Mac Guckin de Slane). *Journal Asiatique* III: 5–60; 187–210; 291–308; 325–353.

———. 1847–1851. *Histoire des Berbères et des dynasties musulmanes de l'Afrique septentrionale* (ed. William Mac Guckin de Slane). 2 Voll. Algers: Imprimerie du Gouvernement.

———. 1857. *Muqaddimat Ibn Khaldūn*. Il Cairo: Būlāq.

———. 1858. *Prolégomènes D'Ebn-Khaldoun* (ed. M. Quatremère). Paris: Benjamin Duprat.

———. 1862–1868. *Les Prolégomènes d'Ibn Khaldoun* (ed. William Mac Guckin de Slane). Paris: Librairie orientaliste Paul Geuthner.

———. 1867–1868. *Kitāb al-'Ibar* (ed. Naṣr al-Hūrīnī). Il Cairo: Būlāq.

———. 1950. *An Arab Philosophy of History* (ed. Charles Issawi). London: Murray.

———. 1951. *Ta'rīf bi-Ibn Ḫaldūn wa-riḥlatuhu ġarban wa-šarqan* (ed. Muḥammad Tawit al-Tanji). Cairo: Lajnat al-Ta'lif wa-al-Tarjamah wa-al-Nashr.

———. 1958. *The Muqaddimah: An Introduction to History* (ed. Franz Rosenthal). 3 Voll. New Jersey: Princeton University Press.

———. 1967–1968. *Discours sur l'histoire universelle*, (ed. Vincent Monteil). 3 Voll. Beyrouth: Commission libanaise pour la traduction des chefs-d'oeuvre et Sinbad.

———. [1959] 1990. *Šifā' al-sā'il li-tahḏīb al-masā'il* (ed. Abū Yaarub Marzouki). Tunis: al-Dar al-Àrabiyah lil-Kitāb.

———. [1980] 1995. *Le voyage d'Occident et d'Orient* (ed. Abdesselam Cheddadi). Paris: Sindbad.

———. 2002. *Le Livre des Exemples. I. Autobiographie, Muqaddima* (ed. Abdesselam Cheddadi). Paris: Gallimard.

———. [1967] 2005. *The Muqaddimah: An Introduction to History* (ed. Franz Rosenthal), abridged edition. Princeton: Princeton University Press.

———. 2012. *Le Livre des Exemples, II. Histoire des Arabes et des Berbères du Maghreb* (ed. Abdesselam Cheddadi). Paris: Gallimard.

———. 2017. *Ibn Khaldūn on Sufism. Remedy for the Questioner in Search of Answers* (trans. Yumna Ozer). Cambridge: The Islamic Texts Society.

A. Verza, *Ibn Khaldūn and the Arab Origins of the Sociology of Civilisation and Power*, https://doi.org/10.1007/978-3-030-70339-4

(B) Other Works

Abdesselem, Ahmed. 1983. *Ibn Khaldūn et ses lecteurs*. Paris: Presses Universitaires de France.

Abou-Tabickh, Lilian. 2019. *Al-'aṣabiyya in Context. Choice and Historical Continuity in Al-Muqaddima of Ibn Khaldūn*. Toronto: Ph.D. Thesis, Department of Political Science.

Abun-Nasr, Jamil. 1975. *A History of the Maghrib*. Cambridge: Cambridge University Press.

Ahmad, Zaid. 2003. *The Epistemology of Ibn Khaldūn*. London: RoutledgeCurzon.

Ahmed, Akbar S. 2005. Ibn Khaldūn and Anthropology: The Failure of Methodology in the Post 9/11 World. *Contemporary Sociology. Essays on Ibn Khaldūn* 34 (6): 591–596.

Al-Araki, Magid. 2014. *Ibn Khaldūn a Forerunner of Modern Sociology. Method and Concepts of Growth and Development*. Oslo: Høgskolen i Oslo og Akershus.

Alatas, Syed Hussein. 1986. *The Problem of Corruption*. Singapore: Times Books International.

Alatas, Syed Farid. 2011. Ibn Khaldūn. In *Wiley-Blackwell Companion to Major Social Theorists*, eds. George Ritzer and Jeffrey Stepnisky, 12–29. Malden, MA: Wiley-Blackwell.

———. 2013. *Ibn Khaldūn*. Oxford: Oxford Centre for Islamic Studies.

———. 2014. *Applying Ibn Khaldūn. The Recovery of a Lost Tradition in Sociology*. London: Routledge.

———. 2020. The Contemporary Significance of Ibn Khaldūn for Decolonial Sociology: Methodological and Theoretical Dimensions. *Tajseer. Qatar University Press* 1 (2): 75–98.

al-Azmeh, Aziz. 1981. *Ibn Khaldūn in Modern Scholarship: A Study in Orientalism*. London: Third World Research Centre.

———. 1982. *Ibn Khaldūn. An Essay in Reinterpretation*. New York: Routledge.

———. 2003. *Ibn Khaldūn: An Essay in Reinterpretation*. Budapest: Central European University Press.

Albarrán, Javier. 2019. Holy War in Ibn Khaldūn. A Transcultural Concept? *Journal of Medieval Worlds* 1 (1): 55–78.

al-Fārābī, Abū Nasr. [X-XI century]1986. *Kitāb al-millah wa nuṣūṣ ukhrā* (ed. Muhsin Mahdi). Beirut: Dar-El-Mashreq.

———. [X-XI century]1998. *On the Perfect State* (trans. Richard Walzer). Chicago: Great Books of the Islamic World.

al-Idrīsī, Muḥammad. [1154] 2008. *Il libro di Ruggero*. Palermo: Flaccovio.

Alighieri, Dante. [1316] 1988. *La Divina Commedia: Purgatorio*. Milano: Garzanti.

al-Jabri, Mohammed 'Abed. [1976, 1991] 1996. *La ragione araba*. Milano: Feltrinelli.

al-Mas'ūdī, Abū al-Hasan 'Alì. [X century]1861–1877. *Muruj al-Dhahab,* 9 Voll. (eds. Charles Barbier de Meynard e Abel Pavet de Courteille). Parigi: Imprimerie Imperiale.

al-Mubaššir b. Fātik, Abū al-Wafā. [1048–1049] 1958. *Muḫtār al-ḥikam* (ed. Franz Rosenthal). Madrid: Badawi.

Alvarus of Córdova, Paulus. [IX century]1844–1855. *Indiculus luminosus*. In *Patrologia Latina*, Vol. 121, sez. 35, ed. Jaques Paul Migne, 513–556. Paris: Garnier.

al-Yaaqubi, Husayn. 2006. The Banū Khaldūn: From Seville to Tunisia. In *Ibn Khaldūn. The Mediterranean in the 14th Century. Rise and Fall of the Empires. Studies*, ed. Noemí García Millán, 316–331. Seville: Fundación José Manuel Lara.

Amri, Laroussi. 2008. The Concept of 'Umran: The Heuristic Knot in Ibn Khaldūn. *The Journal of North African Studies* 13 (3): 345–355.

Anderson, Jon W. [1983] 1984. Conjuring with Ibn Khaldūn. In *Ibn Khaldūn and Islamic Ideology*, ed. Bruce B. Lawrence, 111–121. Leiden: Brill.

Aristotle. [350 B.C.]2013. *La generazione e la corruzione*. Milano: Bompiani.

Arnheim, Rudolf. 1974. *Arte e percezione visiva*. Milano: Einaudi.

Aron, Raymond. 1967. *Les étapes de la pensée sociologique*. Paris: Gallimard.

Asín Palacio, Miguel. [1919] 2014. *Dante e l'Islam*. Milano: Luni editrice.

Aubert, Bruno. 2016. Au delà d'Ibn Khaldūn. La tragédie arabe n'est pas fatale. *Esprit* 5: 53–59.

Augustin of Hippo. [413–426] 2011. *La città di Dio*. Milano: Mondadori.

Ayad, Kamil. 1930. *Die Geschichts- und Gesellschaftslehre Ibn Ḫaldūns*. Stuttgart und Berlin: Cotta.

Baali, Fuad. 1986. *Ilm al-'Umrān and Sociology: A Comparative Study*. Kuwait: Annals of the Faculty of Arts, Kuwait University.

———. 1988. *Society, State, and Urbanism: Ibn Khaldūn's Sociological Thought*. Lanham: University Press of America.

Baali, Fuad, and Brian Price. 1982. Ibn Khaldūn and Karl Marx: On Socio-Historical Change. *Iqbal Review* 23 (1): 17–36.

Babès, Leïla. 2011. *L'utopie de l'islam. La religion contre l'État*. Armand Colin: Paris.

Baeck, Louis. 1994. *The Mediterranean Tradition in Economic Thought*. London: Routledge.

Baldissera, Eros (ed.). 2006. *Dizionario compatto italiano arabo e arabo-italiano*. Bologna: Zanichelli.

Banfield, Edward C. 1958. *The Moral Basis of a Backward Society*. Glencoe, Ill.: Free Press.

Barnes, Harry E. 1948. Ancient and Medieval Social Philosophy. In *An Introduction to the History of Social Philosophy*, ed. H.E. Barnes, 3–28. Chicago: Chicago University Press.

Barnes, Marian. 2012. *Care in Everyday Life: An Ethic of Care in Practice*. Bristol: Polity Press.

Barry, Brian. 2001. *Culture and Equality*. Cambridge: Polity Press.

Basile, Fabio. 2008. *Immigrazione e reati "culturalmente motivati". Il diritto penale nelle società multiculturali*. CUEM: Milano.

Baudrillard, Jean. [1976] 2010. *La società dei consumi*. Bologna: Il Mulino.

Bauman, Zygmunt. [1999] 2003. *Modernità liquida*. Roma-Bari: Laterza.

Becker, Howard, and Harry E. Barnes, [1938] 1961. *Social Thought from Lore to Science*. 3 Voll. New York: Dover.

Ben Salem, Lilia. 1972. La notion de pouvoir dans l'oeuvre d'Ibn Khaldūn. *Cahier Internationaux de Sociologie*: 293–314.

Bencheick, Jamel E. 1965. Esquisse d'une sociologie de la religion chez Ibn Khaldūn. *La Pensée* 123: 3–23.

Benhabib, Seyla. 2002. *The Claims of Culture. Equality and Diversity in the Global Era*. Princeton: Princeton University Press.

Boccaccio, Giovanni. [1353] 1995. *The Decameron* (trans. G. H. McWilliam). 2nd ed. London: Penguin Books.

Bombaci, Alessio. 1949. Postille alla traduzione della *Muqaddimah* di Ibn Ḫaldūn. *AION* III: 439–472.

———. 1969. *Letteratura turca*. Firenze: Sansoni.

Bosquet, Georges-H. 1969. Marx et Engels se sont-ils intéressés aux questions islamiques? *Studia Islamica* 30: 119–130.

Botsman, Rachel, and Roo Rogers. 2010. *What's mine is yours. The rise of collaborative consumption*. Harper Business: New York.

Boukraa, Ridha. 2008. The Khaldunian concept of 'Umran/Ijtimaa in Light of the Current Paradigm of Post-Modern Society. *The Journal of North African Studies* 13 (3): 317–326.

Boulakia, Jean David C. 1971. Ibn Khaldūn: A Fourteenth-Century Economist. *The Journal of Political Economy* 79 (5): 1105–1118.

Bourdieu, Pierre. 1984. *Distinction: A Social Critic of the Judgement of Taste*. London: Routledge.

Bouthoul, Gaston. 1930. *Ibn-Khaldoun. Sa philosophie sociale*. Librairie Orientaliste Paul Geuthner: Paris.

———. 1934. Ibn Khaldoun. Préface à la nouvelle édition des Prolégomènes. In Ibn Khaldūn, *Les Prolégomènes d'Ibn Khaldoun* (ed. William Mac Guckin de Slane). Paris: Geuthner.

Bozarslan, Hamit. 2014. *Le luxe et la violence. Domination et contestation chez Ibn Khaldūn*. CNRS Éditions: Paris.

Brunschvig, Robert. 1947. *La Berbérie orientale sous les Hafsides*. Adrien Maisonneuve: Tome II. Paris.

Butterworth, Charles. 1972. Averroës, Politics and Opinion. *The American Political Science Review*: 894–901.

Campanini, Massimo. 2004. *Introduzione alla filosofia islamica*. Roma-Bari: Laterza.

———. 2005a. *Studies on Ibn Khaldūn*. Milano: Polimetrica.

———. 2005b. *Ibn Khaldūn: la Muqaddima, la storia, la civiltà, il potere*. In *Studies on Ibn Khaldūn*, ed. Massimo Campanini, 9–48. Milano: Polimetrica.

———. 2007. *Averroè. Bologna: il Mulino.*

———. 2017. *Averroes. The Decisive Treatise*. Piscataway, NJ: Gorgias Press.

———. 2019. *Ibn Khaldūn. Passato e futuro del mondo arabo*. La Vela: Viareggio.

Cantù, Cesare. 1887. *Storia Universale*. Torino: UTET. https://archive.org/stream/storiauniversal07cantgoog/storiauniversal07cantgoog_djvu.txt. Accessed 17 Sept 2020.

Capezzone, Leonardo. 2020. The City and the Law. Aspects of Ibn Khaldūn's critique of the philosophers. *Philological Encounters* 5: 4–24.

Celarent, Barbara. 2013. Taha Hussein, La philosophie sociale d'Ibn Khaldoun. *American Journal of Sociology* 119: 894–902.

Chambliss, Rollin. 1954. *Social Thought: From Hammurabi to Comte*. New York: Dryden Press.

Chaouch, Khalid. 2008. Ibn Khaldūn, in Spite of Himself. *The Journal of North African Studies* 13 (3): 279–291.

Chardin, Jean-Baptiste. 1686. *Travels into Perse and the East Indies*. Vol. I. London: folio.

Cheddadi, Abdesselam. 1980. Le système du pouvoir en Islam d'après Ibn Khaldoun. *Annales. Économies, Sociétés, Civilisations* 35: 534–550.

———. 1994. Ibn Khaldūn. *Prospects: The Quarterly Review of Comparative Education* 24 (1–2): 7–19.

———. [1980] 1995. Lectures d'Ibn Khaldūn. In Ibn Khaldūn, *Le voyage d'Occident e d'Orient, Autobiographie* (ed. Abdesselam Cheddadi), 9–26. Paris: Sinbad.

———. 1999. *Ibn Khaldūn revisité*. Rabat: Éditions Toukbal.

———. 2006. *Ibn Khaldūn. L'homme et le théoricien de la civilisation*. Paris: Gallimard.

Coltman Brown, Irene. 1981. Ibn Khaldūn and the Revelation from the Desert. *History Today* 31: 19–25.

Comte, Auguste. 1855. *Positive Philosophy*. New York: Calvin Blanchard.

———. [1852] 2009. *Cathéchisme positiviste*. Paris: Sandre.

Cooley, Charles H. [1902] 1962. *Human Nature and the Social Order*. New York: Charles Scribner's Sons.

Croce, Benedetto. 1932. Recensione di M. K. Ayad, *Die Geschichts–und Gesellschaftslehre Ibn Ḫaldūns*, Stuttgart, Berlin, Cotta. *La critica* XXX: 213–214.

Cruz Hernández, Miguel. 2003. Siete interrogantes en la historia del pensamiento. *Revista Española de Filosofía Medieval* 10: 69–73.

Dale, Stephen Frederic. 2015a. *The Orange Trees of Marrakesh. Ibn Khaldūn and the Science of Man*. Cambridge, MA: Harvard University Press.

———. 2015b. Return to Ibn Khaldūn–Again. *Review of Middle East Studies* 49 (1): 48–55.

Darwin, Charles. 1871. *The Descent of Man*. London: Murray.

De Angelo, Carlo. 2014. Tribunali religiosi e tribunale arbitrale: l'offerta "giudiziaria" islamica in Inghilterra. *Diritto e religioni* 18 (2): 387–410.

de Jouvenel, Bertrand. 1945. *Du pouvoir, histoire naturelle de sa croissance*. Genève: C. Bourquin.

de Paw, Cornelius. 1774. *Recherches philosophiques sur les Américains ou Mémoires intéressants pour servir à l'histoire de l'espèce humaine*. Berlin: Georges Jacques Decker.

de Tocqueville, Alexis. 1835. *De la démocratie en Amérique*. Paris: Charles Gosselin.

DeBoer, Tjitze J. [1901] 1965. *The History of Philosophy in Islam*. New York: Dover.

Denaro, Roberta (ed.). 2006. *Le mille e una notte*. Donzelli: Roma.

Dhaouadi, Mahmoud. 2005. The 'Ibar: Lessons of Ibn Khaldūn's 'Umrān Mind. *Contemporary Sociology, 34/6: Essays on Ibn Khaldūn*: 585–589.

———. 2011. Ibn Khaldoun, sociologue avant la lettre. *Sciences Humaines* 15 (6): 1–5.

Dozy, Reinhart. 1869. Compte-rendue des "Prolégomènes d'Ibn Khaldoun", texte Arabe par E. Quatremère, traduit par de Slane. *Journal Asiatique* XIV (6): 133–218.

Duesenberry, James. 1949. *Income, Saving and the Theory of Consumer Behaviour*. Cambridge, MA: Harvard University Press.

Duguit, Léon. [1901] 2003. *L'État, le droit objectif et la loi positive*. Paris: Dalloz.

Durkheim, Émile. 1885. Schaeffle, A., Bau und Leben des sozialen Körpers: Erster Band. *Revue Philosophique* 19: 84–101.

———. 1893. *De la division du travail social*. Paris: Presses Universitaires de France.

———. 1912. *Les formes élémentaires de la vie religiouse*. Paris: Alcan.

———. 1994. *Course in Sociology, Opening Lecture*. In *Émile Durkheim on Institutional Analysis*, ed. Mark Traugott. Chicago: University of Chicago Press.

———. [1895] 1999. *Les règles de la méthode sociologique*. Paris: Flammarion.

Easterlin, Richard A. 1973. Does Money Buy Happiness? *Public Interest* 30: 3–10.

———. 1974. Does Economic Growth Improve Human Lot? Some Empirical Evidence. In *Nation and Households in Economic Growth. Essays in Honour of Moses Abromowitz*, eds. Paul A. Davis and Melvin W. Reder, 89–125. New York and London: Academic Press.

———. 2001. Income and Happiness: Towards a Unified Theory. *The Economic Journal* 11: 465–484.

Egan, Timothy. 1995, September 3. Many Seek Security in Private Communities. *New York Times*: Front Page.

El Fadl, Khaled Abu. 2001. Islam and the Theology of Power. *Middle East Report* 221: 28–33.

Enan, Mohammad Abdullah. [1941] 2007. *Ibn Khaldūn: His Life and Works*. Kuala Lumpur: The Other Press.

Engels, Frederick. [1894] 1975. *On the History of Early Christianity*. In Marx & Engels, *On Religion*. Moscow: Progress.

Fakhry, Majid. 1970. *A History of Islamic Philosophy*. New York: Columbia University Press.

Fei Tzu, Han. 1939. *The Complete Works of* Han Fei Tzŭ: *A Classic of Chinese Political Science* (trans. Wen-Kuei Liao). London: Probsthain.

Ferrero, Guglielmo. 1896. Un sociologo arabo del secolo XIV: Ibn Khaldoun. *La riforma sociale* 6: 221–235.

Fineman, Martha. 2004. *The Autonomy Myth. A Theory of Dependency*. New York: The New Press.

Fischel, Walter J. 1952. *Ibn Khaldūn and Tamerlane*. Berkeley: University of California Press.

———. 1958. Ibn Khaldūn on the Bible, Judaism and the Jews. In *Goldziher Memorial Volume*. Part II, eds. Samuel Lowinger et al. Jerusalem: Rubin Mass.

Fleischer, Cornell. 1983. Royal Authority, Dynastic Cyclism and "Ibn Khaldūnism" in Sixteenth Century Ottoman Letters. *Journal of Asian and African Studies* 18: 198–220.

Flint, Robert. [1893] 2010. *History of the Philosophy of History*. Memphis, TN: General Books.

Forte, Francesca. 2005. Per una nuova storiografia khalduniana. In *Studies on Ibn Khaldūn*, ed. Massimo Campanini, 181–199. Milano: Polimetrica.

———. 2020. *Ibn Khaldūn: Antologia della Muqaddima*. Milano: Jaca Books.

Francesca, Ersilia. 2005. Ibn Khaldūn e "la Ricchezza delle Nazioni". Lo sviluppo economico secondo la Muqaddima. In *Studies on Ibn Khaldūn*, ed. Massimo Campanini, 75–99. Milano: Polimetrica.

Frazer, James. 1890. *The Golden Bough*. London: Macmillan.

Fromherz, Allen James. 2010. *Ibn Khaldūn: Life and Times*. Edinburgh: Edinburgh University Press.

Fukuyama, Francis. 1995. *Trust. The Social Virtues and the Creation of Prosperity*. New York: Free Press.

———. 2018. *Identity: The Demand for Dignity and the Politics of Resentment*. New York: Farrar, Straus and Giroux.

Furet, François. 1982. *L'atelier de l'historien*. Paris: Flammarion.

Gabrieli, Giuseppe. 1923. Saggio di bibliografia e concordanza della storia di Ibn Ḫaldūn. *Rivista degli Studi Orientali, X*: 169–211.

Gabrieli, Francesco. [1930] 1984. Il concetto di 'aṣabiyya' nel pensiero storico di Ibn Khaldūn. In *L'Islam nella storia*, ed. Francesco Gabrieli, 211–252. Bari: Dedalo.

Gamarra, Yolanda. 2015. Ibn Khaldūn (1332–1406): A Precursor of Intercivilizational Discourse. *Leiden Journal of International Law* 28: 441–456.
García Lizana, Antonio. 2006. Tradición y progreso: las claves del futuro. *Cuadernos de CC.EE. y EE.* 50–51: 159–176.
Gardet, Louis. [1977] 2002. *Gli uomini dell'Islam*. Milano: Jaca Book.
Gates, Warren E. 1967. The Spread of Ibn Khaldūn's Ideas on Climate and Culture. *Journal of the History of Ideas* 28: 415–422.
Gaudemet, Jean. 1962. Esquisse d'une sociologie historique du pouvoir. *Politique* 19–20: 195–234.
Gautier, Émile Félix. [1927] 1952. *Le Passé de l'Afrique du Nord*. Paris: Payot.
Gellner, Ernest. 1981. *Cohesion and Identity: the Maghreb from Ibn Khaldūn to Émile Durkheim*. In *Muslim Society*, ed. Ernest Gellner. Cambridge: Cambridge University Press.
———. 1995. *Anthropology and Politics. Revolution in the Sacred Grove*. Oxford: Blackwell.
Ghini, Agnese. 2011. *Casa, tecnologia, ambiente*. Rimini: Maggioli.
Gibb, Hamilton A.R. 1933. The Islamic Background of Ibn Khaldūn's Political Theory. *Bulletin of the School of Oriental Studies* VII: 23–31.
Gibbon, Edward. [1776] 1996. *The History of the Decline and Fall of the Roman Empire*. London: Penguin Classics.
Gierer, Alfred. 2001. Ibn Khaldūn on Solidarity ("Asabiyah")–Modern Science on Cooperativeness and Empathy: A Comparison. *Philosophia Naturalis* 38: 91–104.
Girard, René. [1961] 2002. *Menzogna romantica e verità romanzata*. Milano: Bompiani.
Gobineau, Joseph Arthur, comte de. 1853–1855. *Essai sur l'inégalité des races humaines*. Paris: Firmin Didot Frères.
Goodin, Robert E. 1985. *Protecting the Vulnerable. A Reanalysis of Our Social Responsibilities*. Chicago: Chicago University Press.
Goodman, Lenn Evan. 1972. Ibn Khaldūn and Thucydides. *Journal of the American Oriental Society* 92 (2): 250–270.
———. 1999. *Jewish and Islamic Philosophy: Crosspollinations in the Classic Age*. New Brunswick, NJ: Rutgers University Press.
Goumeziane, Smaïl. 2006. *Ibn Khaldoun, un génie maghrébien*. Paris: Non lieu.
Gozzi, Gustavo. 2008. Neutralità dello stato, libertà religiosa e fondamento dei diritti. In *Diritti umani. Trasformazioni e reazioni*, ed. Silvia Vida, 85–108. Bologna: Bononia University Press.
Gumplowicz, Ludwig. 1925. *Soziologische Essays*. Innsbruck: Universitäts- Verlag Wagner.
Hackman, Richard. 2009. Why Teams Don't Work. Interview with Diane Coutu. *Harvard Business Review* 87 (5): 98–105.
Haidt, Jonathan. 2012. *The Righteous Mind*. New York: Vintage Books.
Haleem, M.A.S. Abdel (trans.). 2004. *The Qur'an*. Oxford University Press.
Hamès, Constant. 1999. Islam et Sociologie: Une rencontre qui n'a pas eu lieu? In *Sociology and Religions. An Ambiguous Relationship*, eds. Liliane Voyé and Jaak Billiet, 171–182. Leuven: Leuven University Press.
Harper, Kyle. 2020, April 2. The Coronavirus is Accelerating History Past the Breaking Point. *Foreign Policy*. https://foreignpolicy.com/2020/04/06/coronavirus-is-accelerating-history-past-the-breaking-point/
Hart, Herbert L.A. 1961. *The Concept of Law*. Oxford: Oxford University Press.
Hashemi, Morteza. 2019. Bedouins of Silicon Valley: A Neo-Kantian Approach to Sociology of Technology. *The Sociological Review* 67 (3): 536–551.
Hassan, Faridah Hj. 2006. Ibn Khaldūn and Jane Addams: The Real Father of Sociology and The Mother of Social Works. *Congreso Ibn Khaldūn*, November 3–5, Madrid. http://www.docsford.com/document/6091263. Accessed 17 Sept 2020.
Heath, Eugene, and Byron Kaldis. 2017. *Wealth, Commerce and Philosophy: Foundational Thinkers and Business Ethics*. Chicago: The University of Chicago Press.
Hegel, Georg Wilhelm Friedrich. [1837] 1902. *Lectures on the Philosophy of History*. London: Bell and Sons.
Hillenbrand, Carole. 2016. *Islam. Una nuova introduzione storica*. Giulio Einaudi: Torino.

Hobbes, Thomas. [1651] 1985. *Leviathan*. London: Penguin.
Hodgson, Marshall G.S. 1974. *The Venture of Islam: Conscience and History in a World Civilization*. Chicago: University of Chicago Press.
Hopkins, Nicholas. 1990. Engels and Ibn Khaldūn. *Alif. Journal of Comparative Poetics* 10: 9–18.
Hopley, Russell. 2016. Plague, Demographic Upheaval and Civilisational Decline: Ibn Khaldūn and Muḥammad al-Shaqūrī on the Black Death in North Africa and Islamic Spain. *Landscapes* 17 (2): 171–184.
Horrut, Claude. 2006. *Ibn Khaldūn, un Islam des "Lumières"*. Paris: Les Éditions Complexes.
Hosseini, Hamid. [1995] 2003. Understanding the Market Mechanism before Adam Smith. In *Medieval Islamic Economic Thought*, ed. Shaikh M. Ghazanfar, 88–107. London: Routledge Curzon.
Hourani, Albert. 1962. *Arabic Thought in the Liberal Age 1798-1939*. Cambridge: Cambridge University Press.
Hughes-Warrington, Marnie. 2008. *Fifty Key-Thinkers on History*. London: Routledge.
Hume, David. [1779] 1976. *The Natural History of Religion*. Oxford: Oxford University Press.
Huntington, Samuel P. 1996. *The Clash of Civilization and the Remaking of World Order*. New York: Simon & Schuster.
Hussein, Taha. 1918. *Étude analitique et critique de la philosophie sociale d'Ibn Khaldoun*. Paris: Pedone.
Ibn Taymmiyya. 1981. *Dar' ta'āruḍ al-'aql wa-l-naql*. Cairo: Dār al-Kutub.
Ibraham, Hilmi. 1988. Leisure, Idleness and Ibn Khaldūn. *Leisure Studies* 7: 51–57.
Illich, Ivan. 1977. *Nemesi medica. L'espropriazione della salute*. Mondadori: Milano.
Irwin, Robert. 2018. *Ibn Khaldūn. An Intellectual Biography*. Princeton: Princeton University Press.
Isma'il, Mahmud. [1976] 1996. *Nihāyat usṭūrat naẓarīyāt Ibn Khaldūn: muqtabasah min Rasā'il Ikhwān al-ṣafā*. Al-Manṣūrah: 'Āmir lil-Ṭibā'ah wa-al-Nashr.
Issawi, Charles. 1950. Preface. In *An Arab Philosophy of History*, ed. Charles Issawi. London: Murray.
'Izzat, 'Abd al-'Aziz. 1947. *Ibn Khaldoun et sa science sociale*. Cairo: Université de Fouad.
———. 1952. *Étude comparée d'Ibn Khaldūn et Durkheim*. Cairo: al-Maktabat al-Anglo al-Misriyya.
Kahlaoui, Tarek. 2008. Towards Reconstructing the *Muqaddimah* Following Ibn Khaldūn's Reading of the Idrisian Text and Maps. *The Journal of North African Studies* 13 (3): 293–306.
Kahneman, Daniel. 2004. Felicità oggettiva. In *Felicità e economia. Quando il benessere è ben vivere*, eds. Luigino Bruni and Pier Luigi Porta, 75–113. Milano: Guerini e associati.
Kalb, James. 2004, February 14. Ibn Khaldūn and Our Age. *Turnabout*. http://antitechnocrat.net/node/23. Accessed 17 Sept 2020.
Kalin, Ibrahim. 2016, December 10. Ibn Khaldūn has a Message for Us. *Daily Sabah Columns*. https://www.dailysabah.com/columns/ibrahim-kalin/2016/12/10/ibn-khaldun-has-a-message-for-us. Accessed 17 Sept 2020.
———. 2017a, January 6. Al-Fārābī Prayer. *Daily Sabah Columns*.https://www.dailysabah.com/columns/ibrahim-kalin/2017/01/07/al-farabis. Accessed 17 Sept 2020.
———. 2017b, January 21. Remembering Ibn Khaldūn and Toynbee: Challenge and Response. *Daily Sabah Columns*. https://www.dailysabah.com/columns/ibrahim-kalin/2017/01/21/remembering-ibn-khaldun-and-toynbee-challenge-and-response. Accessed 17 Sept 2020.
Kalpakian, Jack. 2008. Ibn Khaldūn's Influence on Current International Relations Theory. *The Journal of North African Studies* 13 (3): 357–370.
Kant, Immanuel. 1785 (1998) *Groundwork of the Metaphysics of Morals*. Cambridge University Press.
Kantorowicz, Ernst. 1989. *Les deux corps du roi. Essai sur la théologie politique au Moyen Âge*. Paris: Gallimard.
Khosrokhavar, Farhad. [2002] 2005. *Suicide Bombers: Allah's New Martyrs*, London and Ann Arbr, MI: Pluto Press.

Kittay, Eva F. 1997. Human Dependency and Rawlsian Equality. In *Feminists Rethink the Self*, ed. Diana T. Meyers, 219–266. Boulders, CO: Westview Press.
Krugman, Paul. 2013, August 25. The Decline of E-Empires. *New York Times*. http://www.nytimes.com/2013/08/26/opinion/krugman-the-decline-of-e-empires.html. Accessed 17 Sept 2020.
Kymlicka, Will. 1995. *Multicultural Citizenship. A Liberal Theory of Minority Rights*. Oxford: Clarendon Press.
Labica, Georges. 1968. *Politique et religion chez Ibn Khaldūn*. Alger: SNED.
Lacoste, Yves. [1966] 1998. *Ibn Khaldoun, Naissance de l'Histoire, passé du Tiers Monde*. Paris: La Decouverte.
Laffer, Arthur. 2004. The Laffer Curve: Past, Present, and Future. *Executive Summary Backgrounder No. 1765*: 1–18. s3.amazonaws.com/thf_media/2004/pdf/bg1765.pdf. Accessed 17 Sept 2020.
Lagarde, Georges de. [1934] 1956–1970. *La naissance de l'esprit laïque au déclin du Moyen Âge*. Louvain: E. Nauvelaerts.
Lahbabi, Mohamed-Aziz. 1987. *Ibn Khaldūn: notre contemporain*. Paris: L'Harmattan.
Lakhsassi, Abderrahman. 1979. Ibn Khaldūn and the Classification of the Science. *The Maghreb Review* 4 (1): 21–25.
Lambton, Ann K.S. [1954] 1980. *Theory and Practice in Medieval Persian Government*. London: Ashgate.
Laroui, Abdallah. 1987. *Islam et modernité*. Paris: La Découverte.
———. 1999. *Islam et Histoire*. Paris: Flammarion.
Lavisse, Ernest, and Alfred Rambaud. 1898. *Histoire générale*, Tome X. Paris: Armand Colin & Cie.
Lawrence, Bruce B. 1983. Ibn Khaldūn and Islamic Ideology. *Journal of Asian and African Studies, XVIII* 3–4: 154–165.
———. 1984. *Ibn Khaldūn and Islamic Ideology*. Leiden: Brill.
———. 2005. *Introduction to the 2005 Edition*. In Ibn Khaldūn, *The Muqaddimah: An Introduction to History* (ed. Franz Rosenthal), abridged edition, vii–xxv. Princeton: Princeton University Press.
Leaman, Oliver. 2005. Foreword. In *Studies on Ibn Khaldūn*, ed. Massimo Campanini, 7–8. Milano: Polimetrica.
Lefebvre, Henri. 1965. *Sociologie de Marx*. Paris: Presses Universitaires de France.
Lelli, Giovanna. 2020. *Knowledge and Beauty in Classical Islam: An Aesthetic Reading of the Muqaddima by Ibn Khaldūn*. London: Routledge.
Leopardi, Giacomo. [1898] 2014. *Zibaldone*. Milano: Mondadori.
Lévy-Strauss, Claude. [2000] 2016. *Corsi e ricorsi: In Vico's Wake*. In *We Are All Cannibals*, ed. Claude Lévy-Strauss, 133–138. New York: Columbia University Press.
Lewis, Bernard. [1986] 1999. *Semites and Anti-Semites: An Inquiry into Conflict and Prejudice*. New York: Norton.
Titus Livius. [I century A.D.]1997. *Storia di Roma*. Milano: Newton Compton.
Lombardi, Marco. 1997. Le follie di Spagna. In *Percorsi europei*, ed. Maria Grazia Profeti, 167–192. Firenze: Alinea.
Lucretius. [Ist century B.C.]2004. *On the Nature of Things (De Rerum Natura)*. New York: Dover Publications.
Luzzati, Claudio. 2016. *Del giurista interprete: linguaggio, tecniche e dottrine*. Torino: Giappichelli.
Machiavelli, Niccolò. [1532] 2005. *Il principe*. Torino: Einaudi.
Mackenzie, Catriona, Wendy Rogers, and Susan Dodds, eds. 2014. *Vulnerability: New Essays in Ethics and Feminist Philosophy*. Oxford: OUP.
Mahdi, Muhsin. 1957. *Ibn Khaldūn's Philosophy of History*. Chicago: University of Chicago Press.
Maimonides, Moses. [1180–1190] 2000. *The Guide for the Perplexed*. New York: Dover.
Malik, Kenan. 2015. The Failure of Multiculturalism: Community versus Society in Europe. *Foreign Affairs* 94 (2): 21–32.

———. [2013] 2016 *Il multiculturalismo e i suoi critici. Ripensare la diversità dopo l'11 settembre*. Roma: Nessun Dogma.
Martinez-Gros, Gabriel. 2012. L'État et ses tribus, ou le devenir tribal du monde, Réflexions à partir d'Ibn Khaldoun. *Esprit* 1: 25–42.
Marx, Karl. 1848. *Manifesto of the Communist Party*. London: Burghard.
———. [1859] 1970. *A Contribution to the Critique of Political Economy*. Moscow: Progress Publishers.
Maunier, René. 1915. Les idées sociologiques d'un philosophe arabe au XIV siècle. *Revue internationale de sociologie* 23: 142–154.
Mauss, Marcel. 2006. *Techniques Technology and Civilization*. New York: Berghahn Books.
McKenzie, Evan. 1994. *Privatopia: Homeowners' Associations and the Rise of Residential Private Government*. New Haven: Yale University Press.
McNeill, William H. 1976. *Plagues and Peoples*. New York: Anchor Books.
Mead, George Herbert. 1934. *Mind, Self and Society*. Chicago: University of Chicago Press.
Megherbi, Abdelghani. 1971. *La pensée sociologique d'Ibn Khaldoun*. SNED: Alger.
Mill, John Stuart. [1859] 1991. *On Liberty and Other Essays*. Oxford: Oxford University Press.
Miller, John H. 1975. *Ibn Khaldūn and Machiavelli: an Examination of Paradigms*. Manhattan, KS: Master's Thesis, Kansas State University.
Montesquieu, Charles-Luis de Secondat, baron de. 1748. *De l'ésprit des lois*. Amsterdam: Chatelain.
———, baron de. [1734] 1876. *Considérations sur les causes de la grandeur des Romains et de leur décadence*. Paris: Garnier Frères.
Montgomery Watt, William. 1961a. *Muḥammad*. Oxford: Oxford University Press.
———. 1961b. *Islam and the Integration of Society*. Bristol: The Burleigh Press.
Monticelli, Luca. 2003. Le "cultural defense" (esimenti culturali) e i reati "culturalmente orientati". Possibili divergenze tra pluralismo culturale e sistema penale. *L'Indice penale* 6: 535–586.
Morgan, Lewis Henry. 1877. *Ancient Society*. New York: Holt.
Nagel, Thomas. 1986. *The View from Nowhere*. Oxford: Oxford University Press.
Namatianus, Rutilius. [415] 1992. *Il ritorno*. Torino: Einaudi.
Nassar, Nassif. 1964. *Le maître d'Ibn Khaldūn, Al-Ābilī*, 103–114. XX: *Studia Islamica*.
———. 1967. *La pensée realiste d'Ibn Khaldūn*. Paris: Presses Universitaires de France.
Nicholson, Reynold A. 1907. *A Literary History of the Arabs*. Cambridge: Cambridge University Press.
Norenzayan, Ara. [2013] 2015. *Big Gods. How Religion Transformed Cooperation and Conflict*. Princeton: Princeton University Press.
Norton, David F., and Jacqueline Taylor (eds.). [1993] 2011. *The Cambridge Companion to Hume*. Cambridge: Cambridge University Press.
Nussbaum, Martha C. 2006. *Frontiers of Justice: Disabilities, Nationalities, Species Membership*. Cambridge, MA: Harvard University Press.
Okin, Susan Moller. 1999. *Is Multiculturalism Bad for Women?* Princeton, NJ: Princeton University Press.
Oppenheimer, Franz. 1922–1935. *System der Soziologie*. Jena: G. Fisher.
Orsi, Renzo, Davide Raggi, and Francesco Turrino. 2013, December 13. Ridurre le tasse si deve. *Lavoce.info*. http://www.lavoce.info/archives/15593/ridurre-le-tasse-pressione-fiscale-curva-di-laffer/. Accessed 17 Sept 2020.
Ortega y Gasset, José. [1934] 1976–1978. Abenjaldún nos revela el secreto: pensamientos sobre África Minor. *Revista del Instituto Egipcio de Estudios Islámicos en Madrid* 19: 95–114.
Owens, Mitchell. 1994, August 25. Saving Neighbourhoods One Gate at a Time. *New York Times*. http://www.nytimes.com/1994/08/25/garden/saving-neighborhoods-one-gate-at-a-time.html?pagewanted=all. Accessed 17 Sept 2020.
Pandolfi, Francesco. 2016, Febbraio 26. Pattuglie in Bolognina: questa è casa nostra e la rivogliamo. *Il resto del Carlino*. http://www.ilrestodelcarlino.it/bologna/cronaca/ronde-bolognina-commercianti-1.1923559. Accessed 17 Sept 2020.

Parekh, Bhikhu. 2000. *Rethinking Multiculturalism. Cultural Diversity and Political Theory*. Cambridge, Mass.: Harvard University Press.
Pareto, Vilfredo. [1917] 1988. *Trattato di sociologia generale*. Torino: UTET.
Parise, Goffredo. [1974] 2013. Il rimedio è la povertà. In *Dobbiamo disobbedire*, ed. Silvio Perrella, Milano: Adelphi.
Parisi, Francesco. 2008. Colpevolezza attenuata in un caso dubbio di motivazione culturale. *Rivista italiana di diritto e procedura penale* 3: 1447–1456.
Parolari, Paola. 2017. *Sharīʻah* e corti islamiche in Inghilterra tra mito e realtà. Pluralità di ordinamenti giuridici e interlegalità nelle società multireligiose e multiculturali. *Materiali per una storia della cultura giuridica* 1: 157–192.
Parsons, Talcott. 1951. *The Social System*. London: Routledge.
Patriarca, Giovanni. 2009, December 20. Il prologo della modernità. Filosofia della storia e scienze sociali in Ibn Khaldūn. *Dialegesthai*. https://mondodomani.org/dialegesthai/gpa02.htm. Accessed 17 Sept 2020.
———. 2019. El eterno retorno de la Asabiyyah. Ibn Jaldún y la teoría política contemporánea. *Daimon. Revista International de filosofía* 76: 139–153.
Perra, Margherita Sabrina, and Elisabetta Ruspini. 2015. Femminismi e contro-femminismi? Un tentativo di riflessione a partire dal movimento americano Women against Feminism. *Sociologia Italiana – AIS Journal of Sociology* 5: 97–122.
Petrarca, Francesco. [1349] 2009. *Letters on Familiar Matters (Rerum Familiarum Libri)*. New York: Italica Press.
Pettit, Philip, and Geoffrey Brennan. 2006. *The Economy of Esteem*. Oxford: Oxford University Press.
Phillips, Anne. 2007. *Multiculturalism without Culture*. Princeton: Princeton University Press.
Piccardo, Hamza (ed.). 1994. *Il Corano*. Roma: Newton & Compton.
Pines, Shlomo. 1970. Ibn Khaldūn and Maimonides, a Comparison between Two Texts. *Studia Islamica* 32: 265–274.
Pišev, Marko. 2019. Anthropological Aspects of Ibn Khaldūn's Muqaddimah: A Critical Examination. In *Bérose–Encyclopédie internationale des histoires de l'anthropologie*, 1–21. Paris: Bérose. http://www.berose.fr/article1777.html?lang=fr. Accessed 17 Sept 2020.
Pizzi, Giancarlo. 1985. *Ibn Ḫaldūn e la Muqaddima: una filosofia della storia*. Milano: All'insegna del pesce d'oro.
Plato. [390–360 a.C.]2007. *La Repubblica*. Milano: BUR.
———. [390–360 a.C.]2014. *Theaetetus*. Oxford: Oxford University Press.
Polybius. [144 a.C.]2001–2006. *Storie*, Vol. 1–8. Milano: BUR.
Pomian, Krzysztof. 2006. *Ibn Khaldūn au prisme de l'Occident*. Paris: Gallimard.
Ptolemy. [II century B.C.]1940. *Tetrabiblos (Quadripartitum)*, ed. Frank E. Robbins. Cambridge, MA: Loeb.
Rabi', Muḥammad Mahmoud. 1967. *The Political Theory of Ibn Khaldūn*. Leiden: Brill.
Rawls, John. 1993. *Political Liberalism*. New York: Columbia University Press.
———. [1971] 1999 (rev. ed.). *A Theory of Justice*. New York: Oxford University Press.
Raz, Joseph. 1986. *The Morality of Freedom*. Oxford: Clarendon Press.
———. 1994. Multiculturalism. In *Ethics in the Public Domain*, ed. Joseph Raz. Oxford: Clarendon Press.
———. 2020, May 5. Joseph Raz's Response to Covid-19. *Tang Prize*. https://www.tang-prize.org/en/media_detail.php?id=1382. Accessed 17 Sept 2020.
Renan, Ernest, and Djamal ad-Din al-Afghani. 1883. *Le journal des débats*: 1–17. http://blogs.histoireglobale.com/wp-content/uploads/2011/10/Renan-al-Afghani.pdf. Accessed 17 Sept 2020.
Risé, Claudio. 2016. *Sazi da morire*. Cinisello Balsamo: San Paolo.
Ritzer, George, and Jeffrey Stepnisky. 2011. *Wiley-Blackwell Companion to Major Social Theorists*. Malden, MA: Wiley-Blackwell.

Rizkiah, Kholifatul, and Abdelkader Chachi. 2020. The Relevance of Ibn Khaldūn's Economic Thought in the Contemporary World. *Turkish Journal of Islamic Economics* 7 (2): 70–90.

Rosenthal, Erwin. 1932. *Ibn Khaldūns Gedanken über den Staat. Ein Beitrag zur Geschichte der mittelalterlichen Staatlehre*. Oldenbourg: Munich.

Rosenthal, Franz. 1958. *Preface to Ibn Khaldūn*. In Ibn Khaldūn, *The Muqaddimah: An Introduction to History* (ed. Franz Rosenthal). Vol. I, xxix–cxv. Princeton: Princeton University Press.

———. 1984. Ibn Khaldūn in His Time. In *Ibn Khaldūn and Islamic Ideology*, ed. Bruce B. Lawrence, 16–24. Leiden: Brill.

———. 1987. Ibn Khaldūn. In *Encyclopedia of Religion*, ed. Mircea Eliade, 565–567. New York: Macmilllan.

Rostow, Walt Whitman. 1960. *The Stages of Economic Growth. A Non-Communist Manifesto*. Cambridge: Cambridge University Press.

Russell, Bertrand. [1946] 1996. *History of Western Philosophy*. London: Routledge.

Sahlins, Marshall. [1972] 1980. *Economia dell'età della pietra*. Milano: Bompiani.

Said, Edward. 1978. *Orientalism*. London: Penguin.

Sailer, Steve. 2003, January 13. Cousin marriage conundrum. *The Unz Review*. https://www.unz.com/isteve/cousin-marriage-conundrum/. Accessed 17 Sept 2020.

Salama, Mohammad. 2011. *Islam, Orientalism and Intellectual History. Modernity and the Politics of Exclusion since Ibn Khaldūn*. London York: I. B. Tauris.

Salisbury, Jean de. [1159] 2009. *Metalogicon* (ed. Daniel McGarry). Philadelphia: Paul Dry Books.

Sarton, George. [1927] 1962. *Introduction to the History of Science*. Baltimore, MD: Williams and Wilkins Company.

Sartori, Giovanni. 2000. *Pluralismo, multiculturalismo e estranei*. Milano: Rizzoli.

Schacht, Joseph (ed.). 1974. *The Legacy of Islam*. Oxford: Clarendon Press.

Schumpeter, Joseph. 1954. *History of Economic Analysis*. New York: Oxford University Press.

Scruton, Roger. 1997. *Society of Strangers: Education for Citizenship in the Post-Modern World*. London: University of London, Institute of United States Studies.

Seligman, Adam B., and David W. Montgomery. 2019. The Tragedy of Human Rights: Liberalism and the Loss of Belonging. Society 56: 203–209.

Sen, Amartya. 2006a, February 27. The Uses and Abuses of Multiculturalism: Chili and Liberty. *The New Republic*. http://www.pierretristam.com/Bobst/library/wf-58.htm. Accessed 17 Sept 2020.

———. 2006b. *Identity and Violence*. London: Penguin.

Servigne, Pablo, and Raphaël Stevens. 2020. *How Everything Can Collapse*. Cambridge: Polity.

Shachar, Ayelet. 2001. Two Critics of Multiculturalism. *Cardozo Law Review* 23: 253–297.

Shackleton, Robert. 1961. *Montesquieu*. London: Oxford University Press.

Silvestre de Sacy, Antoine Isaac. 1810. *Extraits de Prolégomènes d'Ebn Khaldoun*. In *Relation de l'Egipte par Abdellatif, médecin arabe de Bagdad*, ed. Antoine Isaac Silvestre de Sacy, 509–524 (translation); 558–564 (Arabic text). Paris: Treuttel & Würtz.

———. [1816] 1843. Ibn Khaldoun. In *Biographie universelle ancienne et moderne*, ed. Antoine Isaac Silvestre de Sacy, Tome XX. Paris: A. Thoisniers Deplace.

———. [1826–1827] 2012. *Chrestomatie arabe, ou extraits de divers écrivains arabes*. Paris: Ulan Press.

Smith, Adam. [1776] 2008. *An Inquiry into the Nature and Causes of the Wealth of Nations*. Chicago: University of Chicago Press.

Sorokin, Pitirim A. [1947] 1962. *Society, Culture, and Personality*. New York: Cooper Square.

Soyer, Mehmet. 2010. *Examining the Origins of Sociology: Continuities and Divergencies between Ibn Khaldūn, Giambattista Vico, August Comte, Ludwig Gumplowicz, and Emile Durkheim*. Master Thesis. Denton: University of North Texas.

Soyer, Mehmet, and Paul Gilbert. 2012. Debating the Origins of Sociology: Ibn Khaldūn as a Founding Father of Sociology. *International Journal of Sociological Research* 5: 13–30.

Speake, Jennifer. [2003] 2014. *Literature of Travel and Exploration. An Encyclopedia*. London: Routledge.

Spengler, Joseph. 1964. Economic Thought of Islam: Ibn Khaldūn. *Comparative Studies in Society and History* 6: 268–306.
Spengler, Oswald. [1918–1923] 2007. *The Decline of the West*. Oxford: Oxford University Press.
Spragens, Thomas A. 1976. *Understanding Political Theory*. New York: St. Martin's Press.
Stearns, Justin. 2007. Contagion in Theology and Law: Ethical Considerations in the Writings of Two 14th Century Scholars of Naṣrid Granada. *Islamic Law and Society* 14 (1): 109–129.
Stowasser, Barbara. 1983. *Religion and Political Development: Some Comparative Ideas on Ibn Khaldūn and Machiavelli*. Washington, DC: Center for Contemporary Arab Studies.
Strauss, Leo. 1941. Persecution and the Art of Writing. *Social Research* VIII (4): 488–504.
———. [1939] 1998. *L'insegnamento esoterico*. In Leo Strauss, *Gerusalemme e Atene*. Torino: Einaudi.
Strauss, Leo, and Joseph Cropsey. [1963] 1972. *History of Political Philosophy*. Chicago: Rand McNally and Co.
Stuurman, Siep. 2015. Common Humanity and Cultural Difference in the Sedentary-Nomadic Frontier: Herodotus, Sima Qian, and Ibn Khaldūn. In *Global Intellectual History*, eds. Samuel Moyn and Andrew Sartori, 33–58. New York: Columbia University Press.
Tainter, Joseph. 1957. The Meaning of 'Political' in Political Decisions. *Political Studies* 5 (3): 225–239.
———. 1988. *The Collapse of Complex Societies*. Cambridge: Cambridge University Press.
Talbi, Mohamed. 1973. *Ibn Ḫaldūn et l'histoire*. Tunis: Maison Tunisienne de l'Édition.
———. 2002. Ibn Khaldoun. *Encyclopédie de l'Islam*, t. III, 849–855. Leiden: Brill.
Taleb, Nassim Nicholas. [2012] 2013. *Antifragile. Prosperare nel disordine*. Milano: il Saggiatore.
———. 2016. The Most Intolerant Wins: The Dictatorship of the Small Minority. *Medium.com*. https://medium.com/@nntaleb/the-most-intolerant-wins-the-dictatorship-of-the-small-minority-3f1f83ce4e15#.gtww575wa. Accessed 17 Sept 2020.
Taylor, Charles. 1992. *Multiculturalism and the Politics of Recognition*. Princeton: Princeton University Press.
Thucydides. [IV century B.C.]1989. *The Peloponnesian War* (trans. Thomas Hobbes). Chicago: The University of Chicago Press.
Tillion, Germaine. 1966. *Le Harem et les Cousins*. Paris: Seuil.
Touraine, Alain. 1997. *Pourrons-nous vivre ensemble? Égaux et différents*. Paris: Fayard.
Toynbee, Arnold. [1934] 1962. *A Study of History. Vol. III: The Growths of Civilizations*. New York: Oxford University Press.
Triki, Fathi. 1986. *L'Esprit historien dans la civilisation arabe et islamique*. Tunis: Maison Tunisienne de l'Édition.
Trujillo, Isabel. 2003. *Imparzialità*. Torino: Giappichelli.
Turchin, Peter. 2006. *War and Peace and War: the Rise and Fall of Empires*. New York: Plume.
———. 2013, August 26. Ibn Khaldūn on the Rise and Decline of Corporate Empires. *Clyodinamica. A Blog about the Evolution of Civilizations*. https://evolution-institute.org/blog/ibn-khaldun-on-the-rise-and-decline-of-corporate-empires/. Accessed 17 Sept 2020.
Turner, Bryan S. 1971. Sociological Founders and Precursors: the Theories of Religion of Émile Durkheim, Fustel de Coulanges and Ibn Khaldūn. *Religion* 1: 32–48.
Turroni, Giuliana. 2002. *Il mondo della storia secondo Ibn Khaldūn*. Roma: Jouvence.
———. 2005. Ibn Khaldūn: penseur classique de l'islam laïque. In *Studies on Ibn Khaldūn*, ed. Massimo Campanini, 123–144. Milano: Polimetrica.
———. 2014. 'Umrān. La civilisation dans la théorie khaldûnienne. In *Encyclopédie de l'humanisme méditerranéen*, ed. Houari Youati, encyclopedie-humanisme.com/?Umran. Accessed 17 Sept 2020.
Van Gennep, Arnold. [1910] 1920. *La formation des légendes*. Paris: Flammarion.
Vanoli, Alessandro. 2004. Recensione di G. Turroni. *Filosofia politica* 1: 139–141.
Veblen, Thorstein. 1899. *The Theory of the Leisure Class*. New York: Dover Thrift.
Ventura, Raffaele Alberto. 2015, July 8. Facebook e il declino dell'Occidente. *Prismo*. http://www.prismomag.com/zuckerberg-legge-ibn-khaldun/. Accessed 17 Sept 2020.

———. 2020a, April 2. Ibn Khaldūn 2020: Medieval Lessons on Social Collapse. *Medium*. https://medium.com/@raffaele.ventura/ibn-khaldun-2020-medieval-lessons-on-social-collapse-bfbd7cacec3c

———. 2020b. *Radical choc. Ascesa e caduta dei competenti*. Torino: Einaudi.

Verza, Annalisa. 2000. *La neutralità impossibile*. Milano: Giuffrè.

———. 2008. Islam e diritti umani: tra rigidità strutturali e radici interne. In *Diritti umani. Trasformazioni e reazioni*, ed. Silvia Vida, 211–225. Bologna: Bononia University Press.

———. 2012. Lost in Translation: Human Rights Between Western Secularism and Islamic Scripturalism. In *Liber Amicorum René Foqué*, eds. Marie-Claire Foblets, Mireille Hildebrandt, and Jacques Steenbergen, 657–670. Brussels: Larcier.

———. 2013. Western and Islamic Values: A "False" Contraposition. *ARSP* 99 (2): 173–185.

———. 2014a. Principio di sussidiarietà e universalità dei bisogni: il riaccendersi tecnologico della fiducia. *Notizie di Politeia* 116: 14–35.

———. 2014b. The Rule of Exposure. *From Bentham to Queen Grimhilde's Mirror. ARSP* 4: 450–466.

———. 2015a. "Quest" identitaria mediata dal web, (cyber)bullismo e stratificazione sociale alla luce di un singolare caso di "devianza" di massa. *Studi sulla questione criminale* 2-3: 129–150.

———. 2015b. Ansia panottica e "treadmill effect" nell'utopia eudaimonistica delle nuove tecnologie. In *Filosofia del diritto e nuove tecnologie*, eds. Raffaella Brighi and Silvia Zullo, 89–103. Roma: Aracne.

———. 2016. L'*hikikomori* e il giardino all'inglese. Inquietante irrazionalità e solitudine comune. *Ragion Pratica* 1: 243–257.

———. 2017. La compattezza etico-sociale e il ciclo delle civiltà. Cultura occidentale e multiculturalismo contemporaneo alla luce della lezione di Ibn Khaldūn. *Materiali per una storia della cultura giuridica* 1: 223–247.

———. 2018. Il concetto di vulnerabilità e la sua tensione tra colonizzazioni neoliberali e nuovi paradigmi di giustizia. In *Vulnerabilità. Analisi multidisciplinare di un concetto*, eds. Orsetta Giolo and Baldassare Pastore, 229–251. Roma: Carocci.

———. 2019. Vulnerabilità e forme "altre" di radicalizzazione. L'echo chamber delle comunità online di odio misogino e antifemminista. *Notizie di Politeia* 136: 57–69.

———. 2020. "Mascolinità tossica" sul web: la "cultura" dell'odio antifemminista online. In *Postfemminismo e neoliberalismo*, eds. Annalisa Verza and Silvia Vida, 157–196. Roma: Aracne.

Vico, Giambattista. [1725] 1977. *La scienza nuova*. Milano: BUR.

von Hammer-Purgstall, Joseph. 1812. *Über den Verfall des Islam nach den ersten drei Jahrhunderten der Hidschra*. Wien: Anton Schmid.

———. 1818. *Extraits d'Ibn Khaldūn*. In *Fundgruben des Orients*, ed. Joseph von Hammer-Purgstall, Vol. 6, 301–307, 362–364. Wien: Anton Schmid.

von Hemsö, Gråberg, and Chevalier Jakob Grefve. 1835. An Account of the Great Historical Work of the African Philosopher Ibn Khaldūn. *Transactions of the Royal Asiatic Society of Great Britain and Ireland* 3 (3): 387–404.

von Kremer, Alfred. 1879. Ibn Chaldun and seine Kulturgeschichte der Islamischen Reiche. *Sitzungberichte der Kaiserlichen Akademie der Wissenschaften, Philosoph.-histor. Klasse* 93: 581–634.

Voyé, Liliane, and Jaak Billiet. 1999. Introduction. In *Sociology and Religions. An Ambiguous Relationship*, eds. Liliane Voyé and Jaak Billiet, 9–16. Leuven: Leuven University Press.

Walzer, Richard. 1963. Aspects of Islamic Political Thought: Al-Fārābī and Ibn Xaldūn. *Oriens* 16: 40–60.

Walzer, Michael. 1994. *Thick and Thin. Moral Argument at Home and Abroad*. Indiana: University of Notre Dame Press.

Weber, Max. [1922] 1978. *Economy and Society: An Outline of Interpretive Sociology*. 2 Voll. Berkley: University of California Press.

West, Ed. 2015. *Asabiya, What Ibn Khaldūn, the Islamic father of social science, can teach us about the world today*, e-book. https://www.amazon.co.uk/*Asabiyya*h-Khaldun-Islamic-father-science-ebook/dp/B0133Y2XSG/ref=sr_1_1?ie=UTF8&qid=1438364083&sr=8-1&keywords=*Asabiyya*h. Accessed 17 Sept 2020.

Wittgenstein, Ludwig. [1921] 1989. *Tractatus logico-philosophicus*. Torino: Einaudi.

Woodley, Michael A., and Edward Bell. 2012. Consanguinity as a Major Predictor of Levels of Democracy: A Study of 70 Nations. *Journal of Cross-Cultural Psychology* 44 (2): 263–280.

Wright Mills, Charles. 1939. Language, Logic and Culture. *American Sociological Review* 4: 670–680.

———. 1956. *The Power Elite*. New York: Oxford University Press.

Index

A. Verza, *Ibn Khaldūn and the Arab Origins of the Sociology of Civilisation and Power*, https://doi.org/10.1007/978-3-030-70339-4

Printed in Great Britain
b[redacted]

54368045R00159